Global Success
International Business Tactics
for the 1990s

Dr. Carl A. Nelson

LIBERTY HALL
PRESS™

LIBERTY HALL PRESS books are published by LIBERTY HALL PRESS, an imprint of McGraw-Hill, Inc. Its trademark, consisting of the words "LIBERTY HALL PRESS" and the portrayal of Benjamin Franklin, is registered in the United States Patent and Trademark Office.

FIRST EDITION
SECOND PRINTING

Library of Congress Cataloging-in-Publication Data

Nelson, Carl A., 1930–
Global success : international business tactics for the 1990s / by Carl A. Nelson.
p. cm.
ISBN 0-8306-3506-8
1. Export marketing—United States. 2. Small business—United States. I. Title.
HF1416.5.N45 1990
658.8′48—dc20
90-30037
CIP

For information about other McGraw-Hill materials, call 1-800-2-MCGRAW in the U.S. In other countries call your nearest McGraw-Hill office.
TAB Software Department
Blue Ridge Summit, PA 17294-0850

Questions regarding the content of this book should be addressed to:
Reader Inquiry Branch
TAB BOOKS
Blue Ridge Summit, PA 17294-0850

Vice President & Editorial Director: David J. Conti
Book Editor: Pat Mulholland-McCarty
Book Design: Jaclyn J. Boone
Production: Katherine G. Brown

Contents

Preface

As the author of this book I want you to take away more than notions of how to increase business profits and improve earnings.

It is business that initiates international trade; international trade is free enterprise; and free enterprise leads to greater global welfare. It wasn't that long ago that merchants (businessmen) were the least esteemed of any class. However, interdependence has brought them new respect. The modern global business paradigm crosses national borders where we find some companies with greater power than some nations. Therefore business leaders must constantly ask themselves, what's the purpose of the enterprise? Short term stock valuation? Immediate returns on capital invested? Or is it long term social good?

For twenty years my work took me to the Pacific Rim. I lived in Japan for two years and often visited the "Four Tigers"—South Korea, Hong Kong, Singapore, and Taiwan. I observed how a mixture of planning, free enterprise, and exporting changed those nations. In the past, economic growth theory advocated "pushing" the development of the domestic market, but, the "new economic growth model" I observed worked in reverse. By making things and selling those things wherever in the world people could afford them, foreign currency was brought back to improve the welfare of the domestic population. International trade "pulled" the newly industrialized nations (NIC) into the mainstream of economic growth.

From this export-oriented mechanism have come growing similarities among world cultures and that portends greater harmony and less chance of war. It would seem then that greater interdependence of nations is good for business and mankind.

Acknowledgments

I ACCEPT FULL RESPONSIBILITY FOR ANY FAULTS THIS BOOK MIGHT HAVE AND gratefully share any praise for its virtues with the following persons who gave freely of their time to critique and otherwise offer comments to improve the book:

Harold Sheble, former Marketing Manager, Solar Turbines; John W. Pfeiffer, East-West Marketing Consultant, Carlsbad, CA; Karl J Biniarz, Vice President and Manager, Dai-Ichi-Kangyo Bank of San Diego, CA; James M. Murray, President, The Timberock Company; Michael A. Lapadula, Vice President Marketing, Loral Terracom; Frank Rugnetta, Manager, Worldwide Sourcing, Solar Turbines, Inc. (Subsidiary of Caterpillar, Inc.); William D. Ingram, President of KevTon, Inc.; Mr. Ralph Jones, Manager, Effectiveness Training, Inc.; Mr. George Muller, Deputy Director, Office of Export Trading Company Affairs, International Trade Administration, U.S. Department of Commerce; Gary L. Kaplan, Director and Mary Abbott, Paralegal Specialist, Trade Remedy Assistance Office, U.S. International Trade Commission; Claire Buchan, Office of the United States Trade Representative; David J. Conti, Vice President and Editorial Director, Liberty Hall Press, a division of TAB BOOKS; Renan Komurcuoglu, Susan Topham and Jackan Gutu, international researchers; and finally, my wife Barbara who read, coddled, and encouraged as the work developed.

Introduction

THE NATIONS OF EARTH ARE INTERDEPENDENT. IT IS NOT A CONDITION THAT will happen in the future. Call it "Space Ship Earth," the "Global Village," the "World Economy," the "Pacific Century," but no matter what it's called it is here and it is a condition that will continue to dominate world economics into the twenty-first century and beyond.

As a result of this interdependence phenomena, the opportunities for world trade expansion have never been greater. Kids in Pakistan wear Levis, the Chinese have television, and Americans stretch their budgets by purchasing less expensive goods from overseas.

Everyone has observed the success of Japan and the "Four Tigers" (Singapore, Hong Kong, Taiwan, and South Korea). In addition to them, businesses from all over the world have invaded the United States markets. Now managers of more and more small- and medium-sized American businesses are saying: "Hey! I'm going to get into your market, too. I'm going to challenge you on your own turf."

Global Success: International Business Tactics for the 1990s presents the game plan to win the international trade game. It is the business manual—the how-to's to strike-back and compete in the age of global interdependency. It is valuable reading for anyone interested in cross-border business.

This book is about "international business tactics" and is intended for forward-thinking people: entrepreneurs, managers and decision makers, and even those persons who have only a general interest in international trade. It will be particularly useful for those in small- and medium-sized manufacturing and service companies who recognize our world has changed and are ready for new challenges, ready to become a "global business."

This book is also a crossover book—it can be used as a how-to guide for the growing manager, or a college level text, or a reference for the business executive. For those who are venturing into the global arena for the first time it will show you how to succeed in an interdependent world and win the trade game. For those of you who are already in international business, large or small, the book will bring focus to your current work and expand your horizon. Anyone who reads this book will learn how to overcome international obstacles by adopting the secrets of top American companies.

Global Success: International Business Tactics for the 1990s deals with service companies as well as manufacturers and covers a wide range of specific information brought together for the first time in one book. Such things as culture, vaulting barriers to franchise, or taking advantage of production-sharing opportunities are often found in separate texts but in reality global business is synergistic. Each chapter presents, in a "how-to" format, a tactic (pawn or rook) on the international trade chess board which you can use to gain your overall profit strategy. It is packed with specific information, names, addresses, and telephone numbers to lead you into greater international business success. This book is designed to assist the international businessperson to win the trade game by using the right mix of business tactics.

Least we forget the lessons of the past, the prolog of this book, titled "prelude to success," synopsizes the history of U.S. international trade. It explains the "Yankee Trader Spirit" which propelled America to become the world's greatest trading nation. From this chronicle covering 200 years in a few pages, seven lessons are drawn about how to reverse dangerous trends.

Chapter 1 focuses trade expansion opportunities in terms of the Quadrant four companies—the thousands of small- and medium-sized manufacturers and service firms not yet in the trade game. It then develops a game plan which offers three strategic elements and eleven practical business tactics.

In Chapter 2 you will learn the importance of the first business tactic: understanding "culture" as it relates to international business success, and the do's and don'ts country-by-country.

Global businesses are marketing and sourcing (importing) worldwide, so the next two chapters explain how top companies are exporting and importing.

Chapter 3 is about international marketing (exporting) and offers a pragmatic method of how to decide whether to "do it yourself," form associations under the Export Trading Company Act of 1982, or work with intermediaries. The chapter also explains who to hire as key personnel and how to develop a practical strategic and tactical international market plan.

In Chapter 4 you will learn how international sourcing is done routinely in most of today's manufacturing companies.

Organizing the firm to keep up with changing times is the subject of Chapter 5. It reveals how modern manufacturing adjusts in a changing global environment.

Chapter 6 explains how to enter a global service industry just waiting to absorb the know-how that keeps two-thirds of all Americans employed.

Chapter 7 shows you how to find and deal with General Trading Companies (GTCs), Export management companies (EMCs), or the "new" Export Trading Companies. The latter are the fledgling firms that are destined to become America's answer to the giant Japanese Sogo shoshas.

Chapter 8 sheds light on one of America's most misunderstood trade laws, the Export Trading Company Act of 1982. In reality this legislation offers untapped creative opportunities. The chapter also reveals the secrets of the Sogo shosha.

Gaining, preserving, or enhancing market share in a credit- and barrier-constrained trade environment compels creative strategies. Europe 1992 and other emerging market-unions are forcing managers to aggressively think of new ways to remain competitive in a changing world. Chapter 9 takes the position that international trade barriers are hurdles to leap over not obstacles to prevent your entry. You will learn how to "partner" and form "strategic alliances" which will allow you to vault over the traditional cultural and marketing barriers as well as visible and invisible tariffs. These often stand in the way of those managers who are teetering on the decision should I or should I not enter the international market. You will also learn how to use counter-trade, Foreign Trade Zones, or benefit from franchising and direct mail.

Production sharing is the fastest growing industry in the world today. Chapter 10 explains off-shore assembly and production, and compares the Mexican Maquiladora with Singapore's Program.

As a result of *perestroika* and *glasnost*, more and more Communist (nonmarket) countries are adjusting toward free markets and free enterprise. In Chapter 11 you will learn how to do business with these controlled economies in order to profit from growing east-west trade.

Chapter 12 explains how to get your "beef" to the right person in the U.S. government to obtain relief from illegal and unfair international trade practices.

The appendices of this book are themselves the material of first-hand references for the global executive. To better prepare and plan for an international business trip, they include complete listings of world holidays, foreign currencies, foreign management titles, foreign business titles, and the names, addresses, and telephone numbers of the American Chambers of Commerce abroad. In addition the appendices include a complete listing of U.S. Foreign Trade Zones (FTZs), and important contractual forms, such as elements of an agent/distribution agreement, international licensing agreement, and the application form for an Export Trade certificate of review.

When you are finished reading this book you will not only know how to expand your international dealings but where to go and who to contact for help.

"Economies grow and mature, just as human beings do. They have an infant phase, called agriculture. Then they go through adolescence, or the industrial stage. Then they reach maturity and become post-industrial economies, symbolized by the McDonald arch."

Steve Schlosstein
Trade War

Prolog
Prelude to Success

THIS BOOK IS ABOUT WINNING THE INTERNATIONAL TRADE GAME, BUT TO win any game—be it baseball, basketball, or economic competition—the players need an orientation. Knowing as did Santayana that, "Those who cannot remember the past are condemned to repeat it," business leaders ask, "Where are we? Where did we come from?" Only when the past is understood can a strategy for the future be assembled.

An abbreviated version of United States' trade history is presented in this prolog. At the end of the reading, lessons are drawn which set the tone for the remainder of the book and allow the development, in Chapter 1, of a proactive game plan for winning.

A GRAPHIC SNAPSHOT

During the short two hundred years of American history the country transitioned from an underdeveloped nation by climbing through its industrial age, and emerging as a leader in the high technology post-industrialized era. Figure P-1 shows, by way of graphic representation, those changes in terms of deficits and surpluses of the balance of merchandise trade.

OUR ROOTS

During her first eighty years, the United States was, by today's standards, an underdeveloped country and the volume of trade, though brisk, was commensurately small. The early years of American independence was in fact a period of

1

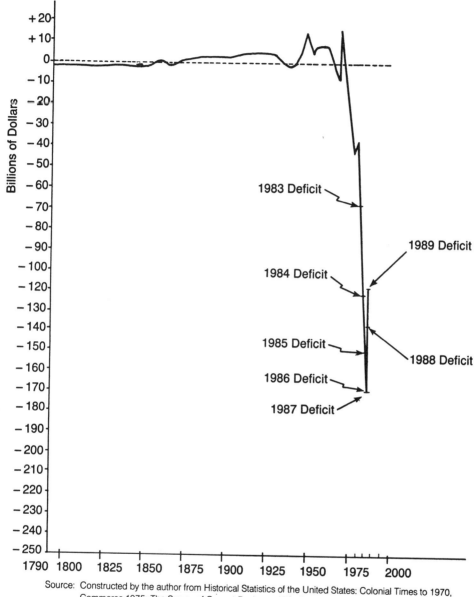

Source: Constructed by the author from Historical Statistics of the United States: Colonial Times to 1970,
Commerce 1975; The Survey of Current Business, U.S. Chamber of Commerce 1983 and Wall
Street Journal.

Fig. P-1   Merchandise Trade Balance—Birth of the Nation to Present.

business depression. General economic problems were compounded by small, but chronic imbalances of payments. In order to solve their trade struggle, the "new" Americans had to reach out to distant markets.

Before the Revolutionary War, the colonies were one of England's trade partners, a very junior partner at that. Transition to a sovereign nation proved a rude shock to American merchants accustomed to the commercial privileges offered to members of the Empire. British islands in the West Indies were immediately ordered closed to American vessels, and trade with England became less profitable because of new duties and restrictions imposed by the scorned mother country.

Post-independence economic conditions forced ship owners to seek out new trading opportunities. In the same years that some American merchants were attempting to repair their commercial ties with Britain, a number of other equally enterprising New England "Yankee" Traders rose to the crisis by sponsoring pioneering voyages to South Africa, India, and East Asia. Thus the merchants of the new nation began to compete in the international marketplace.

Some of the sponsors were peddlers from early New England who roamed far and wide through the American colonies and beyond. Those peddlers won a great reputation for getting high prices. People often said that someone was as "shrewd as a Yankee" or "clever as a Yankee."

The risk takers

Yankee Traders were sometimes merchants, sometimes sailors, sometimes a bit of both, but they were always risk takers. One of those Yankee Traders was the man Jesse Hurd who had been a shipmaster in his younger days, but did not go to sea after 1800. Letters were sometimes addressed to him as Jesse Hurd, Merchant and sometimes as Captain Jesse Hurd.

New York, 25 March, 1813

Mr. Jesse Hurd,

Dr Sir, we send you by sloop Marshall 1 anchor for the schooner you are building which we have charged to you. We wish you to write us what progress you make in building the schooner also whether you have procured the hemp. It is reported 100 new licenses have been granted in France to import Colonial produce from America and Croze & Richard have furnished one for the schooner you are building. Considerable quantities of sugar and coffee have lately come in here from Havana and prices have fallen and we think a good freight might be obtained for the schooner to France in a few weeks and recommend your using all the dispatch you can. We are

yours,
Nathal. L. & Geo. Griswold

PS. The trade from Baltimore to France is nearly cut off by the British. Thus perhaps this may increase shipments from this place. NL & GG.

Beginning about 1800, Jesse Hurd kept a store in Middle Haddam, Middle Haddam Landing, or Chatham—all names designating the same Connecticut River Village. Jesse Hurd also owned one of the several shipyards.

Middle Haddam storekeeper-shipbuilder-Yankee Trader Jesse Hurd was able to obtain capital to invest in new voyages by giving notes, and using his profits to supply the interest and pay off the loans. In this way or by buying a fractional interest in a particular ship for a particular voyage, he and others in the village cooperated to sell the goods they manufactured by investing in the enterprises of the very ships they helped to build.

Almost all of Hurd's ships were sent to New York where they were loaded with cargoes for the West Indies, Cadiz, Lisbon, Bordeaux, Canton, or West Africa. Success of a trading voyage depended principally upon the captains of the ships who expedited commerce in addition to being Master of the vessel. Picture Jesse Hurd wearing a tall beaver hat and carrying an ivory-headed cane as he made his way from the New York Merchant's Exchange to the Tontine Tavern to give parting instructions to one of his Captains a day or two prior to the sailing.

The letter that trader Hurd gave to his Yankee Captain would have been phrased in broad terms, leaving the Master ample room for maneuver. The instructions sometimes expressed no more than pious hopes of what might be achieved in the course of the voyage. But if success of the voyage was in the hands of the Captain, commercial success was in the hands of the merchant. Credit was the basis for commercial success.

Our Yankee Trader reputation

Concern for the ability to finance a new adventure, to preserve the safety of the one underway, or to stave off a sudden crisis became a part of the Yankee Trader frame of mind and dominated mercantile thinking well into the nineteenth century. According to the merchant's code, the cardinal sin lay not in slaving (which many of them engaged in), smuggling, or privateering, but in the inability to deliver on promises. The merchant's word is and has to be his bond.

Global trading

An example of early global trading was when the Niantic, one of Jesse Hurd's vessels, set sail for Canton, China on October 29, 1836. The Captain reported there was little social life and amusements, because Yankee Traders were barred by Imperial edict from going about in China. Merchants glimpsed the mysterious and colorful Orient only on trips through the harbor. He spoke of entering and leaving the great harbor of Canton, and passing by the island that only five years later became the colony of Hong Kong. Two years later Niantic returned with her holds loaded with profitable goods.

In the beginning America was a debtor nation, but a spirit grew among the merchants. They called it the Yankee Trader spirit and their reputation became the watchword of trustworthiness, adventure, high spirit, and boldness. Yankee

Traders cooperated to send their tall ships throughout the world with their holds full of American goods, in search of trade. They went anywhere they could turn an old dollar for a new. Their willingness to accept risk was the foundation which launched the tradition of a great trading nation.

CIVIL WAR PERIOD

From April 12, 1861, when Southern artillery shelled Fort Sumter in Charleston harbor, until April 9, 1865 when Confederate General Robert E. Lee surrendered his ragged exhausted army, American industrial goals shifted to war-fighting. It was alternately known as the War Between the States, or the War of Secession, but it was the war that drove the nation into bankruptcy, depression, and extreme international trade deficits. Neither the North nor the South could sustain the effort without importing great amounts of goods and because everything that was manufactured went to the war effort, there was nothing left to export. Deficits, deficits, deficits.

POST CIVIL WAR

As a result of men like Jesse Hurd, America first plodded, then surged ahead in its quest for new sources of products and markets. Then, after the interruption of the Civil War which cemented the union of states, America shot back into international trade like the sparks from a six-shooter. America changed from an agrarian society to a nation that made things: railroads, ships, bridges, clothes, cars, then airplanes. And the search for markets spilled beyond the borders. The industrial revolution exploded and propelled the country, except for the Great Depression, into almost 90 years of international trade surpluses.

BETWEEN THE BIG WARS

We call the United States' current trade problem the new game of international competition because the country dealt with trade problems before. The aftermath of World War I brought a time not unlike today. They were the years when most European nations were heavily in debt to the United States. They were the years, much to the chagrin of many Americans, when all except "brave little Finland" defaulted those debts outright. They were called the "interval years" and it was a time of intense competition from foreign-made goods. They were the years of the Great Depression when the major trading nations attempted to buoy trade levels by cut-throat competition and the application of higher and higher barriers. "Beggar-thy-neighbor" tactics, the method of increasing the exports of one country at the expense of other countries using exchange rate depreciation and unprovoked tariff increases, became commonplace and the United States' trade balances became deficits.

Responding to mounting domestic pressure to protect American jobs yet remain competitive, the nation's legislators began searching, very much as they are today, for solutions to the trade problems. The outgrowth of that protectionist period was a series of barriers to international trade. America almost lost the old game because it took actions that helped plunge the nation and the world into a decade of depression, despair, and unprecedented international merchandise trade deficits.

THE REGRESSIVE LAWS

At the time this economic warfare began, the United States had several federal, as well as many state laws that forbade anti-competitive agreements, monopolies, and attempts to monopolize. The Sherman Antitrust Act, passed in 1890, as well as the Clayton Antitrust Act, and Federal Trade Commission Act (FTC), both passed in 1914, were designed to ensure a competitive business environment and thereby benefit American consumers. They were not written to apply to foreign activities of United States' companies but because of the stiff penalties for non-competitive collusion (treble damages) these acts became what we now call institutional barriers. They were seen as obstacles and many Americans felt they stifled trading growth.

The Shipping Act of 1916 provided for regulation of ocean freight forwarding. It forbids these service organizations from having a "beneficial interest" in shipments that they serve. The definition does not cover divisions of manufacturing companies that export their own goods directly through an ocean carrier.

The Trading with the Enemy Act of 1917 gave the President of the United States the power to control export sales during war time. A 1933 amendment extended his power to periods of national emergency. This change gave the President the power to use America's manufacturers as peacetime instruments of economic war.

The Forney-McCumber Tariff Act of 1922 didn't impose particularly high tariffs but targeted potential new imports and allowed the president to change tariff rates up or down by as much as 50 percent.

The Smoot-Hawley Act was passed in 1930 by the Hoover administration. At the time, foreign products like Madeira wine and olive oil from Southern Europe were spilling into the country. Congress decided American farmers needed protection so it raised the tariff on wine, oil, and just about everything else so high that more than a score of nations retaliated against American goods by jumping on the protectionist bandwagon. The resulting ill will and trade dislocation were important factors in retarding worldwide economic recovery.

The Buy-American Act of 1933, was touted as an anti-depression measure, but it contributed to inflation and remains on the books today.

To prevent recurrence of bank speculation in corporate stock which led to the Great Crash, the Glass-Steagall Act was passed in 1934. No longer could banks invest in corporate equities and commercial enterprises. In the eyes of many, the result was the loss of capital for trading when the nation needed it most.

THE TRADE-STIMULATING LAWS

In order to stimulate international trade, the United States passed the Export Trade Act of 1918, better known as the Webb-Pomerene Act. This law amended the Sherman Act and section 7 of the Clayton Antitrust laws for purposes of conducting export trade. The Webb-Pomerene Act exempted trade associations established and registered with the Federal Trade Commission for the sole purpose of engaging in export trade of ''goods, wares, or merchandise,'' so long as that trade did not restrain trade or influence artificial prices within the United States. In other words, for international trade purposes, it allowed firms to team up and form associations and to fix prices for foreign trade goods (but not services) without violating the United States' antitrust laws.

The Export-Import bank of the United States (Eximbank) was created in 1934 to aid in financing and to facilitate exports.

The Edge Act was passed which allowed a corporation formed under Title 12 United States Code Sec. 611-31 to engage in international banking and financial operations.

SANITY RESTORED

On balance, the tariff and other barrier policies of the 1920s and early 1930s turned out to be more of a deterrent than a stimulant to international trade and contributed to the Depression of the 1930s.

But good sense began to prevail in 1934, the year that Secretary of State Cordell Hull saw passage of the Reciprocal Trade Agreements Act, which he conceived. It led the movement toward lower tariffs by giving the President of the United States authority to enter into reciprocal trade agreements with foreign governments to reduce tariffs without the necessity of ratification by the Senate. This act also incorporated the Most Favored Nation (MFN) principle, which has served as the cornerstone of the United States trading system ever since. Under the MFN principle, the benefits of any bilateral tariff reductions negotiated by the United States are extended to all MFN countries. The idea is by making such concessions other nations might give similar treatment to United States exports in their country. Eventually this bilateral approach developed into the multilateral method of trade negotiations.

As a result of, or possibly in spite of this strange mixture of legislative depressants and stimulants, the United States came out of the slump of post World War I, the depression subsided, and the country prepared for the next World War.

THE BIGGER WAR

During World War II the products carried around the globe by our courageous soldiers, sailors, and marines became linked to the word "Yankee" which had now become a term of endearment among the people of those nations saved from despotism. "Made in U.S.A." came to mean quality as well as quantity because the United States war effort resulted in even greater home profits which were reinvested in even greater industrial capacity, plant and product development.

POST WORLD WAR II

The United States emerged from World War II as the recognized leader in international trade. As the United States' trade success grew, products displaying the initials "U.S.A." sold themselves and our balances zoomed to unprecedented highs. For the next twenty years, international trade surpluses grew at a rate of 20 percent a year. This lulled the country into a feeling of comfort.

THE CRASH

Few remember why or how it happened. It just crept up on us. The years following World War II were beguiling. Of all the major industrial nations only the United States had a manufacturing base left intact and as a result, dominated world markets. But in 1971, the trade balances went negative and have remained so for almost two decades—the longest and most severe period of international trade decline in United States' history.

In 1971, when the balances first went negative, authorities discounted the problem. They called it an anomaly to an otherwise positive trend. The trade deficits, which continued for the next few years, were similarly shrugged off. They said it was a result of the Organization of Exporting Oil Countries (OPEC) and the high cost of imported oil. In 1975, the experts rubbed their hands and gleefully said, "I told you so," because the balances had once again righted themselves by jumping to a record high and everyone thought the problem was solved.

But their happiness was short lived, because the United States has run annual deficits of $20 billion or greater since 1975. Could it be that our Yankee Trader heritage failed the nation? What could have caused the abrupt change from a nation of unprecedented surpluses to a nation of record-breaking deficits?

THE MULTIPLE CAUSES OF THE DECLINE

The decline didn't begin in 1971. It began much earlier. It was in the mid-1960s, about twenty years after World War II, that our share of world trade began to slip. To understand why the United States got caught from behind let's look at what happened after that war.

Multiple factors contributed to the erosion of trade. The first factor was the creation of the United Nations Monetary and Financial Conference which met at the fashionable Bretton Woods Resort in New Hampshire. There amid the majestic White Mountains representatives of forty-four nations, who knew that economic wars frequently beget shooting wars, engaged in protracted discussions that developed a two-pronged plan. First, an international loan fund of more than $8 billion to help stabilize national currencies and facilitate payments across international borders. Second, a world bank capitalized at about $9 billion to provide loans to needy nations, primarily for reconstruction and economic development.

It was the vision of United States policymakers that gave birth to the International Monetary Fund, the United Nations, the World Bank, and Bretton Woods all of which became the basic economic order of the world and stimulated growth.

The competition

The next major factor that contributed to trade erosion was the program called *Government Aid and Rehabilitation in Occupied Areas* (GARIOA), better known as the *Marshall Plan*. It was initiated in Germany but the same economic stimulation techniques were also used in Japan. It was the policy the United States adopted to focus its resources on the economic growth of the countries left torn and disrupted from the war. At the same time the country took an altruistic approach to trade by opening its borders to imports, which contributed to an increased standard of living in other parts of the world.

The Marshall Plan was a good policy for the times, but Generals Marshall and MacArthur may have done their jobs too well because out of the ashes of war Germany and Japan rose to become our competitors.

The rise of Japan

The Japanese learned most completely. Their manufacturing strategy adopted the pages about growth economics right out of the best textbooks. In 1949, they gave birth to the Ministry of International Trade and Industry (MITI) which began to control and orchestrate their ''industrial policy.'' The strategy that organization adopted focused on the country's international comparative advantage and, among other things, placed emphasis on value-added industry and exports. They began by copying the ideas of others, making things in thousands of small firms and selling them cheap in the countries of the world where the consumers had money to spend. In the early 1960s they made a calculated decision. They refused to be relegated to a labor-based economy. They saw no future in exporting only direct labor because so many countries that did so ended up as beggar nations. Instead, Japan made the strategic decision to focus on high-technology. They worked out the tactics of their strategy and began to give tax credits, special depreciation incentives, assistance to smaller exporters, special subsidies, infant-industry protection, and overseas market development, all under the watchful eye of MITI's "Industrial Policy."

As their manufacturing base grew their education system began to turn out increasing numbers of engineers and scientists. Then they increased their Research and Development (R&D) effort and began to design their own products. Above all they listened to the American expert, W. Edwards Demming, when he taught them about statistical quality controls.

Demming is a statistician who has become an international business legend, but is still best known in Japan where he has been treated with reverence since their reconstruction days. It was his advice, to eager Japanese companies, which triggered their extraordinary economic rebirth. His message to the Japanese was simple: tally defects; scrutinize them; trace the source of the problem; make corrections; and record the results. Today Demming is considered an American national treasure by other quality control gurus.

Massive infusions of capital, the Marshall Plan, and the alchemy of the Bretton Woods conference ushered in a new era. Because economic integration and free movement of goods and capital were encouraged, Japan staged a "miracle" in economic and political strategy.

More competitors

Japan is but one of the United States' major competitors but not the only one. Other countries have contributed nearly a third of the economic growth of the Asian rim. Using the Japanese model, the Newly Industrialized Nations (NICs), rose from the mud of agrarian societies and the ashes of war. The Japanese model, they observed, was the "new model for economic growth." Instead of concentrating on agrarian reform and policies that stimulated only production for the domestic market, they went the route of a mixture of free enterprise coupled with five-year industrial plans. They encouraged production sharing, began to manufacture things, and exported those products to the locations of the world where people had spendable incomes, like the United States. The result was jobs, and an infusion of foreign currency.

Characteristics of these countries have been low inflation, low deficit spending, low tax bite, and low unemployment. Another characteristic has been that many of these countries have developed highly sophisticated private and semiprivate trading organizations that are accepted by the business community as a necessity for excellence in export promotion. Such organizations as the Japanese Sogo Shosha (discussed in Chapter 8) and the state owned trading companies of Taiwan and Brazil provided aggressive international market reach for a wide range of smaller foreign firms.

The combined exports to the United States from the "Four Tigers" of Asia—Taiwan, Hong Kong, South Korea and Singapore—grew 48 times, a spectacular growth from such a low post-war base. By 1980, 15 of the 50 largest banks in the world were Asian. Over the period 1960–1978 only China's gross national product (GNP) grew at less than 5 percent a year.

By the early 1980s, Trans-Pacific trade exceeded Trans-Atlantic trade. The United States depended less economically on Europe than it did on Asia. East Asia overtook Europe as the nation's chief supplier of manufactured goods. United States' imports from that region exceeded other imports nearly three to two. They flooded our market with well-made, low-priced imports. The loss of control of major business enterprises to foreign interests resulted in a decline in large sectors of the manufacturing industry. Asian countries accomplished this through a vigorous emphasis on exporting—they live by trade.

The flip side

At the same time that the new competitors took advantage of America's open border—an "unmanaged" trade policy to penetrate and capture market share—they kept their own borders closed. Complex interstate (government) controls, such as high tariffs, and institutional barriers, such as multi-tiered distribution systems prevented Americans equal access to their markets.

GATT

Another factor of the United States' international trade decline was the General Agreement on Tariff and Trade (GATT) established in 1947. It basically defined the rules of conduct and emphasized a mechanism for orderly expansion of trade. GATT was to provide a means whereby nations could make concessions through multilateral bargaining. Membership in GATT meant assurances that smaller countries would be treated as fairly in world markets as any other nation; therefore, the United States, as a major power, no longer had the edge. To further exacerbate the problem, the 1962 Kennedy round of GATT talks erroneously treated Japan as a Lessor Developed Country (LDC). Fifteen years later Japan was producing 8.5 million cars and trucks a year compared to United States 12.5. Between 1963 and 1980 Japan's exports to the United States grew over 23 times by value, nearly doubling the growth rate of imports from France and tripling the imports from Britain.

Back in the U.S.

At the same time overseas leaders were making arrangements for a strong post war recovery and the invasion of our market, American manufacturers were not giving great importance to exports. The United States had its own vast domestic market, and the country in the late 1940s, 1950s and even into the 1960s, was still benefiting from the wartime label "Made in U.S.A." American manufacturers didn't need the Yankee spirit, because their products sold themselves.

Following the war, the United States entered a period of high consumption. After all, the nation had sacrificed and the people deserved the good things of life. As a result of United States dollar appreciation, citizens traveling abroad felt rich. They traveled even more and further magnified the losing game. This led to low rates of saving, which led to low capital investment in research and development. Table P-1 gives a comparison of savings figures for 1980.

Table P-1 Savings 1980.	
Country	Savings as a share of National income
Taiwan	33.4
Singapore	28.4
Japan	8.1
Republic of Korea	16.5
Italy	12.7
France	11.8
Britain	7.2
United States	4.3

Sources: National statistical year books.

Low saving rates were not caused just by frivolous post World War II spending. The post-Vietnam War era began to shrink pocketbooks, and housewives, who are the principal consumers in any nation, began to look for bargain prices. By the late-1970s the consuming family began to see what was happening as cost competitive products of equal or better quality began showing up on the shelves at a time when the United States was facing double-digit inflation. They came from Asia, but also from every other corner of the world which learned that "Yuppies" (young urban professionals) and "Dinks" (dual income no kids) had money.

Enter, the service economy

About this same time another phenomena began to change American business. Mr. Akio Morita, President of Sony Corporation, said, "A major contributing factor to Japan's phenomenal economic challenge is due to the 'laziness' of the United States worker." He was referring to what writers of the time spoke of as a slippage of the work ethic. What happened had nothing to do with laziness. The country was moving rapidly toward a white collar work as a natural result of more education and less reliance on a blue collar force as a major factor in competition.

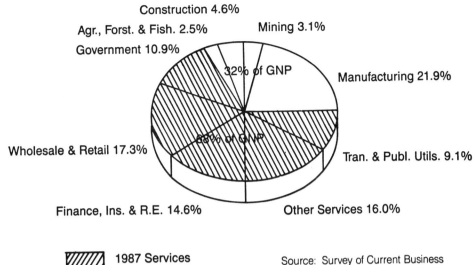

Construction 4.6%
Agr., Forst. & Fish. 2.5%
Government 10.9%
Mining 3.1%
32% of GNP
Manufacturing 21.9%
Wholesale & Retail 17.3%
68% of GNP
Tran. & Publ. Utils. 9.1%
Finance, Ins. & R.E. 14.6%
Other Services 16.0%

[/////] 1987 Services   Source: Survey of Current Business

Fig. P-2   U.S. GNP breakdown by Industry—1987.

Automation and robotization, with their inherent capability to eliminate human downtime or non-work time began replacing people who normally had to wait while management set up machinery for new products.

Knowledge and capital became a growing substitute for labor in American manufacturing. New industries began to emerge that were information and knowledge based. Service industries grew until, as shown in Figs. P-2, P-3, and P-4, they represented more than two-thirds of the United States' Gross National Product. People in the service industries wanted manufactured products and they found them on the shelves marked "Made in Taiwan," "Made in Italy," and "Assembled in Mexico." Americans were now dependent on products from other nations, i.e., interdependence.

As shown in Table P-2, even though manufacturing continued to account for roughly 80 percent of United States and world trade, the United States' share slipped.

___Table P-2 Share of World Manufacturing Trade.___			
	1970	*1980*	*1987*
U.S.	14.9%	13.0%	10.5%
Japan	9.4	11.2	13.0
European Community	46.2	45.6	43.1
East Asia tigers*	2.3	5.4	9.1

Hong Kong, Taiwan, Singapore, and South Korea
Source: General Agreement on Tariffs and Trade (GATT)

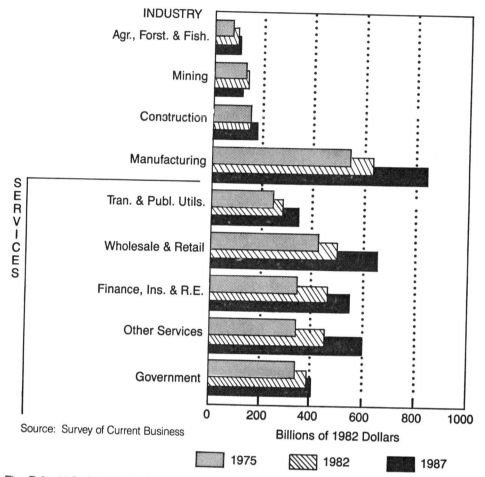

Fig. P-3   U.S. GNP by Industry (Dollars Increase).

The new reality

Countries like Japan, Korea, and Taiwan with their planned economies did look east toward the wealthiest market in the world and did push their goods to a price-hungry American consumer. But what really happened was more complex.

As a result of the changes described earlier, the United States became deeply and irrevocably involved in the growing global economy. Economic realities had changed. The United States had entered the post-industrial age and her competitors had become more sophisticated. They closed most of the technology gaps that once gave the United States the edge over foreign industries, and they began to capture both domestic and international markets once dominated by United States firms.

In the mid-1970s when interdependency first became apparent, professional managers of the major multinational corporations recognized what was happen-

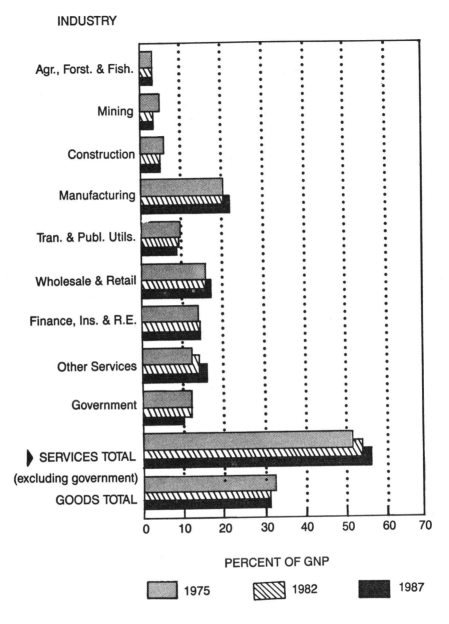

Source: Survey of Current Business

Fig. P-4   Industry Percent of U.S. GNP (1975, 1982, 1987).

ing. These are the largest 200 to 300 firms that do 90 percent of the United States' total international business. They saw that trade in manufactured goods was growing worldwide at 7.8 percent, while trade of similar United States manufactured goods was only growing 5.1 percent.

A rising tide of the United States' manufacturers went the direct foreign investment route. Large corporations began to form international networks by building subsidiaries overseas, to take advantage of offshore production using cheaper labor rates, and then importing the goods back to the United States.

Other manufacturers began sourcing foreign components which they integrated into their exportable products, thus improving their competitiveness, but contributing to growth in imports.

Some industries, particularly the techno-intensive manufacturers, began spending above-average shares of revenue on R&D for new products and better processes, such as artificial intelligence (robotics) to maintain their competitive edge.

Service companies began to spring up to benefit from America's comparative advantage in education and the knowledge intensive industries.

American farmers recognized the changing trends of the world and adjusted to a global market. Producers were keenly aware of the vital importance of world markets and one in every four acres of farmland produced for export. During that period, United States' farm export performance had generally been impressive, but by the mid-1980s even that had taken a downturn.

But many Americans overlooked the change to an interdependent global economy. Producers from all over the world began penetrating the U.S. market at the same time that many of America's small- and medium-sized manufacturers remained entrenched in their own domestic market.

LESSONS LEARNED

Over the span of 200 years, America has come a long way in international trade. Beginning as a stepchild of England, the United States blossomed to become the world's greatest trading nation only to fall into chronic debt. No other national problem has proven more persistent, and completely resistant to more cures by statesmen and business leaders alike than the erosion of national competitiveness.

Understanding the lessons of history and applying them with grit and determination is the solution. It's the foundation of this book.

Lesson 1: Free enterprise and capitalism are well—it really works. In the short 200 + years since the founding fathers put their thoughts on paper advocating an experiment with freedom that philosophy has permeated the world. It has proven that the invention of free enterprise and market economics is stronger than the paternalism of socialism. The Communist experiment with utopia failed and free enterprise has proven to be so good that other nations have adopted it and are competing favorably using American rules.

By the mid-1970s the United States realized it was no longer the lone competitor in world markets, nor was it the lone competitor in its own market. Some viewed the change to internationalism as the coming of age of the Newly Indus-trialized Countries (NICs), but others saw it as a reactive response on the part of foreign nations rather than a proactive one. Those people believe internationalism happened to fill a gap in a changing America.

But the world also changed. Many of the have-nots of less than two decades ago were now countries to be reckoned with. Japan, leading the way of other nations that had been destroyed by war, proved that market theory economics worked.

International trade equals free enterprise equals market theory. After World War II, the United States promoted its belief in the capitalistic economic system. Using those root beliefs, the competitors became more sophisticated, closed the technology gap, and captured world markets once dominated by United States' firms.

Lesson 2: Trade involves the two-way flow of goods. This is a lesson America learned from the Great Depression of the 1930s. Jan Pen, the Dutch economist was right when he said, "Free trade between free nations furthers the welfare of both . . . exports are profitable for the exporter, but the country as a whole profits from imports."

Imports are a vital part of the American economy because the consumer is the beneficiary. Imports also contribute to sound trade relations, stable international relations, and elevate the standard of living around the world, all the while creating additional business opportunities.

To retreat from the lessons of history to a time when the United States produced most of what it consumed and put up tariff walls to exclude others is an uninteresting thought. It is not free enterprise and is not reality—it is a dangerous trend. The United States is now inextricably involved in the world economy.

Lesson 3: Accepting imports without reciprocity is altruistic. Following World War II, the United States freely accepted imports and the result has been an increased standard of living throughout the world. It's been good for world economic growth but not in all ways good for the United States. There are limits, and those limits are reciprocity. America must defend its rights in international trade and demand equal access to competitors' markets.

Lesson 4: Maintain a high-tech industrial base. The lesson of the two great wars was the necessity, for national security and reasons of our own self interest, to maintain an expandable industrial base at the cutting edge of technology. Old technology wins yesterday's wars, but new technology prevents wars and stimulates the future growth of great nations.

Lesson 5: Strive for free trade. International trade is very regulated. Free trade does not exist, and "fair trade" smacks of protectionism. Nevertheless the concept of "free trade," as idealistic as it is, is a goal worth striving for. Therefore, the United States must stick by and strengthen GATT as the primary element of the international trading system. Multilateral negotiations and Most-Favored-Nation principles worked for Cordell Hull's America of the 1930s and with patience can work for the world of the 21st century.

Lesson 6: The term international "trade" is obsolete. Trade connotes bartering—a business method seldom used in modern business. The word trade implies a defensive strategy, but "marketing" is a proactive word and changes a business' focus to offense.

Recently a group of American high school students was asked to describe international trade. One said, "Isn't it like, ya know, tak'n a boat load of wheat to Japan and trading the wheat for a boat load of cars?"

Jesse Hurd would be amazed to hear students explain it that way. For having learned about today's marketing methods, he would be the first to argue that in describing modern international business one should mentally substitute the word "marketing" everywhere the word "trade" appears. He would also encourage the application of marketing principles in our schools so that youth can take up the challenge and lead the way on a worldwide basis.

Lesson 7: American small- and medium-sized businesses must go on the offensive by thinking beyond the borders. To reverse dangerous trends, the United States must stand by its resolve and continue to promote free trade and free enterprise as a national policy.

Big business needs little help. They are already competing. But smaller manufacturing and service firms must reassess their strategy and get into the international trade game by competing with the rules America invented. This means committing to a game plan and putting into place appropriate international business strategies and tactics.

The remainder of this book offers such a game plan.

1

The game plan

IN THE BEGINNING THERE WAS MAN.

Then man became importers and exporters. In fact, the history of importing and exporting is the history of exploration and economic growth of the world. Man's progress can be measured in terms of toil, travel, and trade.

Then came the invention of telephones, satellite communications, and jet airplanes.

Then came the "age of aspirations."

And then came global "interdependency."

INTERDEPENDENCY

By interdependency we mean the "new world business paradigm" in which there is a growing interchange of goods and financial flows among nations, businesses, and consumers which has expanded trade so that today more than $3 trillion in goods and services move across international borders.

Peter F. Drucker of the Claremont Graduate School suggests that, "From now on any country—but also any *business*, especially a large one—that wants to prosper will have to accept that it is the world economy that leads and that domestic economic (and business) policies will succeed only if they strengthen, or at least do not impair, the country's international competitive position. This may be the most important—it surely is the most striking feature of the changed world economy."

GLOBAL BUSINESSES

Today there are a growing number of these "Global Businesses." A *global business* is one that has an international viewpoint; its employees are often of every ethnic, religious, and national origin; and they market and source wherever it makes good business sense.

How are these global businesses defined? What is an American company? What is a European company, a Japanese company? Frankly, an accurate definition is difficult. Some have crossed suppliers, some investors, some employees, some by position in markets. All we know is that foreign investment is moving rapidly—American firms have ownership in German companies, the Japanese have stakes in Mexican firms, and Brazilian businessmen have alliances in the Far East.

These global businesses have learned how to compete in the age of interdependency. They know it is a time when there is a greater openness of markets and a movement away from the "dangerous trends" of inward looking protectionism, and defensive strategies. They know that the danger is not from without, it's from the inside, from those who are comfortable with security and the status quo. They know that the 21st century will be known as the "World Century" and to remain competitive in a world that is increasingly open, a firm must be outward looking and take advantage of every business tactic and challenge every market opportunity. They know the winners of the global trade game will be the businesses with the best research, best manufacturing, best distribution, best, best, best not on one continent nor one country.

This means modern businesses, particularly small- and medium-sized firms must rethink their approach to international trade by developing a game plan that is proactive and offensive in nature.

MANAGED TRADE

In the prolog you learned that in earlier times goods were purchased at home at the trader's own risk then carried to distant lands to be sold in the currency of that land. Using that currency, the trader or ship captain bought goods to bring back home, hopefully for a profit. That was the way it was for centuries, no tax, no credit, no regulations, and no currency exchange problems.

But the increase in the exchange of goods among nations has brought almost continuous changes in government strategies for ensuring the social welfare of their people and to encourage economic growth.

Richard Whalen, of the Center for Strategic and International Studies, Georgetown University suggested that international trade is a game when he said, "the international struggle is actually a little understood contest [game] among governing elites testing relative ingenuity and skill in devising new political and economic arrangements to offset mounting social and cultural obstacles to productivity."

Unlike those ancient trading days import/export is no longer a free market process—in fact it is very regulated. Even though the United States and several other common markets have no tariff obstacles within their boundaries, there are many tariff and non-tariff barriers between nations, primarily because sovereign nations are protective of their industries.

"Managed trade" by some countries results in national industrial policies that "target" selected industries and markets for development while protecting home businesses from competition.

Regrettably, no supra organization exists to resolve barriers to free trade— the General Agreement on Tariffs and Trade (GATT) has done well, but has not proven as effective as its idealistic founders hoped.

Despite interstate (governmental) controls and structural impediments such as subsidies, tariffs, and antiquated multi-tiered distribution systems, the underlying assumption of this book is that the United States will continue to have a laissez-faire, "unmanaged" trade policy while at the same time attempting to persuade other nations to change their policies toward less regulation. If that happens, total trade volume will be buoyed and everyone will become a winner.

As an individual you can do little about interstate controls. That is for the multilateral trade negotiators, politicians, and GATT. Yet you must press on. Until such time that trade is less regulated, the essential characteristic which will allow you to win the trade game is to work aggressively within existing rules. Take good advantage of every business tactic to remain competitive. Don't get bogged down waiting for the government to solve all the problems.

For those instances when you "butt" against what you consider trade barriers that cause market distortions, Chapter 12 reveals who to contact in the United States Government to explain your "beef," and how to request remedies to regain a "level playing field."

DEVELOPING THE GAME PLAN: Strategy and tactics

"Strategy" and "tactics" are terms most often associated with the military, and are used extensively in war games at the Naval War College in Newport, Rhode Island and the Army War College at Carlisle Barracks in Pennsylvania. However, these terms have been increasingly adopted by the business world and are now used in developing global markets.

Strategy was first developed by military thinkers such as Sun Tzu a contemporary of Confucius who laid the ground work for Chinese military strategy thousands of years ago. It was Sun Tzu who said, "know your enemy better than he knows you." It is also attributed to him that, "one spy in the enemy camp is worth 10,000 foot soldiers."

Another early strategist was Prussian General, Karl Von Clausewitz, who was the first to make a complete study of warfare. He stressed the importance of strategy, which included political, social, and personal factors, as well as tactics, and training to defeat an enemy.

Strategy in the general sense means the science and art of employing political, economic, and psychological forces to gain maximum support for adopted policies. A strategic plan is the integration of smaller pieces (tactics) into a larger purpose.

Grand strategy

Grand Strategy is a term used with the biggest of concepts. For instance, the Grand Strategy of World War II was for the allies to first contain the Pacific theater and concentrate on beating the Nazis in Europe, then re-focus to win in the Pacific.

Strategy

When used alone, the word *strategy* suggests a lesser notion than Grand Strategy, but also large in scope. The Pacific strategy of WWII was to island hop across the ocean to the Philippines then north until finally the Japanese islands could be attacked.

Tactics

Tactic is the art or skill of employing available means or specific actions leading to the accomplishment of an end (strategy). General MacArthur developed the tactics to take back the Philippines Islands. This included the landing at Leyte, the bombardment of Manila, and the drive from the beaches to take the main island of Luzon.

Strategic Planning

President (General) Dwight Eisenhower once said, ''The plan is nothing, planning is everything.''

Modern international business requires the development of a strategic plan which incorporates the tactical steps to implement that plan. All too often companies make the mistake of developing two separate strategic plans, one for the domestic and government market and a separate one for international business. Certainly the approach should be a separate investigation of each, but the total plan should include both, because there is synergy (the whole bigger than its parts), and there are many commonalties. Realistic goals and objectives should be set and a suitable organization plan should be developed with logical tactical steps.

The strategic business plan is simply the measurement of your company and its products and the likely prospects for success.

THE GAME PLAN

Competitiveness in business is defined by three things: 1) The firm's long-run profit performance; 2) the firm's ability to compensate its employees, and; 3) the firm's return on investment to its owners. To do this the products or services of the company must be superior in quality or lower in costs than its domestic and international competitors. But to win the international trade game you must first get into the game.

Strategy #1: Awareness: Recapture the Yankee spirit by thinking beyond the borders

The basic truism of the 1990s and beyond is the interdependence of the nation-states. International trade is an area of business driving toward new horizons. From individuals seeking new careers to those who are at the cutting edge of establishing the fundamental trade rules of outer space, the most important strategy to winning the trade game and reversing any dangerous trends toward protectionism and inward thinking is to understand that interdependence is a reality.

Interdependence requires that business policies be adjusted to the world scene. To be successful in international trade, regardless of the competitiveness of goods or services in terms of price and non-price factors, businesses must substantially improve their global awareness and orientation.

In the past, for all too many managers, international business has been an afterthought. Some just didn't understand the mechanics while for others inertia set in and they were comfortable with marginal profits in a domestic market that was being attacked by foreign producers. Yet others were scared off by the perception of insurmountable obstacles.

Not today! Interviews with business executives reveal very positive attitudes about international business—particularly those companies which have excess plant capacity and a domestic market that is not fully satisfying their needs. Hazah! The pioneer, risk taking, "Yankee" spirit lives!

Things you should know

Some firms have been caught from behind and are not yet aware of what's happening in the United States and the rest of the world. Here's what is really going on:

- Modern manufacturing companies, small-, medium-, and large-size have adjusted to the realities of global competition. Marketplaces are full of consumer products from other nations, the less expensive the better. Women, who do most of the world's household marketing, no longer inspect where a product was made. They respond to "pocketbook" economics.

- Modern service companies are adjusting to the realities of a world of global competition. Service industries like McDonalds are everywhere, fulfilling the wants and desires of people in the consumer marketplace worldwide.
- Many service companies have overseas operations and compete for contracts all over the world.
- Modern marketers fly around the world meeting distributors and developing networks of other contracts. They attend major trade shows and strategically target advertising programs.
- Capital equipment and raw materials purchasers are searching for the best value—worldwide.
- Manufacturer's buyers no longer source only within the boundaries of their own country for component parts. Technology is changing rapidly, so much so that many firms believe they are better off forming multi-year strategic alliances with company's that are experts at staying with the "state-of-the-art" in their industrial specialty.
- A growing number of companies have overseas manufacturing and assembly operations and source raw materials and components from all over the world.
- Globalization is not something that will happen in the future, it has happened. Decision makers now visualize the marketplace in multi-national terms.
- International growth almost always takes longer. Owners know they must have a realistic time horizon and plenty of patience, but they can ultimately expect a good return on capital invested.
- Based on a company's financial condition and other decision factors, top managers form committees to consider a wide range of international business options including exporting, importing, going with a trading company, production sharing, co-investing, and various global marketing strategies.
- Firms then reorganize their company and personnel to manage the options selected.

Even Stanley Tools of New Britain, Connecticut, an old line Yankee company that in the past has been as American as apple pie has adopted the strategy of putting its factories in Europe and the Far East to be nearer their foreign markets.

Of course it is not enough to be aware and interested in international trade. To do something about it—to go beyond wishful thinking, you must understand the changes that have taken place in the United States in terms of who we are, what we make, how we trade, and what we consume.

Who we are. The United States has a higher standard of living than almost any other nation. Americans are generally more educated and their expectations about the division of time between work and play are in many ways more sophisticated. We are an innovative group with excellent research capabilities and incentives for the development of new products, many of which can be classified in the high technology category.

What we make. As a result of the way we are, life in the United States is changing, and the things we make are changing. Shortly after the middle of this century, the United States began manufacturing different things than yesteryear. It is called the "high-tech post-industrial era." Smokestack industries have been replaced by the "clean industries"—incubators of new technology and firms that are users of high-tech.

The best example is the electronics industry. Ralph Thompson, Vice President Marketing for the American Electronics Association characterizes electronics as 70 percent small business. Yet electronics is now the United States' largest manufacturing industry. It is three times larger than the auto industry, ten times the steel industry, and accounts for 6 percent of our national product.

Another thing that has happened is the phenomenal growth of services. They now account for two-thirds of the United States gross national product (GNP) and about 70 percent of United States employment.

United States' products can generally be characterized in four broad sectors. Those quadrants, as identified in Fig. 1-1 are:

- *Quadrant One*—high volume commodities such as grains
- *Quadrant Two*—high volume, highly differentiated products such as automobiles, computers, and TV sets
- *Quadrant Three*—low volume commodities
- *Quadrant Four*—low volume highly differentiated products and services.

How we trade. Major international trading companies typically trade in the Quadrant One, the sector of high volume commodities where profit is greatest.

The IBMs of the world are in Quadrant Two—they need little help to either import or export.

Those that trade in Quadrant Three often form associations, simply because profit margins are too small, and economies of scale are essential.

QUADRANT FOUR

The lower right quadrant in the diagram, shown in Fig. 1-1, the low volume, highly differentiated (technical) product and services area is where the United States needs to facilitate importing and exporting. But it is almost as difficult to

	Commodities	Differentiated Products (Technical systems)
High Volume	**Quadrant One** Typical trading company	**Quadrant Two** Large firms do it themselves
Low Volume	**Quadrant Three** Too expensive to do alone therefore use Associations	**Quadrant Four** Small- & medium-sized manufacturing and service companies What U.S.A. wants to sell

Fig. 1-1   Export Product Sectors.

operate in Quadrant Four as it is in Quadrant Three because of the complexity and expense. Yet it is in this quadrant that 90 percent of American manufacturing and service firms are offering their products. "Quadrant Four" companies are the thousands of small- (from 5 to 250 employees) and medium- (between 250 and 1,000 employees) sized firms that are interested yet have not gotten into the global market.

Small- and medium-sized businesses comprise 97 percent of the more than 14.2 million non-farm corporations. They provide 52 percent of all employment and account for 48 percent of the nation's business output.

Quadrant Four is also the sector where there have been the greatest changes. It is the quadrant of innovation—where high-technology products are spawned. It is also the quadrant where thousands of smaller firms are not yet participating in international trade.

THE PHENOMENA OF CONTENT

World trade is not just about exports, it is about two-way trade—imports and exports and the reality of interdependence is that consumers the world over respond to basic pocketbook economics, not to emotion, or patriotic slogans.

The majority of Americans earn excellent incomes from their high technology and service industries. To maintain the nation's standard of living yet be able to move ahead into the future and compete at the leading edge, the low- and mid-tech consumer gap must be filled. Americans need many inexpensive, but world class products. These products generally have a high labor content and come from two places: 1) companies that have substituted automation for labor, and 2) companies that import low cost parts from countries that have a lower standard of living.

People's attitudes about product content have changed. Once upon a time "Made in U.S.A." meant good old American know-how and quality, unsurpassed in the world. At another time, "Made in Japan" meant cheap, low quality copies. Then came the "phenomena of content." In the 1970s and 1980s products with labels "Made in Hong Kong," "Made in Japan," "Made in Germany," or "Assembled in Singapore," began penetrating world markets and content took on less and less importance to the consumer. The reality of today is that few products have the pure content of one nation. Product content is more often a mixture of labor, raw materials, capital, and know-how—whatever it takes to provide the best product, at the best price, for the consumer who cares little about how it was made. What does count is global name identification: Kodak, Fuji, Mercedes, IBM, etc, etc.

Most businesspeople and economists believe that retaining purity of national content at the expense of competition is protectionism and economic suicide. They believe content is a business decision, not a political decision—what is good for the consumer is good for business.

That is not to say that products designed and created in the U.S.A. aren't in demand in other parts of the world. Quite the contrary. The American movie, television, and video industries have stimulated greater wants for American things than ever before.

Strategy #2: The decision

The next key to winning the trade game is the decision to commit resources and a long-term strategy to maintain long-term competitiveness.

It's a misconception that the only successful international businesses have their own branch offices and plants in foreign countries. Certainly many do, but the vast majority of importers and exporters are just successful domestic manufacturers or service companies.

Many smaller firms are not waiting. When asked about the benefits of international trade, the president of a small electronics outfit explained it this way. "For most companies, expanding the firm's market area to include the entire globe can only benefit the overall sales picture. Some foreign markets will not be as rich or as promising as others. But the potential for even modest sales gains outweighs the associated costs or risks. An increase in volume usually means rising profits as well as an opportunity to utilize excess production capacity. For some products it can often extend the life cycle that was otherwise on the decline.''

That's not to say there will not be barriers in the path of your decision. You could be faced with a formidable list of apprehensions, some perceived, some real.

The misinformed will think of every conceivable reason not to get started, but this book is about reassuring you and assisting you to overcome the real barriers.

In spite of the perceived stones in their path, many Quadrant Four firms have overcome the obstacles. One of those is a small electronics firm near San Diego, California. That company does about $9 million in annual volume, has 65 employees, and almost 100 percent of its sales are in the international market. Now that's a Yankee spirit!

Does a firm have to sell 90 to 100 percent to foreign countries? Of course not. A company may begin international trade by importing less expensive components, but eventually this leads to export opportunities. A firm that exports 15 to 50 percent of total sales has an aggressive program. On the other hand a company that is selling totally overseas is probably missing many sales right here in the United States. After all the American domestic market is still the largest in the world. Why else would the United States be experiencing such fierce competition from foreign manufacturers?

It is important to recognize in today's interdependent business setting that marketing is a global activity and domestic marketing by itself no longer has meaning. Figure 1-2 shows that as a percent of the Gross World Product (GWP) of $14.7 trillion, the United States market, albeit very large, is just one of the world's many markets.

Aggressive American international companies are not deterred by lack of cash flow or inability to form their own foreign department. They search for alternative business arrangements.

Motivation of top managers is the prerequisite to foreign market entry and many join hands with competent trading companies, because they know there is more than one way to compete internationally.

Strategy #3: The tactics

Tactical planning and policy determines how your business fits into the marketplace. This book is designed to assist companies in Quadrant Four by offering a menu of methods to go on the offensive and take advantage of ever-growing international opportunities. Every enterprise should consider a mix of these business tools and organize to maximize profit on a global scale.

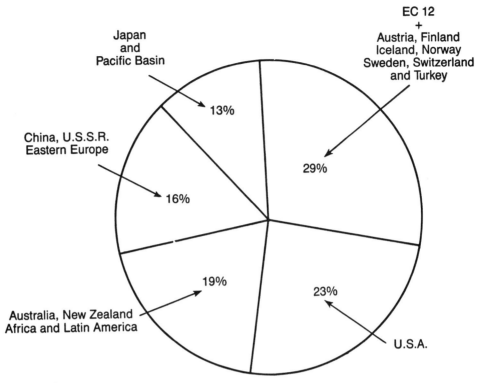

Fig. 1-2   Shares of Gross World Product (GWP).

The future of international trade for the small- and medium-sized manufacturer and service company in the United States is essentially no different than for any firm in any country in the developed world. As the global economy becomes more knowledge intensive and the sunrise (high technology) industries emerge at even faster rates, businesspersons will find the search for markets even more diverse. Regardless of the size of the firm, getting to the markets of a world that has growing interdependence will require economies of scale and knowledge centered arrangements that can bring the most sophisticated international business techniques.

This book offers 11 business tactics. They are not new. They are already on the books. Not everyone will be right for you, but a mix can help you win. They are the tactical keys to winning the trade game.

Break through culture barriers

What is culture? Know the difference between country and company culture. Learn what can happen when in a foreign country for an extended period. Study the do's and don'ts before visiting. Find out about women in foreign cultures.

Market internationally (export)

Know when the firm is ready to enter the foreign market, and what motivates top management. Learn the decision factors that allow businesses to choose the right marketing method. Develop and execute a strategic international marketing program that makes practical business sense.

Source globally (import)

Apply the latest thinking in international purchasing. Learn to look at global sourcing as it fits into the integrated manufacturing system by using Just-in-time (JIT) and Value Analysis (VA) and to develop a Commodity Management Approach (CMA).

Organize manufacturing for world business

Define your strategic boundaries, then integrate forward by partnering and exporting. Organize the firm to support changing international marketing and sourcing and to maximize tax benefits.

Compete in the global services market

Identify the kinds of services that can do business overseas. Learn how to get information, how to develop a market plan then break-in to the market, and what key elements are necessary to win a competitive bid.

Use intermediaries

Analyze the reasons to use intermediaries. Who are they? What do they charge? Learn how to get the most from these experts in international trade.

Form teams to win

Find out how to use the extraordinarily flexible Export Trading Company Act of 1982 (ETCA) to form teams to strike-back on more favorable terms against foreign competitors on their own turf. Learn how to apply for antitrust exemption and how to structure imaginative trade associations.

Vault trade barriers

Examine your options to deal with visible and invisible trade barriers. Use the 1992 union of the European community as a model to apply creative arrangements to circumvent interstate (governmental) controls that stand in the way of free trade. Study ingenious alternatives such as a forfeit financing, countertrade, direct mail, franchising, licensing, co-investing, and how to use a Foreign Trade Zone for profit.

Benefit from production sharing

Compare the advantages of the production sharing countries that have low labor costs. Learn who are the leaders in this growing industry. Review the Mexican Maquiladora case study and compare it to the incentives offered by Singapore.

Develop business with non-market countries

Study the trade prospects with Communist countries. Review United States policy and how non-market trade is organized. Find out who to contact, how to prepare proposals, and how to negotiate.

Level the playing field

Learn how to take your "beef" to Washington, DC to get relief from illegal and unfair import or export practices and interstate controls.

The next chapter addresses the first business tactic—appreciation of culture as it relates to international business success. This is a constant. It applies to all firms contemplating international business, because it is one of the major obstacles which prevents decision makers from entering the global market. By understanding culture, managers have a broader vision of the world, its business opportunities, and how to be a profitable player in various countries.

"Fear and suspicion are obstacles to clear thinking especially on matters where foreigners are concerned."

Jan Pen

2

Break through culture barriers

THE VERY THOUGHT OF DOING BUSINESS IN A FOREIGN CULTURE CAN BE A major barrier for American business decision makers, but it shouldn't be. After all, the original Yankee Traders were known for their curiousness, and inquisitiveness, and isn't it true that all Americans are simply transplanted foreigners? Appreciating cultural differences should come naturally.

It's not that businesspeople don't periodically kick around the idea of doing business overseas, they do. But all too often the prospect is dismissed as too risky, or the market too complicated when the underlying reason is really fear of the unknown. Sometimes it's the mystique that the languages are unintelligible and the people are different—"they" can't be trusted.

Too often American decision makers brush aside culture believing that there are universals and the United States is the model.

Can one culture be superior to another? Political systems, armies, navies, and even economic systems may be superior, but cultures are not.

The best way to appreciate another culture is to "walk in the other fellow's shoes," that is, live in the country and get a feel for the similarities and differences. Short of that, this chapter is the next best thing, because its purpose is to help you break through the culture barrier so you will at least appreciate the concept. You are cautioned that to be effective in your business dealings it is essential to be prepared. Do your homework before you interact in a new country, and then get on with doing business.

This chapter is organized into two parts. The first provides general information about culture as it relates to global business. To assist you with your homework, the second part offers lists of practical "do's and don'ts," country-by-country, within the following regional groupings: America's immediate neighbors (Canada and Mexico), Pacific Rim, Indian Ocean, Europe, Middle Eastern States, Gulf States, non-market (Communist) economies, South America, Central America, and Africa. Additional homework aids are provided in Appendices A, B, C, and D. Appendix A is a listing country-by-country of the world's holidays. By referring to this information you can plan to do business when it does not conflict with commercial holidays. Appendices B, C, and D provide listings of foreign currencies, management titles, and business titles to help smooth your way in international trade.

THE U.S., NO LONGER ISOLATED

You might not think of it as such, but the United States is an island nation. Of course there are neighbors north and south, but the country is separated from the resources it lacks as well as from the major markets of the world by the Atlantic and Pacific Oceans, the Caribbean Sea, and the Gulf of Mexico. The United States is a maritime nation and those major bodies of water are vital to the country's survival but at the same time they serve as natural barriers to trade.

Distance and time caused by the historical use of ocean shipping has prevented Americans from knowing their agents, and foreign business partners as well as they know those at home. From this lack of understanding of another's culture comes mistrust. As a result, some business persons become intimidated and consequently develop what is known as irrational xenophobia, an anxiety or in the worst case, a hatred of things foreign. National boundaries are "safe," even when sales and profit yields indicate otherwise.

The vast size of the United States and its common language is also an obstacle which caused some businesspeople to avoid exposure to foreign lands and cultures. America's melting pot ideology hid the fact that the country had a closed culture where, in the past, foreign trade had been a small percentage of our gross national product (GNP).

But all that has changed. Modern aviation dominates global transportation and the world is much smaller. The economy has become increasingly open to foreign competition. Market barriers have been reduced and competitors have made significant market share gains. The manufacturing base has changed from smoke stack to high tech and national trade performance has been dismal. National survival as well as business survival increasingly depends on reaching out to the people and cultures of the world to sell those goods America manufactures best and in turn exchanging for those that others do best.

Does understanding foreign cultural values really make a difference? You bet it does!

One person who traveled overseas regularly and made friends in many countries, said, "they're more like us than they're different." What he meant was that they like kids, they want them to be educated, they understand business, and they work hard. What he didn't say was the differences are what effect attitudes, so much at times, that some managers won't even consider entering the market to do business with "them."

Top executives acknowledge the problem. Most feel strongly that living and traveling as well as having an appreciation of the many factors of culture and language make a difference in their decision or ability to enter the international market. Most agree that the first step for an American manager is put aside cultural blinders and become more cosmopolitan.

One executive of a major United States' manufacturing company offered, "It routinely takes us as much as sixty hours of preparation for a fifteen minute business meeting." He questions his staff to make certain that they are totally familiar with the customs and history of the country, the company, and even mid-level government officials that they may need to contact.

WHAT IS CULTURE?

Let's get the word "culture" straight in our minds. Most dictionaries give three definitions. It is thought of as the act of developing the intellectual and moral faculties; enlightenment and excellence of taste acquired by intellectual and aesthetic training; and acquaintance with and taste for fine arts, humanities and broad aspects of science as distinguished from ordinary trade and craft pursuits. That's a good definition, but not what we refer to in this chapter.

A second definition refers to culture as the integrated pattern of human knowledge, belief and behavior that depends on man's knowledge and the capacity to pass on that knowledge to succeeding generations. That's not what we are referring to either.

The definition that interests us from a business point of view is that which has to do with diverse groups of people—the customary beliefs, social forms and material traits of a racial, religious or social group.

BUSINESS CULTURE

Culture is a set of meanings or orientations for a given society, or social setting. It's a complex concept because there are often many cultures within a given nation. For you an international business person, the definition is more difficult because a country's business culture is often different than its general culture. Thus, the environment of international business is composed of language, religion, values and attitudes, law, education, politics, technology and social organizations that are different.

Culture gives you a set of codes to deal with phenomena in a social environment. It sets priorities among the codes, and it justifies the need for the culture, usually by means of an associated religion. Whatever a nation's culture is, it works for them. In order to function within it, you must get on the band wagon.

The Japanese do it very well. They learn how to penetrate foreign markets by sending their managers to live and study in "the other fellows shoes." Their mission is to develop relationships with contemporaries that will last for years. The Japanese don't try to change the way of life in the other country, they learn about it. When they go home they are specialists in marketing and production in that country which they researched.

It's a country's culture that regulates such things as sexuality, child raising, acquisition of food and clothing, and the incentives that motivate people to work and buy products. All of these things are, of course, major factors in marketing products. Business culture is secondary to a country's general culture, but provides the rules of the business game and explains the differences and the priorities.

COUNTRY CULTURE

The process of taking the baggage of one's own culture into another is commonly called "cross-cultural communications." The ability to be successful in another culture requires an appreciation of theory, time, some practical rules, and an accommodating attitude. Let's look first at the theory.

Relationships

Relationships developed over a long period of time is the thing that reduces mistrust. To meet this challenge you need to understand the countries, their people, and the cultures where you intend to do business.

Language

Ask a Japanese businessman what language he speaks, and he will say the language of the customer.

Language is the thing that sets humans off from other forms of life. It is the way you tell others about your history, and your intentions for the future. Language is the means of communicating within a culture.

For people in a given culture their language defines their socialization. Sometimes, from the substance of some information it is possible to tell immediately the origin of the speaker. For instance, what is the country of origin of the person who says the following:

> "If y'all play ball—we can interface the system architecture, put on a dog and pony show, then split some knock-out profits."

As you could probably tell, this person is from the southern United States.

There are more than 3000 languages in the world today and probably as many as 10,000 dialects. Obviously, because there are only about 200 nations on earth, many countries have more than one language and culture. Some of the languages within a country have priority. Some are used for business, others are used for training and education. You need to have an appreciation that there are language hierarchies within nations in order to proceed with such every day practices as contract definition.

Some languages have become more dominant than others. On a global basis it is generally agreed that English is the world's major language. Therefore Americans often have an advantage. Because of its dominant role, English is becoming the most useful second language for people of other countries to learn. Although it is not growing in popularity, French is probably the second most useful language in the world. Of course Spanish is essential to do business in Central and Latin America. Languages such as Japanese and Chinese are also growing in importance as these nations grow economically.

The multiplicity of languages and the accompanying cultures in the world economy are having a dynamic affect on global trade. Every time a cultural barrier is crossed there is a potential communications problem and international trade depends on communications. Speaking in the customers language is the cardinal rule of international trade. Probably nothing deserves your attention as an international manager more than the possibility of language confusion and misunderstanding. It is not uncommon that trade is stifled simply because one or both parties to the relationship misinterpreted the meaning of a simple sentence.

For instance when Coca-Cola first introduced its soda to the Asian market, the name was translated with Chinese characters that sounded like ''Coca-Cola,'' but read as ''Bite the wax tadpole.'' Obviously, on a practical basis persuasive communications requires accurate translation for advertisement, packages and labels. A company whose work is poorly translated runs the risk of being laughed at, offending a customer and, in the end, losing the business deal.

Body language

Example 1. Frank had an appointment to meet Isuko at 11:30 in the morning, but he arrived at 12 o'clock. Their conversation was friendly but Isuko harbored a lingering hostility. Frank unconsciously communicated he didn't think the appointment was very important or that Isuko was a person who needed to be treated with respect.

Example 2. It was important that Jose Arriba and Bill Martin develop a cordial relationship for business reasons. At a party, Jose, in Latin fashion moved closer and closer to Bill as they spoke. Bill, interpreting this as an invasion of his space or a pushiness on the part of Jose, backed away. Jose interpreted this as a coldness. Body language, sometimes called the ''silent language'' spoke again.

From these examples you can see the subtle power of non-verbal communication. It's the first form of communication you learn, and you use it every day to tell other people how you feel about yourself and them.

This language includes your posture, gestures, facial expressions, costumes, the way you walk, and even the treatment of time, material things, and space.

People are very sensitive to any intrusion into their spatial bubble. An American's bubble of psychological distance or space is about 18 inches. If someone stands too close to you, you back up. Try it. If you can't back up, you lean away, or tense your muscles. Everyone tries to adjust their space in such a way that he or she feels comfortable. Some protect themselves with a purse, or an umbrella. Others move away to another spot behind a desk or a chair.

The language of the eyes is another age-old way you exchange feelings. You look away from someone who uses their eyes in a way you are not accustomed. Yet the use of eyes varies worldwide by class, generation, region, ethnic, and national differences. Think about it. Eye contact between men and women is measured in seconds and micro-seconds. In some cultures it's taboo to look at all.

Even the way you listen has a silent language of its own. You know immediately whether the person you're talking to is "tuned in." If a person is listening the head will nod, and occasionally the "Hmm" sound will be spoken. The speaker will know the listener wants to terminate the conversation when he or she fidgets and begins to look either at his watch or gaze about the room.

Body language is learned the same way you learned spoken language—by observing and imitating the people around you when you were growing up. You learned gender signals appropriate to your sex by imitating your mother and father.

These patterns of body language vary widely from one culture to another. American women sit with their legs crossed at the knee, or they may cross their ankles. Young Latin males, in their machismo, sit on the base of their spine, with their legs and feet spread wide apart.

People communicate a great deal by their gestures, facial expressions, posture and even their walks. Can body language affect your business dealings? You can bet on it!

Religion

Nothing destroys the development of relationships more than stereotypes of religious attitudes. Religion plays a major part in the cultural similarities and differences of nations. In itself religion can be a basis of mistrust and a barrier to trade.

A religious group took Bristol Meyers to court for selling low quality formula infant milk in a third world country. Both Eastman Kodak and General Motors have been targets of organized religious movements in other countries because of management decisions.

Religion is often the dominant influence for the consumer of products. Such things as religious holidays (Appendix A) determine buying and consumption patterns. Knowing what is forbidden and what a society expects as a result of their various religions affects market strategy.

Values and attitudes

The role of values and attitudes in international business are difficult to measure, but vital to success. Work ethic and motivation are the intangibles that affect economic performance. Values for instance, affect how you view time. The saying is, ''the clock runs in English and walks in Spanish and French.'' One international traveler said: ''The only time the Spanish are on time is for the bull fight.''

In more modern societies time has become a commodity, i.e., ''time is money.'' As an example, the time horizon of many American firms is measured in quarterly profits, yet for most Asian business cultures, the time horizon is measured in terms of 25, 50 or even 100 years. Building international business and trade across national borders just doesn't happen at a big city pace. In countries that have older, more traditional values, time is often measured in the movement of the sun, phases of the moon or relative to planting seasons.

Values of a society determine its attitudes toward wealth, consumption, achievement, technology and change and you must evaluate in terms of the host culture. Researching attitudes about openness and the receptivity to new technology are the essentials of marketing America's changing products.

Japanese Time Horizon: According to James B. Vaughn, Director of California's Office of Trade and Investment for the Asian region, ''. . . Japanese businesspeople have a strong tendency to want to deal with Japanese suppliers. It makes it very difficult for Americans to break into that system.'' He thinks it may take as much as 10 years to develop the business relationships and understand the market. ''It takes a lot of time and a lot of money, and my sense of American business and culture is that it doesn't lead Americans to do business that way.''

Laws and legal environment

The laws of a society are another dimension of its culture. They are the rules established by authority, and society. On the one hand laws provide an opportunity to handle the mistrust of doing business across international boundaries and on the other they can become barriers and constraints to operations. The laws of nations are often greatly different. The fact that most of the world's legal systems can be classified under the two headings of Code law and Common law does not mean identity of laws under those two headings any more than that those are the only two systems. About half of the nations of the world are under a form of either Code or Common law, but the other half are under either Muslim, Communist or indigenous laws. In most cases none of the world's legal systems are pure. Each nation has its own unique laws, nevertheless, one can find more and more similarities and mixtures within each classification.

Complications among national legal systems could drive the feint heart from international trade, but international law is growing and there is a set of adjudication practices that have developed over the years. *International law* is the derived law that in effect minimizes the range of differences among national laws. In the interdependent world of today international law is the growth area in the legal environment. There is no international legislative body that makes international laws. What does exist is a set of agreements, treaties, and conventions between two or more nations that represents the dampening of intercultural conflict.

For most dealings you will be most interested in the law as it relates to contracts, but you should always consider litigation as a last resort. Settle disputes in other ways if possible. Litigation is only for the stupid and the rich, because it usually involves long delays, during which inventories are tied up and trade halted. Law suits are costly, not just because of the money, but also because of the broken relationship that results. Most international commercial disputes can be solved by conciliation, mediation, and arbitration. The International Chamber of Commerce provides an arbitration service that can often be written right into a sales contract for use should the unspeakable happen.

Education

Culture shapes our thoughts and emotions. Your motivation is influenced by your education as well as other things such as values and religion which we have already discussed. The biggest international difference is the educational attainment of the populous. The next biggest difference is the education mix. In some countries such as the United States there is little difference in the mix. Practically all Americans are educated kindergarten through 12th grade. In the United States, education is no longer a function of wealth, but not so in many other countries. It is not unusual to find only the elite of some nations educated to the levels Americans assume for all people. The impact of education is therefore profound on marketing products as well as establishing relationships, because good communications are often based on relative education capacities and standards.

Technology

The most recent change in technology is our growing control over energy and information. The word technology begets concepts such as science, development, invention, and innovation. Some older languages don't even have words to express these concepts. Understanding the technological gap among nations is an essential element to exporting products across borders. Wide gaps still exist between the most advanced nations and those that are still what we call "traditional societies." The implications for you are that such things as training needs for technology transfer, and the impact of that transfer on social environments must be considered. You should always look at technology from the importing country's point of view.

Social organization

International trade cannot be conducted without involvement in foreign social relationships. In order to develop market segmentation and target markets the social organizations of a country must be studied. Insensitivity to the customs of the consumer country will not only result in misinformed decisions but also precipitate resentment and in some cases recrimination.

Nothing is universal in business organizations. There are no universal theories of motivation, leadership style, or consumer behavior. Such theories are figments of American business schools and do not stand up well in practice, nor do they export well. The truth is humans have invented an amazing diversity of institutions.

Social stratification is the hierarchy of classes within a society—the relative power, social priorities, privilege and income of those classes. Each class within a system has somewhat different and distinct tastes, political views, and consumption patterns. Many countries have a socio-religious ideology that allows rank to be intrinsic and inherited biologically. This implies that different categories of humans are culturally defined as if consisting of different worth and potential for performance. Regardless of how you react to such non-competitive socialization, such ideas are predictable in some countries. Faced with such a system of socio-religious rank it is essential that you learn how to deal with it—not attempt to change it.

PRACTICAL APPLICATIONS

Now that you have an appreciation of the theory and fundamentals of culture, let's take a look at the practical side.

Culture affects businesspeople in four ways: (1) Marketing; (2) Negotiating; (3) Culture Shock; and (4) When Just Visiting. It's called "cross cultural communications."

MARKETING

Here is a short list of examples designed to convey the importance of culture and how much difference it makes to how your firm might market its products.

- Four out of five Germans change their shirts only once a week.
- Deodorant usage among men ranges from 80 percent in the United States to 55 percent in Sweden, to 28 percent in Italy, and 8 percent in the Philippines.
- Feet are regarded as despicable in Thailand. Athlete's foot remedies with packages featuring a picture of feet are not well received.
- White is the color of mourning in Japan. The color purple is associated with death in many Latin American countries.

Adapting your product design, labels, and marketing strategy is driven by the consumer's culture.

NEGOTIATING

Culturally, nothing comes less natural to Americans than bargaining. As a nation which operates on a fixed price system, most marketers have grown up with the notion of buying off the shelf at the price offered or don't buy at all. Of course, comparative shopping is native to your buying psychic, so when the international stakes increase and the competition, often nations that are born cultural negotiators, begin to force your hand, your instincts might provide some basis for taking the right action, more likely they will not. Unfortunately, all too many firms wander into international bargaining situations with no plan and no idea how to proceed. For them, its an ad-lib and ad hoc operation all the way. For some, lack of preparation is the result of a sense of corporate superiority, but for most it's pure ignorance of the number and competence of the ferocious competitors out there scouring the world for scraps of business.

The first step in preparing for international negotiations, is to develop a complete assessment of your firm's capabilities. Analyze your strengths and weaknesses, particularly in terms of managerial skills, product delivery, technical abilities, and global resources.

Next, analyze your target—the company or country where you intend to sell your product. Keep in mind that the human and behavioral aspects of your negotiations will be vital.

- Understand the place in the world where you will be traveling.
- Know their culture, history, and political processes.
- Pay particular attention to the importance of face saving to the people of the country where you will be negotiating.
- What is the host government's role in country negotiations?
- How important are personal relations?
- How much time should you allow for negotiations?

In Ethiopia, the time required to make a decision is directly proportional to its importance. This is so much the case that low-level bureaucrats attempt to raise the prestige of their work by taking a long time to make decisions. If you, a foreigner attempted to speed the process, you could innocently downgrade the importance of their work.

The third step is to know your competitors. What is their financial position, their strengths and weaknesses, and what are their capabilities in terms of negotiating gambits?

The last step is to prepare and train the negotiating team. In todays increasingly competitive business world, there is no substitute for extensive advanced preparation and thought. Many companies have taken to role playing their negotiations long before the initial quote is submitted, or the actual marketing of a product begins. Teams are formed and each team is given a set of negotiating alternatives. Each team pretends to represent a product, company, or country which might be the line-up of competitors. With a chalkboard nearby on which a team presents its position, the negotiators go through sufficient rounds to get a sense of the process. Sometimes price is reduced 10 percent, or service warranties are offered. Even specific advertising concepts are discussed. Little is left to chance.

Competence in formulating strategy and negotiating skill is seldom learned from books—both subjects are ruled by so many variables that there is no substitute for experience and knowledge. Nevertheless, preparation and role playing acts as an excellent training devise and serves to sharpen the skills of even the most experienced.

Some key elements of cross-cultural negotiations

- Use the team approach. Take along financial and technical experts. Have someone take notes while the negotiators focus on the action.
- Dress for business. Show by your appearance that the event is of major importance.
- English is often the negotiating language, nevertheless take someone on your team who speaks the opponent's tongue. Rudimentary knowledge of key foreign terms and numbers might ease the process.

CULTURE SHOCK

Most people accommodate to changing situations, environmental conditions and cultures, but some have problems, particularly when facing a long term situation. This phenomena has been identified as "culture shock."

The term *culture shock* was first used by the anthropologist Kalervo Oberg in 1955 to describe problems of acculturation among Americans who were working on a health project in Brazil. Oberg found it to be a "malady, an occupational disease of people who have been suddenly transported abroad." The symptoms of culture shock can be apparent in people who don't even leave their own culture. It's possible for you to put on your blinders in your own home office.

Let's not overstate culture shock. Only about 25 to 30 percent of those going abroad for the first time are unable to adjust to a new culture. And it should be recognized that culture shock is primarily a matter of adjusting to frustration—the psychological dynamics that everyone finds when encountering new and confusing situations. Most of us have experienced the bewildering ambiguity caused by the inability to predict the behavior of others in a new social situation, maybe joining a new church or going to a new school. Anxiety in these situations ranges from mild discomfort to panic, rage, or flight.

Each person reacts differently. Some people jump right into the new situation and adjust easily. Some become aggressive and angry which scholars have labeled "fight." Others try to escape or withdraw. This is called "flight." Yet others "filter" distort or deny its reality. Those that cope best take up what is called "flex" or behavior adjustment.

Fight. This reaction often manifests itself in scoffing at foreign nationals and in the extreme becomes aggressive to the extent that there is overt destruction of life and property.

Flight. In an effort to overcome frustration this tendency is to reject those people who cause discomfort, that is completely avoid foreign nationals and seek the exclusive security of expatriates from their home country.

On the other hand the complete opposite might happen. By literally joining the host culture, you could relinquish your own cultural identity, thus never resolving the conflict between the two cultures.

When flight becomes chronic, it often leads to alcoholism, and even mental illness.

Filter. A person engaging in filter reaction tends to glorify things in America. As if they were wearing special glasses, they forget the harsh reality that the United States has homelessness, racism, and crime.

Flex. This is the reaction you should be encouraged to adopt. By suspending judgment of the foreign cultures, new cues can be learned and used as guidelines for behavior.

Dr. Sunny Chung, Ed.D., a counselor for international students in the Office of Student Affairs at United States International University suggests that there are five distinct stages of culture shock and that she experienced all five when she came from South Korea to live in America:

Stage One: *Honeymoon.* This is often a happy time when the new arrival falls in love with the new culture.

Stage Two: *Disintegration.* This is the period of immersion into new problems with language, transportation, shopping, food and everyday life. During this period common feelings experienced are: mental fatigue, bewilderment, alienation, depression and withdrawal.

Stage Three: *Reintegration.* Acceptance of the new culture takes place and some negative feelings about the foreign culture is healthy.

Stage Four: *Crisis.* You may experience deep frustration, a loss of self identity, confusion, and anger or in some extreme cases even feel suicidal.

Stage Five: *Autonomy and independence.* This is a period of acceptance and adjustment with small bouts of residual culture shock. At this final stage the person becomes fully capable of accepting and drawing nourishment from cultural differences. These people become expressive, creative and relaxed enough to enjoy humor.

Knowing something of another culture helps smooth the way to adjustment and prevents unrealistic expectations. On the other hand, when you understand and are conscious of your own cultural conditioning you can begin to see that American customs and ways are not ''natural'' for all people.

Overcoming culture shock requires a willingness to try as well as learn about foreign cultures.

JUST VISITING

Most business trips are usually short term and culture shock doesn't have time to set in. Nevertheless, it's important to understand as much about the culture of a country as possible, even when just visiting. To begin let's look at some generalities—some ideas that will help you make a good impression no matter where you're doing business.

Saving face is not just an Asian concept; although, it is particularly sensitive in those countries. Avoiding embarrassment to others, particularly ranking persons is essential wherever you are in the world.

People of any country like to talk about their own land and people. If you ask questions which show genuine interest—it will cultivate their respect towards you. But no one likes critical questions such as: Why don't you do it this way? Or, how come you do it that way? Above all, they don't want to hear how much better it is where you come from.

First impressions do count, and the wrong first impression can stop your business deal in its tracks. Bad first impressions are all but impossible to overcome.

1. SMILE! It's the universal business language and saves many problems.
2. But smile right. The smile in which the lips are parted in a sort of an ellipse around the teeth comes across as phony and dishonest. Smile easy—the kind where the full teeth are exposed and the corners of the mouth are pulled up. This kind of smile says, "Hi, I'm sure pleased to meet you!"
3. Grooming is important all over the world. Studies indicate that most people are more attracted to others who are neat, well groomed, and dress crisply.
4. Flash your eyebrows. That is, in most cultures raising the eyebrows almost instinctively in a rapid movement and keeping them raised for about a half-second is an unspoken signal of friendliness and approval.
5. Lean forward. Liking is produced by leaning forward.
6. Look for similarities. People tend to like others who are like them, so common experiences and interests are often a starting point for producing liking.
7. Nod your head. People like other people who agree with them and are attentive to what they are saying.
8. Open up. A position in which your arms are crossed in front of your chest may project the impression you're resisting the other person's ideas. Open, frequently outstretched arms and open palms project the opposite.

WOMEN IN INTERNATIONAL TRADE

In the battle of the sexes, American women are way ahead. There's more opportunity and freedom for women in United States business than almost any other country in the world. More than three million women own businesses—22 percent of all smaller firms—grossing more than $40 billion annually.

Nevertheless, around the world, it's the same old viva la difference. American women experience "culture shock" in almost every other place outside the United States. Even today, they are forbidden to drive cars or ride bicycles in Saudi Arabia. In Japan, the regard for women in business is still many years behind the United States. Even though a few have broken into middle management, general acceptance is still similar to the mindset of the United States in the 1950s.

Obstacles confronting women in the United States domestic marketplace are still substantial. That bias requires them to overcome more hurdles than men. It is not surprising then that there is a diversity of views about female participation in the still over-whelming male-dominated business worlds of other countries.

It is only recently that greater numbers of women have begun starting up or running their own businesses, but as the number has increased in the United States, the number involved in import-export has proportionately increased.

For the most part, businesswomen figure out ways to overcome the obstacles by simply end-running the problem and going to more receptive markets. Women doing business in most Middle Eastern countries often arrange for men to handle their direct negotiations with Arab businessmen.

One woman, on arrival in Egypt, moves directly into a hotel room and from there directs the negotiations of her Egyptian associate. She meets the principals involved only when the deal is essentially complete.

In spite of the difficulties, there are many success stories, and women in the international market place are encouraging other women to join them.

Ann Hughes, Deputy Assistant Secretary of Commerce for the Western Hemisphere offers, "Is it more difficult for women? You bet it is!" Secretary Hughes goes on to say that, "By far the most common path for enterprising women (to enter the international market) that I have talked to around the country, do it through retailing. Typically a woman starts by importing products for sale in her own shop. As the business grows and she travels more extensively, she begins to see opportunities for selling American products abroad and soon we have an exporter."

One woman in the private sector, the president of a bank Export Trading Company (ETC), reports, "there is a lot more opportunity than we were aware of, especially to do business in the People's Republic of China." She finds that in some markets having a male associate with extensive exporting experience who introduces her as president of the company opens doors. "It gives me more stature and credibility."

Another woman manager, a twelve-year veteran as export manager believes she detects a change in the attitude toward women. She says, "The situation has slowly improved. More women are coming into the field." Her advice to women considering international trade is to take advantage of the educational opportunities now available at adult schools and colleges, and attend import-export seminars.

Another export manager says, "Don't let being a woman hinder you (in international trade). You are a woman only to yourself." She suggests signing mail and telexes with your initials and last name. No one knows whether C. J. Moore is a woman or a man.

The chief negotiator for a major trading company claims that the kinds of problems she encounters on the job have nothing to do with being a woman. Rather, the problems are all about cultural differences, "When negotiating contracts, I have to be very conscious of the fact that the environments in which I do business are culturally and politically different."

A partner of a firm in the male-oriented field of providing management services for overseas engineering and construction says, "You just have to use a little common sense. For instance, the Saudis aren't ready to accept women engineers and contractors, but they are in the Philippines and Indonesia.''

Women have a strong role in Africa, both in the home and in business. Yet visitors should remember that in Muslim and Buddhist nations, the religious stricture against mixing the sexes socially is still very strong. One woman traveling as chief emissary for her company was surprised after meeting with men all day to be placed at a table with their wives that evening at dinner. On the other hand, some women executives find this an advantage. Sometimes they find out more about the country and company from the wives than from the men.

One women gives this advice. At presentations, conversations and sales meetings, avoid using ''I did'' or ''I know.'' She says it's better to use ''We do this,'' or ''Our company does this.''

Tips for women

- ✎ Never give a man a gift, no matter how close the business relationship. A small gift for his family might be acceptable.
- ✎ Give gifts from the company, never from you.
- ✎ If you are married, use Mrs. when overseas. Even if you don't at home.
- ✎ Avoid eating or drinking alone in public. Use room service, or invite a woman from the office where you are doing business to join you at a restaurant.
- ✎ If the question of dinner arises and is useful to cement the deal, avoid any doubts by inviting your counterpart's family.
- ✎ Make a point to mention your husband and ask about your male counterpart's family. Some businesswomen who are not married invent a fiance or steady back home.
- ✎ Try not to be coy about flirtations. Turn them off immediately with a straightforward, ''no.''
- ✎ Be aware of the culture, and dress to fit as closely as your wardrobe will permit. Conservatism works.

OTHER MINORITIES IN TRADE

''New'' Americans, who have already faced the difficulties of entering into a new culture in their adopted country, often have a natural expertise and understanding of their original culture which helps them source or market products overseas.

For minority groups, other than women, i.e., Blacks, Hispanics, Asians, American Indians, and others, many of the expected obstacles turn into advantages. In most of Africa it is an advantage to be a black American. Most newcomers to the United States have the advantage of speaking and understanding another language and culture. Getting off the ground is often easier because contacts are already in place.

Tips for minorities

✎ Don't get caught in the "racial discrimination trap." Every country has discrimination of one kind or another so avoid discussions of this sort.

✎ Do be proud of your heritage and use it to your best business advantage, but do your homework and know your own country's history as well as that of your ancestors.

✎ Do dress conservative—business dress is similar all over the world.

✎ Do use your multi-lingual capabilities.

ABOUT JOKES

The people of every country enjoy humor and they all have their funny stories, but explaining complicated jokes to businesspersons who don't share your culture can be very tricky. Here are a few do's and don'ts:

1. Do remember that each culture reacts differently to jokes.
2. Don't tell foreigners a joke that depends on word play or punning.
3. Do be careful about the subject of your joke. It could be taken seriously in a culture different than your own.
4. Do be informed about the sensitive issues in the country where you are visiting.
5. Do ask to hear a few local jokes. They will give you a sense of what's considered funny.
6. Do tell jokes, everyone enjoys a good laugh.

DO'S AND DON'TS: Country-by-country

The remainder of this chapter lists, country-by-country, suggestions that could help your day-to-day business in a foreign land. The lists are not exhaustive, but do, in most cases, touch on the major cultural characteristics.

THE U.S.' IMMEDIATE NEIGHBORS

Canada

All too often we take for granted the people who live north and south of our shared borders. Yet, these nations, Canada and Mexico, are rich in colorful heritage. Here are a few ideas to stimulate your consciousness.

1. Do be aware that Canadians are sensitive to comparisons with the United States.

2. Do take time to learn the geography of Canada and its rich history and linkages to Great Britain and France.
3. Part of Canada speaks French and another part speaks English. Do know where you are and avoid becoming involved in any disparaging discussions.
4. Possibly because of their heritage, Canadians tend to be more conservative than United States citizens.
5. In conversation, safe subjects are sport, commerce, and geography.
6. Do shake hands on greeting and departing.
7. Do make appointments and be punctual.
8. If invited to a home for a meal, do present an inexpensive gift to the host.
9. Do expect to be entertained in restaurants and clubs.

Mexico

1. Do expect Mexicans to be cosmopolitan, yet be aware of the strong national pride they all take in their rich heritage.
2. Don't draw comparisons with the United States or discuss illegal aliens.
3. Do attempt to learn the language. Mexicans appreciate the effort.
4. Do have a cosmopolitan frame of mind when doing business in this country.
5. Do expect meal hours to be similar to those of southern Europe, i.e., breakfast: 7–8 A.M.; lunch 2–3 P.M.; supper: 8–10 P.M.
6. Appointments are scheduled; however, it is not unusual that they are made from 30 minutes to 1 hour in advance of the time the meeting will actually take place.
7. Greetings among men who know each other usually include a hug as well as a handshake.
8. Do be careful with presents. Inquire in advance.
9. Working hours in this country are 8 A.M.–2 P.M.; 3 P.M.–5 P.M.
10. Mexicans rarely work on Sundays, a day reserved for church and family.
11. Unless a close friend, do not call a person at home.
12. Nothing is more important to the Mexican than his family, which includes not just the immediate members, but also aunts, uncles and cousins several times removed, as well as all the members of his in-laws' families.

PACIFIC RIM

Historically, Americans have been dominated by European cultures, but recently our international business growth has migrated toward the west, so let's begin with Asia.

Excluding the southernmost countries, i.e., Australia and New Zealand which have closer cultural ties to England and the United States, the Asians are extremely sensitive to "loosing face," the behavioral characteristic of maintaining self-esteem. Go slow and learn about the culture.

Australia

1. It is not unusual to be invited to the home of your Australian business associate. When visiting a household, a modest bunch of flowers for the hostess or a bottle of wine is an acceptable gift.
2. Australians generally like Americans, and are much like us, but keep in mind their proper British origin.
3. Eating anything but ice cream on the streets is not proper.
4. Promptness is important.
5. Winking at women, even to express friendship, is improper.
6. Outward signs of emotion, such as hugging, are not considered manly and are avoided.
7. When yawning, one always covers the mouth, and excuses himself.
8. A clenched fist with a raised thumb, as in the American hitchhiking sign, is a vulgar gesture.
9. If an Australian is asked to do something, he will endeavor to please, if told what to do he may reject the command.
10. Men keep their emotions to themselves.
11. Sportsmanship is very important and is often cheered, even in a losing team.
12. Australian beer has a higher alcohol content than American beer, so be careful!
13. At parties or get togethers, it is not uncommon for the men to congregate among themselves and the women among themselves.
14. Tipping is not always necessary; it is often expected at better restaurants.

Hong Kong

1. Reserve and tact are highly stressed.
2. When invited to dinner the guest usually takes a gift of fruit, candy, or cookies to the hostess and presents it with both hands.
3. After entering a home, visitors are usually offered tea, a soft drink, or warm water.
4. Before starting a meal, guests should recognize the older members of the family.
5. Sincere compliments are given and appreciated, but denying them is the Chinese way of accepting them.

6. If one receives a gift, he or she tries to give a gift in return.
7. It is very impolite to open a gift in front of the one who gave it. If, for good reason, you wish to open it, make sure you ask the givers permission.
8. When social appointments are made, a half hour courtesy time is allowed for most people. Business appointments are generally on time.
9. When sitting, visitors should place their hands in their lap and be sure not to wiggle their legs.
10. Blinking the eyes at someone is impolite.
11. The open hand rather than the index finger should be used for pointing.
12. Call for a waiter with your palm down, never up.
13. Police officers with red shoulder tabs speak English.
14. Tipping is not expected.

Japan

1. Japanese don't expect Americans to act exactly like they do, but awareness of manners and customs is important in the conduct of business.
2. Do be polite and considerate.
3. Do observe how the Japanese act.
4. Don't expect the Japanese to use English, although many will.
5. Do try using some Japanese language phrases even if you only know a few greetings like "kon-nichi-wa" or "kon-ban-wa." The result will be that the Japanese will feel closer to you.
6. Do speak slowly and wait for the translator.
7. Bring a small gift for the people you will be doing business with—the Japanese are gift givers.
8. To approach a business, you may do well to obtain a *shokai-sha*, or at the very least a letter of introduction from the embassy. This person may later become a mediator or *chukai-sha*. Bank officers make excellent mediators and chukai-sha.
9. Take a group with you at negotiations. You'll be making a deal with five or six Japanese.
10. Japanese deal through trading companies (Sogo Shosha) and they earn their profits as a percentage of sales. They are motivated by sales.
11. In Japan you rarely negotiate directly with the decision maker. Therefore, the lesser employees take copious notes verbatim. They'll spend hours on what seems to be a very minor subject. For that reason negotiations take a lot of time.
12. Don't expect a lot of feedback from your business counterpart. Its not that they are secretive, its just not in their culture to be direct. The Japanese are much more subtle than Americans.
13. Do expect that if a Japanese answers "maybe" or "probably" to your

question, the likelihood of positive action will be great, even higher than when Americans respond in the same manner. If the same Japanese were to answer "I'm thinking about it," your expectation should be that approximately 80 percent of the time the result will be yes.

14. Ask a question three times in Japan and the third answer will be the honest response.

15. Never call a Japanese by his first name unless invited to do so. Use Mr. or "San" after the name. San is appropriate for both men and women, married or single.

16. Don't wear your shoes in Japanese houses.

17. Normally don't smoke on Japanese trains; however, night trains and express trains often have special smoking sections.

18. Don't soap up in a Japanese bath. Washing is done outside of the tub. The Japanese-style bath is for soaking.

19. Don't tip waiters. A 15 percent gratuity is included on the bill. However in night clubs and bars, customers sometimes will leave a tip.

20. The Japanese bow (ojigi) is famous the world over and is very convenient because it can be used for greeting, thanking, leave taking, or apologizing. It can be used when saying "Good morning" (ohayo), "Hello" (konnichiwa), "Good evening" (konbanwa), "Thank you" (arigato), "Goodbye" (sayonara), or "Sorry" (sumimasen or gomennasai).

21. Bows are used for expressing appreciation, making apologies, requests, greetings and farewells.

22. The Japanese have differing greetings for different situations: They wave their hand to say hello to a friend, give a quick bow of their head in passing, but the direct business bow is deep, and considered an extremely polite bow.

23. The depth of the business bow depends on your status and rank to the other person. Japanese are familiar with the handshake and often shake at the same time that they bow.

24. When passing in front of people, do excuse yourself by stooping slightly and holding out your hand with the edge downwards as if you were cutting your way through.

25. Do exchange business cards.

26. Don't try to use dollars in Japanese stores.

27. Do try the Japanese food.

28. Do slurp your noodles called *ramen, udon, soba,* and do slurp Japanese tea.

29. Do not slurp other foods such as Spaghetti or coke.

Here are a few Japanese body languages:

1. Scratching the head is a way of hiding confusion or embarrassment.
2. Folding the arms implies that a person is thinking hard.
3. Holding up the index fingers like horns on either side of the forehead indicates that a third person (a boss or wife) is angry.
4. Holding a clenched fist beside the head and suddenly opening the fingers expresses the opinion that a person is ''paa'' (stupid or crazy).
5. Holding a clenched fist in front of the face in imitation of a long nose implies that the person under discussion is, like the long-nosed goblin ''tengue,'' a conceited braggart.
6. Touching the index fingers together like swords clashing indicates that people are quarreling.
7. The gesture of applying saliva to the eyebrow shows that you are not taken in by the tall story your friend is telling you.

South Korea

1. Meeting the right person in Korea depends on having the right introduction; therefore, avoid popping in or trying to make direct contact.
2. Koreans like to know your company and your position in that company. Take plenty of business cards.
3. After the exchange of business cards, place them on the table in front of you then proceed with the meeting.
4. The real level of understanding of English may be less than courtesy implies. Speak slowly, emphasize important points.
5. Koreans are considered to be good negotiators, but be patient and don't push your position too hard. Sensitive issues and details should be deferred to be worked out by your staff or middlemen.
6. In Korea, legal documents are not as important as human rapport, relationships, mutual trust and benefit.
7. For the Korean businessman the important thing about a contract is not so much what it stipulates, but who signs it and the fact that it exists.
8. Try to personalize your business relationship. Learn as much about your counterpart as possible—family status, hobbies, philosophies, birthdays, etc.
9. Friendships are highly valued, as is modesty.
10. Like in Japan, entertainment plays an important role in any Korean business relationship. When offered, it should always be accepted, and in some way reciprocated.
11. The giving of small gifts is an accepted practice.
12. Emotional considerations and face are often more important than western logic.

13. A man greets his male friends by bowing slightly and shaking hands. Women usually do not shake hands.
14. One should pay complete attention to the person they are greeting.
15. When visiting a Korean home one should wait to be urged two or three times before entering.
16. Shoes are always removed.
17. Talking or laughing loudly is often offensive.
18. Do not open a gift at the time it is received.
19. Pass food with the right hand, with the left supporting the right fore-arm.
20. Don't be surprised if you are offered dog meat, deer antlers, snake soup, blood worm soup and other exotic dishes. You need not eat your fill, but at least take a taste—who knows, you might like it.
21. Tipping is usually expected in modern tourist hotels.
22. In meetings and on formal occasions one should cross their legs one knee over the other, soles and toes pointed downward. On very formal situations do not cross the legs at all. Hands should remain in sight at all times.
23. Korean men often hold hands in public. It's normal!!
24. Putting one's arm around another's shoulders or slapping a person on the back is reserved for close friends.
25. Both hands are used when giving or receiving objects to another person.
26. Reluctance to accept high honors is the mark of a true Korean gentleman.
27. Do use the Korean greetings and language. It is much appreciated.

New Zealand

1. In informal situations the people are very casual and easygoing, but again, like the Australians, remember their British connection. In situations requiring formality they are very formal and expect others to conduct themselves properly.
2. The greeting "how do you do?" is used in formal meetings.
3. Always use people's titles when addressing them in informal situations.
4. Shaking hands is acceptable at all meetings.
5. Gifts such as flowers are not expected of guests but it is not improper to give them.
6. Visitors should not excessively compliment their host on such items of decor and clothing as the host might customarily feel obligated to give the item as a gift. This is especially true among the Polynesians.
7. The Continental style of eating is used in New Zealand. The check, at a restaurant, is often paid to the waiter at the table.

8. Children are required by bus company regulation to stand and allow adults to be seated if there are insufficient seats.
9. New Zealanders are very proud of their country. Comparisons with the U.S. or other countries is not appreciated.
10. Cover your mouth when a yawn cannot be suppressed.
11. Friday night is the major social night.
12. Tipping is not necessary unless one receives special service beyond normal duties. To offer a waiter or porter money for preferential treatment could offend them.
13. Tea is a ritual in New Zealand—morning and afternoon. If you are invited for tea it probably means ''supper.''
14. Drug stores are called ''chemists'' shops.

Philippines

1. Initial greeting should be friendly and informal.
2. The everyday greeting is a handshake for both men and women.
3. When one greets a young child, he or she should allow the child to show respect rather than lower themselves to the child's level.
4. Older people should be shown great respect and allowed to take the lead.
5. When in another person's home, guests should direct questions to the father.
6. The word hostess should not be used.
7. Do not use the curled finger gesture to call or motion a Filipino towards you. It is extremely offensive. Use the entire hand, palm down.

Singapore

1. Because of the great diversity of cultures in Singapore greetings usually depend on age and nationality of the person. The handshake is the most common gesture of greeting with the addition of a slight bow for Orientals.
2. Great respect is paid to the elderly. The door is held open for them. On buses, one gives his seat to an elderly person before he gives it to a woman.
3. Westerners are expected to be punctual.
4. Shoes are removed before one enters a mosque and sometimes a home.
5. Compliments are appreciated, but usually denied for modesty's sake.
6. Like most other Asian countries, gifts are not opened at the time they are received.
7. Touching another's head is impolite.

8. Legs are crossed one knee over the other. The foot or sole is never pointed at anyone.
9. Hitting the fist into a cupped hand shows very poor taste.
10. When beckoning someone the whole hand palm down is waved.
11. A slight bow when entering, leaving or passing a group of people shows courtesy.
12. Never become drunk in public.
13. Don't litter! One cigarette discarded on the street can cost you S$50.00 or a night in jail.
14. Wear neat, clean clothing.
15. Risque magazines such as Playboy, Penthouse are taboo. A court could fine you upwards of S$500.00.

Taiwan

1. This island nation off the coast of mainland China is a vigorous land of business enterprise.
2. Do avoid discussing China.
3. Do make appointments and arrive on time.
4. By American standards they take longer making business decisions.
5. The handshake is the normal form of greeting.
6. Like many other Asians they entertain in restaurants. These meals are commonly heavy drinking affairs with many courses.
7. The toast is *kampai*, which means bottoms up.
8. Taiwanese business people are generally formal. They respect titles, and the elderly. Thank-you notes are appreciated.
9. Do be prepared to exchange business cards.
10. Gifts are presented with both hands and are not opened in the presence of the giver.

INDIAN OCEAN

These countries, which extend west from Singapore and rim the north Indian Ocean comprise Bangladesh, India, Indonesia, Malaysia, Pakistan, Sri Lanka, and Thailand have been influenced by a mixture of British and Chinese cultures.

Bangladesh

1. This nation, East Pakistan until December 16, 1971, is an infant state compared to most. Nevertheless, after a rocky start it is a place of growing business energy. Knowing its history will be impressive.
2. It will be unusual to be entertained at home.
3. Wives usually are not invited to accompany their husbands.
4. British influence still exists particularly about being on time.

5. Do shake hands with men, but only nod to women—if the hand is extended, of course, you may shake it.
6. Avoid political talk.

India

1. Understanding the religions of this nation is a must before doing business.
2. The handshake is an acceptable greeting but you should expect and may use the *namaste* greeting as well. This is formed by placing the palms together fingers pointed up near the chin and nodding the head.
3. Hindus believe the cow is sacred. Muslims eat no pork.
4. Muslims as well as Hindus generally keep their women hidden away in the kitchen although this is less pronounced among Hindus.
5. When greeting a women avoid touching—not even a handshake. Use the *namaste*.
6. Do make appointments and be punctual.
7. Do use the right hand to pass food.
8. Do talk about sport, travel, art, literature, Indian culture.
9. Don't talk about poverty, homelessness, etc.

Indonesia

1. Do make appointments and be on time in this country.
2. Do expect that business will take time, sometimes long and frustrating.
3. Do use the handshake when greeting.
4. Do remove your shoes when entering any holy place.

Malaysia

1. This is a land of mixed religions. Do expect to be among Buddhists, Hindus, and Muslims.
2. Do remove your shoes when entering a home or holy place.
3. Do respect the elderly—they do.
4. Do be on time and make appointments.
5. It is advisable not to touch a woman on greeting—a slight bow or nod will do.
6. The handshake is common among men.
7. Do expect to be entertained at a restaurant.
8. The left hand is never used to touch food, particularly among Muslims.

Pakistan

1. This is another nation where the use of the left hand to touch food is a no-no.

2. Do not expect pork, it is forbidden, but do expect some highly seasoned beef, lamb, or poultry.
3. Alcohol is not encouraged, although it might be offered in very private situations.
4. The traditional greeting is the handshake, but close friends may embrace.
5. Appointments are necessary.
6. Working hours are 9 A.M. to 4 P.M.
7. Lunch is the business meeting meal.
8. Again, do not shake hands or otherwise touch a woman in public.
9. Do avoid name familiarity.
10. Stick to titles and last names until you have established yourself, although this is a very friendly nation and first names are used early-on.
11. For elders use ''Aap'' and for casual friendships and young adults use ''Tum.''
12. Avoid politics especially domestic politics.
13. Gifts are welcome, particularly if it is something for their children.

Sri Lanka

1. Greetings vary from ethnic group to ethnic group and from caste to caste. Again remember their British influence—common English greetings are acceptable.
2. Titles are very important. It is proper to address acquaintances by their titles unless otherwise invited.
3. Sri Lankans are careful of the types of food they eat. Before inviting a Sri Lankan to an American meal check with the Embassy or Consul for the types acceptable.

Thailand

1. ''WAI'' is the customary greeting of placing the hands together in praying position before the face and slightly bowing or nodding the head. This is both a mark of respect and greeting equivalent to a handshake.
2. Always respect the Royal family.
3. The King's Anthem is customarily played after plays and other events—it is bad manners not to stand at erect attention.
4. Never step on Thai currency, as the King's image is embossed on it.
5. Remove your shoes before entering Thai homes, shrines or temples. Place your shoes' soles down when removing them.
6. It is all right to take pictures of temples, but it is considered rude, in poor taste, and contrary to their religious attitudes to take photographs of persons in informal dress such as swimming suits using a temple as a

back-drop. Certainly you would expect the taking of nude pictures in front of a temple to incense the Thai people, and it did when one foreign magazine attempted to do so.

7. Avoid loud talk.
8. Be patient.
9. Avoid pointing with the finger—it is offensive to the Thais.
10. Do not use profanity.
11. Never touch a Thai on the head or shoulders. To a Thai, the head is a sacred part of the body and is considered off-limits for touching—to them the soul resides there. Don't even pat a child's head.
12. Conversely, the feet are a most unworthy part of the body. To point a toe, sit cross legged, or show the bottoms of the feet is offensive.
13. The proper greeting in this country is the *wai*, which is similar to the Indian *namaste*. Place your hands palms together at chest level and nod your head.
14. Do make appointments and be on time.
15. Expect business decisions to take a long time.
16. When invited to dine, don't decline and say you dislike their food. It is better to taste it, but if you decide not, then make up another excuse not to eat it at all.
17. Gifts are proper, but wrap them.

EUROPE

Before we begin, a few general statements about the do's and don'ts in Europe.

Do be on time. Punctuality is at the top of the list of not only good business practice but good manners. Most Europeans are not as familiar as Americans at first meeting. First names are used only after developing a long relationship. If a person has a title, don't forget to use it just as a matter of course—to show respect.

Austria

1. This is a country with great pride in their own accomplishments. Never refer to them as Germans—they have distinctly different customs and values.
2. Do arrange business appointments in advance and try to be punctual.
3. Flowers or a small gift is appropriate if invited to a home for dinner.

Belgium

1. Do not be surprised to see men embracing.
2. Greetings are often accompanied by kisses on the cheek—three times,

alternating cheeks; although, on a business meeting it is customary to greet and say goodbye with only a handshake.

Denmark

1. Danes like their drink *aquavit*. Be careful it is potent.
2. Toast by saying the word *skoal*.
3. July and August are the months when the Danes vacation—don't expect to do heavy business during the summer months.
4. Punctuality is expected.

England, Scotland, and Wales

1. Of course you know that these three countries comprise Great Britain. When Northern Ireland is added, the four become the United Kingdom.
2. The British generally dress and talk very conservatively.
3. When searching for a non-controversial subject, try sport or animals. Don't talk politics, or about the Queen.
4. Titles are cherished and used even among old acquaintances.
5. Do not vent your emotions, save it for the privacy of the hotel room. The British public school system teaches self-discipline and control.
6. Scotch is the whiskey you drink. If you mean bourbon don't ask for whiskey.
7. Dinners are often similar to our ''dining-in's,'' very formal, and seldom at home. Expect the host to give grace before the main course, then toast Her Majesty's health. You may wish to toast the President of the United States. After the toasts, you may smoke but not before.
8. Invitations to these dinners often specify ''black tie'' which means dinner jackets and long dresses.

Finland

1. The Finns are generally not very formal people.
2. Do make appointments in advance and be on time.
3. This is a country that likes their saunas, so be prepared for a relaxing evening.

France

1. Do expect business to be conducted in a formal way.
2. Don't expect to be invited home, but if so do take flowers or candy.
3. Do be on time for your appointments.
4. The handshake serves as the standard greeting, but don't be surprised to see kissing on the cheeks.

5. In some cultures, particularly Asian, socializing comes first, but the French tend to get right to business. They may take their time making the decision, but they are forthright and direct in their intentions.
6. The French are known for their fine food, but don't be surprised if you are offered snails and horse meat.

Greece

1. This is a country of generosity and sincerity. Do expect to be invited home for dinner.
2. Age is revered in Greece. The elderly are served first, addressed with respect, and have authority.
3. Punctuality is less important here than in most European countries, but you should not be the offender. Do make appointments and call if you are to be late.
4. Be prepared for a handshake, a hug or even a kiss at each meeting.

Italy

1. This is also a less formal country than many of the northern European nations.
2. Expect to spend a lot of time at lunch, and expect to get some business done during this meal that sometimes takes two or three hours.
3. Although punctuality is not an Italian virtue, don't pick up the habit.
4. The Italians do take business very seriously, so be on time and do make appointments.
5. Do be careful of your gestures. The Italians find the upward hand or fingers offensive.
6. Learn the titles of the people you are doing business with and use them. Most college graduates have a title.
7. Shaking hands is part of the culture here. Expect it often and vigorously.

Netherlands

1. The Dutch are formal in their business dealings.
2. Do be on time and make appointments.
3. Do expect that 100 percent of the people of this country speak English. It is bad form to ask if somebody speaks English—it is assumed and they don't even like to be questioned about it.

Norway

1. You may be invited to a Norwegian home, if so take a small gift.

2. Be on time.
3. Do talk about sports and travel, but don't talk about social status or other personal topics.

Spain

1. Put away your American clock and join in this entirely different cultural application of time. You will start later and have the main meal in the middle of the day. You should expect to work later.
2. The "siesta" is a break in the middle of the day when most stores and businesses close, usually from approximately 1:30 until 4:30 P.M. Most people go home to join their families, and even take a short nap. Others spend the time in restaurants with their friends.
3. Because the day is already shifted, expect to eat supper well after nine or ten o'clock when the restaurants open. This meal often extends well into the next morning.
4. Do use the handshake, but don't be surprised to see hugs (*abrazos*) among men who are friends or even only business associates.
5. Spanish attitudes about punctuality is changing. Once, it was almost impolite to arrive on time, but now most business meetings begin reasonably on time.
6. Do take a small gift if invited to dinner.

Sweden

1. Sweden is a nation of progressive, even liberal thinking about society and politics. Read up on the latest innovations and don't be afraid to use these as topics of conversation. Don't make comparisons between the United States and Sweden.
2. Make sure you know something of the cultural differences between the other Scandinavian countries of Norway, and Denmark. Other terms you should be familiar with are *Norden*, which adds Finland and Iceland to the Scandinavian list, and *Fennoscandia*, a term often used to describe Finland and the Scandinavian Peninsula.
3. Do indulge yourself of the famous *smorgasborg*, an assortment of cold and hot foods placed on a table for self-service. Eat the foods in the order your host suggests which is usually fishes, followed by cold meats, then hot dishes, then finally desserts.
4. Do make appointments and be punctual.
5. The Swedes traditional toast is *skoal*.
6. Do wait until your host toasts you. Toasts are initiated by seniority.
7. Watch your host carefully and replicate his or her *skoal* motion.
8. Drunk driving is a no-no, so be careful. It is wise to designate a driver who will not drink.

Turkey

1. Because of its location and its historical background, Turkey has always attracted many foreigners. Istanbul, which connects the two continents of Asia and Europe, is the heart of business.
2. This country stresses business and economic development both domestic and international.
3. Turkey with a population of more than 50 million is considered one of the more competitive markets of the future.
4. Appointments are necessary. Be punctual.
5. Firm handshaking is customary.
6. To use a few Turkish words, eases the atmosphere even if those few are the limit of your vocabulary. Try *merhaba* for hello; and *merci* or *tesehkur* for Thank you.
7. Turkish people are sensitive that they are not confused with Arabic nations, particularly in regard to religion. Unlike the Arabic countries, religion is free and is not emphasized—do not mix religion with business relations.
8. Expect to be invited home or to a nice restaurant for dinner. Do not try to pay the bill. It would be considered offensive to do so because you are the guest.
9. If you are invited home for a meal the host will push food toward you and insist you eat more than normal. It is their way of showing hospitality.
10. Turkish cuisine is world famous. Try the shish kebob, doner (gyros), boklaw and of course the Turkish coffee.

West Germany

1. Berlin is actually a neutral state.
2. Always preface the words Germany and Berlin with "East" or "West" as appropriate.
3. This is a country of conservative thought, attitudes, and bureaucratic approaches. Do make appointments and be punctual—it is essential.
4. Do use the handshake. It is important in both business and personal relationships.
5. Until invited, never take the liberty of using a first name.
6. The body language (psychological) distance of most Germans is 18 inches or more.
7. Do not expect to establish a close relationship during a short duration. They maintain relationship distance until they are sure business will be long term.
8. Do be careful to use titles.
9. Use your last name when answering the telephone.
10. Do expect Germans to respect authority and older people.

11. Do respect the "line of command" in a German company.
12. Do expect invitations.
13. If invited to an intimate dinner with a family or couple, do take a gift such as flowers or candy.
14. Do expect breakfast to consist of breads, no meats.
15. Do expect lunch to be the big meal of the day.
16. Expect Germans to drink in the evening. Beer and wine consumption is among the greatest in the world.
17. Do not expect Germans to greet strangers. "Hello" is reserved for acquaintances.
18. Topics of conversation are politics, sports, and business.
19. Do expect presents and gifts with business associates, particularly during the Christmas season.
20. Do expect working hours during the work week for government and banks to be: 9 A.M. – 12 P.M., lunch 12 P.M. – 2 P.M., 2 P.M. – 4 P.M. Shops are closed everywhere from 1 P.M. – 3 P.M. The Germans work Saturdays from 9 A.M. – 1 P.M., but do not work Sundays.

MIDDLE EASTERN STATES

This group of states is composed of Egypt, Israel, Iran, Iraq, Jordan, Lebanon, Saudi Arabia, and Syria.

Egypt

1. Time is less important in this country than it is in the United States; nevertheless, do make appointments.
2. On greeting, do expect to shake hands, but also hug and kiss on the cheek.
3. Avoid politics in conversation.
4. Do expect the major meal of the day to be lunch. Business meetings often take place over lunch.
5. Do not expect to be invited home for lunch, but if you are, do expect the meal to be served in one large bowl from which everyone will eat.
6. Egyptians have difficulty saying "no." Instead, expect that they will postpone things by saying "we will see."
7. Do be careful of gifts. Know the receiver well before offering a gift, otherwise it could be perceived as an attempt to bribe.
8. Office hours are 8 A.M. – 2 P.M., lunch break is for 3 hours during which people usually go home, then return to the office by 5 P.M.

Israel

1. Customs in this Jewish state differ from those of its surrounding Arab neighbors. Whereas Friday, and in some cases Thursday, is the day of

rest in Arab states, from nightfall Friday until nightfall Saturday is The Sabbath in Israel. Therefore the work week is from Sunday through Friday.

2. When planning a trip for business purposes, do make appointments in advance.
3. *Shalom* is the greeting word, and a handshake is expected. Don't put a lot of stock in titles; they're more casual about this than even the Americans.
4. Politics, American and Israeli are often topics of conversation.

Iran

1. This is a nation that is tired of war and ready to rebuild. There is a growing need for foreign business.
2. Appointments for private sector business are essential; however, this is less important in the public sector.
3. Punctuality is less important in this country than others.
4. Do use the handshake for welcoming and greetings. Hugging and kissing is done only between friends. Instead of actually kissing, cheeks are touched during the greeting embrace.
5. Iranians do not expect foreigners to speak their language (Persian), nevertheless do use the common words: *selam* for hello, and *merci* or *mutshakeram* for thank you.
6. Avoid conversation about politics and war, particularly Iraq.
7. Meals are usually big gatherings where the main dishes are rice and chile Kebob.
8. Iranians are interested in foreign people and like to invite them home.
9. Business is often discussed over meals in restaurants.
10. It is not traditional to exchange gifts in business relations, but they are not refused.
11. Government working hours are 8 A.M. – 3 P.M. with one hour for lunch.
12. Private sector hours vary and depend entirely on the owner.
13. Businesses are closed every Thursday (normally for a half day) and all day Friday.
14. Women in the business sector must cover their hair and wear conservative shirts and blouses. Most Iranian women, especially followers of Homeyani also wear a *chodor* (a long black dress).
15. Alcohol is prohibited but some people, in violation of the law, do drink it at home. It is not served at hotels.

Iraq

1. Iraq has been at war for nine years and is seeking business to rebuild the nation.

2. Do make appointments and try to be there 10 – 25 minutes early to give the impression that you care.

3. Do initiate a greeting with a handshake, then follow-up with small talk about how much you like your stay, the food, the climate or historical places.

4. Do use first names.

5. Expect to be invited to lunch or dinner in a restaurant.

6. Do prepare yourself for traditional food, especially at lunch time, which is the main meal and may be anytime between 1 P.M. and 5 P.M. You will most likely be served lamb cooked or fried with heavy corn oil.

7. It is not a good idea to give presents to government officers—they become offended. Private sector persons can accept and exchange gifts.

8. Working hours are: 9 A.M. – 2 P.M. (government); lunch 2 P.M. – 4 P.M.; and after lunch 4 P.M. – 8 P.M.

9. Alcohol is available, but it is illegal to drive under the influence—jail can result.

10. Do not smoke in an office.

Jordan

1. Jordan has the highest literacy rate in the Middle East; therefore do expect to find the people you deal with in the business sector to be highly educated.

2. Do be aware that Jordan imposes high border tariffs on such luxury items as T.V. and cars. For instance imported cars have as much as 300 percent duties.

3. Be aware that about 75 percent of the population of this country are Palestinians who have also become citizens of Jordan, or were born in Jordan.

4. Appointments are necessary. Foreign businesspeople should be punctual.

5. People in this country do not like to talk about politics with foreigners. Do talk about family and traditional issues such as recreation and sightseeing.

6. Foreign business people are usually invited for dinner at either a restaurant or home where business is a satisfactory topic.

7. Jordanians do expect presents, but this is an opportunity to promote your products with samples for gifts.

8. Do expect to be made comfortable by your Jordanian counterpart. They will place you in an excellent hotel and take you sightseeing and to restaurants. They give you great importance if they perceive you sincere and nice.

9. Working hours are: 9 A.M. – 1 P.M.; lunch for 2 hours; then work again from 3 P.M. – 7 P.M.

Lebanon

1. Because of war, business in this country has come to a standstill.
2. Do expect that once conditions normalize, this country will return to its traditional place as one of the business capitals of the world.
3. Unlike other Arabic countries, Lebanon has the only Christian/Arab Government—50 percent of the population is Christian and 50 percent is Moslem.

Syria

1. Syria is a nation that has imposed high tariffs on most imports, therefore, little business is done with foreign firms.
2. Due to low wages, living conditions in Syria are very low.
3. French is the second language.

GULF STATES

This group of countries comprise Bahrain, Kuwait, Sultanate of Oman, Qatar, Saudi Arabia, United Arab Emirates, and North and South Yemen. This grouping of states has several cultural characteristics which are presented as a group of traits. Individual cultural differences are specified separately.

Common cultural characteristics

1. Essentially, the people of these nations all come from the same tribe; therefore, they have many common cultural characteristics.
2. Do expect people to be very conservative, especially their external appearance.
3. Don't expect religion in these nations to be separate from politics. Politics is religion and vice versa.
4. Do expect presents and gifts as a sign of appreciation.
5. If you receive a gift, you should give one in return.
6. Do expect the working hours to be regulated by prayers. Everyone goes home and businesses are closed during prayers which is five times a day. Every work place has a small praying area or mosque.
7. Do expect alcoholic beverages to be prohibited.
8. Do expect lunch to be the main meal of the day.
9. If you are served lamb (the most prestigious meat), or turkey, you are being treated very special.
10. Do expect women to be treated significantly different than in the west.

They remain in the background, and are forbidden to drive or ride bicycles.

11. Do make appointments, but do not expect that the meeting will happen on time.

12. Do expect to do business with contracts, even though in earlier times the word, a handshake, and the reading of the Koran represented a promise.

13. Do not admire somebody's personal property or children. If you do, it could be considered giving them the evil eye.

14. During a business meeting, do expect to be served coffee, tea, and later coffee again. The drinking cups are generally very small and the server will continue to pour until you shake the cup forwards and backwards signifying you have had your fill.

15. Do expect the second serving of coffee to signal the end of the meeting whether the contract is concluded or not.

16. To keep wealth in the family, do expect to find inter-family marriage to be common, especially in Saudi Arabia. First cousin marriages are most common, and relationships between families are very strong.

17. Do not be surprised to find two men kissing and hugging. This is a sign of strong friendship and has no sexual connotation at all.

18. Do expect higher class society to kiss the lower class person twice on the cheek. If the person is especially loyal or valuable, he or she will receive an additional kiss right after the second kiss.

Bahrain

1. This small Kingdom is located on an island in the Persian Gulf, but is connected to the mainland by a highway.

Kuwait

1. As a result of income from oil, Kuwait has the second highest per capita income (greater than $10,000/year) in the world after the U.A.R.

2. In spite of the high incomes, do expect to find this country in serious need of social and economic development.

3. Do expect the quality and reputation of products to be very important. These people like to buy expensive goods. Giving high priced gifts is very common.

4. Do expect loyalty to be held in high regard.

5. Do expect the topics of conversation to be casual such as where they spent their last vacation and what they purchased while away.

6. Do be careful about political discussions. They often become diatribes about the conflict between Arabs, Palestinians and Jews.

7. Do expect rice, lamb meat and seafood to be the main dishes.
8. Although the people are not formal and often use first names, they do like to use titles such as Doctor or Engineer.

United Arab Emirates (U.A.R.)

1. U.A.R. has the highest per capita income in the world.
2. Life and people in this country are very similar to the other Gulf States, especially Kuwait.

Yemen

1. This country is considered among the least developed countries of the world.

NON-MARKET (COMMUNIST) ECONOMIES

Albania, Bulgaria, China, Cuba, Czechoslovakia, East Germany, Hungary, Mongolia, North Korea, Vietnam, Poland, Rumania, Russia or Soviet Union, Vietnam, Yugoslavia, comprise the nations whose economies are strongly influenced by communistic political thought. Of course, since the peaceful revolution of 1989, many countries on this list are changing their economic and political positions. They are organized culturally because business intercourse for most American firms is just now beginning to grow. Chapter 11 discusses the way to do business in these countries.

Albania

Business in Albania? Maybe not, but the people of every country have something and want something.

1. Do make business appointments far in advance and be punctual.
2. Do not talk about politics—sports and geography are good subjects.
3. Do take pictures of the colorfully clothed people.
4. Do not try to take pictures of military or police installations.
5. Gifts are welcome if invited to a home.

Bulgaria

1. This is a Communist country, so don't discuss politics, religion, or social conditions.
2. Do address men or women as comrades—with their last name, of course.
3. Head gestures are the reverse of our culture. A head shake means yes, and a nod means no.
4. Candy, flowers, or wine make excellent gifts if invited to a home.

China

1. The Chinese are a formal people.
2. Do respect titles and the elderly.
3. Do refer to the country as the "People's Republic of China" or simply as "China."
4. Do not use expressions such as "Red China," "Mainland China," or "Communist China."
5. The Chinese approach to business is subtle, and often indirect compared to the American "lay-all-your-cards-on-the-table approach."
6. Foreign business delegations are usually welcomed at the airport by a person of equivalent stature. Similarly, they attach great importance to seeing their guests off.
7. Do take a large supply of business cards—they are exchanged frequently in China.
8. In Chinese practice, the surname precedes the personal name, and married women do not use their husband's name.
9. When Chinese enter a room for a meeting it is in protocol order. Therefore they assume the first foreigner to enter the room is the delegation head.
10. The leader of the guests is seated to the right of the main Chinese host.
11. Meetings generally being with small talk. Safe subjects are the weather, how many visits you have made, and what Chinese cities you might have visited.
12. Avoid mentioning Taiwan, but if it comes up do not refer to that country as the "Republic of China" or as "Nationalist China." "Taiwan Province" or simply "Taiwan" will do.
13. When it is your turn to state your business, pause frequently and speak slowly to allow the interpreter a fair chance to keep up.
14. Negative replies are considered impolite in most oriental cultures. When in doubt say "maybe" and clarify later.
15. Chinese prefer to know in advance exactly what will be discussed—like us, they don't like surprises.
16. Don't be surprised if you are invited to frequent banquets over lunch or dinner—it is a polite Chinese gesture, and an opportunity for a good meal at state expense.
17. The visitor need not reciprocate this hospitality while in China, but should be prepared to entertain his Chinese hosts if and when they come to visit you.
18. Although there are exceptions, like the bigger hotels, generally the Chinese consider tipping an insult.
19. At these banquets, Chinese hosts are expected to arrive before the guests and seating is rigidly by rank.

20. It is the responsibility of the hosts to serve their counterparts from the platters. Of course the guest of honor is served first by the principal Chinese host. It is perfectly polite to serve yourself once the dish has been first served.

21. The cardinal rule when you are finished eating a particular course is to leave some food on your plate else your host will continue to serve you and you will be expected to eat.

22. The Chinese understand if you elect to pass on duck blood soup, sea slug, duck brains, or fish stomach.

23. As you grow in the art of Chinese banqueting you will soon learn that drinking plays no small part. People who do not drink should not feel compelled to imbibe. But do return toasts with soda or some other drink.

24. At the end of a toast all are expected to rise and say *ganbei*, the equivalent of "bottoms up," then turn the glass upside down to demonstrate that all has been consumed.

25. Stay on safe subjects at banquets. Food, geography, climate, or art are generally non-controversial. Public embarrassment is considered a major breach of etiquette so be careful not to pose questions to ranking Chinese that puts him on the spot.

26. Gifts from foreigners are generally politely declined—the Chinese have rigorous rules about bribery and corruption and the offering of lavish gifts may embarrass the intended recipient.

27. A presentation to the business organization as a whole is a better idea.

28. In China friendship probably means good working relationships rather than personal relations, which are very hard to establish.

29. Leave your tuxedo at home. The Chinese don't care what their foreign guests wear. However, women should not wear revealing, see-through blouses and should not wear shorts.

Cuba

Times change and doing business in Cuba is not as farfetched now as it once was.

1. Do dress comfortably—Cuba lies within the tropics, and because of the northeast trade winds has a pleasantly warm climate. Nevertheless, be prepared for a rainy season from May to October.

2. Do remember that this country still operates on the Spanish clock with siesta time from about 1:30 P.M. til 4 P.M.

3. For conversation—politics no, sports yes.

4. Leave your English at home and be prepared to do business in Spanish.

Czechoslovakia

1. Be punctual for your business appointments.
2. Avoid politics by talking about sports.
3. Do be careful not to photograph military or police installations.
4. Small gifts exchanges are welcome, but don't overdue and embarrass.

East Germany

1. The name of this country is the German Democratic Republic of just GDR.
2. To these people the label East or West doesn't exist. East Berlin is just Berlin.
3. You may not visit a manufacturing plant without a permit issued by the Ministry of Foreign Trade.
4. Needless to say, don't get into political discussions in this Communist country.

Hungary

1. Because of the state-run trading organization, make your appointments well in advance and be on time.
2. Do expect to be entertained in restaurants.
3. If invited to a home, an appropriate gift might be flowers for the woman and Western liquor for the man.
4. Do avoid politics, but be sure to talk about art in this nation that has had many world-famous composers and writers.
5. Do take pictures of the colorful folk costumes.
6. Do not photograph military or para-military personnel or installations.

North Korea

The reunification of the Koreas may never happen, but the possibility of doing business with North Korean firms becomes more of a reality each year. The customs of the two countries are similar; therefore, most of the same do's and don'ts are found under the heading for South Korea. Prior to visiting North Korea, in addition to this list, do review those of South Korea as well.

1. Do remember that this is a centrally controlled economy and many of the business practices differ in that regard from South Korea.
2. Make your appointments far in advance and be on time.
3. In this country you will need a translator. English is seldom spoken. Speak slowly, emphasize important points, and avoid colloquialisms.
4. Friendships are highly valued, as is modesty.
5. Emotional considerations and saving face are often more important than western logic.

6. When visiting a Korean home one should wait to be urged two or three times before entering.
7. Shoes are always removed.
8. Talking or laughing loudly is often offensive.
9. Do not open a gift at the time it is received.
10. Pass food with the right hand, with the left supporting the right fore-arm.
11. Both hands are used when giving or receiving objects to or from another person.
12. Do use the Korean greetings and language. It is much appreciated.

Poland

1. Don't expect to hurry your business in this state-owned economy. The bureaucracy requires that decisions be reviewed at various levels of the hierarchy.
2. Set up your appointments well in advance and be on time.
3. The Polish drink hard liquor and lots of it, even while doing business.
4. Do be careful of your conversation. It's okay to talk about the United States and your family, but don't talk about World War II.

Rumania

1. Appointments well in advance are required in this state managed economy.
2. Romanians are generally very punctual, you should be too.
3. Trade with the West has been commonplace since the 1960s so expect a high level of understanding and appreciation for free enterprise.
4. Expect negotiators to be clever businesspeople.
5. Do not expect to be invited to a Romanian home. Should it happen, take flowers for the hostess, and a small gift for the family.
6. Sport, art, music, and travel are good topics of conversation.

Russia or Soviet Union

1. The full name is Union of Soviet Socialist Republics, or Soviet Union. It is often referred to as Russia, but it is really a country of many customs and languages. "The Soviet Union is not a country, but is a world," according to an old Russian saying.
2. Do not exchange money with an ordinary citizen. It is against Soviet law and the penalty could be the cancellation of your visa. Do exchange at official offices.
3. Plan your trip and make appointments well in advance.
4. Be punctual.

5. Do expect the greeting to be a handshake. Kisses and hugs are occasionally seen among friends.
6. Expect negotiations to go slowly in the centrally controlled trading organization.
7. The Soviets are sports fans, so don't hesitate to use sport as a topic of conversation. Avoid politics, but do talk about painting, literature, or music in this land often more famous for its talented people than its industry.

Vietnam

1. Once two sovereign nations, this controlled economy now does less business with the West. Nevertheless, recent changes offer increased opportunity.
2. The Vietnamese are formal people.
3. Do respect titles and the elderly.
4. Do refer to the country as the ''Vietnam.''
5. Foreign business delegations are usually welcomed at the airport by a person of equivalent stature. Similarly, they attach great importance to seeing their guests off.
6. Expect to be greeted with a bow and a handshake.
7. When Vietnamese enter a room for a meeting it is in protocol order. Therefore, they assume the first foreigner to enter the room is the delegation head.
8. The leader of the guests is seated to the right of the main Vietnamese host.
9. Meetings generally begin with small talk. Safe subjects are the weather, travel, and cities you might have visited.
10. When it is your turn to state your business, pause frequently and speak slowly to allow the interpreter a fair chance to keep up.
11. Negative replies are considered impolite in most oriental cultures. When in doubt say ''maybe'' and clarify later.
12. Vietnamese prefer to know in advance exactly what will be discussed—like us, they don't like surprises.
13. At banquets, Vietnamese hosts are expected to arrive before the guests. Seating is rigidly by rank.
14. It is the responsibility of the hosts to serve their counterparts from the platters. Of course, the guest of honor is served first by the principal Vietnamese host. It is perfectly polite to serve yourself once the dish has been first served.
15. The cardinal rule when you are finished eating a particular course is to leave some food on your plate or else your host will continue to serve you and you will be expected to eat.

16. The Vietnamese understand if you elect to pass on duck blood soup, sea slug, duck brains, or fish stomach.
17. Stay on safe subjects at banquets. Food, geography, climate, or art are generally non-controversial. Avoid mentioning the war.
18. Gifts from foreigners are generally politely declined—a presentation to the business organization as a whole is a better idea.

Yugoslavia

1. This is a nation of growing business opportunity.
2. Do make your appointments well in advance.
3. Do be on time, even though Yugoslavs put less priority on punctuality than others.
4. You might be invited to a home in this country, so check out gift giving customs. Wine and flowers are always welcome. The men like whiskey.
5. Conversation topics are less constrained in this country, because they get away to Western nations often for business. In the beginning, sport, family and travel are still recommended topics.

SOUTH AMERICA

Generalizing is dangerous; however, in an attempt to conserve the limited space of this book several observations about cultural commonalties of this region of the world are offered:

1. *Machismo* is the concept that men are superior to women. This is an extremely strong feeling among the people of the nations south of the U.S. border. Being manly is constantly on the minds of men and it is important to them that they appear brave and have great self-confidence.
2. In general men and women shake hands on greeting and departure. Close friends often hug and pat each other on the back.
3. Women friends often greet each other with a kiss on the cheek.
4. The clock generally runs on southern European time, that is lunch and supper are usually taken about two hours later than in the United States.
5. America is not an exclusive term for those that live in the United States. It includes those that reside in Central and South as well as North.
6. Family ties, the church, and business loyalties are extremely strong and highly valued by South Americans. Nothing is more important.
7. People of these nations go to great lengths to avoid offending. How something is said is more important than what is said. A businessperson will avoid being brisk or ''businesslike.'' Instead he or she will try

to make each conversation friendly and warm even though the deal is being made at the same time.

8. Aristocratic top executives and governmental ministers will seldom negotiate with you at the outset. Instead expect middle-class middle managers to lay the ground work.
9. Whom you know is what generally matters more than what you know.
10. Be patient in business matters. Don't expect immediate results.
11. Show your humanity—Latins expect and want to see it.

Argentina

1. Do expect to be greeted with a handshake.
2. Expect to make appointments and be on time.
3. Do take or arrange for delivery of a gift for the hostess if invited home for dinner.
4. Sports and art are acceptable conversation topics. Do avoid politics and religion.

Columbia

1. This is a nation that loves sport, particularly soccer and the bull fights.
2. Because of Columbia's high altitude, expect your body to need time to adjust.
3. Do expect time to be less important than establishing a good relationship. Negotiations can wait until you know your business partner.
4. Do expect to be greeted with the handshake.

Bolivia

1. Do expect a handshake in personal greetings.
2. Eating on the street is not good manners; Often the food found there is not of good quality.
3. Do watch your manners—considered very important.
4. Do make appointments.
5. Do be on time for meetings even if others are late.
6. Do dress in moderate, conservative taste.
7. Direct eye contact influences positive communications in this country.
8. Do expect a closer body language distance. Expect patting on the shoulder as a sign of friendship.

Chile

1. Do expect Chileans to greet one another with an "abrazos," or hug, but you will, at least at first receive only a handshake.

2. Do expect to be entertained at public restaurants and hotels.
3. Don't be late to appointments.

Peru

1. Do expect to be greeted with a handshake, but Peruvian men will exchange hugs.
2. Expect to make appointments and be on time for business—being late a casual half-hour is expected.
3. Do take or arrange for delivery of a gift for the hostess if invited home for dinner.
4. Sports and art are acceptable conversation topics. Do avoid politics.

Uruguay

1. Do expect Uruguayans to work hard on projects that interest them but they do not consider being efficient, keeping busy, and learning to conquer the material environment virtues in themselves.
2. Do expect personal relationships to be valued highly and in most cases preferred to impersonal, functional connections.
3. Do expect men to be well dressed, but in a conservative manner.
4. Do expect women to have extensive political and legal rights—they are generally accepted as equals in social and cultural life and often in the political, business and financial world.
5. Do expect to find career women, and those that you meet to be exceptionally talented people.
6. Do expect the urban educated elite to know some English, but you should count on doing business in Spanish.

Venezuela

1. This is a country that holds great store for titles and position. Instead of saying, ''Mr. Johnson.'' The Venezuelan would say, ''Engineer Johnson.''
2. Do make appointments.
3. Smaller firms are less formal.
4. Because of the hot weather do dress casually.
5. Conversation among men, when not talking business, is usually about women.
6. Do expect to be invited out to discuss business. Luncheons at nice restaurants are common.
7. Do expect the color black to be considered the most fashionable color among women, and subdued colors fashionable for men's suits.

8. Do expect, as a result of their far-reaching mixture of races, that this nation has greater opportunity, and that it is less tradition-bound, and has less class prejudice than most other Latin American cultures.
9. Do expect to learn that business training in this country puts high value on spiritual and social aptitudes.

Brazil

1. The language of this country is Portuguese. Try to learn some and don't worry about making mistakes. Brazilians appreciate your efforts even if your vocabulary is small. English is spoken by many of the well-educated.
2. Do expect Brazilians to be casual about work. But, don't mistake this attitude for laziness or indifference. They just consider time and work to be necessary evils rather than essential parts of life.
3. Do expect men to value their manliness. It is all important to be brave and display great self-confidence in every situation.
4. Do expect the body language to be different. It is simply friendliness for a Brazilian to stand close to you when he speaks, to pat your shoulder or back, or even to rearrange your tie or scarf. Don't misinterpret this familiarity.
5. Do expect family ties to be extremely strong and very important.
6. Do dress discretely and in good taste. Shorts are worn only at the beach.
7. Do be soft-spoken and gentle-mannered.
8. Do knock on office doors, but after knocking once, stand back and wait.
9. Don't knock on the door of a Brazilian's home. Stand back and clap.
10. Do conduct yourself properly in public.
11. Do speak about the things you admire about Brazil, such as its culture and arts and the nations progress in developing its resources.
12. Don't make a circle with your fingers to show that everything is OK. This is considered an extremely vulgar gesture in Brazil.
13. Do use the "thumbs up" sign when things go well.
14. Don't snap your fingers. This is also considered vulgar.
15. Don't eat on the street or on public transportation.
16. Don't yawn or stretch in public.
17. Don't over tip. Most restaurants will add 10 percent to the bill. Leave another 5 percent and you'll be fine.
18. Don't overpay for domestic help or other services.
19. Although definitely a male-dominated society, machismo in this country takes a milder, more subtle form than is generally found in neighboring Hispanic America.

20. Do expect Brazilians to be very fashion conscious, but actually casual dressers. A suit and tie for men, and suits and skirts or dresses for women are the office standard.

Paraguay

1. Do expect to be greeted the first time with *mucho gusto* (pleased to meet you). Thereafter, the greeting will be "good morning" or "good evening."
2. Do be on time for appointments even though strict punctuality on the part of the Paraguayans is not demanded.
3. Do discuss family, sports, current events and the weather, but avoid politics.
4. The national pastime of this country is conversation. Do not expect as great a division between work and play as in the United States
5. Do expect business hours to extend from early morning until late afternoon with a midday break for siesta.
6. Do expect compliments to be given freely and expressively, but they should be about personality traits rather than about objects or appearance.
7. Never use the United States "okay" sign or make a sign with crossed fingers—these are considered offensive.
8. Do sit erect, with both feet on the floor. Crossing of legs is acceptable but only with one knee over the other.

Ecuador

1. Do expect this to be a nation of strong feelings of nationalism.
2. Do expect the work week to be six days, eight hours a day.
3. Don't expect dignitaries to eat in public.
4. Do expect to be greeted with a handshake.
5. Although punctuality is not essential, it is impressive.
6. Do avoid political topics and any issues or subjects that imply the superiority of the United States.
7. Do control your body language. Don't fidget with the hands, answer with the head or move your feet unnecessarily while seated.
8. Do dress well. All people of this nation, rich or poor attempt to be well-dressed in public.
9. Do avoid sun glasses except when actually needed.

CENTRAL AMERICA

In general you should expect the people of the modern nations of Central America, the narrow bridge of land that connects the continents of North and South

America, to reflect a blend of cultures. Great early civilizations once existed in this area of the world providing a rich heritage.

El Salvador

1. Do expect to find this nation the most industrialized of all Central American countries.
2. Do expect to be greeted with a handshake, but friends are hugged with regularity.
3. Do expect the clock to run on hispanic time, that is lunch in the late afternoon—about 2 P.M. and late supper—about 9 or 10 P.M. or even later.
4. Do exercise great care in traveling in this country—ask about conditions.

Belize

1. This is the smallest nation in Central America.
2. Do recall the British colonial history of this nation and expect a residual of those ways.
3. Do make and be on time for appointments.
4. Do expect to be greeted with a handshake.
5. Do dress comfortably for this hot and humid nation.

Honduras

1. Greetings are often hugs for friends and acquaintances, but expect a handshake to be the norm on first arrival.
2. Topics of conversation might include the ancient civilization and fascinating history of the country.
3. Do dress comfortably.
4. Do make appointments.
5. Do expect to be entertained in public restaurants.

Nicaragua

1. This is the largest country in Central America.
2. Do expect the way of life in this country to be similar to that of other Central American countries—primarily agrarian and in general they speak Spanish and follow the ways of the Roman Catholic Church.
3. Do respect appointments, but don't be surprised if precise time is not kept.

Costa Rica

1. The name means "rich coast" in Spanish and its people are mostly of European (Spanish) descent.
2. Do expect the people to be very literate.
3. Do expect to be greeted with the handshake, but expect women to kiss cheeks of each other on greeting.

Panama

1. Do expect the people of this nation to refer to their country as the Crossroads of the World for it lies on the traditional trade routes between North and South America.
2. Do expect that many Panamanians speak English.
3. Don't talk about politics, and do be sensitive to Panama's nationalism.

AFRICA

This, the second largest continent, is rich in natural resources and has always been the source of minerals and raw materials such as diamonds, cobalt, copper, gold, manganese, and uranium. However, the nations of this great continent are just coming into their own as industrial traders.

More than 800 languages are spoken in Africa; therefore, there are at least 800 different cultures. Nevertheless, most business continues to take place in the urban areas and there the various cultures become fused, for the sake of business.

While it is dangerous to generalize, this section is organized into five regions: West Africa; East Africa; North Africa; South Africa; and Central Africa. These groupings lend themselves to logical cultural statements that are useful for the foreign businessperson.

Do keep in mind that all the new countries were once old European colonies; therefore, throughout Africa there are strong remnants of those cultures interlaced with the new. There are lingering sensitivities about colonization so do be careful to avoid those discussions in conversation. In general international politics and the positive achievements of the country you are visiting are good topics.

West Africa

West Africa includes Nigeria, Mali, Togo, Niger, Senegal, Guinea, Ivory Coast, Ghana, Cameroon, Gambia, Sierra Leone, and Benin.

1. Greetings by handshake, not hugs are the order of the day in these countries.

2. Do use both hands when shaking hands with old people, i.e., left hand grasps the right wrist or forearm as you shake with the right hand.
3. Do expect a flexible schedule with regard to appointments. Even confirmed appointments can be cancelled at the last minute, even without your consent.
4. Don't be surprised if business meetings are held in the home.
5. Do carry a gift when you are invited home.
6. Do expect that cursing is considered rude and can alienate your business contacts.
7. Do be straightforward—honesty pays well in this region.
8. Don't wear short pants to an office or home meeting.
9. Do expect that old people are highly respected.
10. Do expect old people to be seated first.
11. Do expect women to be first in walking, entering, sitting and exiting.
12. Do accept whatever is offered—it is a way of expressing appreciation and it is considered impolite not to accept.
13. Do wash your hands before a meal in anticipation of eating finger food.
14. Don't lick your fingers or make noise when eating.
15. Do pay a lot of attention to family eating styles and the order in which people eat.
16. Don't ask your host to split the bill. In these countries when they invite, they pay. When you invite, you pay. No half-half.
17. Do refrain from discussing political matters.

East Africa

East Africa includes Kenya, Uganda, Tanzania, Ethiopia, Somalia, Burundi, Ruanda, and the Sudan.

1. Do make appointments and be on time.
2. Don't hug when meeting your host, use the handshake.
3. Don't smell of alcohol at business meetings.
4. Avoid complimenting business associates. Compliments are not popular.
5. Don't try to impress your business contacts. Avoid limousines and chauffeurs.
6. Never disguise your full identity.
7. Honesty and truth are highly valued as a basis of a good business relationship.
8. Do be careful of protocol procedures and proper addresses and titles. When in doubt consult your embassy.
9. Do be respectful of tribal traditions. Check with your host when in doubt.

10. Do respect National Flags, to do otherwise is a reminder of colonial times.
11. When invited for a meal, do not offer to share or pay the bill.
12. Do expect to be served food and drink without being asked.
13. Do graciously accept that which is served. It is a sign of appreciation.
14. Don't rest your feet on tables and chairs—a sign of bad manners.
15. Don't be too inquisitive.
16. Avoid dominating the conversation.
17. Avoid interrupting during a conversation.

North Africa

North Africa includes Morocco, Algeria, Libya, Tunisia, and Egypt.

1. Do make appointments, but do not try to schedule them when they fall on their national holidays.
2. Don't hug. It is not accepted.
3. Don't stare at people.
4. Do talk slowly and avoid being loud.
5. Do not be shy about asking your host to pose for a group photo, but do avoid taking pictures of buildings, people or places without checking with your host.
6. Don't be in hurry in business meetings.
7. Do expect most businesspeople in this region to be very trusting of foreigners.
8. Do not attend a business meeting with alcohol on your breath.
9. Do accept invitations for meals at home, often on short notice.
10. Do respect that women sit before men.
11. Do respect their currencies.
12. Avoid talking politics.
13. Do respect family traditions and practices.
14. Do be patient with bureaucratic hassles. It may take longer than expected to get your money out of the country.

South Africa

South Africa includes Zimbabwe, Mozambique, Botswanna, Zambia, Angola, Namibia, Swaziland, Lesotho, and South Africa.

1. Do make appointments and be on time, but remember to observe public holidays.
2. Don't hug when greeting—use the handshake.
3. When you are met by both husband and wife, do shake hands with the man first, then the wife.

4. Do give old people greater respect.
5. Do use both hands when shaking hands with old people, i.e., left hand grasps the right wrist or forearm as you shake with the right hand.
6. Do remove your hat when talking to older people, seniors, and government officials.
7. Do check with your embassy about titles of leaders, Chiefs, and other seniors.
8. Don't ask people what tribe they belong to.
9. Do avoid smelling of alcohol in public or at business meetings.
10. When invited for a meal pay great attention to eating instructions and habits.
11. Do wash your hands before a meal—you may need to eat with your fingers.
12. Unless you are left handed, always use the right hand to greet others, to receive, or give something.
13. For women: Do not cross your legs; use minimal eye contact.
14. Do expect to exchange gifts.
15. In conversation avoid teasing, gossiping, rumors or discussions of politics.
16. As a guest, don't refuse drink, fruit, or food when offered. It's polite to offer and to accept.
17. Do be patient about governmental bureaucracy.
18. Don't attempt to bribe.

Central Africa

Central Africa includes Zaire, Congo, Gabon, and Chad.

1. Do expect to be greeted with a handshake, hugging is highly unusual.
2. Do remember that old people talk, sit, walk in and walk out first.
3. Do make and keep appointments, on time, but don't be surprised if appointments are cancelled without notice. Be patient.
4. Public holidays are observed by everyone, particularly independence days.
5. Do be careful to get names and pronunciations correct.
6. Do show respect to flags, and national currencies. They are national symbols of remarkable respect.
7. Do stop walking when the national anthem is played.
8. Don't talk down or joke about the government, local culture, or styles.
9. On the first visit, do not ask about a person's family. It's okay on the second visit.
10. Do expect meetings to be held in either an office or at a hotel.
11. Don't dress in shorts or other casual dress for a business meeting, a home visit, or a meal.

12. Don't refuse a home invitation.
13. Don't mix pleasure with business.
14. In conversation: don't betray a shared confidence; don't tease; don't curse; and don't pretend to know it all.
15. For women: don't over-talk men.
16. Do check with your embassy to learn how to identify police, public transportation, etc.

You might think that culture will take care of itself after technical business studies and analysis are complete, but maintaining your competitiveness means changing your viewpoint and adjusting strategy to the demands imposed by the new world environment. The environment of today is interdependence. To cope and compete in international markets, one must factor foreign cultures into business strategies.

The next chapter develops international marketing from A to Z.

3

Market internationally (export)

IN THE PAST THE UNITED STATES' DOMESTIC MARKET HAD BEEN SO lucrative and had so few foreign competitors that small- and medium-sized firms seldom looked beyond their shores to sell their goods. If they did sell overseas, the buyers came to America, because in those days "Made in U.S.A." sold itself.

Let's face it, in those days the nations recovering from the "Big War" manufactured very little themselves and foreign consumers had precious little money. On the other hand, the United States had a giant industrial base untouched by the ravages of that war, and its people were relatively affluent.

TIMES HAVE CHANGED

Since about 1960, world trade grew at more than twice the rate of the United States' economy. Most countries mounted an emphasis on manufacturing and extended their marketing reach to target the United States. At the same time foreign markets were less saturated, because in many instances the foreign push into the United States market had been to the exclusion of their own.

Post World War II industrial recovery, particularly in Europe and Asia substantially increased the opportunity to find buyers with money. People of the world became richer and better off, consequently the foreign marketplace grew faster than the United States domestic market and the opportunities for overseas sales have never been better.

STRIKE BACK

Now is the time for *service* companies as well as *manufacturing* firms, to strike back and aggressively push into foreign markets to become "global businesses." Why? Because there are substantial profits to be made.

IS YOUR FIRM READY?

In today's interdependent world a company's strategic plan should include consideration of a marketing effort on a global scope. Your first step, regardless of whether your company is in services or manufacturing, should be to consider your growth pattern. The second step is to assess your company's potential for success.

What are your long range growth goals?

Does your firm as a whole have maturity? Has it been in the marketplace long enough to sustain entry into new markets? These questions must be answered and they relate to commitment, attitudes, plant capacity, personnel, finances, and environment.

Top management motivation and commitment

This issue starts at the top. Are you, the management, resolved to enter the international market with staying power? Or is the effort lukewarm, just waiting to wilt at the first resistance.

The internationalization process begins when top management becomes committed and motivated. The need for profitability improvement, the receipt of over-the-transom orders, the gaining of special knowledge about foreign opportunities, and the prestige of international operations are all factors in stimulating top management to decide to move into global operations.

Of course commitment to enter the foreign market must be backed up with common sense and logic. Here are 14 reasons why you should consider marketing internationally as a business tactic:

1. **Profit.** Some say that a strong dollar prevents the taking of reasonable profits, yet the relative value of currencies is only one factor in the calculation of profit. In fact, quality, service, and consumer acceptability are often larger measures of product sales success than price.
2. **Break ground for hardware.** Software offered by service and consulting firms often breaks ground for the subsequent improvements and the entry of high-technology hardware.
3. **Develop trust.** Service companies gain ancillary sales based on relationships and trust developed by having a presence in and knowing the capabilities of foreign nations.

4. **Expansion of marketing base.** Expanding your firm's market area can only benefit the sales picture and although some foreign markets are not as rich as the United States' domestic market, they are often quite profitable. Some overseas markets provide for greater profit margins than the sale of the identical product in the United States and in many cases provide an increased market share by beating the competition to the foreign country. A wider base of sales distribution can also minimize fluctuations in domestic conditions. Expanding into foreign markets can be a source of growth for your company if it is facing a domestic market which has matured and is trending toward a downturn.

5. **Extension of product life.** Often, as a result of less developed technology in foreign countries your firm can, by exporting, extend the life cycle of a product that may have reached the obsolescence stage in domestic market.

6. **Excess capacity.** By expanding your market to foreign countries your production can increase beyond the limits set by the domestic market. The benefits of this are obviously better utilization of your labor and capital by reducing unit production costs, more effective use of management and technology, and lower overall operating costs. Thus exports can increase volume, amortize overhead and absorb excess capacity.

7. **Sales stability.** Where your company's product line is subject to seasonal demand, exporting to a foreign market can counterbalance that seasonality, thus stabilizing sales, generating efficiencies in production, cash flow and employment.

8. **Diversify risk.** There are different perceptions of what is considered the risk of doing business overseas. Some explain it as a financial risk while others might say it's the risk of producing then finding out that the market dried up simply because of political changes. Another might explain the risk as the ever changing global economic and political environment. Competing in only one economy can make your firm dependent on that economy. By diversifying into more than one economy you can insulate yourself from the dangers of that single dependency. This is particularly true when foreign markets are in earlier stages of product life cycle than the domestic market.

9. **Defend the domestic market.** By competing in the international market against other multinational firms your company may improve its marketing skills and thereby be in a better position to protect your own domestic market in the long term.

10. **Penetrate trade barriers.** Establishing production and marketing operations overseas may allow your firm to enter markets that are not otherwise open competitively.

11. **Lower offshore production costs.** Establishing production offshore may allow your company to take advantage of lower labor rates and raw

materials costs, thus making products more competitive in world markets.

12. **Encouragement of imports and foreign investment by some foreign governments.** As a way of developing their own economies, many host governments welcome foreign operations and trade. Often these are joint ventures or technical arrangements serving to gain markets within the country.

13. **Tax and other incentives.** Governments, including the United States, offer distinct advantages for companies that sell or lease their goods to customers in foreign countries.

14. **Intellectual property protection.** By establishing an office overseas a service company can monitor its intellectual property while carving a new market.

Time horizon and profit attitudes

Does your firm have the staying power and mental toughness to make a foothold and grow in a foreign culture even to sustain losses in the short-run to gain long-term profits?

This is an internal problem and unique to each company. Internalization requires a longer time horizon than many investors prefer. Americans all too often are looking for a fast return on their money. In the international scene you should expect profits and certainly excellent growth, but it takes longer.

For some firms, costs and profit margins are less important than total long run profit potential. For example, it might be smarter in the long run for your company to sell more at a smaller profit margin than to sell a few at a higher margin but only be in the market for the short haul. The Japanese and Koreans have used the "long haul" concept over and over to gain entry into the United States market.

Plant capacity

The key here is the product volume the firm can venture with reasonable safety. Don't plan expansion into a new market based on a heavy outlay for capital equipment. Instead, calculate the number of additional units your firm can produce from the existing fixed costs over and above average sales. Your loss due to production is then only the per-unit cost of materials and man hours.

Personnel

Are your key people willing to put in the time and investment? Do you have a pool of creative and experienced marketing personnel and a research staff?

Size and financial position

More than any other obstacle, the size of your firm and finances will determine your ability to make international market entry. Your company's financial picture in the domestic market frequently determines its capability to make the initial investment. You should have sufficient reserves or see sufficient cash flow to satisfy borrowing the necessary working capital to kick-off an international department and begin market penetration.

The high cost of exporting is frequently a perception. Obviously it is more expensive to fly to Kenya from Colorado to establish a market for goods than to fly to New Jersey. On the other hand, the long run profit opportunity could be greater in Kenya. Each situation is different. As one executive of an excellent international company said, "Expense scares off the beginner, but it is trivial compared to the potential market."

All business ventures require a financial commitment in terms of investment. In the case of entering a foreign market, the primary costs are management, travel, overhead, promotion, advertising, and administration. A rule of thumb for expansion into any new venture is to have a steady profit margin trend for a period of one to three years. The profit we earn from sales is called "return on investment" and each project undertaken by the firm should be expressed in the likelihood of attaining the company's target return. This should always be better than bank interest rates ("cost of capital") otherwise the investment should not go forward. (It would be better and safer to leave your money in the bank.)

Environment

Modern business strategists spend as much time analyzing the environment concept as any other. In general terms, what is meant by *environment* is the overall climate for your business including the domestic economy, the political climate, the world economy, and international competition.

IN THE PAST

Most American firms have entered the global market only as a sequence of events over time. In other words, companies came to the business of importing or exporting only as an afterthought. This staged process, often taking many years, generally began only when smaller firms were successful in the domestic market. The stages of entry typically followed a pattern similar to this:

1. At some point in the firm's life it became engaged in extra-regional expansion, widening its experience and "market consciousness." For some it began with a search for cheaper raw materials or components. During this period the small firm began to fill some unsolicited (over-the-transom) orders but still had not engaged in a serious international plan.

2. Soon the firm began to investigate exporting. If the investigation was successful, the small firm began to experiment. At first it was interested only in overseas sales of its surplus products but was without resources to fill overseas orders on an ongoing basis.

3. If the experimentation was successful the firm became an experienced exporter by actively soliciting overseas sales. Therefore, it was willing to make limited modifications to its products and marketing procedures to accommodate the requirements of overseas buyers.

4. The exporting firm eventually made major modifications in its products as well as its marketing practices in order to reach more buyers.

5. Finally, the firm developed new products for existing or new overseas markets and diversified its markets to other countries.

HOW TO CHOOSE THE RIGHT MARKETING METHOD

Today the firm that considers entering international business does not have to wait for the slow, step-by-step process to take place. Starting a new department can be expensive as well as time consuming, but you can get into the international market without investing a large sum of capital. There are three "forks-in-the-road" to get your products overseas.

1. Take the right fork and "do-it-yourself" (most expensive but most control). Developed here and in Chapters 5 and 6.

2. Take the middle road and "let a trading intermediary do it for you" (fastest and least expensive to start, but gives up control). Chapter 7 deals with this method.

3. Take the left fork by forming an association of firms under the Export Trading Company Act of 1982 (shares costs and control). This is explained in Chapter 8.

Each of the methods have merit and each have limitations. Do not discard any choice until you have done a solid analysis. In fact, a mix of these methods may be your best bet.

This section of the chapter shows how to make the decision.

Do-it-yourself (direct)

Your firm uses the direct method when you develop your own market plan and set up your own international sales department to deal with foreign distributors, agents or overseas marketing subsidiaries. Using this method your company is responsible for shipping its own products overseas.

Typically, the do-it-yourself method requires the full time effort of a trained department manager, a sales representative and suitable administrative support.

Let a trading intermediary do it (indirect)

The quickest way to get into the global market is also the least expensive. Many small- and medium-sized firms also use this method to get started.

This approach means dealing through an international trading firm that acts as a sales intermediary (middleman). The trading company develops the market plan and acts as the manufacturing company's international department. These intermediaries normally assume responsibility for moving products overseas. Chapter 7 discusses General Trading Companies (GTCs), Import-Export Management Companies (EMCs), Webb Pomerene Associations, and the newly formed Export Trading Companies (ETCs).

In many cases letting a trading company do it is the smartest way, but it often means giving up some control and means the manufacturer or service company must play by team rules. The Japanese use this method predominantly. More than 75 percent of Japanese exports are handled through what are known as Sogo shosha (see Chapter 7).

Form a marketing association under the
Export Trading Company Act of 1982 (ETCA)

Many small- and medium-sized firms are using this method. Chapter 8 explains how to form an Export Trading Company (ETC) with other manufacturers or service companies to compete under this Act.

THE DECISION FACTORS

How does the small firm decide whether to do-it-themselves, work with a trading company, or form an ETC?

Global market reach

Global market reach is the organization, offices, and contacts in other countries to support the gathering of intelligence and execute a sales effort. Market reach would be considered "limited" if a firm or trading company had contacts in only one or two foreign countries. On the other hand, a "comprehensive" global reach would be the capability to market a given product in every country where that product has logical buying potential.

International marketing personnel

Does your firm have trained international marketing personnel? The consideration here is the expense of hiring well-experienced people versus having a trading company do the marketing.

Team spirit (control)

This factor involves the question of how well your firm can accept a hands-off approach to the marketing of your products by a trading company. This can become a major factor in the case of a high-technology product where an engineering background is essential to providing after sales support.

Studies have shown that the relationship between a trading company and its clients is critical. Given a long term investment in an intermediary's expertise, team spirit is that intangible belief that the agent is at all times working in the manufacturer's best interest, even though in specific instances it may not seem so. The relationship is even more difficult when one realizes that international marketers are not door-to-door salesmen. Because the time horizon for doing business internationally is by its very nature longer than for domestic business there are often long periods when nothing seems to be happening. International business generally takes a great deal of patience and as a result, confidence and a team spirit is more difficult to sustain.

Occasionally a manufacturer signs on an intermediary to market the company's product, but after some time passes has the temptation to go around the middleman. This is self-defeating and contractually dangerous. On the other side of this matter, because there are no professional standards for qualifying or licensing, the small manufacturer should exercise due care in selecting the proper trading company. If your firm cannot accept an intermediary as an equal, do it yourself.

The financial decision

The critical decision is the financial decision. The major fixed cost of your own international department are the personnel. At least three employees working full time are usually required to market products in several countries. A minimum foreign sales department will require an export sales manager, an export sales representative, and an administrative person. Table 3-1 shows these typical costs on an annualized base.

CASE STUDY

This case analysis is designed as a model to show you how to make the financial decision. It is assumed the firm considers the international marketing department a profit center.

Assume Company X sells its product for $10.00 a unit, but it only costs $2.50 to make. An intermediary will buy at 50 percent off recommended retail price (not unusual) or at $5.00 a unit and resell it overseas. If company X had developed its own export department it could sell the product to an overseas distributor at only 30 percent off list price or at $7.00 a unit. For this example profit

_____Table 3-1   Export Sales Department costs (Annual)._____

Function	Cost
Export Sales Manager	$40,000
Sales Representative (Bonuses not included)	$30,000
Administration (Secretary)	$24,000
Travel & Entertainment	$20,000
Promotion & Advertisement	$35,000
Admin costs (Telex, etc.)	$30,000
Benefits Package (at about 15% of salaries)	$11,000
Market Intelligence	$10,000
*Traffic manager	
*Communications Manager	
*Engineering Services	
*Promotion Assistant	
*Additional Sales Personnel	
Total costs	$200,000
*Expansion personnel	

The total costs in this example were chosen for convenience and are considerably understated.

is defined as retail price times unit sales minus trade discounts, direct production costs, and fixed costs. The break-even decision is described graphically in Fig. 3-1.

The dotted line represents Company X profits at $4.50 ($7.00 – $2.50) selling through the firm's own export department. Note that 44,445 units must be sold before the firm generates enough revenue to overcome the annual export department costs of $200,000.

In contrast, assuming no up front fees (which is sometimes the case), the solid line represents Company X profits at $2.50 ($5.00 – $2.50). At the break-even point the middleman has already generated profits of greater than $100,000 for Company X. Of course, at the intersection of the two curves (100,000 units) the company's own export department would generate more profit. Everything in area A would be losses. Everything in area B would be early profits, and everything in area C would be the advantage of Company X having its own international department provided that several other factors such as market reach, international know-how and market knowledge is available.

Assuming your firm has the finances, a viable product, and definite long range goals, your own foreign sales department can eventually generate sufficient revenues to support the costs. If the firm's financial situation can sustain losses for the short run, it should use the "do-it-yourself" method.

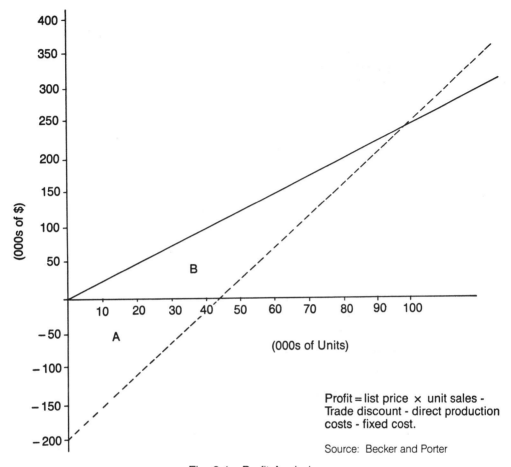

Fig. 3-1   Profit Analysis.

On the other hand, if your company does not have foreign market knowledge nor the immediate finances, yet has international goals, you are better off to go the trading company route or join with others to form an ETC.

There are many excellent, reputable intermediaries. Chapter 7 deals extensively about these firms. It explains who they are, and how to get in touch. Chapter 8 explains how to form trade associations under the ETCA.

INTERNATIONAL MARKETING PROGRAM

Regardless of which method you have chosen, someone has to develop a marketing program, in writing. If you do it yourself, your own staff (or consultant) should do the research and write the plan. If you decide to deal with an intermediary or form an association under the ETCA, they should write the plan. No matter, a plan for your program must be written!

There are two phases to a marketing program. Phase one is the planning stage and phase two is the action stage. The remainder of this chapter is organized to explain these phases.

PHASE 1: The planning stage

There are two major aspects of a written marketing plan: "strategy" and "tactics." As discussed in Chapter 1, these words have been adapted by the business world from military terminology and are used extensively in developing new markets, particularly global markets.

Don't be intimidated by the terms strategy and tactics. *Strategy* is the term for adopted policies. A *strategic plan* is the integration of smaller pieces (tactics) into a larger purpose.

Tactic is the art of skillfully employing available means or specific actions leading to the accomplishment of the strategy.

Strategic planning

Modern marketing requires the development of a strategic plan, then isolating the tactical steps needed to implement the plan.

Your plan should be written as a distinct part of your firm's larger, overall business strategic plan and should define your company's international policy. Realistic goals and objectives should be set and a suitable organization plan should be developed. Above all your plan should be put on paper.

Strategic planning and policy determines how your business fits into the marketplace. The strategic plan is simply the measurement of your company and its products and the likely prospects for success. A firm's total strategic plan has three sub-parts: 1) the domestic commercial plan, 2) the government plan, and 3) the international plan. Don't make the same mistake many firms do by making two separate plans, one for the domestic and government market and a separate one for the international market. Certainly the approach should be a separate investigation of each market, but the total plan should include all, because there is synergy (the whole bigger than its parts), and there are many commonalities. This chapter deals only with the international marketing plan. Table 3-2 is an outline used to explain the process. A similar outline may be used for the domestic and government plan.

STRATEGIC PLAN

This part of the international market plan is the data gathering and thinking stage. Allow plenty of time for this to include many staff meetings which encourage "blue sky" discussions.

_____Table 3-2 Market Plan Outline._____

A. Executive Summary (written only after all other parts of the plan are complete)
B. International Marketing Objective
      a. Leader, follower, challenger, or nicher.
C. Intelligence
    1. Data gathering
    2. Kinds of information
    3. The target market
      a. Segmentation
    4. The players
    5. Interstate (governmental) controls
    6. Strategic alternatives
D. Market Tactics: The Five P's
    1. Pop
    2. Product
    3. Price
    4. Place
    5. Promotion
E. Action Stage
    1. Budget
    2. Contingencies

Intelligence (market research): The need to search and know

In the past, all too many firms have migrated to a foreign market by accident. Today, however, more and more companies are making strategic decisions and entering the international game with a well thought-out plan. The plan is developed from gathered intelligence.

For some the term intelligence is a dirty word. It conjures thoughts of CIA, spys, and dirty tricks. Intelligence is not about secrets, because the "half life" of secrets is very short. You can't run a business on secrets. What you need is the right stuff for an analysis so you can use your brain to make the best business decisions, particularly to minimize or avoid risk.

Intelligence is a good word for the modern businessperson, because the concept goes beyond just information gathering. Modern intelligence not only gathers, it analyzes, then assesses the information from all available sources. The process is quite ethical—it's the users that sometimes lose their sense of values.

Intelligence has great significance for you, the modern manufacturer or service company manager. The correct application and rationing of capital is dependent on information, otherwise, it is wasted on bad decisions. Once the decision is made to enter a given market, research should begin to collect, select, assess and pass on useful information to the decision maker.

Most small- and medium-sized firms do not have a corporate level intelligence gathering capability other than that which might have been developed in their domestic marketing department. Even then, most marketing organizations are often no more than a personal sales effort. Salesman lack the time or the opportunity to be isolated long enough to take on the kind of research and analysis necessary to bring about thoughtful information for decision making.

Most often, the smaller firm is well advised to contract with a private service company that specializes in international research. These firms have the experience to not only gather and sift through the magnitude of information, but also to tailor the analysis to the specific needs of the client.

To unlock the U.S. government's treasure chest of information, call the Office of Business Liaison, Washington, DC. Telephone: (202) 377-3176. Ask for a copy of the *Business Services Directory*.

Data gathering

The American Marketing Association defines *marketing research* (our term is *intelligence*) as "the systematic gathering, recording, and analyzing of data about problems relating to the marketing of goods and services." In other words, it is the process of supplying information for marketing business decisions, and those decisions can be about planning, problem solving, or control of performance.

You should think of this as a building block process wherein the researcher starts with a problem and ends with a presentation of the findings to top management. The methods have been perfected in modern business, and the risk of not doing research is loss of profits and time.

Classically, the approach to market research has seven steps:

1. Define the problem
2. Develop a research plan
3. Identify data sources
4. Collect the data
5. Analyze the data
6. Interpret the data
7. Present the results for application (decision making)

Secondary data

Most research begins with *secondary data*, that is, publications, journals, periodicals, official government documents, etc. In most advanced countries there is a wealth of material, but for most world markets there is a serious shortage of secondary data. Nations with low per capita income have commensurately smaller government budgets to collect and analyze statistical data. For example, some countries have never taken a census. Others have only a few publications that deal with the kind of information you might need.

Primary data

Your intelligence will be focused toward your firm's specific needs. You will want to know what people think about your product, prices, and promotion. *Primary data* is gathered directly from the people who know—the consumer. But people in different countries react differently and have varying views about responding to collection of data. In some countries, responses are driven by the culture—a polite answer is given regardless of the person's real feelings. In others, the suspicion of government is very high, yet in others, illiteracy is the significant barrier. An important way to gather primary data is through American Chambers of Commerce abroad. A listing of addresses for those chambers is available in Appendix E.

Language

In lieu of readily available information researchers might have to design data collection instruments. The sequence for this effort is to design, translate, test, redesign, retest, conduct the study, then finally translate back to the parent language. Obviously, communications and primary data collection is compounded when a country has several languages.

Communications

Probably the most frustrating condition for the international intelligence gatherer is the lack of modern communications in some countries. In many countries consumers don't have telephones and the mail systems are unreliable. Data then has to be developed from a street questionnaire or interviews gathered in popular metropolitan areas, then extrapolated for the country as a whole.

Kinds of information

In general, before moving into the international marketplace, you, the decision maker should look at three things: 1) which markets to enter (strategy); 2) how to enter the markets (tactics); and 3) how to market in the target markets (tactics).

Your intelligence effort should focus on four different areas: 1) the target market; 2) the players; 3) Interstate (government) controls; and 4) strategic alternatives.

Target market

Learn to think like an Admiral or a General, because the beginning step of this effort is the development of a strategy. A world map should be displayed in a room we will call, for lack of a better name, the intelligence center. Using pins, flags, or small magnets you can easily identify countries and cities that are to be your targets. Next, an erasable board should be located nearby. On the board you will list by priority your targets. You might say, "why not just do it all on a computer." There's nothing wrong with using computers. It should be done, but there is something about displays that provide visibility to the intelligence process. The wall display still has its value and is recommended.

Targeting involves finding that part of the total market which a business believes it can serve most effectively. It's impossible for a given company to meet the needs and tastes of all consumers in a particular area. Most products must be aimed at only a segment of the total market population, principally because consumers like to feel that a product is produced for their particular needs. People tend to identify with a product when this psychological bond has been created. Of course there are several other reasons why target marketing is important.

- Targeting focuses the firm's efforts and encourages realistic goals.
- Aiming marketing efforts at everybody is like aiming at nobody.
- Focusing on target countries and consumer groups within that target country makes marketing less expensive and more effective.
- Targeting helps develop a market niche and differentiate the company from the competition.
- Buyers of consequence are not always the end users of a product. It is the buyers that interest you.
- Segmenting the market into sub-targets helps in the identification of the competitors, both foreign and local.

Segmenting

Segmenting prospective markets in international market research requires a two-tiered approach.

First the researcher sorts the available information at a "macro" level. *Macrosegmentation* divides a market by broad characteristics such as geography, demography, development level, host government involvement, personality, behavior, and competition:

- *Geography*: Think first in terms of continents—Europe, Asia, or Australia. Determine which major region offers the most sales appeal. Then segment countries within the continent, thinking of the people, for example, where do they live—rural or urban, near oceans, mountains or plains.

- *Demographics*: Consider the income, age, religion, nationality, and culture of potential customers.
- *Development level*: For instance certain services might be excluded from a country that has a low level of technological development, has a closed business environment, or low level of capital available.
- *Host government involvement*: Some governments are directly involved with the negotiations between sellers and private sector buyers. The role of government should be analyzed on a country-by-country basis.
- *Personality*: Think in terms of *their* self-image; what are *their* psychological needs and tastes.
- *Behavior*: Who will benefit from your product?
- *Competition*: Who is the general competition? Is there any? Is it local or foreign? What is their market share?

The second tier of the segmentation approach is called *microsegmentation*. It is the determination of homogenous customer groups within macrosegments, that is, pinpointing the actual decision makers who buy the product. Factors that define microsegments may include procurement criteria, cultural aspects of buying, procedures employed by firms, the structure of decision-making units within firms, and the competition's techniques. This information allows you to design a promotional strategy that caters to the decision-making unit (DMU).

- *Procurement criteria*: In one company, decisions are made by a committee, in others, only by the president. In some cities, the mayor is the sole fiscal authority, while in others the city or planning manager may be the actual DMU for major procurements.
- *Cultural aspects of buying*: In some countries only the women of the family do the buying, while in others, for certain products, the young people decide for themselves what they will buy.
- *Procedures employed by firms*: Buyers in some firms will only deal with their own national representatives. Some buy as a result of competitive bids developed from formal requests for proposal (RFP).
- *Structure of decision-making units (DMU) within firms*: Some companies require presentations to committees of top management while others give autonomy at certain levels of management up to specific dollar values.
- *Competition's techniques*: Call it industrial spying, call it research, no matter what it's called, an appreciation of local competition and their methods is essential.

The players

Another display, in or out of the computer, should be a list of the customers, suppliers, competitors, government officials, and any others that can affect your program. This should be developed in detail, using names, addresses, background, and decision making power. Remember, when you go international, your competitors now expand by a significant multiple, because you must now think in terms of foreign competitors, not just domestic.

Interstate (government) controls

Many of your tactical decisions will be based on how to maneuver around the obstacles or barriers presented by foreign governments. A rigorous analysis of tariff schedules, taxes, and non-tariff barriers should be developed. Analyze these barriers, not only from your domestic point of view, but also from the point of view of nations that are adjacent to the target market country. Sometimes there are opportunities to flank a problem. (See Chapter 9, Vaulting Trade Barriers.)

The need for in-depth segmentation varies from company to company. Manufacturing companies may find their target DMU is a specific individual, much the same as in their own domestic market. On the other hand, a service company may find that the perceived risk of buying a piece of software is so high that only a top management committee can make the decision.

Ultimately the questions that must be answered are:

- Who is the end user?
- Who is the actual buyer?
- What are the best methods of closing a sale?
- How large a target market can your firm serve?
- What is unique about your product or service?
- What are the company's resources to serve this market?

International marketing objective

The nature of capitalism ensures that if a business enjoys a monopoly position, and if that business is lucrative, there will, sooner or later, be competition. Therefore, if a new firm is entering the market with a standard product or service it is immediately faced with the question of how to obtain a market share. In any business environment, a firm must decide how to position itself in relation to the competition. This analysis applies in the international marketplace as well as the domestic market. Your company can be either a market leader, a challenger, a follower or a business that has its own niche.

Based on the analysis of your intelligence, if your firm can identify a target market and pursue an effective marketing strategy to fill a niche, bigger firms might not be attracted and the competition might be much less. Obviously, the niche must be large enough to be profitable.

MARKETING TACTICS: The five "P's"

Few marketers think of their actions in terms of tactics; however, the success of your work is measured by your ability to adjust to the changes of the marketplace just as the tank commander or ship captain must change their tactics to the battle scene.

In academia—Marketing 101, these methods are called the *market mix* or *variables*—the four "P's:" *product, price, place* and *promotion*. But in reality they are the tactics of winning the trade game. This author has a fifth "P," called "Pop" which will not be explained later, but rather by its nature will be discussed right now!

POP

"Pop" is the characteristic of being responsive to the customer. Action! Right now! It's that quality that makes one company win over others. It's the thing that wins contracts and sells products all over the world. It turns a "looky-loo" into a sale. It is the tone that pervades a company and gives the prospective client a feeling you really care about solving his or her problems. It's answering the mail, today! It's the way you answer the telephone and when you answer the telephone.

Kim Dae-Won is the political and economic editor and deputy managing editor of *Cholla Ilbo*, the local newspaper of Chonju, Korea. During his visit to the United States, in the Spring of 1989, under the auspices of the International Visitor Program of the United States' Information Agency, he commented about "pop." No, he didn't use that term, but he might have if he knew about it. He did reveal a common Korean viewpoint that when a businessperson from his country calls a company in the United States, often to purchase something, the United States' company is not always responsive. He also mentioned that sometimes the calls were made on Saturday when, he chided, "you don't work and we do." "Even in your restaurants," he said, "no one seems to care. There is just not a feeling of urgency or responsiveness in America."

PRODUCT

In general, the same factors used to evaluate a product's potential in the domestic market will determine your success in a foreign market. Much of the common sense business knowledge you have relied on in the domestic market will serve you well internationally. You must still offer a good product at competitive prices

prices that serves a need for a given population. However, not all products marketed in one economy or environment can be marketed in another country at a profit. In Chapter 2 you learned that such things as religion, and cultural preference were major factors. Adapting your product culturally required learning what your market liked. What were their tastes? What turned them off in terms of attitudes, social differences, and language? Obviously there are a range of other business and engineering issues which should also be considered, such as product need, product standards, level of technology, durability/quality, technical specifications, and alternative uses.

Product need

To determine need in a new market, the prudent approach is to observe and examine known buying patterns. Climate, culture, history and habits must be considered. There is universal appeal for leading edge technology that is durable, adaptable, and requires little servicing. However, purchasing power often overcomes appeal and need when the local populations cannot afford to buy the products.

Product standards

Each country has its own product standards such as food and drug laws, safety standards, quality, and technical standards. While most countries are moving toward accepted worldwide practices prudence dictates that a firm entering a new foreign market research the host country's regulations.

Level of technology

Typically, the most advanced products are developed in the most advanced countries. Hi-tech, as these products are known, are exported to the most favorable foreign markets first. Later, as the original countries lose some of the export market, (when other advanced countries begin to produce the product locally) the product should be marketed in less developed countries. Eventually, lower production costs in these countries could reverse the process and the original country may begin to import their own product. This process, commonly known as "product life cycle," is well understood among international businesses and is used to extend sales life. Knowing where a product is in the product life cycle will help you target markets.

Durability/quality

One of the most remarkable consequences of Japanese export success has been the importance of quality. After sales service can be expensive, particularly when repair parts and technicians must travel an ocean away from the factory.

Equipment operations under varying and demanding conditions strain the best engineered parts; therefore, durability becomes a major issue in the design of products for overseas markets.

Technical specifications

Analyze your product in terms of adaptability to a particular foreign country. Each national government establishes and enforces technical standards to ensure products meet safety requirements and are compatible with or interchangeable with locally produced products. As an example, in the United States, the electrical system is based on 120V, 60 Hz, while the majority of the rest of the world uses 220V, 50 Hz. Conversion to the metric system, technical specifications and codes is essential to market in foreign target markets.

Alternative uses

Products in one country are not always used for the same purpose in other countries. One of the most obvious examples is the bicycle. In the United States, they are used almost exclusively for recreation or physical fitness purposes, but in many foreign markets, where automobiles are not affordable to the general public, bicycles are a primary mode of transportation.

PRICE

The first step in setting a price for the overseas market is to establish the policy objectives. As discussed earlier, entering the international marketplace requires commitment. Most firms view foreign market entry as the first step of a long-term effort, so pricing must be consistent with maximizing long-run profits. On the other hand, prices must be attractive enough to stimulate interest by consumers and agents/distributors.

Market costs

Marketing across oceans and international boundaries adds costs to a product. The cost of doing business includes transportation, import duties, foreign taxes, overseas sales representatives, travel, lodging, and paperwork. Begin with your factory output cost, including profit margin, then add-on:

- Packaging for overseas shipment
- Average shipping costs (truck to port as well as ocean or air)
- Insurance
- Documentation
- Banking charges
- Warehousing

- Commissions to foreign distributors
- Import duties
- Cost of currency differential
- Cost of warranty
- Cost of in-country product support

Of course, some of these costs may be borne by the buyer, but it's better to overestimate your costs, than to later underquote and learn you have significant losses.

Market price

When determining your price for the overseas market it is essential to learn as much about the market price as possible then compare that knowledge with your calculation of costs, usually cost-plus profit or (domestic price-plus). This is called *pricing in—costing out*. The comparison of the two, that is, market price minus actual costs-plus, will determine where your product is in the market and whether you can make sufficient profit.

Another method of determining price is called "marginal cost pricing." Figure 3-2 shows that using this technique, prices are set at the point where marginal cost (the incremental increase of cost in producing and selling one additional unit) equals marginal revenue (the incremental increase in revenue). With price set at this point, profits, in theory, are maximized.

Most firms use the domestic cost-plus method because it is very difficult to obtain an accurate picture of the marginal cost and revenue curves with exports.

Market price can be deceiving, because it may be a reflection of foreign domestic manufacturing costs, or other features your competitors have built-in,

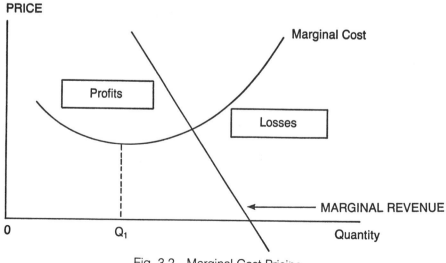

Fig. 3-2   Marginal Cost Pricing.

such as allowance for credit, or services. Make certain you compare apples to apples. Nevertheless, begin with competitive market pricing. Check catalogs, order a competitor's product, or review government price index reports.

The question to be answered is "will your price be competitive overseas?" Regardless of the method used, you are looking for the difference between market price and costs (price in-cost out). When the difference is positive you can begin export marketing secure in the thought that there are profits to be made. If the difference is negative you have two directions to go:

- Reduce the products direct costs by employing cheaper materials or cut some of the product features.
- Position the product at the upper end of the consumer market, cut middleman, or begin manufacturing or assembling the product overseas (see Chapter 10).

Market entry price

Market entry pricing is still another matter. Taking a long-term view of pricing policy does not preclude gaining short term objectives. Gaining market share, recovering an initial cash investment, or forcing competitors, who are experiencing only marginal success, from the market may dictate rapid penetration.

Over the years we have seen the Japanese and Koreans use this tactic. They often enter a market at a price under their nearest competitor, then after traditional buying patterns have been interrupted and market share is gained, they systematically raise the price until profit margins and shares are stabilized. This tactic helps explain why the Japanese and Koreans have established themselves as world-class exporters.

If you decide on this tactic, be careful you are not guilty of what is known as *dumping* (see Glossary and Chapter 12). This is the practice of placing a product in a market at prices much below fair market value (often below domestic manufacturing costs) in order to gain market entry.

PLACE

By *place* we mean the market channel and physical distribution considerations for a product or service. *Market channels* are the steps a product or service follows from the manufacturer to the final consumer, i.e., the means of getting the product before the public.

Earlier in the chapter you learned how to decide which marketing method to use. If you decided to let a trading company market your product you would expect the place considerations to be taken care of by the intermediary firm.

In general, overseas market channels are the same as those in the United States. There are agents, brokers, distributors, retailers as well as the direct means of getting the product to the consumer, such as the mailers or magazine advertisements.

Sales agents or independent representative

Sales Agents are commission representatives (export agents) who typically serve more than one related but non-competitive firm and are paid a commission based on actual sales. This is often the most cost effective way for a firm that has a technical product or has limited marketing resources. Selling through these agents leaves the risks, responsibility of documentation, shipping, and payment arrangements with the seller. They do act as your representative to promote your firms reputation, resolve problems and/or recommend solutions. A contract usually defines the respective rights and obligations for a specific period and can be exclusive or nonexclusive.

Brokers

Brokers usually bring buyers and sellers together by use of worldwide connections and special knowledge of the marketplace. In general, they deal in bulk commodities such as paper or sugar and are often an inexpensive way to dispose of surpluses.

Distributors

A *distributor* is a merchant who normally buys your product at a discount then stores, resells it, and collects payment using an established sales organization in a defined geographic region or territory. A distributor is particularly useful for those products that require after sales service and/or repair and for products which are advertised heavily. It is usually the responsibility of the exporter to provide for the safe shipment to the distributor's warehouse and also provide promotional literature. The distributor in turn uses his means to advertise and/or distribute the materials and product. It is not unusual for the distributor and seller to share the costs of advertising. As with the agent or representative, the length of the association is established by contract which is renewable provided the arrangement proves satisfactory.

Retailers

Foreign retailers are an important channel particularly for mass market consumer products. It is to your advantage to deal direct just as it is to their advantage to deal direct with the manufacturer. Often retailers that are a large chain will insist on their own house label but will buy in large quantities.

Direct marketing

As discussed later in this chapter under the heading of ''advertising,'' direct mail marketing is a growing means of doing overseas selling, and often means working closely with a foreign advertising firm.

State controlled trading companies

This term applies to countries where business is conducted by a few government sanctioned and controlled trading entities. These opportunities are becoming more and more important and are discussed in greater depth in Chapter 11.

Contract protection

Whether you decide to go with an agent or distributor, a contract should be carefully drawn which describes the territories which will be covered and under what exclusive rights and authorities. Such an agreement is discussed in more detail in Chapter 7, and the important elements are listed in Appendix F.

PROMOTION

A series of well-prepared news releases about new products, entry into new markets, or the hiring of new personnel can often provide just as much recognition as an ad campaign for the company that is new to a market. Of course, the copy must use the short and easy-to-read "news" approach, and not appear to be a sales gimmick. Media will publish news free of charge, but they want you to pay for sales related advertising.

The purpose of your market research phase was to gain the necessary information to place your product in the marketplace in the most rational way to maximize sales. After all, communications between seller and buyer, whether it be the international or domestic market has always been the essence of sales success, and the major tactical elements of promotion are advertising, direct mail, and trade fairs.

Advertising

Regardless of your method of marketing, direct or indirect, you will want to maintain some degree of control over the implementation of your marketing program. Advertising is a results oriented business function, and you want the highest yield for your invested dollar.

Your selection of a target market was based on research evidence that there was indeed a large group of customers with needs, and the ability to pay. But before you can develop a budget to implement your market program you must answer several questions.

- Is your goal immediate sales or long-term customer relationship?
- Have you decided on rapid market entry or are you happy with a steady, modest share of the market?
- What is your market? Is it distributors and wholesalers or is it direct to the target market segment?

Developing the message

Begin with the product. Develop a list of the features of your product. Next develop a table of its benefits, satisfaction or advantages. Then compare that information to your research about the target consumers in your market. What are the uses, prices, service considerations, varieties, and maintenance needs of your product? On the consumer side look at frequency to purchase, motivation to purchase, location of purchase, income, local culture, religion, sex, and age of your consumer. Thus the systematic matching of product and features with the target market becomes the structure of the message. Now you can begin to write the copy using these comparisons to formulate appeals to your target consumer.

Of course the message must, out of necessity, be translated into the language of the target market. This will be true even if the target language is the same as yours. For instance, American English is not British Isles English, nor is it Australian English. You need better than a word-for-word translation. Only someone intimate with the culture and language can convert the inferences, nuances, punch, and flair needed to persuade. This is even more difficult when translation is into a completely different language. Remember, on market entry you may get just one chance. If your message has an error that insults the foreign consumer or makes your company the standing joke in the local bar, it may take a long time to recover. You must be just as careful with the instructions that accompany the product so that the user is not confused about how to safely operate the equipment or software.

Media selection

Don't fall into the trap of thinking that the same media you currently use in the domestic market will necessarily prove successful in your foreign market. The media of each overseas location has reached a different stage of maturity. Most developed and semi-developed nations have a full array, such as billboards, bus and trolley posters, magazines, television, radio, newspaper, and point-of-sales displays. On the other hand, in less-industrialized countries the print media will be less available so you might have to rely on trade exhibits or personal selling.

Buyers of different countries often have different ways of evaluating a product. Some need to touch and see the product first hand, others will act on the written word alone, yet others need to examine catalog literature. Because of low standards of literacy in many countries, pictures displayed on buses or outdoor billboards at sporting events and along major transportation routes are extensively used.

Choosing an advertising agency

Most countries have domestic based advertising agencies which handle accounts in foreign countries. On the other hand, there are several multinational agencies and local foreign firms with which you might wish to work. The choice is sometimes a difficult one and often determined by whether you can live with an ad campaign similar to the ads you use in your domestic advertising, or do you need it tailored to the specific target market? Certainly your budget will be a major factor in your decision. A visit to the country, discussions with local businesspersons, distributors, or sales agents will help you decide.

Domestic based. The advantage of the choice of a domestic based ad agency gives you the comfort of convenient communications. You have no language problem so you can talk over progress and trade copy ideas in a quick give-and-take manner. Of course this lends itself to a campaign similar to that used in the domestic market. A disadvantage may be the high overhead costs required to keep overseas offices.

Local foreign firm. A local firm might be experienced in delivering material to the target consumer in their own culture. They might already have promoted a product similar to yours. If your objective is to develop your export activities in a concentrated territory, an agency primarily specializing in that region is the best choice for both economic and service reasons. Copy developed for one country could require only minor adjustment to serve an adjacent one, thus saving the cost of starting over with a new agency in your next target market. The disadvantages may be language barriers and distance factor.

Multinational agencies. If you have selected several countries as target markets you may wish to engage a multinational agency. These firms often have a greater international perspective. If you intend, as a long range goal, to move into markets that are significantly separated and culturally different, the multinational is logical. By choosing one centralized agency you can establish a long-term relationship and avoid the management problem of coordinating among too many external agencies.

Cooperative approach. Rather than undertaking their own campaign, many successful exporters enter into agreements with their selected trading company or overseas distributor/agents to share the costs of advertising. The advantage of the co-op method is the shared cost, and immediate familiarity with local markets and media. The disadvantage is loss of budgetary control.

Direct mail

Do some companies market their products overseas by direct mail? You bet they do. And this method is growing. In many ways, for the small new-to-export business, it can be superior because working capital requirements are often less and budgeted funds can be dispersed in a very rational way. See Chapter 9 for a detailed treatment.

Trade fairs

By their very nature some products need to be seen by potential customers. The flip side to that notion is no matter how much market research you do, it will not tell you everything you need to know about your product's reception in a foreign country.

There is no substitute for taking the product to the market. Advertising, sales letters, brochures and other literature are helpful, but observation of the consumer reactions must be a major tactic in any marketing effort. Trade shows, fairs, and missions provide that opportunity. They are today's "window on the market." The concept is not new. Most Asian and European countries have been doing trade shows, fairs and missions for centuries. By their very nature they provide a unique opportunity to gather intelligence about competitors.

Trade shows, like advertising are results oriented. From the beginning, because you want the highest yield for your invested dollar, you should develop a method of measuring results. The data you will need is:

☞ Cost per visitor

☞ Number of leads

☞ Sales per lead

☞ Total sales at the show

☞ Sales as a result of the show

☞ Number of prospects invited versus those that attend

☞ Comments from attendees

☞ A comparison of your effort vis-a-vis your competitors

Planning for the show. Begin your efforts with result measurement in mind. The key elements of preparing for a trade show are:

☞ *Check it out:* When time permits, first attend a trade show as an observer.

☞ *Where to Exhibit:* From your market research you will already know where your industry shows are held and which ones are most popular. Some specialize in specific products, others promote a range. Inspect lists of previous attendees to be certain your target market (decision-making units DMUs) are likely to be at the one you select.

☞ *Develop a Time Table:* Include the dates for completion of: show space reservations; booth shipment; set-up date; carnet application; pre-show campaign; travel reservations; hotel reservations.

☞ *Pre-show campaign:* Advertise your participation several weeks before the show. Send press releases, flyers, and even formal invitations to potential customers.

☑ *Apply for a Carnet:* This document, arranged through the United States Council for International Business, eliminates the need to pay tariffs or post bonds for the temporary importation of professional equipment and commercial samples. This should be done at least three weeks in advance.

☑ *Booth size:* Your investment in the design of a booth is for the long term. Be sure that it assembles, packs, and ships easy. When installed it should be large enough to comfortably accommodate several people.

☑ *Booth location:* Attempt to position your booth on main isles and near the entrance where the traffic flow is the highest. These locations cost more but the return in terms of leads and sales contacts yield the highest results.

☑ *Literature development:* Keep your general literature simple, but informative. Use plenty of pictures and diagrams. Above all, make certain it is done in the local language.

☑ *Coordination with distributors:* When you can, bring your distributors into your booth. Make them feel a part of the team. As a minimum cut them in on your plans and get their input.

Results. The show is over and you're exhausted. You go immediately to the Riviera for several weeks rest. Right? No, wrong! Now the real work begins. The follow-up period is when sales are made. Get a list of the show's attendees. Compare that with the list of leads you developed at your booth. Needless to say, every person your booth-team made contact with needs to be contacted in some way, if only by a follow-up sales letter. However, many potential contacts on the attendee list never got to your booth, yet they may be the very people you should contact. Remind them of your presence at the show and send them the literature they missed.

Only after the follow-up period has been exhausted can you rest on your laurels and develop the statistical analysis to determine your success. Go back to your original measuring method and lay out the numbers. Don't be blinded by the beauty of the venue. It's all about results.

PHASE 2: The action stage

Now the fun begins—executing the plan. But your efforts should not be random. Instead a systems approach is recommended so that when you are finished the results can be measured.

    A. Systems approach
       1. Budgeting
       2. Measuring Results
       3. Correcting Tactics
       4. Contingency Plans

Budgeting

A strategic market plan is a "wish list" developed by your marketing staff, a consultant, or intermediary. It represents every method they would like to use to get the product to the target market. But few firms can satisfy all tactical elements in terms of resources. Marketing must stand in line alongside research and development (R&D) and production for its fair share of the company's funds. This is when the best planners prioritize the elements of their plan in terms of results. Select from your total plan those elements that you think will bring the greatest, fastest return—for cash flow. Don't give up on the rest of your plan. Execute it as funds become available.

Systems approach

The marketing process should be visualized as a "system" wherein a set of pre-determined inputs (market tactics) are measured and acted upon in such a way that the inputs are continually changed as conditions change. In the international marketplace these tactics are sometimes affected by external as well as internal conditions. The strongest of the firms participating in the international marketplace retain a flexibility about their efforts which allows them to react to these changing conditions.

Measuring results

The elements of every strategic plan must, from the beginning, be developed in such a way that they can be measured in terms of actual sales success. Statistical analysis should drive every step of the marketing plan. Every advertising campaign, every trade show, every distributor must have measurable, quantitative, statistical check points that determine sales success.

Correcting market tactics

Keep in mind that marketing tactics are never "locked in concrete," in fact, the most important thing you should understand about success in winning the trade game, just like the battlefield, is that the five P's are in almost constant change.

The development of any strategic market plan must have safety valves. That is, if one marketing tactic doesn't work, where do we go from here? For instance, if advertising doesn't bring in the desired sales results through the media of one target market, there must be some thought to redirecting those funds to a distribution network or the hiring of agents.

Contingency plans

Every plan should have a set of contingencies or activities, based on a set of "what ifs." Those decisions will not be based on conjecture or emotion, but rather on hard statistical data related to income and profit over a predetermined time objective.

Examples of a contingency plan in international marketing might be:

- If sales in a certain country do not meet your return on investment criteria, turn your product over to a local agent.
- At a certain sales level you will consider severing your ties with an intermediary and establishing your own marketing subsidiary.

International marketing is, in the eyes of the decision makers of many small- and medium-sized firms, an awesome mental picture—the major obstacle to tapping growing market opportunities. But if the activity is approached rationally there are sufficient alternatives such that any company should be able to enter. The most attractive for the firm with limited funds is the trading company alternative which is explained more fully in Chapters 7 and 8.

The next chapter explains how to source (import) on a global basis.

4

Source globally (import)

JUST AS THE MARKETING DEPARTMENT HAS LOST ITS SINGLE-DIMENSIONAL focus, so has the modern purchasing department. International sourcing of components, products and raw materials is done routinely in most of today's global businesses.

THE CHANGES

Two things have happened in the past several decades that have increased the complexity of sourcing (importing) decisions and in turn affected the development of a manufacturing strategy.

First, until recently manufacturing integration concerned make or buy decisions only in the domestic market. From 1945 until about 1965 the United States had the only viable manufacturing base and purchasing meant essentially buying only from other American firms. During the twenty-year period from about 1965 through 1985 foreign firms introduced a growing line-up of improved products. Now the list of world class competitors includes manufacturers on every continent and the window for buying decisions has widened.

The other factor that has added further to this complexity is the "phenomena of content." Whether it be consumer or capital goods, today's purchasers are discriminating and fickle. They care little about where the product is made, only that it have good quality, the right price, and stable production. To compete in the global marketplace with world quality products small- and medium-sized manufacturing firms will, sooner than later, be required to consider a mix of foreign and domestic content.

This has created more complex sourcing decisions that affect the manufacturing process. Worldwide purchasing has become a big player requiring new approaches and redefinition of business boundaries. A firm no longer has the luxury of limiting make or buy decisions only to its domestic country, because good, unemotional business sense requires consideration of international alternatives such as:

- Importing raw materials and component parts
- Manufacturing offshore
- Assembling offshore
- Countertrade arrangements

Each of these alternatives are discussed in detail in later chapters. Chapter 10 explains the great under-tapped, offshore manufacturing and assembly capacity, particularly along America's southern border in Mexico. Chapters 9 and 11 explain countertrade and how to deal with controlled (Communist) economies, respectively.

PURCHASING IS PURCHASING AND IMPORTING IS IMPORTING

The same principals of purchasing that work within the domestic market will generally work in the broader international scope. The complications are searching and advertising, then handling the transactional aspects of importing. This chapter assumes that the reader understands how to conduct an international trade transaction and is familiar with the various cost factors, ''terms of sale'' such as f.a.s., c.i.f., f.o.b., and how to get through the customs maze.

THE DECISION

The decision to enter the world of global sourcing holds two major obstacles for top management. The first is attitudinal. That is, management must commit to give it a go. This requires a cultural adjustment and an understanding that foreigners will now be in the purchasing loop, which brings a new requirement to research and study other countries and learn about their people.

The second important barrier has to do with method. Just like international marketing, there is a ''fork-in-the-road'' for global sourcing. Your firm can ''do it itself'' (direct) or ''let a trading intermediary do it for you'' (indirect purchasing). The wise company considers a mix of methods. For instance, some components or materials are better suited to be handled by your own firm. For others you might be better off to go through an Import Management Company (IMC) that specializes in your needs.

Import management company

These intermediaries often have contacts within the international community or even carry an inventory of components and other materials related to your specialized product line. Usually found near heavily industrialized areas, Import Management Companies (IMCs) survive as a satellite of their surrounding manufacturers by supporting their needs. These firms often buy and sell on their own, but more likely operate as commission agents or brokers for their clients (See Chapter 7 for a more complete discussion of intermediaries).

Just like the marketing intermediary, the more the IMC is made a part of the team, and allowed to understand the manufacturers problems and constraints, the better this method works. Seldom do these IMCs operate as the purchasing department for the manufacturer. More likely they handle only a fraction of the total purchasing effort for a larger firm.

The benefit of these international intermediaries is their search capability. For the new-to-international purchasing firm, the know-how and experience of the right IMC can get the manufacturer a quicker introduction to reliable, stable worldwide sources.

SETTING UP FOR INTERNATIONAL PURCHASING

Most international purchasing begins after a firm's domestic sourcing processes are well established. Normally, an experienced buyer, with some foreign connection or an interest in international travel starts the process.

The learning curve for this method is often quite steep, because the new-to-international buyer must not only learn how to search globally, but also learn the ins-and-outs of importing as well.

To speed entrance into worldwide sourcing, many firms hire someone who already has importing experience.

THE INTEGRATED MANUFACTURING SYSTEM

The complexities of today's modern manufacturing system require a point of view that seeks relationships with companies, foreign and domestic, so as to work as a team to optimize the Just-in-Time (JIT) concept.

JUST-IN-TIME (JIT)

Modern businesses attempt to avoid large inventories and their associated warehousing costs. High inventories represent lost revenue because they are assets not earning even the lowest of market interest rates. Of course, some inventory must be carried, but most companies limit that to no more on the shelf than the minimum required to meet predetermined statistical fill levels.

Most manufacturers have instructed the managers of their purchasing department to move toward a method called Just-in-Time (JIT). The term means just what it says—components and materials needed in the production process arrive precisely at the time the production line needs the item, thus limiting the required inventories and reducing the concomitant costs of production. Underlying the JIT philosophy is the elimination of waste, with waste being defined as anything that adds only cost to a product, and not value.

VALUE ANALYSIS (VA)

Value Analysis is a major part of the JIT process, because by definition only an activity that physically changes a product adds value, machining, plating, assembly, etc. Activities such as moving something to and fro, counting, or storing adds only cost, not value. Enter, stage right, JIT. It turns out value-adding operations comprise only a miniscule portion of the entire operation—some have calculated less than one percent.

As it turns out, JIT has its own set of problems such as quality control, reliability of sources, and cash-flow performance. These are significant barriers to overcome for the domestic buyer and can seem insurmountable when sourcing internationally. Nevertheless, many firms have established sound relationships with overseas firms, often at significant cost savings.

STRATEGIC SOURCING

To achieve the optimum integrated system, many firms have established an office, often a single person, whose task it is to step away from the day-to-day "rat race" of purchasing and look at the total procurement picture. The title commonly used for this position is Worldwide Purchasing Manager (WWPM).

By virtue of his or her separation from the typical headaches of day-to-day buying, the WWPM can take a proactive approach to sourcing instead of being reactive. This same person can include JIT and VA philosophies as part of this new approach to sourcing, and they can even be included at the product design stage. Those that have taken this step have learned one thing. It pays off handsomely in savings through the reduction of costs for primary "cost drivers."

In the past, most purchasers have used the traditional simplistic buying criteria of price, quality, delivery and service for all items and only searched the domestic market. *Strategic Sourcing* is the technique of starting with the "now situation" for the firm's product. It consists of investigating JIT, VA, pricing, supply assurance, adequacy of quality, and a host of services as these criteria relate to the total cost of the product, isolating the significant cost drivers, then searching the world for the right suppliers of those cost drivers.

Cost drivers

In the production process of capital equipment, as well as highly differentiated consumer products, parts can generally be separated into two categories. The first, typically called the "trivial many" (not categorized this way to down grade their importance but rather to expose their costs) are those parts which often account for only about 20 percent of the total product cost. The other category is often referred to as the "vital few" because they are the primary cost drivers of the final product. They are called the "vital few" because they often only amount to 20 percent of the total items, yet can account for as much as 80 percent of the cost. Identified as the "significant cost drivers," it is the "vital few" that receive the concentrated effort through a multi-functional commodity management approach.

THE COMMODITY MANAGEMENT APPROACH

The strategist does not focus on the "trivial many," instead he or she focuses on the "vital few."

When using this sourcing technique, it is important to remember to establish market driven target costs on a "landed basis" so as to be able to compare "apples-to-apples." This is vital when comparing foreign sources with domestic sources. What might seem like a good deal from an overseas supplier might prove to be too expensive when transportation, tariffs, and coordination headaches are included in the calculation of landed cost.

Solar Turbines, Inc. of Southern California has experienced, in the words of Frank Rugnetta, Manager, Worldwide Sourcing, "mind boggling success" using the Commodity Management Approach. There has been as much as 80 percent reduction for some items and routinely 30-40-50 percent reductions in costs for most of their major cost drivers.

Commodity Management Team (CMT)

To analyze the "vital few," the worldwide sourcing manager typically forms and chairs a Commodity Management Team (CMT) made up of key players from design, quality assurance, manufacturing, finance, marketing, and any others needed to satisfy the requirement. Through a facilitation process on the part of the worldwide sourcing manager, the CMT develops marketing, technical, quality and commercial objectives for every major cost driver in the production process in terms of cost, state of the art requirements, quality, supply assurance, product development, financial, managerial, and stability criteria.

The outcome of CMT meetings is the development of a market driven target cost (landed) and with well developed criteria for each of the vital few.

The strategic team then assists in setting up a prioritization for the vital few so that the worldwide sourcing manager can then state purchasing objectives in such a way as to derive a strategic "master purchasing plan." The purpose of this plan is to reduce costs yet maximize the "macro business decision," i.e., in some instances, purchasing must subordinate its goals to achieve what is best for the company.

The analytical method used by the CMT for sorting, choosing, and prioritization is often similar to the Jepner-Treigo decision analysis process. This and other similar methods force the CMT to make rather simple decisions of "must haves" and "wants." These techniques force line managers to assign priorities (usually on a scale of 1–10) to the vital few, component by component in such a way that a ranking can be determined. This kind of decision analysis should not be avoided under the false perception that it requires sophisticated computers. It can be done by small- and medium-sized firms with fairly simple manual number manipulations.

The request for proposal

The traditional steps of purchasing are: (1) issue the Invitation For Bid (IFB) or Request for Proposal (RFP) which defines specifications; (2) wait for responses; (3) analyze then accept the lowest price of responsible bidders.

Now, using the CMT method, the approach is reversed. Members of the line purchasing organization make individual IFB or RFP releases against the "master plan" which defines for the bidders precisely what the target price of each "vital few" component must be in order for them to compete. In other words, the sourcer tells the sourcee what his price must be and explains the objectives that must be met for that price.

One such offering by Solar Turbines, Inc. resulted in 40 bids which were then reduced by an elimination process to a short list of six. Although the RFP was advertised internationally, the final winner was not a foreign company (Japanese and German firms did bid). An American manufacturer won the bid and ultimately entered into a long term strategic alliance with Solar to provide the items in question on a Just-in-Time (JIT) basis. This meant that the winner became a "partner" in Solar's production process and was given proprietary information so that their own production system could be integrated with that of Solar.

Advantages

Lower ultimate costs is the most obvious advantage to using the CMT method, but more important is increased efficiency, reduction of suppliers, synchronous flow, and improved transportation costs.

Disadvantages

The worldwide purchasing approach requires a continual internal dialog of the overall business concept and how specific commodities can best contribute to the overall business objectives. As a result there is a time cost due to the need for increased and continuous training of purchasing and manufacturing personnel.

Search capability

Don't be misled. It is not just the "vital few" that are sourced worldwide. The "trivial many" have excellent potential for foreign sources, but these are generally left to the operational buyer. This means, just as it did for international marketing, that the prerequisite for international sourcing success is intelligence. Modern firms must invest in research, either by their own personnel or with the assistance of a firm that specializes in the collection of international data. Purchasing personnel need information in order to satisfy the Just-in-Time (JIT) requirements of providing the required amount, at the required time, at the lowest ultimate cost, and at the highest quality.

To meet this critical need many larger firms have organized special divisions dedicated to supporting purchasing's needs for such information as worldwide labor costs, raw materials, floating exchange rate information, and tax and tariff implications of overseas sourcing. Smaller firms rely on a cooperative approach where information gathered by overseas marketing personnel is shared.

The next chapter will show you how to organize the manufacturing firm for international marketing and sourcing.

"Our products now are known in every zone,
Our reputation sparkles like a gem,
We've fought our way thru
And new fields we're sure to conquer too,
For the ever onward IBM"

IBM company song

5

Organize manufacturing for world business

THIS CHAPTER IS ABOUT ORGANIZING THE SMALL- OR MEDIUM-SIZED MAN-
ufacturing firm to support the operational choices that best suit the firm's global
business growth.

BLUE RIBBON COMMITTEE

In the beginning a Blue Ribbon Committee should be formed to assess your
firm's readiness to go international. Using the steps suggested in Chapter 3, the
Committee will recommend to top management the best method to enter the
global marketplace. Once formed, this group should be chartered as a standing
committee of the firm to examine the organization on an annual basis.

STRATEGIC BOUNDARIES

The earliest task of the Blue Ribbon Committee is to examine the firm's strategic boundaries. The boundaries of your business are defined by what your firm
does, i.e., what its products are and what others do for it. In other words, what
your firm makes, what it buys and how it sells.

Vertical adjustments to your strategic boundaries are the what and where,
make or buy decisions that relate to the expansion or contraction of single functions or product lines. *Horizontal adjustment* relates to changes of strategic
boundaries through the expansion or contraction of multiple functions or diversification into new industries. This chapter is concerned only with vertical activities, but will discuss both forward and backward integration.

Forward integration is a vertical adjustment synonymous with market power, that is, going on the offensive to increase sales volume. This can be accomplished by opening your own retail stores, or beginning a direct mail operation. Another means to forward integrate might be to export your products or establish an overseas subsidiary in order to be nearer your foreign markets.

Backward integration is the defensive strategy of reducing costs and pro tecting the firm against exploitation from powerful sources of raw materials and product by searching for new, less costly sources or producing the component yourself.

Figure 5-1 depicts business decisions left and right of center. Those to the left are decisions related to reducing production costs, and those to the right are those having to do with expanding markets. Don't be scared off by the term integration. All it means is the consideration of what you do and what others do for you and those decisions are made based on quality, price, delivery, and reliability.

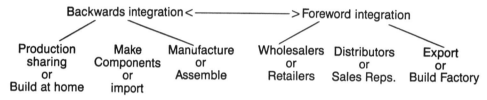

Fig. 5-1   Vertical Integration Adjustments.

GO FOR IT!

The assumption of this chapter is that your Blue Ribbon Committee, chartered to assess your firm's readiness to go international, has studied your company's position and made the following recommendation: "The firm can overcome any obstacle and there is sufficient working capital. We're ready, as the British say to, 'give it a go.' We can do it ourselves. We understand this means long-term commitment with a capital 'C'."

THE GLOBAL BUSINESS

The global business is one that takes on a worldwide point of view and makes no distinction between domestic and international business. In practical terms it may favor one market region over another, but that is probably a result of early growth—emerging from the imprint of its founding country or more probably because of some tax or investment advantage. A global viewpoint eventually invades every business decision that affects the bottom line. People are selected for the organization because of their international viewpoint and experience, products and raw materials are marketed and sourced on a worldwide basis and staffs have global responsibilities.

THE CHANGING ORGANIZATION

As your success in international sales and sourcing grows it's inevitable that you will be faced with reorganization. At the outset you should be aware there's no best method—no standard model. Each global business must design the organization that works best for its product line and global application.

Growth

When international sales volume becomes a significant component of total company business you will, no doubt have already formed a separate export department using one of the ways described later in this chapter. During this growth period you should carefully watch your costs and selling patterns. An export department is primarily a sales department and if a major part of your business originates from one country or a specific area of the world you should consider forming an overseas subsidiary. This subsidiary could be for marketing (export), sourcing (import), for distribution, or it could be a combination assembly and/or manufacturing operation.

PARTNERING

Businesses worldwide are forming relationships that strengthen their position. In Chapter 1 it was referred to as *"new world business paradigm."*

Partnering is the forming of strategic alliances, to increase long term stability and leverage. It is a modern-day tactic useful in both the forward and backward integration process. It is a particularly useful tactic for small- and medium-sized firms which have low volume, highly differentiated products. The formation of subsidiaries, whether wholly owned or joint ventures is explained in detail in Chapter 9. Another option is to license your products for manufacture and/or distribution. That too is explained in Chapter 9.

Your expansion might be in many countries on many continents with many products. When that happens you will have several organizational options available, depending on selling patterns, sales growth and significant legal or tax advantages recommended by your lawyer or accountant.

In selecting the proper organization for your firm the critical elements are:

1. Avoid duplication, i.e., divisions or departments doing the same function.
2. Avoid suboptimization, that is treating international business as a separate segment of corporate business thus preventing their optimal use in the best interest of the total organization.

ORGANIZING FOR INTERNATIONAL MARKETING

Your organization should support the strategic boundaries of your firm. Forward integration ranges from exporting directly, to using a marketing subsidiary for sales coordination among overseas factories.

INTELLIGENCE: The Prerequisite

Organizing for international marketing is all about organizing for selling, which requires creativeness and determination not found in some aspects of business operations.

The prerequisite for any successful international business venture is intelligence. Before your international effort can move forward you must invest in market research, either by your own personnel or with the assistance of a firm that specializes in the field. From this search for broader markets will come a strategic approach. That approach, if you recall from the discussion in Chapter 3, suggests you integrate your market plan into the total business plan and that it cover a time frame of three to five years.

PERSONNEL

The most important aspect of the growth of your international sales effort will be the selection of the right people to carry out your plan. The dominant personal characteristic of these employees will be the ability to work on a team in a multicultural environment.

A typical international marketing department when fully developed, would include an export manager, a traffic manager, a communications manager, an engineering services manager, credit and finance personnel, a sales manager, a promotion assistant, and sales personnel. Of course, not all of these positions are filled at once, instead most companies let their organization develop as their sales and activities increase, hiring only as cash flow will allow their expansion. In the early stages many of these functions can be farmed out to such support organizations as a reliable freight forwarder, or your banker who will review your documentation and give you advice. Fleshing out an entire international marketing department may take several years, nevertheless from the start you should have an understanding of the responsibilities of the key personnel.

Export manager

The single most important position to be filled in any exporting organization is the export manager. The person in this key leadership role will have control, planning, and profit/loss responsibility. He or she will be the person in your organization that, based on interpretation of market intelligence, will set the marketing objectives, coordinate with production, design, service, inventory planning, finance, credit, and will develop the overseas contacts. The export manager should be well trained and fully competent in the fundamentals of international marketing and market planning, including adapting to sensitive cultural differences as they relate to product and market decisions. Above all, the person hired for this job should be an able leader who can work effectively with and motivate the international staff, yet have good rapport with other corporate officers.

Traffic manager

The job description of the traffic manager includes processing all incoming orders, and supervising collection, documentation, packing, insurance, and shipping. In other words he or she is responsible, in general, for all preparation and expediting of goods to fill orders. When searching for someone experienced for this position look for someone who is familiar with documentation, foreign transportation processes, freight forwarders, packing requirements, shipping regulations, and payment methods. Obviously this employee must be someone the export manager can completely depend upon, because the position is so important to executing the transaction.

Communications manager

This position is critical to "sound" relationships with overseas markets, and the proper execution of this job often can reflect well on the company. The communications manager should, as a minimum, understand how to prepare correspondence. While not a requirement, a good working knowledge of several languages is also useful. He or she should have the nicest sense and concern for the nuances of language as they affect the sale of products. Hands-on experience with long distance communications equipment such as telex and facsimile is essential. Another important, and more recent requirement is appreciation for video and other special sales training methods.

Engineering and services manager

As the department grows and sales activity increases, the need to coordinate critical technical design and engineering assistance becomes vital. This is a critical issue! In-country service, response time, and logistic (supply) support is essential to serving an export market. This person must be top drawer because he or she is often the link to protecting the company's reputation in distant markets. This position often serves as the link between the marketing and the international sourcing organizations.

Promotion assistant

Although the export manager acts primarily as a sales manager, the need to follow through on details related to media campaigns, catalogs and coordination of overseas trade fairs often requires an assistant. This should be a high energy, details oriented person, willing to travel and put in long hours in support of the overseas sales effort.

Sales representatives

Personal relationships are most important in international trade. Therefore, the export salesperson should be the kind of person that has a "feel" for finding the key that converts or closes a sale through personal contact with overseas buyers. The relationship between buyer and seller is often more important than price. Most companies are hiring foreign nationals for these positions, because they know and understand the local customs and the language.

Administration personnel

Like any other business operation, there is a basic need to keep order in the house. If nothing else, administrative personnel—secretaries, and clerks serve to allow others freedom to think and not be tied to the office. In the case of an international organization, where the travel time of managers is often much greater than for domestic operations, the office personnel become a major reflection of the company and as such should be multilingual and culturally sensitive as well as proficient in their tasks. It is not unusual that administrative entry-level personnel "step-up" to management positions after suitable seasoning.

Evaluating sales personnel

Your sales staff is so vital to you that from the outset you should have an image of the ideal international salesperson in mind. Among other things this person should:

1. Want to sell!
2. Enjoy travel.
3. Have a desire to deal in a foreign environment and language.
4. Be able to adapt to other cultures.
5. Have a track record or at least exhibit behavioral instincts for the bottom line—the ability to close.
6. Show bounce-back characteristics, the ability to regroup and deal with rejection.

Foreign nationals

Sooner or later you will want to hire foreign personnel, because they offer advantages over the exclusive use of domestic hires. For instance they:

1. Allow you to do business. In many countries, a foreign firm cannot operate unless they use native agents or representative.

2. Are less expensive in terms of both salaries and travel costs.
3. Give your company a home country identity.
4. Can help you avoid cultural and legal barriers.
5. Have an easier time managing other foreign nationals.
6. Are less vulnerable to threats of terrorism.

On the other hand, foreign nationals can be difficult to shed once they become settled into a job. Some foreign laws require severance pay or specific causes prior to firing. Typically they are hired through an employment contract which unless carefully worded can become binding and expensive to break.

Turnover

Personnel turnover in international marketing is more important than turnover in other aspects of your business. The limited number of people involved and the distances can cause catastrophic implications. Make certain top executives visit overseas distributors and foreign employees often to ensure continuity should the unexpected happen. Back-up international data and information so that your market effort will not lose a step due to change of key personnel. Replacement personnel should be hired for their contacts, and having had experience promoting related goods.

THE MARKETING ORGANIZATION

In the early stage of developing an international marketing department the typical company has four options:

1. Expand its own department from a domestic base.
2. Recruit an already experienced staff.
3. Use the Export Trading Company Act of 1982 to form a cooperative export organization (explained in detail in Chapter 8). This law is primarily applicable in support of export operations because of its anti-trust implications, but it also has useful tax implications.
4. Use a mix of organizational support including intermediaries to get the job done.

The start-up organization

Expansion of the international department will be a function of capitalization. As a minimum the organization should have an export manager, a salesperson and administrative support.

Expand from domestic base

Your firm can develop from within by expanding the duties of a few personnel who show an interest in international business. Usually one or more members of the firm's domestic marketing organization have the inclination and ambition to begin forming the new department. Slowly, over time, allow those personnel to become the international department. The key to success is finding a leader personality who is capable of developing a plan, being responsible for training the staff and generally functioning as the export manager. Often a firm will bring in an outside consultant at this point, one that is a seasoned manager and who has had experience with start-ups. Other duties related to export marketing, finance and traffic are spread among the various domestic departments and integrated with their normal activities.

Advantages. Personnel who already know the firm's products, organization, and key employees in other departments bring initial stability to the development of a new department. There is a built-in level of trust that is never there initially when outsiders are hired for a new function. In reality this method of developing from within brings with it some cost savings in the short run. Often only the job descriptions of "old hands" are enriched—not their salaries.

Disadvantages. The flip side to this method of growing from a base of employees from within is that the present staff will have their time diluted and the development of the new department will often take a "back seat" to their normal duties. Two things can suffer: (1) the current job, with the inevitability of error, omissions, and delays that a beginning exporter can ill afford; and (2) the timely start-up of the new department. For the same reasons, when an outside consultant is hired, that person sometimes has a difficult time getting the attention of the current staff due to their overload condition.

Recruit a staff and form a separate department

The second option is the recruitment of a staff that is already trained and has developed a track record at other companies. In this case you would create a separate export department by hiring several key employees to concentrate on the development of export business. The first to be hired would, of course, be the export manager who, with your support, would hire the remainder of the staff using the schedule developed in your strategic plan as modified by the actual growth pattern of world sales activity.

Advantages. By having a separate export department, in charge from the beginning, management can get better data and a feel for the development process. Recruited personnel often have established contacts and relationships with support organizations. The company's image will be enhanced and employee morale within the department should not become a problem.

Disadvantages. Top management of the company must be cautious of new management for international operations that bring with them approaches that are too optimistic, interjecting utopian sales projections based on their experiences with other established firms. This method will require a period of familiarization for new employees to learn how your company operates and about your products.

ORGANIZING FOR TAX BENEFITS

There are no tax incentives for importing. However, United States' tax rules offer what amounts to be about a 15 percent exclusion of the taxable income earned on international sales to the firm that organizes an offshore office through which it passes its export documentation. Here's how it works.

Foreign Sales Corporation (FSC)

Under rules put into effect in January 1985, exporters who wish to take advantage of this incentive, which can be very substantial, must establish a foreign corporation. Called a Foreign Sales Corporation (FSC) under the tax code, this subsidiary organization must maintain a summary of its permanent books of account at the foreign office, and have at least one director resident outside the United States.

Meeting these requirements isn't as difficult as it sounds. Some 23 foreign countries, those which have an agreement to exchange tax information with the United States, and all United States possessions like the Virgin Islands, Guam, and Saipan have already established offices capable of providing direct support as your FSC.

Multiple exporters, up to 24, may jointly own a FSC and through the use of several classes of common stock divide the profits of the FSC among the several shareholders. Of course larger firms can form their own FSC.

Domestic International Sales Corporation (DISC)

Prior to December 31, 1984, the United States tax code provided for another, simpler method to take advantage of all international sales tax deferrals. This method, originally created by the Revenue Act of 1971, is still on the books but is applicable only for those firms whose annual exports are less than $10 million. To take advantage of this method you need not have an overseas presence. Simply form your own local legal entity called a Domestic International Sales Corporation (DISC) through which you pass your export documentation. You may still defer taxes on export earnings, but must pay an annual interest charge on the amount of tax that would be due if the post-1984 accumulated DISC income were included in the shareholder's income.

Small FSC

The tax implications of international trade are important and can be a major factor in how you do business. Small exporters have several options for their foreign sales operations. They may export through a DISC, playing an interest charge on the deferred income or they can join together with other exporters to own an FSC. Another alternative for the small exporter is to individually take advantage of relaxed, small FSC rules, under which they need not meet all of the tests required of the large FSCs.

You should consult an accountant who specializes in international taxes to assist you in setting up whichever organization is applicable and to best advantage for your firm.

Historical Note: The United States changed from DISC to FSC procedures as a result of a dispute between certain other signatories of the General Agreement on Tariffs and Trade (GATT). These nations contended the DISC amounted to an illegal export subsidy because it allowed an indefinite deferral of direct taxes on income from exports earned in the United States. Although not specifically agreeing with its accusers, United States tax law changed on January 1, 1985 to preclude continuing disagreement.

ORGANIZING FOR GLOBAL SOURCING

The modern approach to global business seeks synergism (the whole is greater than the parts). Just as international marketing (exporting) must be integrated with your total company marketing strategy, so must international sourcing (importing) be integrated with your total purchasing and manufacturing strategy.

Intelligence

Good intelligence is as much a prerequisite for purchasing as it is for a successful marketing effort. Before your international effort can move forward you must invest in research, either by your own personnel or with the assistance of a firm that specializes in that field. You cannot assume that sources will find you or that the ''grapevine'' will get the word out to all qualified suppliers.

Personnel

Many international sourcing personnel are experienced domestic purchasing managers who have the inclination to travel and the talent to work with people of other cultures. However, just as in marketing, there is a movement toward foreign nationals in sourcing.

Purchasing director. As a key person under the vice president for manufacturing, this position requires extensive experience not only in purchasing, but also in total business operations. This person is often in-house selected but may come on a horizontal move from a firm offering similar products.

Worldwide sourcing manager (WWSM). The ideal selection for this position would be a person with an engineering degree related to the industry of your product as well as a business degree. He or she would have purchasing background, but most important have a high degree of skill at influencing behavior patterns. This job is only one-tenth buying and requires 90 percent missionary work or the selling of new ideas and approaches.

International purchaser. The modern line purchaser need not have a business degree, although that would be useful. More important is the ability to relate to other cultures and understand the relationship of the buying function to the "macro business objectives." Purchasing represents a major reflection of the company and as such should be multi-lingual and culturally sensitive as well as proficient in their tasks.

Organization

Worldwide purchasing must be keyed to production flow, engineering, research and development, marketing, after market requirements, and material selection, and it plays a growing part in the optimization of an integrated manufacturing system (explained in Chapter 4).

Today's sourcing organization must not only have the capability to purchase materials, goods and services to support in-house manufacturing, but also locate parts and assemblies from sources outside the boundaries of the business, all with the intent to improve profit margins of the business unit as a whole.

ORGANIZATION MODELS

There are several ways to organize your firm to accommodate changes as it grows in the international arena. While there is a rigid pattern, most global companies are organized geographically, functionally or by product line.

Start-up organization

The first organization will either be split off from the domestic marketing or purchasing departments or organized as a new entity. The beginning effort is generally focused on one or two high priority target countries. Figure 5-2 shows how a diagram of this organization might look.

Organizing geographically

You might find early on that your firm is serving several countries that are close to one another in a region yet far from your home base. This is the typical beginning of restructuring the organization by geographical area.

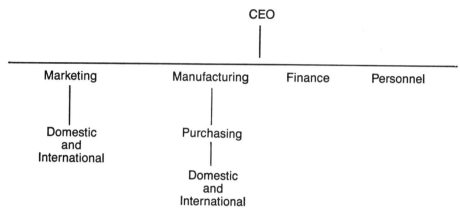

Fig. 5-2   Start-up Organization.

By organizing a headquarters or a "marketing subsidiary" (Chapter 9) in the region there is a common base for management and it becomes easier to communicate, thus optimizing marketing know-how. Figure 5-3 is an example of such a structure.

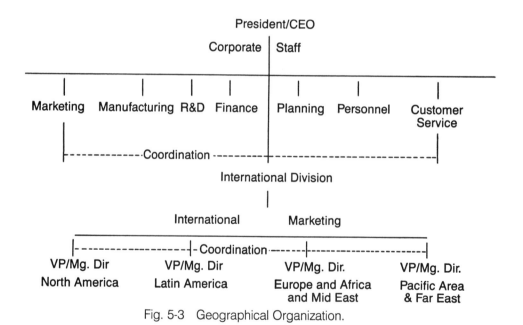

Fig. 5-3   Geographical Organization.

Flat geographic

The main drawback of this geographic organization is the tendency to dilute the global viewpoint. Over time regions begin to take on domestic viewpoints and there is the danger of suboptimization. To overcome this tendency, a strong coordinational management style must be put in place.

One top manager, Michael A. Lapadula, Vice President Marketing for Loral TerraCom, of San Diego, California, overcomes this tendency by keeping a close rein from the corporate headquarters. His organization is flat and tight. He had four subordinate managers in the home office with him, each has a region in which the company does business through sales representatives. The representatives, in each of the 50 countries where Loral does business, are natives of that country, familiar with the people, businesses and government, and their needs. Mr. Lapadula believes his company has ''pop'' (responsiveness) which translates to bigger sales as a result of using representatives. His flat organization looks like Fig. 5-4.

Fig. 5-4   Flat Geographical Organization.

Functional organization

A functional organization lends itself to a firm that has very homogenous lines of products and line executives have global responsibilities. Figure 5-5 is typical of a functional organization.

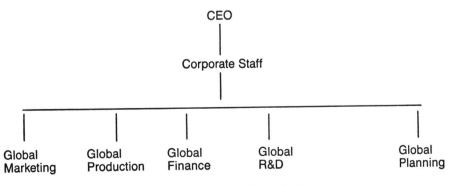

Fig. 5-5   Functional Organization.

Organizing by product

Another means of organization is along the lines of Fig. 5-6 in which each line product has its own international sales organization. This is a world company approach where product groups are responsible for global marketing and sourcing. This method is typical for firms with several unrelated product lines for which their marketing tasks vary more by product than by region.

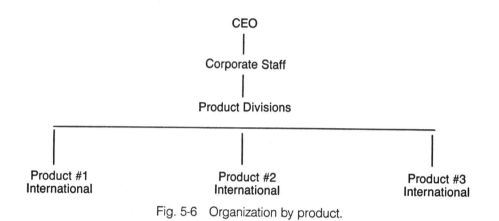

Fig. 5-6   Organization by product.

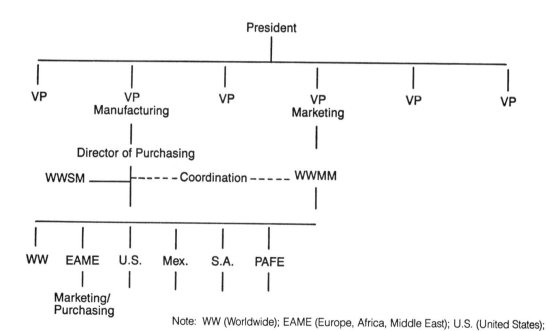

Note: WW (Worldwide); EAME (Europe, Africa, Middle East); U.S. (United States); Mex. (Mexico); S.A. (South America); PAFE (Pacific Area, Far East).

Fig. 5-7   Integrated International Organization.

THE INTEGRATED INTERNATIONAL ORGANIZATION

Figure 5-7 shows an organization structure for an integrated manufacturing system. It shows that the Worldwide Sourcing Manager (WWSM) is at the same level within the organization as the line purchasing managers. He or she is a principal assistant to the purchasing director who is responsible for developing policy and procedures and providing a vision for line purchasers who are closely linked to the Worldwide Marketing Manager (WWMM) and marketing counterparts in the integrated organization.

The next chapter explains how to enter the global services industry.

6

Compete in the global services market

SERVICES, INCLUDING GOVERNMENT, NOW ACCOUNT FOR MORE THAN TWO-thirds of the United States gross national product (GNP). Approximately 70 percent of all United States employment, let me repeat—70 percent of all Americans are working in a service industry. The services industry over the past twenty years has exploded!

The international services market has simultaneously grown to become a multi-billion dollar business, and the United States has the largest share, about 20 percent worldwide.

This chapter is about the kinds of service businesses that lend themselves to the international marketplace, and how to compete.

WHAT KINDS OF SERVICES CAN BE EXPORTED?

Almost all Research and Development (R&D) is done by the developed nations and the United States has the lead in most areas. Much of the professional and technical know-how is common to the United States and is in high demand in Least Developed Countries (LDCs). Many new products, concepts, and procedures being developed are directly applicable to the environments of these countries, particularly in food processing, medical services, agriculture, water resources development, education, and housing.

Your business could be technical and management consulting; legal services; advertising; information; accounting; computer; telecommunications; most kinds of insurance; construction and engineering or several not on this list which are being marketed on a global basis. Let's discuss a few.

Data services

Some call it the information age because data processing services are crucial to individuals and to the operations of businesses, governments and educational organizations. The United States is the world's largest player in the data services business accounting for 40 percent of the world's database suppliers and about 20 percent of the on-line services.

Data processing is used to deliver vital records such as census, death, birth, payroll checks, and the list goes on. Overseas, major United States data processing companies have operations, but smaller firms are moving to compete. Most American data processing firms are serving United States customers with international sales, particularly in neighboring Canada and Mexico.

There are growing barriers to overseas growth that the service company in this business should be aware of such as: Telecommunications regulations, and restrictions on the content of transborder information and data flows.

Health care

Coincidental with the post World War II industrial growth has come a rising standard of living and a demand for better private and public health care service. Commitment to upgrade medical and health care has brought an up-surge of "buy American" equipment as well as buy the know-how to manage health delivery systems.

Venture capital

The story goes that the first venture capital project that affected the United States was when Queen Isabella financed Christopher Columbus. Since that time the process has continued and was instrumental for much of the early development and industrialization of the United States. The current boom in the United States developed during the 1970s and 1980s as a result of improved tax laws and has proven to be the engine of new growth, particularly in Boston and California's Silicon Valley. Recognizing venture capital as the locomotive of United States innovation, other countries have become interested in the venture capital industry. Consequently, many United States venture capital supplying firms are looking into overseas opportunities where the rewards will match the risk.

Entertainment

Worldwide distribution of pre-recorded music and the motion picture industry, including feature entertainment, television films, video tapes, video cassettes and video discs is dependent on foreign markets as valuable sources of income. Companies serving the entertainment industry should be aware of trade barriers such as import quotas, subsidies, excessive taxes, and a recent up-surge in piracy resulting from new technologies such as video-recorders and cable and satellite television which make duplication and interception easy.

Life insurance

Foreign premiums for United States life insurers amounted to $1.6 billion in 1984 and are expected to grow at double-digit rates in the decades ahead. Because insurance is a heavily regulated industry, it is critical to research each country's laws and attitudes. Nevertheless, there are solid business opportunities for those who have patience and are innovative.

Management consulting

This category includes training and supervision of personnel, management of facilities, economic and business research, finance, market analysis, strategic planning, and other management services. Governments, private industry, and other organizations hire these firms for a fee or on a contract basis. The international activity of management and consulting services firms has grown rapidly in recent years and will continue to prosper. Net foreign receipts for United States consulting and technical services increased at an average annual rate of over 20 percent between 1978 and 1985. Like other services industries, expansion overseas is sometimes impeded by non-tariff trade barriers such as ownership restrictions, foreign exchange controls and discriminatory taxation policies, all of which require innovative business operations.

Franchising

The same factors that spurred the growth of franchising in the United States domestic market, i.e. new jobs, new entrepreneurs, and new services, has also propelled its movement into overseas markets. More than 300 United States business format franchising companies operated more than 27,000 outlets in foreign countries in the mid-1980s and the future will see an increase in the variety and growth. In general, foreign laws and regulations have not been overly restrictive, because franchising tends to foster ownership and employment. (Franchising is developed in more detail in Chapter 9).

Tourism

Herman Kahn, the late futurist, predicted that by the year 2010, tourism will be the world's largest industry. Already worldwide tourism receipts exceed $150 billion and for many countries it is a major source of foreign exchange earnings. Tourism translates into a booming service industry in terms of travel, lodging and restaurant related businesses as well as such spin-offs as rental cars, and food and beverages.

Business services

Advertising, accounting, construction and engineering continues to show a surplus of export activity for United States firms operating overseas. In addition to a continuing growth projected in the developed world, there is much contract work available in third-world nations and it is often financed with the help of international development organizations.

BREAKING IN

Given that a company is established in the domestic market and has the resources, the first step is some early "homework." What is going to be offered overseas? Some minor working capital outlay and time should be allocated to determine the price, delivery, quality, warranty, and after-sales—which should be blended together to create a desirable offering. Keep in mind that distances, communications, language, culture, and government regulations are some of the forces that play a part in the offered package.

As a rule of thumb, if a service is competitive in the United States domestic market, then it may have some overseas potential.

Caution: The excitement of entering "exotic" markets could push your service firm into the international arena before you are ready. As a general rule, a firm in a given service industry should be mature in the domestic market before attempting to go overseas. It is important to take a realistic view of the firm's financial, management, and personnel resources. Unless there is a reasonably stable foundation, the firm may not be ready. Unlike trading a mechanical product, many times the costs to get a soft product into a foreign country are higher than in the domestic market.

HOW TO ORGANIZE

Large American service companies, such as the "Big Eight" accounting firms have been in the overseas market for many years. Nevertheless there is room for the growing smaller firm, and many go it alone. In order to compete it may be necessary to network a group of specialized companies into a cohesive organization. Many organizational forms can be used; however, for a group of local service companies, the Export Trading Company (ETC) organized under the Export Trading Company Act of 1982 could be considered a valuable method to market services worldwide. Chapter 8 addresses the anti-trust aspects of this relatively new law and shows how it can be used to your advantage to make big profits overseas.

Personnel

In the early stages of developing an international service business most firms assign the responsibility to a project manager (PM) who becomes an expert in the new market and brings the information to the corporate organization and line managers.

Usually the project manager also is assigned to be the manager of a competitive proposal and as such, sees the venture through to the successful end. PMs are often given profit and loss responsibility as well as the authority to select and assign employees.

It is not unusual that experienced personnel from the parent company kick-off a venture in a new country; however, soon after start-up foreign hires are often brought into the operation. The benefits are market, culture, and language knowledge as well as the wise suggestion to the host country that the firm is a good citizen and intends a home identity.

Caution: Review Chapter 2, and fully understand the importance of sending culturally sensitive employees to live or represent your firm in a foreign country.

THE MARKET PLAN

A market plan, based on sound market research, should lay-out the country or countries the firm intends to penetrate, in terms of sequence, and market communications methods. For instance, your service might require procurement decisions. In one city, decisions might lie with a committee, in another the decision-making unit (DMU) might be the mayor, i.e., he or she might be the sole fiscal authority. In the United States, sales people gather this information from their own experiences in dealing with customers. In the international marketplace, unless the service firm already has a sales force presence, it might be necessary to include in the plan the development of a relationship with some local representative, client, or associate (consider contacting an overseas Chamber of Commerce, listed in Appendix E). The plan should include some understanding of the competition, both domestic and by other international firms. The resultant plan will lead to an estimated budget, which will need top management approval.

MARKET RESEARCH

Again, intelligence is the prerequisite for a plan designed for successful penetration of a new market. Service firms should have a clear understanding of foreign business environments and potential customers before committing themselves to the international marketplace. The need to invest time and money in market research cannot be emphasized enough.

First step

What are your goals? Analyze your firm using the same criteria developed in Chapter 3.

Second step

Locate the regions and nations with the best potential to reach those goals. In other words, where are the best market/buyer segments?

Third step

Analyze the international barriers and learn the DMUs of the service. To get the answers to these big questions, service companies often must piece together information gleaned from a number of different sources. Unlike data about manufactured products, comprehensive data about services in many countries often is not available. This is true even in the United States. Therefore, services must often use the concept called ''derived demand.''

Derived demand

Demand for a service buyer's industrial end-product or consumer goods determines what services and equipment the firm needs to produce the product.

Two methods are used to arrive at derived demand: *complementary* and *substitute*. By examining trends in complementary or substitute product areas that are closely linked to their expertise, consultants and other service industry firms can often determine their best overseas markets.

Complementary. Examples of complementary product areas might be:

1. A service company that provides clean overalls, rags, and smocks on a turn-around basis would examine machinery and hardware sales in order to find the DMU of the end-user market.

2. Suppliers of computer software can utilize the trade statistics that show flows of computer hardware.

3. An agricultural consultant dealing in farm management might analyze sales of tractors, farm chemicals, and irrigation equipment.

Substitute. Substitute product indicators are sometimes harder to find and may not always lend itself to the services area. Examples might be:

1. A company with a new industrial technology which negates the need for certain raw materials would search for markets where those raw materials are now being sold.
2. Firms in a certain country use obsolete methods and it can be shown that your product can speed up the process and be more efficient and cost effective.

The bottom line of your research should be to answer the question: Is it feasible or desirable to expand into the overseas market?

KEY ELEMENTS TO WIN BIDS

There is a gamesmanship to winning government contracts and subcontracts no matter what country makes the offer. The keys to winning are: understanding the bid process and then developing an appropriate strategy.

Types of bid instruments

Most countries use procedures similar to those used by the United States government, issuing such advertisements as IFBs (Invitation For Bids) and RFPs (Request for Proposals).

IFB (Invitation For Bids)

These bid instruments are the simplest and fastest means for a government to make purchases of either manufactured goods or services. Awards are ordinarily made to the lowest bidder. Formal advertisement is made through one or more of the public publications described later.

RFP (Request For Proposals)

These are used when a government wants a contractor to design the product or service and depends heavily on the skills of the contractor. In these cases governments cannot afford to rely on only the lowest bid because there are often technical requirements which also must be met. Generally, RFPs are in two parts: (1) the technical proposal; and (2) the cost proposal. Governments evaluate the technical proposal before cost is considered. Usually those contractors that are technically competent are then asked for a best and final offer.

Two-step procurements

This is the method used by some governments to get the most technically qualified bidder at the lowest price. It usually goes like this: A government first asks for technical proposals without pricing. Once those with the best technical proposals are determined, a second proposal is submitted as a sealed bid.

Sole source

These procurements bypass normal competitive bidding processes and allow a government agency to give the project to one contractor. These can be justified when:

- There is only one source for a highly specialized product or service or it is proprietary.
- The skills or qualifications are unique and no one else can do the job less expensively.
- An emergency exists and a purchase must be made in less time than a normal offering would allow.

Unsolicited

Contractors can submit a proposal for a sole source award. These must be for things that are unique and proprietary.

Bidders mailing lists

In addition to monitoring publications where you might find advertisements for the service your firm offers, you can write appropriate agencies in other governments and get on their bidders lists. Sometimes these lists represent those companies that have met some prequalification requirements, thus representing a "blue ribbon" list of contractors.

Strategy

The submission of a bid in response to an IFB or RFP is as much a sales effort as if you were selling a product in the market. As stated earlier, gamesmanship or proposalship wins bids, not through luck, but rather through an intelligent, persuasive effort.

Most of your competitors will be able to show that they can do the job, but to win the contract you must show, by compelling evidence, that you are the best contractor for the client.

The minimums

Your proposal must at least:

- *Be timely:* The bid must be to the agency that advertised no later than the exact time set to open the bids.

- *Conform to the requirements and specifications of the offer.* Don't impose new conditions.

- *Minimize clerical and technical mistakes.* Some governments allow for opportunities to correct, but for some, they are grounds for disqualification.

Beyond the minimums

Capturing the bid means more than just being able to do the job. Your proposal must be organized for the greatest impact to the reader; it must show how you are more technically qualified; it must appear to be within the ball-park for cost; and must include a counter to what you believe will be the competitor's proposal. Above all, it must take into account cultural and language differences.

SOURCES AND CONTACTS FOR BUSINESS

Although much of the current information about opportunities is gained by having representation in target market areas in order to keep close touch with decision makers, there are many sources of public offerings. The following section shows a partial list of suggested organizations and publications that provide information or contract for services.

UNITED STATES GOVERNMENT SOURCES

There is great emphasis placed by state and federal governments to stimulate the service industries to enter international trade. Therefore, the first place to look is Washington, DC and your local state house.

United States Department of Commerce

The first point of contact to obtain information from the United States government is the Office of Business Liaison, United States Department of Commerce, Room H5898C, Washington, DC 20230, Telephone: (202) 377-3176. This office serves to guide businesses and individuals through the maze of the federal government. Professional staff answers questions about government programs, services and policies and provides a variety of published materials. This office can put you in touch with the right people. Ask for a copy of the *Business Services Directory*.

Here is a list of valuable phone numbers at the Commerce Department for service industry offices:

Office of Service Industries	(202) 377-2587
Office of General Industrial Machinery	(202) 377-5455
Office of Major Projects and International Construction	(202) 377-5225

Office of Special Industrial Machinery	(202) 377-0302
Office of Consumer Goods	(202) 377-0337
Bureau of the Census	(301) 763-4100
Office of International Economic Policy	(202) 377-3022

The Commerce Department also offers *Commerce Business Daily*, an up-to-date document which provides notification of Requests for Proposals from United States government agencies as well as some foreign governments. The price is approximately $160.00 a year (first class mailing), or $81.00 (second class).

Commerce Business Daily
Superintendent of Documents
Government Printing Office
Washington, DC 20402

United States Embassies and Consulates

Overseas offices in the United States embassies and consulates in more than 140 countries are prime sources of information about service industry opportunities. The best source for the names and addresses of the currently assigned people is the booklet titled: *Key Officers of Foreign Service Posts—A Guide for Business Representatives*. It costs about $2.00 a single copy and can be ordered from your nearest government bookstore.

United States Agency for International Development (USAID)

This agency, which coordinates development projects worldwide, has developed a computerized database to help service companies to compete for consulting opportunities. Called Aid Consultant Registry Information System (ACRIS), it provides a readily accessible data bank of firms who are interested in doing business with A.I.D. To get on the list contact:

OSDBU/MRC
United States Agency for International Development
Washington, DC 20523
Telephone: (703) 875-1551

Trade and Development Program (TDP)

This organization stands alongside USAID as an agency under the umbrella of The International Development Cooperation Agency (IDCA). Its function is to assist American service providers such as large construction companies to compete for international contracts. Telephone (703) 875-4357.

National Science Foundation

The National Science Foundation does not maintain a formal bidders list, but is frequently interested in small firms that are innovative, and have developed a research and technology orientation for important scientific and engineering problems.

> NATIONAL SCIENCE FOUNDATION
> Room 511-A
> 1800 G Street, N.W.
> Washington, DC 20550

INTERNATIONAL ORGANIZATION SOURCES

There are many international organizations involved in various aspects of development programs that use the services industry. The following is a list of the major organizations.

United Nations

The United Nations system of organizations represents a vast global market for potential suppliers of services. Required services cover a wide spectrum, from expert input or consulting assistance on economic and engineering feasibility studies to preparation of contract documents complete with designs, specifications, and cost estimates. Key members of the system are:

United Nations Development Programme (UNDP). The world's largest channel for multilateral technical and pre-investment cooperation.

> UNITED NATIONS DEVELOPMENT PROGRAMME
> One United Nations Plaza
> New York, NY 10017
> Telephone: (212) 906-5000

United Nations Industrial Development Organization (UNIDO). A vehicle for technology transfer between developed and less developed nations.

> UNITED NATIONS INDUSTRIAL DEVELOPMENT ORGANIZATION
> P.O. Box 707, A-1011, A-1070
> Vienna, Austria
> Tel: 26310

Department for Technical Cooperation for Development (DTCD). Funds surveys and feasibility studies.

> DEPARTMENT FOR TECHNICAL COOPERATION FOR DEVELOPMENT
> United Nations
> New York, NY 10017
> Tel: (212) 754-8947

Food and Agriculture Organization (FAO).

FOOD AND AGRICULTURE ORGANIZATION
Via delle Terne di Caracalla
00100 Rome, Italy
Tel: 57971

International Telecommunications Union (ITU).

INTERNATIONAL TELECOMMUNICATIONS UNION
1211 Geneva 20, Switzerland
Tel: 995111

Inter-Governmental Maritime Consultative Organization (IMCO).

INTER-GOVERNMENTAL MARITIME CONSULTATIVE ORGANIZATION
101-104 Piccadilly
London, WIV OAE, England
Tel: 499 9040

International Fund for Agriculture Development (IFAD).

INTERNATIONAL FUND FOR AGRICULTURE DEVELOPMENT
Via Del Serafico 107
00142 Rome, Italy
Tel: 54591

International Atomic Energy Agency (IAEA).

INTERNATIONAL ATOMIC ENERGY AGENCY
Vienna International Centre
P.O. Box 100
A-1400 Vienna, Austria
Tel: 2360

The World Health Organization (WHO). Employs consulting firms that specialize in education, environment, health, and water supply.

THE WORLD HEALTH ORGANIZATION
1211 Geneva 27
Switzerland

The Inter-Agency Procurement Services Unit (IAPSU). This is the inter-agency unit that helps the UNDP and its partner agencies procure essential project inputs. No less than 12 member organs and 16 specialized agencies use the IAPSU.

INTER AGENCY PROCUREMENT SERVICES UNIT (IAPSU)
Palais des Nations
CH-1211 Geneva 10
Switzerland

Development Forum Business Edition (DFBE). The primary source of information on business opportunities in the United Nations system is Development Forum Business Edition (DFBE) which is published 24 times a year. Enquiries regarding subscriptions should be directed to:

Development Forum
Business Edition
United Nations
Palais des Nations
CH-1211 Geneva 10
Switzerland

or

DEVELOPMENT FORUM LIAISON UNIT
Room E-1055
World Bank
1818 H Street N.W.
Washington, DC 20433
U.S.A.

Yearly subscriptions are approximately U.S. $250.00.

World Bank Group. The World Bank Group consists of the International Bank for Reconstruction and Development (IBRD), the International Development Association (IDA), and the International Finance Corporation (IFC).

International Bank for Reconstruction and Development (IBRD). Promotes economic development by extending loans for high-priority programs and projects.

International Development Association (IDA). Extends loans to member countries with per capita GNP of about $700.

International Finance Corporation (IFC). Encourages growth of productive private enterprise by developing agencies by extending loans.

The World Bank's clients are developing countries which borrow about $11–12 billion annually. Although the Bank just loans money and does not award bids, it does require transparency, that is, public visibility of the bidding process. Each program and project is a discreet investment by the bank, but can represent a large number of contracts or business opportunities. Information about the various projects are advertised in

Development Business
United Nations
G.C.P.O. Box 5850
New York, NY 10163-5850

or

The Monthly Operational Summary
The Johns Hopkins University Press
Journals Division
701 W. 40th Street
Suite 275
Baltimore, MD 21211

Subscriptions to the *Monthly Operational Summary* are $95 a year.

International Monetary Fund (IMF). Provides short- and medium-term financial aid to countries in external deficit. Tel: (202) 477-2945.

Asian Development Bank (ADB). Provides conventional and concessional loans, technical assistance, and investment promotion to developing Asian countries.

CONSULTANTS SERVICES DIVISION
Asian Development Bank
P.O. Box 789
Manila, Philippines 2800

Inter-American Development Bank (IDB). Contributes to the accelerated development of member countries by providing loans.

OFFICE OF PROFESSIONAL SERVICES FIRMS
Inter-American Development Bank
808-17th Street, NW
Washington, DC 20577

African Development Bank. Helps formulate projects and loan applications to promote investment in public and private capital in Africa.

INFORMATION OFFICE
African Development Bank
B.P. 1387
Abidjan, Ivory Coast

OTHER SOURCES

Service firms should always search the private sector in their area of specialization. The best informed are quite often those companies and organizations competing in similar work areas.

Trade and professional associations

Trade and professional associations are often the most valuable source of not only information but contacts through networking. There seems to be an infinite number of associations—at least one for every endeavor, and many of those have international affiliations. Two resource guides for associations are:

National Trade and Professional Associations of U.S. and Canada
Columbia Books, Inc.
1350 New York Ave., Suite 207
Washington, DC 20005
Tel: (202) 737-3777

Encyclopedia of Associations
Gale Publishing Co.
Book Tower
Detroit, MI 48226
Tel: (301) 961-2242

American Chambers of Commerce Abroad

The primary role of these overseas organizations is to promote business. They can be very helpful, particularly for business leads, advice, and referrals. A list is provided in Appendix E.

The next chapter explains how to use intermediaries such as General Trading Companies (GTCs), Export Trading Companies (ETCs), and Export Management Companies (EMCs).

"We buy and sell everything under the sun, except people and coffins."

Sogo shosha executive

7

Use intermediaries

THE UNITED STATES EXPORTS MORE THAN $250 BILLION WORTH OF GOODS and services annually. Of that, about two-thirds has been handled directly by manufacturers, roughly 15 percent by American General Trading Companies (GTC), and another 10 percent by foreign trading companies. The remainder, about 6 percent, is handled by the more than 4000 major Export Management Companies (EMCs) and the "new" Export Trading Companies (ETCs) that have formed since 1983.

SMALL- AND MEDIUM-SIZED FIRMS

By some estimates, total United States trade could double in less than ten years if 30,000 small- and medium-sized companies with exportable products increased their export volume by as little as 5 percent. One way for them to do this could be through greater use of intermediaries.

American businesspersons are an independent lot and dealing with international intermediaries has, all too often, not been the most cherished business arrangement. Many small- and medium-sized companies endure the slow, step-by-step build-up, wasting time and money, or prefer to not even enter the game at all because they are too stubborn to do business with an intermediary.

One international expert with more than twenty years trade experience recently said, "Often, when I visit a manufacturing company that has told me they are in international trade, I find a part-time high school girl handling the paperwork and filling orders that came by mail. Seldom are they actively marketing their products, yet the owner thinks the company is in the international marketplace. They could use the services of a trading company."

Intermediaries have been the backbone of Japanese international trade success. They have their giant Sogo shoshas which trade more than $350 billion of goods each year. Now the Koreans, Taiwanese, Europeans, as well as countries in South America depend more and more on the expertise of trading companies. Few foreign manufacturers try to market their goods internationally by themselves because they need the economies of scale and marketing expertise that intermediaries provide.

Most American trading companies are reputable businesses. For small- and medium-sized firms, given a high level of trust, they are the best way to get started, and are essential for the United States' growth in international trade. Small- and medium-sized companies not yet involved in international trade could do well to consider using an intermediary.

In Chapter 3 you learned how to make the rational business decision of whether to enter international trade by the direct method (do-it-yourself), form an Export Trading Company (ETC), or go the indirect route by using an intermediary. This chapter explains who the United States' trade intermediaries are, how to find them, and how to use one to your best advantage. The next chapter is about how to form trade associations and trade intermediaries using the Export Trading Company Act of 1982 (ETCA).

WHAT IS AN INTERMEDIARY?

Defining the various intermediaries that operate in international trade in the United States is difficult. The United States Department of Commerce defines them in terms of exports, excluding, as if they didn't exist, those that specialize in importing.

An *intermediary* is a firm that acts to market or broker goods manufactured in one country to companies and governments in another.

In the United States there are several arrangements available to a small- or medium-sized firm that decides to use the indirect method. There are six general categories of intermediaries operating in the United States:

- *General Trading Companies (GTCs)*. These firms, as their name implies, import and export a broad range of goods, cutting across many product lines and marketing to many countries. There are both foreign and American GTCs operating in the United States.

- *Export Trading Companies (ETCs)*. These are new companies (since 1983), formed under the Export Trading Company Act of 1982. They can be bank or non-bank owned and have broad antitrust benefits. They may be creatively organized to stimulate exporting, but they may import goods as well.

- *Import/Export Management Companies (I/EMCs)*. These are America's traditional intermediaries. Most often referred to in literature as EMCs, they are usually smaller firms that specialize by: (a) exporting or importing, (b) product/industry, and (c) market areas.

- *Webb-Pomerene Associations*. These associations have been formed under a 1918 law that limits their activities to export only, and specific antitrust benefit.
- *Multi National Corporations (MNCs)*. Some very large corporations that compete on a global basis take on, as an additional business unit, the exportation of goods for others.
- *Piggybacking*. This is a method of exporting whereby a company with complementary products convinces a larger firm, often an MNC, to act as intermediary.

WHAT CAN THEY DO FOR YOU?

Intermediaries are independent organizations that often act as the exclusive sales department for noncompetitive manufacturers. Although there is some loss of control, these organizations come very close to behaving like your own export department. Even the loss of control can be tempered by asking for frequent performance reviews.

These firms work simultaneously for a number of manufacturers for a commission, salary, or retainer plus a commission. They work through their own overseas network of distributors and market your products overseas along with other allied but noncompetitive product lines. Most intermediaries provide a wide range of services including:

- Strategic Market Planning
- Market research
- Shipping
- Advertising
- Documentation
- Channel distribution selection
- Insurance
- Financing
- Exhibit your products in trade shows

In short, the intermediary essentially domesticates your overseas sales by taking full responsibility for the export end of your business, relieving you of all the headaches of doing it yourself. A good intermediary takes a personal concern in your company, managing the entire scope of the international marketing effort for long-term development and profit.

These firms will solicit orders from foreign clients, correspond on your stationery, and sign off on letters or telexes and invoices in the name of the principal (manufacturer), as your export manager. The manufacturer bears the risk of non-payment, but the intermediary assists the manufacturer with the details of the transaction and gets paid a commission on the export sale.

Most sales initiated by the intermediary need approval of its client company. This way manufacturers retain greater control of the marketing of their product overseas, especially when they maintain their own brand names.

What the manufacturer wants

In the early stage, the manufacturer should search for the right intermediary, that is, one that handles similar product lines. Having narrowed the search to several that can do the job, the final selection should be based on finding the company which has/will:

1. Develop strategic market plans similar to that suggested in Chapter 3.
2. International experience.
3. Product knowledge.
4. Overseas network.
5. Geographic coverage.
6. No conflict of interest.
7. A trustful relationship with the manufacturer, i.e., to be perceived as member of the team.

What the intermediary wants

A manufacturer should not be surprised to learn that many large, successful intermediaries have more to say about who selects who than the manufacturer. What manufacturers and intermediaries want and get are two different things. Everything is negotiable and no one works for nothing. Here is a list of what intermediaries want:

1. A product that has a ready market.
2. A product that has staying power.
3. An advance (call it retainer or earnest money) against time spent doing research and developing a strategic market plan.
4. Sufficient margin to cover handling costs and make a reasonable profit.
5. Freedom to develop a strategic plan and execute the plan, hands-off.
6. Products in the intermediary's area of expertise.
7. A trustful relationship with the manufacturer, i.e., to be perceived as member of the team.
8. Realism in expectations.

9. Free marketing support, i.e. samples, advertising, trade show participation, etc.
10. Kept informed about company progress, policy changes, or production delays.

INTERMEDIARY COMPENSATION

Basically the intermediary offers two things: (1) time, and (2) expertise. The manufacturer should expect to compensate fairly and reasonably for these services.

The way an agent is compensated depends primarily on how "bullish" the intermediary feels about the product. If the intermediary believes the product is unique and very salable, the intermediary will probably work for the manufacturer on a straight percentage of sales basis. On the other hand, if the middleman firm feels there will be a lot of development work required, it will ask for a retainer and you pay the extraordinary expenses of market entry.

In return for their services the intermediary will usually want your best domestic commission. The agent receives a commission that is generally based on invoice cost of the products being represented. This could range from 10 percent for consumer goods to 15 to 20 percent for industrial products. The commission can also vary between 7.5 percent and 20 percent of the wholesale distributor price. In this method the intermediary is like an internal export department. The manufacturer invoices the foreign customer directly and carries out financing required.

Example

Product cost:	$5.00/unit
Retail price	$20.00/unit
Distributor Price:	$10.00/unit @ 50% Discount
Intermediary @ 20% off:	$2.00 (comm. + handling costs)
Manufacturers Profit:	$3.00

Overseas distributors want your best United States discount plus as much as an extra 15 percent discount, especially if they are handling high technology electronics.

In addition to commissions some intermediaries ask their clients to share 50–50 on trade show costs, others require a $1/3$, $1/3$, $1/3$ cost split between the middleman, the client, and overseas agents. It is not unusual for intermediaries to ask contributions for advertising and promotion. This is usually at least equal to the proportional amount the manufacturer spends in the United States for domestic sales. The agent should match the contribution.

Retainers are required by many intermediaries, particularly when the introduction of a new product must have heavy advertising and promotion to gain market share.

WHY USE AN INTERMEDIARY?

A discussion of the decision process has already been provided in Chapter 3. For a refresher, the primary reasons for using intermediaries are:

1. They conserve financial resources (out-of-pocket cash flow) that would otherwise be consumed during the years your firm took to develop its own international marketing department.
2. Export sales come quicker because intermediaries already have agents, distributors and customers in place.
3. You learn by observing the professionals in order to eventually develop your own international department.
4. Intermediaries save you time by concentrating their effort on your overseas sales thus allowing you to concentrate on your domestic market.

GENERAL TRADING COMPANIES (GTCs)

The term General Trading Company (GTC) is used in two ways in this book:

1. A trading firm that regards itself, or is regarded by others, as a general trading company whatever its definition might be.
2. Those firms who have extensive overseas networks and offer one-stop diversification by product, market area, and function.

In the broad sense, the term applies to a firm that buys goods in one national market to resell at a profit in foreign markets. In this context, trading company has an identical meaning with trading house, although the latter has the historical connotation of the European export merchant while the former does not.

In a specialized sense, the term has been used to describe a handful of Japanese trading companies that have extensive marketing networks all over the world. Of course, many Japanese firms export their own products, but most deal through their Sogo shosha. Just as in the United States, the Japanese have other trading companies (some have estimated there are as many as 5000, similar to our EMCs) of varying sizes. But the dominant ones, the Sogo shosha are large and handle a great range of products and turnover of goods.

Today, the major difference between the average American intermediary and the largest general trading companies in the world is about $50 – 60 billion. The largest United States Export Management Companies (EMCs) have annual sales of about $60 million while the largest Japanese Sogo shosha have sales of about $60 billion. Sogo shosha are truly among the most significant phenomena of contemporary world commerce.

Since the mid-1970s the importance of large general trading companies has grown rapidly. Japan's success has caused the concept to spread around the world. Since about 1975, the Korean Government has encouraged their establishment. By the early 1980s eleven giant enterprises, called Chonghap-mooyeok-sangsa were in place. Most, like Samsung, Hyundai, and Daewoo are closely affiliated with groups of large Korean corporations called Chaebol (similar to Japanese Zaibatsu) and are competing as general international trading companies. Like the Japanese Sogo shoshas, they have become highly prestigious companies and already account for about half of their country's exports.

The Brazilian government helped set up both private and public trading companies in 1976. Their progress has been slower than that of Korea, but by the early 1980s accounted for more than 20 percent of Brazilian exports.

The Chinese word for these economic concentrations is Caifa and they are developing them industry by industry. Although the Sogo shoshas are the largest and best known, multi-product general trading companies also exist in Finland, Canada, Hong Kong, Sweden, Switzerland, Singapore, and Taiwan.

History of Trading Companies. It is probable that there have always been trading companies. The earliest English overseas trade organization, the Merchants Staple, was organized in the 14th century as a way to replenish the royal treasury. The Company of Merchant Adventurers was formed in 1505, the Russia Company in 1553, and Levant Company in 1581—all were traders in search of spice. Home governments not only gave the companies exclusive right to trade, but also protected them with armies and naval forces. The East India Company conquered a subcontinent, ruled over 250 million people, raised and supported the largest government and standing army in the world. They even deployed 43 warships. American history books are full of tales about the Virginia and Plymouth Trading Companies—they discovered the New World.

U.S. GENERAL TRADING COMPANIES (GTCs)

In the United States, the largest general trading companies have traditionally been those that import and export raw materials and commodities, such as grains.

You should expect these firms to trade in their own name, buying and selling or representing your product in various markets worldwide. They generally take title to the goods they export and provide a "one-stop" exporting service in terms of insurance, financing, and shipping.

The largest and most advanced commodity and raw materials dealers are Phillip Brothers division of Philbro, Cargill, and Continental Grain. Here is a partial list of other general trading firms:

CONTITRADE SERVICES/MERBAN
Americas Corporation
277 Park Ave.
New York, NY 10172

CICATRADE U.S., INC.
500 Park Avenue
New York, NY 10022

M. GOLODETZ & CO., INC.
666 Fifth Ave.
New York, NY 10020

WOODWARD & DICKERSON, INC.
937 Haverford Road
Bryn Mawr, PA 19010

PHILLIP BROTHERS, INC.
1221 Avenue of the Americas
New York, NY 10020

UNITED STATES TRADING CO.
1605 New Hampshire Ave., NW
Washington, DC 20009

EXPORT TRADING COMPANIES (ETCs)

Prior to 1982, the United States did not have a law that allowed business arrangements to be formed to avoid antitrust for the joint exportation of products and services or that permitted banks to take an equity position in trading companies. Before that time, Export Management Companies (EMCs), Webb-Pomerene Associations and a few large General Trading Companies (GTC) were the only intermediaries available to assist manufacturers.

Now, you can take your products or services to a new kind of American middleman called Export Trading Companies (ETCs). You can even form your own association of companies using a new law that enhances your global marketing competitiveness and gives you excellent protection from antitrust. The methods to form these business arrangements under this law, the Export Trading Company Act of 1982, are explained in detail in the next chapter.

There is even a special office in the Department of Commerce, the sole purpose of which is to help you learn who the current Export Trading Companies (ETCs) are or help you form one yourself. That address is:

OFFICE OF EXPORT TRADING COMPANY AFFAIRS
International Trade Administration
Room 1223
U.S. Department of Commerce
Washington, DC 20230
Telephone: 202-377-5131

Since its passage, two new types of trading companies have been formed. In the first instance Bank Holding Companies have developed what are now known as Export Trading Companies (ETCs). Most of these fit the generic definition of General Trading Companies (GTCs) in that they handle a wide range of products, buy and sell in their own right, assist in financing and act as a one-stop export-import organization.

In the second instance, associations have formed under the same law to handle a narrower grouping of products. These also are called Export Trading Companies, yet have used the law expressly to minimize their exposure to United States antitrust laws.

Bank trading companies

Most of the newly formed trading companies have remained operational; however, some have fallen by the wayside. This does not mean that the concept does not work. It only means that under the free enterprise system some start-up companies succeed and others, for an unlimited list of reasons, fail. Table 7-1 is a list of the Bank Trading Companies. It is presented here to assist you to make contact. It shows that as of 1989, forty-six Bank Holding Companies had been certified to establish Export Trading Companies, of which thirty were operational.

Table 7-1   Bank Holding Company Affiliated Export Trading Companies (ETCs).

Bank Holding Company	Export Trading Company	Status
Security Pacific Corporation San Francisco, CA	Security Pacific Export Trading Company Los Angeles, CA	Not Active
Citicorp, New York, NY	Citicorp International Trading Company New York, NY	Not Active
First Interstate Bancorp, Los Angeles, CA	First Interstate Trading Company Los Angeles, CA	Operating
Walter E. Heller International Corp. Chicago, IL	Heller Trading Company Chicago, IL	Closed
First Kentucky National Corp. Louisville, KY	First Kentucky National Trading Company Louisville, KY	Inactive
Union Bancorp, Inc. Los Angeles, CA	StanChart ExportServices Los Angeles, CA	Operating
Croker National San Francisco, CA	Croker Pacific Trade Corporation San Francisco, CA	Closed
Ramapo Financial Corp., Wayne, NJ; Ultra Bancorp, Bridgewater, NJ; New Jersey National, Trenton, NJ	Bancorp's Int'l Trading Corp. Somerset, NJ	Operating

——————————————Table 7-1. Continued.——————————————

Bank Holding Company	Export Trading Company	Status
State Street Boston Corp., Boston, MA	State Street Trade Development Corp., Boston, MA	Not Active
International Bancshares Corporation Loredo, TX	IBC Trading Company Loredo, TX	Not Active
United Midwest Bancshares, Inc., Cincinnati, OH	United Midwest International Corp. Cincinnati, OH	Closed
U.S. Bancorp Portland, OR	U.S. World Trade Corporation Portland, OR	Operating
First Chicago Corporation Chicago, IL	Sears World Trade, Inc. Company Chicago, IL	Not Active
Hongkong and Shanghai Banking Corporation Hong Kong	Equator Trading Company Hartford, CT	Operating
Security Pacific/Rainier Bancorporation (Joint Ven) Seattle, WA	Rainier International Trading Company Seattle, WA	Operating
Shawmut Corp. Boston, MA	Shawmut Export Corporation Boston, MA	Operating
BankAmerica Corp. San Francisco, CA	BankAmerica World Trade Corporation San Francisco, CA	Not Active
Chase Manhattan Corp. New York, NY	Chase Trade, Inc. New York, NY	Operating
Bankers Trust New York, NY	Bankers Trust Int'l Trading Corporation New York, NY	Operating
First National State Bancorporation Newark, NJ	First International Trading Company Newark, NJ	Operating

Bank Holding Company	Export Trading Company	Status
Society Corporation Cleveland, OH	Export Partnership for International Trade, Inc. Cleveland, OH	Sold
Fleet Financial Group, Inc. Providence, RI	Fleet Trading Company Providence, RI	Inactive
First National Bancshares, Inc. Houma, LA	First Export Corporation Houma, LA	Operating
Manufacturers Hanover Trust Corporation New York, NY	C.I.T. International Sales Corporation New York, NY	Merged/ dissolved
First Union Corp. Charlotte, NC	First Union Export Trading Company Charlotte, NC	Operating
Alaska Mutual Bancorporation, Anchorage, AK	Mutual International Corporation Anchorage, AK	Operating
FrontierBancorp. Vista, CA San Diego, CA	Interbank Trading Company San Diego, CA	Not Active
Florida Park Banks, Inc. St. Petersburg, FL	Park Services International, Inc. St. Petersburg, FL	Closed
Capital Bancorp Miami, FL	Capital Trade Services, Inc. Miami, FL	Operating
CoreStates Financial Lancaster, PA	CoreStates Export Trading Company Philadelphia, PA	Operating
North Valley Bancorp, Redding, CA	North Valley Trading Co. Redding, CA	Operating
Maryland National Corporation Baltimore, MD	MN Trade Corporation Baltimore, MD	Operating

_____Table 7-1. Continued._____

Bank Holding Company	Export Trading Company	Status
Summit Bancorp Summit, NJ	Bancorp's International Trading Corp. Summit, NJ	Operating
MarineCorporation Milwaukee, WI Rolling Meadows, IL	Marine Financial Services, Inc. Milwaukee, WI	Operating
Ramapo Financial Corp, Wayne NJ; Ultra Bankcorp, Bridgewater, NJ; The Summit Bancorp; New Jersey National, Trenton, NJ (Joint Venture)	Florida Interbank Trade Company, Inc. Jacksonville, FL	Operating
First Wisconsin Corp. Milwaukee, WI Rolling Meadows, IL	InterContinental Trading Co., Inc. Rolling Meadows, IL	Closed
Commerce Union Corp. Nashville, TN	Commerce Trading Corp. Nashville, TN	Operating
Valley National Corp. Phoenix, AZ	Valley International Trading Company Phoenix, AZ	Operating
Manufacturers Hanover Corporation New York, NY	Manufacturers Hanover World Trade Corporation, New York, NY	Operating
Marine Midland Banks, Inc. New York, NY	Marine Midland Trade New York, NY	Operating
United Bancorp of Arizona Phoenix, AZ	United Bank Export Trading Company Phoenix, AZ	Operating
Interfirst Corp. Dallas, TX	Interfirst World Trade Corporation Dallas, TX	Operating
Irving Bank Corp. New York, NY; Bank of New York, (Joint Venture)	Irving International Trade, Inc. New York, NY	Operating

Bank Holding Company	Export Trading Company	Status
Merchants National Corporation Indianapolis, IN	Merchants Export Development Corp. Indianapolis, IN	Operating
Norinchukin Bank Norinchukin, Japan	Zen-Noh Grain Export Corporation Metairie, LA	Operating
Sovran Financial Corp. Norfolk, VA	Commerce Trading Co. Nashville, TN	Operating

Source: Federal Reserve, Washington, DC, May 1989

Certificated trading companies

Just like the Bank Holding Trading Companies, some of the firms originally organized to minimize their risk under United States anti-trust laws no longer operate today. Nevertheless there are many excellent firms you should consider for your export business. To assist you to make contact, Table 7-2 is a list of the Trade Companies and Associations certified under the Act. It reveals that as of May 1989, 99 (non-banking) specialty associations have been certified under the act to compete internationally, of which 83 are operating.

Table 7-2   Certificate of Review Holding Export Trading Companies (ETCs)

Company Name	Location	Status
International Development Institute	Alexandria, VA	Operating
Int'l Market & Procure Services, Inc.	Butler, PA	Not Op
U.S. Farm Raised Fish Trading Co.	Jackson, MS	Not Op
Universal Trading Group, Ltd.	St. Louis, MO	Not Op
Intex International Trading Company	Houston, TX	Operating
International Trailer Sales, Inc.	N. Kansas City, MO	Operating
Trade Development Corp. of Chicago	Los Angeles, CA	Operating
DMT World Trade, Inc.	Waukesha, WI	Operating
Texas First Int'cont'l Trading Co.	Dallas, TX	Not Op
Barlar International, Inc.	Dallas, TX	Operating
United Export Trading Association	Laredo, TX	Operating
U.S. Export & Trading Company	Carlsbad, CA	Operating
SOR, Inc.	Olathe, KS	Operating
Carpenter Body Works, Inc.	Mitchell, IN	Operating
TWP Company, Inc.	Washington, DC	Operating

_____Table 7-2. Continued._____

Company Name	Location	Status
Gate Group, U.S.A., Inc.	Ft. Lauderdale, FL	Operating
Micro Products Company	Chicago, IL	Operating
VEXTRAC, Ltd.	Norfolk, VA	Operating
International Raw Materials, Ltd.	Philadelphia, PA	Not Op
Crosby Trading Company	New Orleans, LA	Not Op
Am-Tech Trading Co., Inc.	Jackson, MS	Not Op
Harold L. Porter Associates Int'l	Ceredo, WV	Operating
Farmers Rice Cooperative	W. Sacramento, CA	Operating
Fleetwood Int'l (Balfour Maclaine Int.)	New York, NY	Operating
Export Trading Company	Schaumburg, IL	Operating
United Export Trading Co., Inc.	Los Angeles, CA	Operating
Opti-copy, Inc.	Lenexa, KS	Operating
Watsand International, Ltd.	Lake Bluff, IL	Operating
Northwest Fruit Exporters	Yakima, WA	Operating
Equinomics, Inc.	New Orleans, LA	Operating
The Aries Group, Ltd.	Arlington, VA	Operating
AEON International Corp.	Marion, IA	Operating
Carolina Western, Inc.	Greenville, SC	Operating
Savannah Sales Corp.	Savannah, GA	Operating
Alco World Trade, Inc.	Miami, FL	Not Op
Kerex, Inc.	Nashville, TN	Operating
Apparatex Int'l Trade	New York, NY	Operating
Great Agassiz Basin Export Trade	Fargo, ND	Operating
Stone Export Trade	Chicago, IL	Operating
Gerhardt's Export Trade	Chicago, IL	Operating
Med-Tech Int'l	Washington, DC	Operating
N.B. Carson & Co.	Salem, MA	Operating
First Agri. Manufacturer's Export	Birmingham, AL	Operating
Quality Exporters	Grenada, MS	Operating
Int'l Continental Agri-Tech	Florence, MS	Operating
Chlor/Alkali Producers Int'l	Pittsburgh, PA	Operating
Global Operations Co.	San Francisco, CA	Operating
Sealaska Timber Corp.	Ketchikan, AL	Operating
World-Wide Sires, Inc.	Hanford, CA	Operating
Marine Midland Bank, N.A.	Washington, DC	Not Op
Comet Rice, Inc.	Greenville, SC	Operating
Amatex Export Trade Association	Greenville, SC	Not Op
Henny Penny Corp.	Eaton, OH	Not Op
Aloha Marketing Services	Kailua-Kona, HI	Not Op
Wrangell Forest Products	Wrangell, AK	Operating
Georgetown Export Trading	Washington, DC	Not Op
Irrigation Components International	Mobile, AL	Operating

Company Name	Location	Status
Basler Electric Company	Highland, IL	Operating
Greys Harbor Export Importing Co.	Aberdeen, WA	Operating
California Dried Fruit Export Trading	Washington, DC	Operating
American Pecan Company	Atlanta, GA	Operating
Pacific Northwest Fish Export Assoc.	Seattle, WA	Operating
U.S. Shippers Association	Wilmington, DE	Operating
National Association of Export Co.'s	New York, NY	Operating
International Shippers Association	Seattle, WA	Operating
Abreu de la Mota & Associates	New York, NY	Not Op
East-West Trade Association, Inc.	Rockville, MD	Operating
Stream Shippers Association	Los Angeles, CA	Operating
American Wood Chip Export Assoc.	Portland, OR	Operating
Safety Equipment Export Trading Co.	Arlington, VA	Operating
Millers' National Federation	Washington, DC	Operating
American Film Marketing Assoc.	Los Angeles, CA	Operating
Eximark Corporation	Wilmington, MA	Not Op
National Machine Tool Builders Assoc.	McLean, VA	Operating
Crann Corporation	Beaverton, OR	Operating
U.S. Business & Industry Develop.	Easton, CT	Operating
Rocky Mountain Export Trading Co.	Missoula, MT	Operating
Cal. Cherry Export Assoc./San Joaquin	Sacramento, CA	Operating
The North Dakota Export Trade Co.	Grand Forks, ND	Operating
Calcined Petroleum Coke	New York, NY	Operating
U.S. Hide, Skin & Leather Assoc.	Washington, DC	Operating
Southwestern Fisheries Assn.	Tallahassee, FL	Operating
Aluminum Recycling Export Assoc.	Washington, DC	Operating
Michael R. Mace dba Mutual Tra. Svc.	Billings, MT	Operating
Olde South Traders, Inc.	Tallahassee, FL	Operating
TradeNet International of Wash., DC	Washington, DC	Operating
Global Marketing Assoc.	Wilmington, DE	Operating
Hammer-Davis Inter., Inc.	New York, NY	Operating
U.S.A. Book-Expo, Inc.	Millwood, NY	Operating
Port of Montana Port Auth.	Butte, MT	Operating
Michigan Export Dev. Auth.	State of MI/Lansing	Operating
Abdullah Diversified Marketing	Nashville, TN	Operating
National Tooling and Machine Assoc.	Ft. Washington, MD	Operating
CISA Export Trade Group	Worthington, OH	Operating
American Cast Metals Assoc.	Des Plains, IL	Operating
The Ferrous Scrap Export Assoc.	Washington, DC	Operating
Wood Machinery Manuf. of Amer.	Philadelphia, PA	Operating

Source: Office of ETC Affairs, Department of Commerce, April 1989

EXPORT MANAGEMENT COMPANIES (EMCs)

Export Management Companies are also sometimes known as Import/Export Management Companies (I/EMCs), Combination Export Managers (CEM) or Export Distributors.

The term export management company is used to describe a trade intermediary which is usually small, privately held, sometimes undercapitalized, and product- or area-specific. More important, most EMC's neither take title to the goods they export nor provide a "one-stop" exporting service, although that is not the case among the larger ones.

Export Management Companies (EMC) are currently the predominant means for the smaller-sized firm to enter the international trade arena, and the most common form is the commission agent. There are approximately 4,000 EMCs operating in the United States.

Some are relatively large, with annual sales as high as $50 million, and handling as many as 50 to 100 United States manufacturers. These companies cut across a wide swath of industries and export to most of the world's markets.

Another group is smaller with annual sales ranging from $500,000 to $5 million. These EMCs represent a few carefully selected clients.

Then, because there is no licensing requirement, there are an untold number (thousands) of very small companies (often home based) with fewer than five employees handling goods on their own account and maybe that of one or two smaller manufacturers.

EMC as an agent

Sometimes the EMC works as a commission agent of the manufacturer and uses the manufacturer's name. For this method all correspondence, invoicing and literature use the logo and stationery of the manufacturer being represented.

EMC as a distributor

EMC also can act as an independent distributor, buying and selling the products, but marketing in the name of their principal. When an overseas order is received, it places the order with the manufacturer, pays cash to the manufacturer, resells the goods to foreign buyers, and invoices them directly. Usually the EMC buys at domestic net wholesale prices less a percentage that approximately equals the manufacturer's domestic-sales overhead. The EMC then marks up the price sufficiently for it to cover handling costs and make a satisfactory level of profit. The EMC pays its overseas distributor or representative a commission and carries the cost of credit required by foreign buyers. Most EMCs acting as distributors work closely with their manufacturers with regard to pricing and customer relations, especially if the product is technical and requires installation and/or after sales service.

EMC as a consultant

Sometimes EMCs act only as consultants to a manufacturer, providing their international marketing expertise to the company's international department. For this they receive a retainer/fee or a combination retainer/commission. Often they are rewarded on a project basis.

Import/Export Management Companies are not without weaknesses. Most of these weaknesses are found in the export firms themselves but they sometimes have problems in their relationship to clients. Most often this relates to lack of trust on the part of the manufacturer (Cronin 1982). Other causes of ineffectiveness on the part of EMCs have been high unit costs, deficient personnel depth, and inability to provide market services beyond selling. As you can tell, picking the right Export Management Company is critical, but it is a two-way street. Trust and team work is the answer.

FINDING AN EMC

EMCs are real hands-on experts, but many do not advertise or band with others as much as they ought. Therefore, finding the right one for your product can sometimes be a chore in itself. The first stop in your search for an EMC would be your local international trade association. Other EMCs belong to one or more of the professional Export Management Company associations listed below:

EXPORT MANAGERS ASSOCIATION OF CALIFORNIA (EMAC)
14549 Victory Blvd., Suite 5
Van Nuys, CA 91411
(818) 782-3350

NATIONAL FEDERATION OF EXPORT ASSOCIATIONS (NFEA)
1511 K Street NW, Suite 825
Washington, DC 20005
(202) 347-0966

AMERICAN ASSOCIATION OF EXPORTERS AND IMPORTERS
11 West 42nd Street
New York, NY 10036
(212) 944-2230
(FAX) 212-382-2606

Other sources of information might be trade publications, or your local United States Department of Commerce representative. Don't hesitate to make direct contact with the Office of ETC Affairs at the Department of Commerce in Washington, DC, Telephone: (202) 377-5131. A publication that lists many EMCs by geographic and product sector is called *Partners in Export Trade: The*

Directory for Export Trade Contacts. It can be ordered from your nearest government bookstore or from the Superintendent of Documents, United States Government Printing Office, Washington, DC 20402-9325, S/N 003-009-00512-4, $11.00.

Once you have identified several EMCs which have experience with your product or at least products that are complementary, gain an appointment or write to explain your situation. EMCs are always looking for new lines, but don't be surprised if they select you instead of you selecting them. They don't waste time on something that doesn't show profit potential or a firm that won't give them adequate backup support.

Other EMC arrangements

Besides the dominance of the Export Management Companies (EMCs), and a smaller number of General Trading Companies (GTCs) in the United States there are several other options open to the manufacturer wishing to expand into overseas markets. Each option represents a link in the market channel and each has inherent advantages and limitations.

Export commission agents

A number of United States international intermediaries operate as representatives of overseas buyers. These companies are usually only interested in specific lines of goods. These "Commission Houses" as they are also called will not buy your merchandise, but are capable of matching buyer and seller. For this service, the agency receives a fee from their foreign clients.

Country controlled export agents

These are foreign government agencies of quasi-governmental agencies that locate and purchase goods.

Export brokers

Like the export commission agent, the broker will not buy your goods, but does smooth the groundwork because of their knowledge of markets and contacts. They will save you money and time by locating and putting you in direct contact with interested buyers, but for that your broker will receive a commission on sales. Some brokers have a wide network of contacts both commercially and geographically, while others focus on narrow industrial and geographic segments of the world.

Export consultants

By their nature, consultants bring expertise you need only on an occasional basis. The firm that is inexperienced in international trade would do well to employ a consultant in the initial stages of entry. Once you have established your own international organization the consultant has lost value. The consultant's importance derives from experience in every facet of a project particularly market analysis, personnel selection, product evaluation, promotional strategies, tax implications, and legal considerations. Consultants work on a fee based retainer or commission, or a combination. Their seasoned experience and judgment more than pay for their fee.

Export merchants

This is the old, established term to describe a trader, usually serving as an agent for the manufacturer, who plays the role of the principal in transactions with foreign customers. In the 1800s, European export merchants took over most of the responsibilities of the manufacturers by providing a wide range of services in trading, and the term *export merchant* was gradually replaced with *trading house*. As a result of this evolution, the trading house now offers multiple services related to trading, such as providing the manufacturer with cash to cover the cost of the goods, giving credit to the customer on its own account, and taking on the financial risks by assuming the title of the transactions.

Think of an export merchant in the same sense you would of any other domestic sale. These companies simply buy your goods at the door and you know little about the eventual marketing or shipping. Most often there are no ties between you and this international entrepreneur; therefore, they may buy once and never be seen again. For you it only means additional sales volume without the problems of overseas documentation, or coordination.

WEBB-POMERENE ASSOCIATIONS

The Export Trade Act of 1918, better known as the Webb-Pomerene Act was passed by the United States Congress in order to allow manufacturers more flexibility to cooperate for international sales. This act amended the Sherman Act and a section of the Clayton Antitrust Act.

Under this legislation, trade associations can be registered with the Federal Trade Commission for the sole purpose of engaging in export trade of ''goods, wares, or merchandise'' so long as they do not restrain trade within the United States.

Simply put, the Webb-Pomerene Act allowed American firms to team up to form cartels and fix prices for foreign goods without violating the United States antitrust laws.

The Webb-Pomerene Act is still on the books and is an exception to antitrust laws that prohibit competitors from acting jointly. The intent of the act is to help smaller firms acquire economies of scale by combining to compete more efficiently against foreign cartels. By working together they can conduct market research of foreign markets, and reduce unit costs of international distribution with higher volume than going it alone. Webb-Pomerene Associations (WPAs) can fix prices and set up quotas for overseas markets.

The limitations of the Webb-Pomerene Act are:

- It is only applicable to the export of goods or merchandise and does not apply to the exporting of services or licensing transactions.
- There is no binding antitrust preclearance.
- Not limited to single damages—could be assessed treble damages for an antitrust violation.
- Must engage solely in exports.
- Does not provide for the payment of attorney's fees by plaintiff, should plaintiff lose the case.

Between 1918 and 1965, a total of 176 associations were registered in the United States, of these only 130 ever functioned. Until about 1930 these associations accounted for approximately 12 percent of total United States exports. By mid-1978 the number of WPA's had declined to 30 and the share of exports had fallen to only 1.5 percent. For the past 10 years these trade associations have remained stalled. As Table 7-3 indicates, there were only 36 active WPA's in 1981.

Joining a Webb-Pomerene Association should not be overlooked because it is still an option for the new-to-export firm, however, the numbers of WPA's that have survived are small and they are predominantly in the agriculture and raw materials. Table 7-3 lists the 35 WPAs that were doing business in the United States as of 1981.

Table 7-3   Webb-Pomerene Associations
(36 Registered as of 1981).

Name	State	Number of Members	Product line
Afram Films, Inc.	NY	7	Films
Amatex Export Trade	SC	23	Textiles
American Barter Trade	WA	4	Agriculture
American Cotton Export	TN	31	Cotton
American Frozen Food			Frozen Food
American Motion Picture	NY	9	Motion Pictures

Name	State	Number of Members	Product line
American Peanut Export	GA		Peanuts
American Poultry Int'l			Poultry
American Wood Chip Ex	OR	6	Wood Chips
ANV Export Corp.			
California Avocado Exp	CA	5	Avocados
California Dried Fruit	CA	27	Dried Fruit
California Rice Export	CA	4	Rice
Citrus Shippers United	CA	29	Citrus Fruit
Interiors International	MA	4	House Products
Kaolin Clay Export	NJ	3	Clay
Motion Picture Export	NY	9	Motion Pictures
North Coast Export Co.	CA	7	Lumber
North Coast Exp. Coop.	CA	7	Lumber
North West Dried Fruit	OR	6	Dried Fruit
Onion Export Associates	NY		Onions
Pacific Agric. Coop	CA	14	Agriculture
Phosphate Chemicals Exp.	NY	4	Phosphate Chem
Phosphate Rock Export	FL	6	Phosphate Rock
Pulp, Paper Paperboard	PA	16	Paper Products
Renoun Shippers, Inc.			
Sulphur Export	NY	2	Sulphur
Talmex Export Corp.	CA	6	Tallow
Texas Produce Export	TX		Produce
Tobacco Export Assoc.	TX		Tobacco
U.S. Ordinance Prod.	DC	4	Ordinances
U.S. Poultry Export			Poultry
West Coast Perishable	CA	13	Perishables
Wood Fibre Exports			Wood Fibre
Wood Fibre Marketing	GA	67	Wood Fibre

Source: Federal Trade Commission, 1981

MULTINATIONAL CORPORATIONS (MNCs)

Several major multinational corporations (MNCs) have their own trading companies which handle large volumes of goods for themselves and others. The eleven largest MNC trading companies, in approximate order of their export amounts are: General Motors, Ford Motors, General Electric, United Technologies, du Pont, IBM, Chrysler, Caterpillar Tractor, Eastman Kodak, Boeing, and McDonnell Douglas.

PIGGYBACKING

Piggybacking might be the cheapest way to export. Larger companies with excess marketing capacity or a desire for a broader product line take on additional products for international distribution. The generic term for such activities is "complementary marketing," but the common name is "piggybacking."

There are several reasons why large firms may be interested in piggybacking your products:

1. These firms look for those products that are noncompetitive and add to the basic distribution strength of the large company itself.
2. Exports to existing markets can be increased at little additional expense.
3. Relationships with foreign clients can be improved by satisfying their requests for additional products.
4. Expansion of foreign markets may be easier with a more complete line.
5. Most piggyback arrangements are undertaken when a large manufacturer wants to fill out its product line or keep its distribution channels for seasonal items functioning throughout the year.

Piggybacking can work well for products that are complementary to the exporting firm's line. Example: Sports carrying bags might be a good piggyback with a company that manufactures racquets.

Companies may work together either on an agent or merchant basis, but by far the greatest volume of piggyback business is handled on an ownership (merchant), purchase-resale arrangement. Most will be satisfied to work with you at your best distributor price. Some exporting manufacturers ask for an extra discount above your best distributor price and extra time to pay. Such requests are not out of line if the exporter is going to strongly promote your product or if they need extra time due to foreign customer's delay in paying. In every case it is recommended that a formal contract or letter of understanding exist between you and the exporter.

Finding a piggybacker

Your search should begin in your own industry by contacting your industry association or trade magazines. The United States Department of Commerce can sometimes be helpful, but don't be surprised to learn that information is limited about who is or who is not piggybacking. Your search may require a company-by-company inquiry before you find the right firm.

Here are two firms that often permit piggybacking:

GENERAL ELECTRIC TRADING COMPANY
570 Lexington Ave.
New York, NY 10022

ICC INTERNATIONAL
720 Fifth Ave.
New York, NY 10019

Piggyback limitations

Piggybacking has its drawbacks and is not for every product. Because margins are so narrow in most basic commodities, it seldom works well in those industries. Another problem is that some international firms look at piggyback products as an add-on to the basic distribution strength of their own company. In other words, the small firm is at the mercy of the major manufacturer. Don't link up in a piggyback arrangement outside your own business area without some excellent reason. If you cannot find a piggybacking manufacturer, it is better to go with an EMC or ETC.

NEGOTIATING AN INTERMEDIARY AGREEMENT

It is recommended that you always enter into a written agreement with an intermediary. The minimum points that should be reflected in the document are:

☞ The products covered.

☞ The initial duration of the agreement.

☞ Grounds for termination and period of notice.

☞ How and when the EMC will be paid.

☞ Commissions

☞ Discounts

☞ Support to be provided by manufacturer, i.e. samples, trade show participation, literature, etc.

☞ Pricing policy and arrangements for future changes.

☞ Terms of sale.

☞ Use of patents, trademarks, etc.

☞ Rights to appoint sub-distributors.

☞ Warranty policy.

☞ Returned goods.

(See Appendix F for a more complete list of the major elements of an Agency/Distributor agreement.)

The next chapter explains how to use the Export Trading Company Act of 1982 as a business tactic to team up to win the international trade game.

A rich country makes for a strong army."
Old Chinese proverb

8

Form teams to win

AMONG THE VARIOUS LAWS PASSED BY CONGRESS IN THE PAST DECADE TO stimulate the United States resurgence in international trade none has been less understood than the Export Trading Company Act of 1982 (ETCA). Many business leaders are not even aware of its existence. Many others believe it only has to do with forming giant intermediaries like the Japanese Sogo shoshas. In fact, the law is very flexible and may be used in many creative and ingenious ways. It is just what the doctor ordered to allow more small- and medium-sized service and manufacturing companies to become global businesses. It is so powerful that firms can join together to form cartels and fix prices to compete beyond the borders of the United States.

THE SEARCH FOR A NEW ARRANGEMENT

Congressional and presidential investigations were launched in the late 1970s to find the causes of the United States trade dilemma. To their dismay it was learned that the Japanese already had sophisticated marketing organizations, the Sogo shoshas, which were regarded as a key element in that country's rapid economic growth after World War II and its great success in international trade.

Japanese manufacturers, along with their banks had already taken equity positions in trading companies. These Japanese trading firms were operating as veteran world traders at a time when, after examining America's trade statistics, the spirit of the legendary Yankee Trader seemed to be in hibernation.

A major revelation for Congress was the news that the Sogo shosha had already penetrated the American marketplace. The Secretary of Commerce, at the time (the late) Malcolm Baldrige pointed out that Mitsui, one of the largest

Sogo shosha, was not only a major United States importer, it had become our sixth largest exporter. In the words of ex-Commerce Secretary Pete Peterson, "they are probably the world's most efficient marketing channel."

A VISION

In 1979, Senator Adlai E. Stevenson III, fathered the idea that adoption of the Sogo shosha concept could help United States exports. The intent of the bill he introduced during the first session of the 96th Congress was not just to copy the Japanese but to offer trading company models as tools to set American exporting in the 1980s and 1990s in motion. These new business entities would be called Export Trading Companies (ETCs) and could be United States versions of the Sogo shosha, but more important, the legislation provided for ingenuity to form entities unique to the American situation.

The senator believed that modern, more efficient exporting arrangements were long overdue for American international trade and that bank supported trading companies could provide such expertise. Thus, the basic reforms of his new legislation were to provide:

- Coverage for the service industry, not previously protected under the Webb-Pomerene Act
- Broader general antitrust exemptions
- Needed skills and financial resources brought together by authorizing the participation of banks

Secretary Baldrige had the same vision as Senator Stevenson. He spoke of these new business arrangements in terms of domesticating foreign sales by making terms and conditions as similar as possible to those of domestic sales. These new Export Trading Companies would be organized as independent, privately-owned, profit-motivated corporations. They would have product expertise and the source of this knowledge would lie with experienced persons from specific industries. The investors would be other trading companies such as Export Management Companies (EMCs) and banks.

Baldrige saw the trading company taking title to goods and acting as a "one-stop" exporter, but this would not preclude it from selling the product on a commission basis or performing more specialized export services. The ETC would meet the specific needs of foreign buyers by supplying products at foreign buyer specifications, extending credit in a form acceptable to overseas buyers, clearing shipments through customs, paying duties, freight, and quote landed and duty-paid prices. These new organizations would be large enough to hire their own sales representatives and/or establish overseas offices in foreign markets. Secretary Baldrige saw the requirement for a substantial commitment of human and financial resources. ETCs would handle a large volume of sales in relation to capital in order to earn adequate return on equity. Capital to sales ratio would be between 1:10 and 1:20. In order to obtain large sales volumes for the long-term, the ETC would represent a diverse range of products. Two and three way trade could be ancillary operations.

TEAMWORK

Everyone knew that winning the game would require teamwork. But in the words of (the late) Professor John Donaghue, of United States International University, American, private and public sector organizations must learn to do better at an all for one, one for all attitude.

> "We have forgotten how to cooperate—how to be team players. In a country where everyone grows up playing team sports like baseball, basketball, or football, it seems incredible that the thing we are now paying consultants huge sums of money to teach in industry, is teamwork."

The professor, as did Baldwin and Stevenson, believed that to win the game of international competition required more cooperation and less competition among American businesses. To increase teamwork, manufacturers and others should consider joining together to take advantage of the Export Trading Company Act of 1982 (ETCA).

As allowed under this revision of antitrust laws, American businesses may increase the number of trade related joint ventures.

Using this Act, public and private sectors may close ranks to take several initiatives to stimulate international trade. Corporate networks may be linked to educational institutions for Research and Development (R&D)—promoting research of streamline American logistic systems and to adapt products and services to world markets.

Capital, either pooled from cooperative industries or gathered from banks, may be required for this new teamwork. Capital may be essential to develop the computerized information systems needed to support not only marketing information, but to bring about efficiencies of physical distribution. Financing may also be required to attract a share of the United States most talented people.

Firms with like products or even distinctly unlike products in combinations may, under the ETCA, share the costs of international trading and extend their reach to global markets. Combinations may be better equipped to get the products of small- to medium-sized firms (lower volume, highly differentiated, knowledge centered) to the market.

Banks, airlines, freight forwarders and other international businesses that already had networks of established offices throughout the world may be well suited to be associated with the trading companies in order to provide global market reach.

This chapter is organized into two sections. The first section reveals the origin, history, and methods of the Japanese model. The second section explains how to organize an ETC to your best advantage. At this point you may choose to skip to the second section; however, to completely understand the ETC concept you are urged to take time to read about the Sogo shosha.

ORIGIN OF THE SOGO SHOSHA

In this section of the chapter you should gather sufficient background to understand the underlying concepts of the largest general trading companies as they operate today, enabling you to take greater advantage of America's laws.

The origin of the Sogo shosha preceded that of the American ETC by more than 100 years, dating back to the early 1870s. They have always had ties to the formation of the great business empires known by the pejorative name of *Zaibatsu*.

In the last years of the eighteenth century the Russians, English, Portuguese, and Spanish all tried to win re-entry into Japan, but it was the Yankee Traders who were the most interested of all in opening the Japanese ports. Whaling vessels and clipper ships on great circle routes across the Pacific passed close to the shores of Japan. The Yankees needed to stop at Japanese ports to replenish food and water, but before that could happen the law that decreed death to any foreigner entering the land had to be changed. Every foreign country was unsuccessful until the Americans decided to force the doors.

Commodore Perry, in his "black ships," steamed into Tokyo Bay in July 1853 and delivered a letter from the President of the United States demanding trade relations. He then withdrew to the Ryuku Islands for the winter. But he returned in February 1854 and, under threatening guns, the Tokugawa signed a treaty which opened two ports and allowed a certain amount of regulated trade. In 1856 the United States negotiated a full commercial treaty. Foreigners were finally permitted residence at five ports with free and unrestricted trade.

Following the opening of the ports, dissident elements particularly the Samurai began to press Tokugawa to honor the emperor and expel the barbarians. Tokugawa lost the confidence of the nation, and the historians and Shinto propagandists all persuaded the Edo regime to step aside. The end of the regime came when a new Shogun, the son of the Tokugawa Lord Mito took his seat in 1867. He voluntarily surrendered actual rule to the Emperor. There was some resistance but the bloodless coup we now know as the "restoration of empirical rule" or the "Meiji restoration" took place in the fall of 1867. The forty-five years of the Meiji was a time to study, borrow and assimilate those elements of western civilization which the Japanese chose to adopt. Naval methods were borrowed from England. They learned about armies from Germany. From France they adopted the law, and ironically, from the United States they took business organizations and Yankee Trader methods.

In 1876, the authorities decided to pension-off the Samurai. They prohibited them from ever again wearing their traditional two swords and sent them off with relatively small lump sums. It meant the end of the Samurai as a class with feudal privileges. Some of the more able rose fast in the government, while others used their lump sum payments to start successful business enterprises. The government also aided many new industries with loans or by various other means. Relatively small fortunes were skyrocketed into great economic empires which branched out in all directions. Since then most have been transformed through mergers, dissolutions and regroupings. Each group expanded its empire like an octopus, forming mazes of interlocking cartels and companies with at least one big firm in each industry. Typically one finds a financial institution and a broad range of manufacturing firms all controlled by a single parent company. Of course, linked to each group is a trading company—thus Sogo shoshas were born.

It shouldn't surprise anyone to learn that the Japanese patterned these concentrations of economic power after American trusts. Mitsui, a wealthy merchant family from the Tokugawa period created one of the largest. Mitsubishi was developed by a Samurai family. Iwasaki was a merchant firm of the Edo period.

THE ZAIBATSU

The great business empires which were coming to be known by the disparaging name Zaibatsu (means plutocracy, government by the rich, or giant trust), found the Diet a convenient bargaining ground. Firms such as Mitsui and Mitsubishi often dominated the leadership of the parties. As we've already learned, the aftermath of the depression of 1929 brought worldwide protective tariffs. This seemed to spell disaster for Japanese industry and trade. The Japanese believed the only answer to rising protectionism was to resume its colonial expansion and win the sources of needed raw materials. The result was World War II and the eventual sweep of the United States Navy through the Pacific until the defeat of Japan was complete in 1945.

Because of their power and pre-war influence, the occupation authorities, in a 1946 edict ordered the giant conglomerates dissolved. However, after the occupation officially ended in 1952, some of the former Zaibatsu regrouped, but in a somewhat different form. This happened as a result of a 1953 revision to Japan's antitrust law which raised the limit of stock investment by a financial institution in a domestic corporation from 5 to 10 percent of capital. Bank-centered conglomerate groups now known as Keiretsu or "affiliations" included banks and trading companies and assumed the old leadership roles played by holding companies before the war.

Sogo shosha growth was spurred by events of the 1970s. The oil crisis marked a major turning point. To offset the high cost of imports the Japanese quickened the development of their global reach. As a result of this extension the

Sogo shoshas now account for about 10 percent of world export trade, and their third country business makes them genuine global trading companies. They search all over the world, using their international offices to meet the needs of their customers.

The Japanese militarists of the 1930s called their dream of domination the Greater East Asian Co-Prosperity Sphere and their actions precipitated a major war. Since World War II the Japanese have achieved their growth to world power without firing a shot.

HOW DOES A SOGO SHOSHA WORK?

How do Japanese trading companies differ from western export-import firms? The giant Sogo shoshas possess the power to create substantial amounts of credit and they have invested in a network of offices abroad, thus providing a supported infrastructure to control global market reach. This allows them to also participate in third country trade.

The role of the Japanese general trading company is complex and has at least eleven major functions:

- *Financial services*: They extend credit, make loans, provide loan guarantees, and develop venture capital.
- *Information services*: They have up-to-date information on clients about the world.
- *Risk reduction services*: They offer foreign exchange management, letters of credit, and insurance.
- *Organization and coordination services*: They take on complex projects and pool capital to share risks.
- *Auxiliary services*: They offer documentation, freight forwarding, and customs information.
- Because of economies of scale their services are at a cost reduction and have greater capital efficiency.
- *Human resources*: They devote immense efforts to hiring and training the best employees.
- *Financial resources*: Sogo shoshas amass phenomenal amounts of capital.
- *Global commercial network*: Sogo shoshas have as many as 150 overseas offices giving them extended global reach.
- *Communications systems*: Sogo shoshas have communications and intelligence networks that rival the United States Defense Department and the CIA.
- *Capital formation*: They develop incentive capital from outside the manufacturing sector, particularly in support of small- and medium-sized firms.

In 1975 the 10 largest Sogo shoshas had total sales of $155 billion, accounting for 56 percent of Japan's exports and imports, 18 percent of domestic wholesale trade and 31 percent of the country's gross national product. For the fiscal year ending March 31, 1977, Mitsubishi and Mitsui had annual sales of more than $30 billion. Marubeni, Itoh and Sumitomo had sales of $20 – 22 billion, and Nissho did a volume of $15 billion. By 1980 the largest Sogo shosha bought and sold $60 billion worth of goods, a sales volume greater than the two-way trade between the United States and Japan. By 1983 sales of the big ten had grown to more than $370 billion.

Sogo shoshas have strong ties to and maintain the trust of manufacturers by forming "President's Clubs" where the CEOs meet to exchange ideas. They are product specialists, have strong foreign sales networks under their control, and have depth and continuity of management. The Sogo shosha is integrative in nature, that is, they are capable of dealing with imports as well as exports.

Sogo shoshas rely on economies of scale and have huge staffs of experts in every sub-field of trading, with broad knowledge of languages and foreign markets. Each industrial group in Japan possesses one of these organizations. Manufacturing firms are not large enough to handle the information systems necessary to organize complex trade transactions. Therefore, the Sogo shoshas vacuum up information about foreign economies and act as the central nervous system for businesses tuned to the outside world. On a typical day each giant Sogo shosha sends over 20,000 messages through the most modern mainframe computers and satellites. They also feed their information to the government.

People

It is in the area of human skills that the Sogo shoshas stand most significantly apart from their United States counterparts. A career in international trade is not high on the priority list of an American student. But in Japan learning international business is as prestigious as learning the law, engineering or medicine. The trading companies invest heavily in finding and competing for the best university graduates each year. New employees are first sent to a special short training program. Then they are placed for on-the-job development in various line and staff positions. Later they attend three months of another training program in which top officials of the firm are intimately involved. During these intense sessions they are taught the goals and objectives of the firm. They learn the company's organizational structure and its values. They learn to place the company first wherever in the world they may be. Only after about six months, when they are well seasoned, are final job assignments made.

Because of their size and the enormous number of transactions the Sogo shosha rather than banks are important sources of capital for small Japanese exporting firms. The Sogo shosha take a small percentage of each transaction rather than a conventional mark-up on the products they sell. They profit by generating large trade flows.

Using Sumitomo Trading Corporation as an example, Fig. 8-1 shows that the typical organization, Zaibatsu or other "bank-centered" groups, the mightiest conglomerates in Japan, have a Sogo shosha as the core trading company. In fact, the Sogo shosha acts as the coordinator-secretariat of joint projects of the conglomerate group to which it belongs.

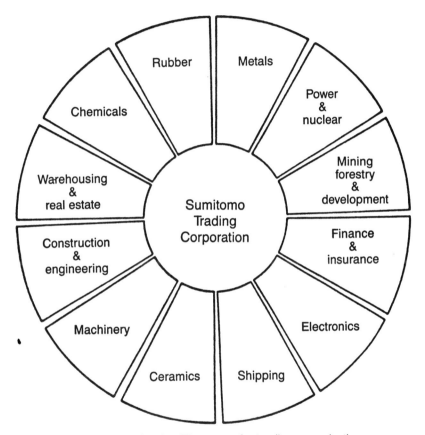

Fig. 8-1   Sogo shosha: The core of a trading organization.

The largest Sogo shoshas possess intimate capital, financial, and business ties with firms of the respective conglomerates. Group firms are the largest shareholders of their respective group Sogo shosha. Group banks, trust banks, and insurance companies are most important in terms of ownership of the shares. In addition, Sogo shoshas also own affiliates which are mostly medium- and small-sized companies. Table 8-1 shows the major shareholders of today's largest Japanese trading companies.

————————————Table 8-1   **Japanese Sogo Shosha.**————————————

Firm name	Shareholders
Mitsubishi	Tokio Ins., Bank of Tokyo, Mitsubishi Bank, Mitsubishi Trust, Meiji M. Life Ins.
Mitsui	Bank of Tokyo, Fuji Bank, Mitsui Bank, Taisho Ins. Nippon Life Ins.
C. Itoh	Dai-Ichi Bank, Sumitomo Bank, Tokio Ins., Bank of Tokyo, Nippon Life Ins.
Marubeni	Sumitomo Bank, Fuji Bank, Taiyo Kobe Bank
Sumitomo	Sumitomo Bank, Bank of Tokyo
Nissho	Iwai Dai-Ichi Bank, Tokyo Ins., Bank of Tokyo, Sanwa Bank, Daiwa Bank.
Toyota	Sumitomo Bank, Asahi Ins., Mitsui Bank, Tokai Bank
Toyo	Menka Mitsui Bank, Taisho Ins., Daiwa Bank, Tokai Bank
Kanematshu-Gosho	Tokio Ins., Bank of Tokyo, Taiyo Bank
Nichimen	Tokio Ins., Bank of Tokyo, Sanwa Bank, Daiwa Bank.

Source: Omar Sawaf, Harvard Business School data for 1977–78

HOW TO USE THE ETCA

This section is the ''how-to'' section of this chapter. In it you will learn how to organize and how to become certified as an Export Trading Company formed under the ETCA (copies of the Act can be obtained from the Office of Export Trading Company Affairs, Room 1223, United States Department of Commerce, Washington, DC 20230).

The preamble

''To encourage exports by facilitating the formation and operation of export trading companies, export trade associations, and the expansion of export trade services generally.''

The four titles (synopsis)

Title I: *General Provisions.* This section provides a description and intent of the Act and provides several useful definitions.

Title II: *Export Bank Services.* This section explains that bank holding companies, bankers banks, and Edge Act Corporations can participate in the financing and development of export trading companies in the United States. It provides for the method of regulation through the Federal Reserve System, the rules

Title III: *Export Trade Certificates of Review*. This section provides a method to obtain voluntary preclearance for antitrust protection. The Act doesn't confer these benefits—rather it provides antitrust protection when domestic competitors participate in joint activities which in turn can lead to the benefits.

Title IV: Foreign Trade Antitrust Improvements. Clarifies the jurisdictional reach of the Sherman Act and the Federal Trade Commission Act to export trade.

NOTE: Only two titles, II and III, of the ETCA are discussed in this chapter. You should review all of these titles to see how they might apply to your export activity.

THE ADVANTAGES

This law affords your firm several advantages, all of which come by way of joint export activities.

- *Barriers*: Firms can end-run non-tariff trade barriers by sharing costs of difficult foreign government labeling, packaging and quality requirements.

- *Bidding*: By teaming-up, firms can respond to foreign orders which might exceed the capacity or capability of any single firm.

- *Capital*: Greater funds in the form of equity can be brought to export activities by bank participation.

- *Economies of Scale*: Joint venture agreements between domestic companies to compete internationally bring increased efficiency.

- *Immunity*: By gaining advanced certification from the Department of Commerce, joint activities, even price setting can gain immunity from federal and state criminal and civil prosecution for export activities.

- *Market Research*: Firms that join together can share the costs of foreign market research, and travel.

- *Market Entry and Development*: Firms with complementary products can achieve cost reductions of advertising, trade shows, missions and other joint activities.

- *Shipping*: Carriers will negotiate lower discounts and longer rate contracts because joint arrangements can provide needed volume and scheduling guarantees.

HOW TO DEVELOP AN ETC

The Export Trading Company Act of 1982 (ETCA) provides a framework for innovators and risk takers to step forward to assist smaller firms to participate in the international trade game. For those associations formed without bank equity, there is no binding definition of an ETC. Instead of each firm supporting the overhead of its own export department, they can join together, even forming cartels to fix prices beyond American borders, thus benefiting from economies that effect the bottom line. A common staff with one international distribution network can make a large profit difference.

For those formed as bank ETCs, an export trading company is defined as a company which does business under the laws of the United States or any state, which is exclusively engaged in activities related to international trade. It is one which is organized and operated principally for purposes of exporting goods or services produced in the United States by unaffiliated persons providing one or more export trade services. This has been interpreted to mean that less than 66.6 percent of the sales of goods or services involve importing, barter, third party trade, and related activities (measured in consecutive two-year periods). In other words, only one-third of revenues must come from exporting.

STRUCTURING AN ETC

The Export Trading Company Act of 1982 (ETCA) supports an unlimited number of formation options. Groups interested in combining would do well to first consider these strategic implications:

- What is the environment for international trade?
- What are the objectives? Profit or economic stimulation?
- What does the investor expect to gain?
- Should products be sourced locally, regionally, or nationally?
- Where will the products be marketed? The world, a continent, or a region?

MODELS

The ETCA is worded in sufficient breadth to allow the formation of many imaginatively modeled trading companies. Some of which are presented here.

Combinations formed by banks

Many of the needed ingredients for a successful trading company are found in banks. Access to capital and handling international financial transactions are among the skills they possess. But bankers are not generally characterized as risk takers; therefore, this model requires careful development of some of the missing elements. Risk taking, the entrepreneurial nature of traders, must be blended into the equation with banking capital, access to products, and the ability to move goods from seller to buyer. Figure 8-2 shows what this organization might look like.

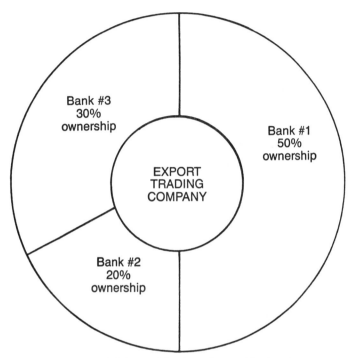

Fig. 8-2   ETC combinations formed by banks.

Combinations of small- and medium-sized manufacturing firms

Figure 8-3 shows a model wherein firms have equal partnership and share a common staff for the export function. A fraternity of C.E.O.s in a city or industry would most likely develop this kind of business relationship. In Japan, "Presidents Clubs" are often developed around the Sogo shosha. A close relationship of the decision makers is essential for any model.

Project-specific combinations of quadrant four service companies

This model holds great promise to take advantage of the ETC legislation. Most often these are not long term business arrangements and therefore are suitable for smaller firms. A joint venture partnership may be formed for the purpose of bidding for international projects. This model is most common for that kind of

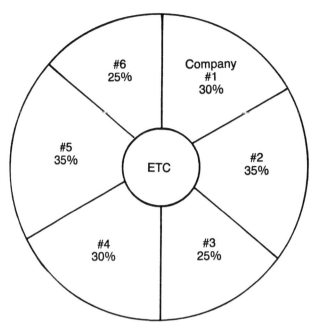

Fig. 8-3   ETCs formed by combinations of small- to medium-sized manufacturing firms.

service company that offers management, engineering or construction. Figure 8-4 is an example.

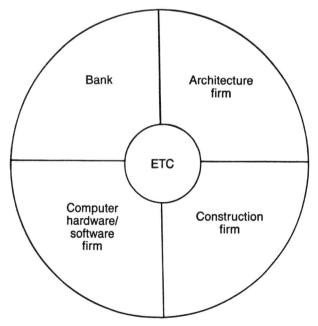

Fig. 8-4   Project-specific combinations of service companies.

Combinations of shipper's associations

A shipper's association is simply a group of shippers that consolidate or distribute freight for the members in order to obtain volume transportation rates or service contracts. Shippers associations can minimize its antitrust exposure thus realizing lower transportation costs previously available only to larger shippers.

Combinations formed by export service firms

The largest Export Management Companies (EMCs) have offices throughout the United States and abroad. They often take title to goods, and already operate essentially as full-scale trading companies. As a result of their expertise they are excellent candidates for combinations with other service firms, including banks or with groups of producers. Figure 8-5 offers a model of such combinations.

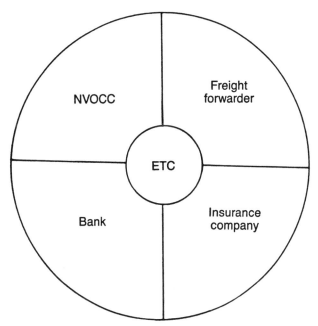

Fig. 8-5   Combinations formed by Export Service Firms.

Combinations for technology licensing

The licensing of patents, trademarks, know-how, and technology are intangible economic outputs and as such are within the definition of export trade and are eligible for certification under Title III of the ETCA. This makes licensing arrangements the best method for innovators to effectively exploit technological advance.

Public sector combinations

One model of an ETC would be organized like a public utility serving a specified region. Because port authorities have a vested interest in promoting the flow of goods through their facilities they are often the organizations that have the most to gain from this approach. States and cities with jurisdiction over a sea or airport are also likely to be interested. Typically the objective of this model is to stimulate economic development by serving the small- and medium-sized manufacturers and agricultural producers in the region. Figure 8-6 shows a way this may be done by combination of a city government, port authority, a community college, and several local banks. A substructure of associations of product specific firms might also take an equity position.

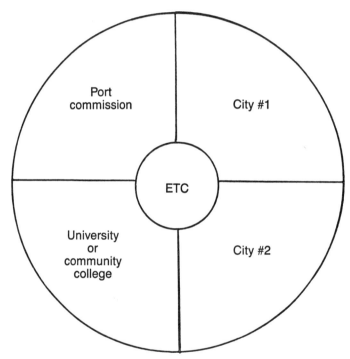

Fig. 8-6   Public Sector Combinations.

Combinations to form "Export" cities

An idea of businessman Leo Engle is to create cities in the United States similar to those he developed in Europe whose function is to be the showcase for exports. Buyers are flown in from all over the world to see in one area, the goods the United States has to offer. Figure 8-7 shows how those linkages can be formed.

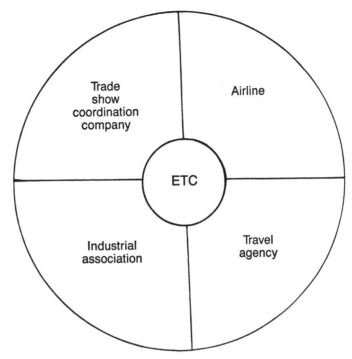

Fig. 8-7   Export City Combinations.

Combinations through trade associations

This model is a by-product of existing industry associations such as food, electronics or chemical manufacturers. Some of these organizations already provide market intelligence and research for their members. Buying and selling of goods overseas is a natural extension. An obvious advantage of this model is that the association has strong potential for attracting new-to-export firms.

ORGANIZING AN ETC

The key variable in developing an ETC is the range of services to be offered. It can be a one-stop full service organization or it can be limited to specific functions. Three general forms of specialization or combinations can be visualized:

1. Perform all export marketing services. In other words, be a "one-stop" operation.
2. Buy and sell on their own account, thus achieving economies of scale or
3. Specialize in foreign government procurement contracts. This company would put together the right mix of goods and services to fill large valued foreign government contracts.

Products

Single product associations such as cotton, grains, or poultry have traditionally been the role of Webb-Pomerene Associations, but the ETCA could equally serve this purpose. Multiple product lines such as a combination of agricultural products, business equipment and electronics require a larger staff and increased training requirements.

Domestic coverage

Export trading companies could be organized to source products or provide trading services on a national, regional or local basis.

Global reach

The international focus and reach of its distribution network is a special strategic consideration. Export attention can be diverse. It can be on a worldwide basis or localized to a region like the Pacific basin or Latin America.

Activities

Selection of activities is a strategic decision and is a fundamental part of the start-up and operation of an ETC. A trading company can export, import, enter into third country transactions, barter or countertrade, or conduct switch trade. The decision is related to those activities that will make the business profitable and are likely to be those that have historically been offered to customers of a given region.

Investors

Like the start-up of any business, the first convincing step for investors is development of a comprehensive, professional business plan. Investors must believe through research that there is a market, that the concept is well thought through, and the very best management will be put in place. Potential investors, whether they be banks or manufacturers want to hedge their risk by being assured that the venture has the best possible chance of success. Large money center banks and other financially strong institutions like regional banks, insurance companies, and foreign trading companies are likely candidates. Short term profits cannot be the objective for this investment. International trade takes time and progress must be measured against long term objectives.

For the public sector, economic stimulation in terms of regional incomes and employment usually has greater consideration than profit.

In other words, the ETC can be everything the General Trading Company (GTC) and the Export Management Company (EMC) can be and more. In fact, the only limitation of the concept is imagination and innovation.

HOW TO BECOME CERTIFIED

A concept of export trade certificates of review was developed under this legislation. The purpose was to clarify the extent which United States' law applies to export trade transactions. To clarify the reach of United States law, Congress adopted language that expressly states that an anticompetitive act is not illegal under the Sherman or Federal Trade Commission (FTC) Acts in this country unless there is: ''Direct, substantial, and reasonably foreseeable effect in the United States.'' Title IV clarifies the jurisdictional reach of the Sherman and Federal Trade Commission Acts.

Bank ownership

As a result of Title II of the ETCA, banking laws were modified to permit bank holding companies, banker's banks, and Edge Act corporations to share in the ownership of Export Trading Companies. The intent was that manufacturers, bankers and the government would team up and work together just as the Japanese have done with their strong support of the Sogo shosha. This is a fundamental change in the general principle of separation of banking and commerce, which had previously been provided under the Glass-Steagal Act of 1934. Clearly the intent was to encourage bank holding companies to take strong interest, and get involved in the development and control of international trade.

A bank holding company, their subsidiary Edge or Agreement corporations, and banker's banks, as eligible investors, must give the Board of Governors of the Federal Reserve System 60 days prior written notice of any investment in an export trading company or any changes in activities. The export trading company in which the bank is subsequently invested must abide by the rule that it derives more than one-third its revenues in each two-year period from export of goods and services produced in the United States.

Certificates of review

Under Title III of the ETCA, any person, including an ETC, can obtain, in advance, from the Department of Commerce, with concurrence of the Justice Department, a certificate that provides virtual immunity from federal and state antitrust actions for the export activities specified in the certificate.

Certification does not prevent actions, but does serve to provide disincentives to government and private litigants from litigating antitrust suits against certified activities. Under this act only single damages are available, and an unsuccessful plaintiff is required to pay the defendant's attorney's fees.

Exporters do not have to form an export trading company to gain antitrust protection under Title III. In fact, no particular organizational arrangement is required. That's not to say that a group of individuals or firms seeking a certificate of review for a joint venture might not wish to set up a separate entity for that purpose. Additionally, there is no requirement that an entity receiving a certificate must be engaged in export, on the other hand, the protection provided by the certificate can cover only that part of the business related to exporting.

The reverse is also true that exporters are not required to obtain a Title III antitrust certificate of review in order to form an Export Trading Company. The certificate program is entirely voluntary and is not a business license.

The ETCA does not replace the Export Trade Act of 1918, better known as Webb-Pomerene Act (WPA). An association of businesses formed to take advantage of the WPA must register with the Federal Trade Commission. This exempts the association from the Sherman Act for the sole purposes of engaging in export trade of ''goods, wares, or merchandise'' so long as that trade does not restrain trade or influence artificial prices in the United States. The Webb Pomerene Act is well suited for dealing in agricultural products and raw materials, but it does not provide for firms that deal in services.

Existing Webb-Pomerene associations may continue to report to the Federal Trade Commission (FTC) to maintain their protection under Title III of the ETCA. Any association of manufacturers formed for the sole purpose of exporting must also register with the FTC. If a trading company or association does countertrade or importing it does not qualify under Webb-Pomerene, but should apply for a certificate of review under the ETCA. Thus potential penalties under section 7 of the Clayton Act can be reduced or eliminated. Only exporters of ''goods, wares, or merchandise'' can be exempt under Webb-Pomerene; therefore, ''service industries'' should apply for a certificate of review under Title III of the ETCA. Table 8-2 provides a comparative listing of the features of the two Acts.

The ETCA makes a substantive change in the Sherman Act and the Federal Trade Commission (FTC) Act. The ETCA codifies what most courts have already recognized, i.e. United States antitrust jurisdiction should not apply to activities in foreign commerce that have no impact on United States competition or consumers. In order for the Sherman Act to apply, anticompetitive conduct involving foreign exports or wholly foreign transactions must have a ''direct, substantial, and reasonably foreseeable effect'' on any import trade or on the export trade of a person engaged in such export trade in the United States. The same language is also applied to unfair methods of competition under the FTCA. In other words, this title guarantees that American courts will not entertain antitrust cases that do not substantially affect United States commerce.

_____Table 8-2   Comparison of the ECTA and the WPA._____

ETCA	*WPA*
The ETCA can cover the export of goods and services, including the licensing of technology.	The WPA covers exports of goods.
Title III of the ECTA is for any person or entity including a single firm.	The WPA is limited to associations.
The ETCA does not limit the domestic or import business of the certificate holder.	The Webb Act requires exporting only.
The ETCA provides binding antitrust pre-clearance.	The WPA acts as only a defense to an antitrust suit that has been brought.
The ETCA limits awards in private actions to single damages, not treble.	The WPA does not limit private actions to single damages.
Title III allows payment of attorneys fees to the prevailing defendant.	WPA does not allow this payment.

In the case of firms other than banks that wish to associate, the advantage of a certificate of review is the removal of ''grey area'' conduct. The application procedure is equally reasonable as for a bank. A certificate of review from the Secretary of Commerce gives virtual immunity from the risk of antitrust under federal and state antitrust laws. These protections extend to the certificate holder's export trade, export trade activities, and methods of operation that are covered by the certificate and conducted while the certificate is in effect.

A listing of the companies already certified under the Act is provided in the appendices.

MAKING THE APPLICATION

The general procedures are not complex for application to Federal Reserve Board, in the case of a bank wishing to invest in an Export Trading Company. Neither is it difficult to obtain a certificate of review, in the case of anyone wishing to gain specific protections from liability under antitrust laws. Here's how it is done.

Federal Reserve Board (FRB) approval

Bank holding companies wishing to invest in an ETC must apply to the Federal Reserve Board's review under Title II of the ETCA. You can call the Federal Reserve Board ETC office for assistance (telephone: 202-452-3786). To meet the requirements of Board Regulation K, the FRB needs the following information (See appendix for a complete checklist for FRB approval):

☞ Name of applicant

☞ A brief description of the proposed investment

☞ Financial information

☞ Country exposure

☞ Any additional information for investment in joint ventures

☞ Compliance with foreign requirements

Applying for certification

Anyone who wishes a certificate of review must file an application to the Office of Export Trading Company Affairs, International Trade Administration, Department of Commerce. Prior to submission you should take advantage of the free preapplication counseling offered by the ETC Affairs Office in Washington, DC (telephone: 202-377-5131). You must satisfy the following general requirements (A copy of the form is provided in Appendix I):

☞ Names and addresses of applicant, members, and their controlling entities

☞ Basic legal documents, organizational information and annual reports for applicant, members, and controlling entities

☞ Description of goods, services, and conduct proposed to be certified (include SIC numbers where available)

☞ Description of market for goods and services proposed to be certified, including principal United States geographic market(s) for sales by applicant and members; dollar value of domestic and foreign sales by applicant, members and their controlling entity (also total value of United States sales by all companies if known)

☞ Statements on intention concerning exchange of confidential business information and intention concerning reentry of exported goods and services into the United States

☞ The specific export trade, export trade activities, and methods of operation for which you are seeking certification

☞ Proposed nonconfidential summary of application for publication in the Federal Register

☞ Draft proposed certificate

By the mid-1970s, Congress had learned, belatedly, the reality of America's international competitive problem. But it was not until the late 1970s that Congress began the search for a new business arrangement that could, trustfully, attract small- and medium-sized firms to international trade. In the Export Trading Company Act, Congress provided a powerful tool to extend global market reach through stronger capitalization and economies of scale.

Small- and medium-sized firms that don't consider taking advantage of this opportunity are missing a chance to become a ''global business'' at minimum capital risk.

The next chapter of the book explains how to leap over tariff and non-tariff barriers using countertrade, licensing, franchising, joint ventures, and Foreign Trade Zones (FTZs).

9

Vault trade barriers

THERE ARE BARRIERS TO INTERNATIONAL TRADE THAT YOU CAN SEE, THAT IS
they are printed on paper in the customs regulations of every country, and there
are those you cannot see.

VISIBLE BARRIERS

What are the visible barriers? Tariffs are one kind, quotas are another (even
though, except for national defense items, they are prohibited under GATT),
and excise taxes another. The most visible, of course, is an embargo which
stops the flow of trade altogether.

INVISIBLE BARRIERS

Barriers you cannot see, the invisible tariffs, are also a reality at the borders of
every country. You just can't find them on the customs books. *Non-tariff barriers*, as they are called, are more complex and the list is very long. Here are some
of the interstate (governmental) controls and structural impediments:

- Controls on foreign currency
- Restrictions on government procurement
- Domestic subsidies
- Restrictive customs procedures
- Technical standards
- Selective export subsidies

- Anti-dumping regulations
- Unnecessary and restrictive health and administrative limitations
- Controls over foreign investment
- Discriminatory foreign exchange rates
- Import Licensing
- Restrictive Customs procedures
- Inefficient and antiquated multi-tiered distribution systems.

A more comprehensive listing of trade barriers is found in the United States Government book titled *Foreign Trade Barriers*. It describes them country-by-country. The book can be ordered from your nearest government bookstore or from the Superintendent of Documents, United States Government Printing Office, Washington, DC 20402-9325, $17.00, S/N 041-001-00326-0.

It is these barriers, visible and invisible, attributed, in Chapter 1, to Richard Whalen that makes international trade a game. Without the barriers, as impossible as that might be, free trade and global business would grow to massive unregulated volumes.

Nations use many reasons for the barriers, some legitimate, others arbitrary. Most often used are:

- Balance of Payment problems
- Economic Development
- Infant industry argument
- Technology transfer
- Industrial policy

BAD NEWS, GOOD NEWS

The bad news is that there are barriers—lots of them. International trade is very regulated. The good news is that you can do business despite much of the regulation.

Gaining access to markets is as much the responsibility of private business as it is government and you as a businessperson have two ways to deal with both visible and non-visible tariffs. In the first instance, assuming the barrier is reasonable, it is your obligation to figure out a way to do business that will work in spite of the trade barrier's existence. This is not a suggestion that you break the law. Quite the contrary, it is by organizing arrangements to accommodate, jump or circumvent the tariff or non-tariff barrier you stay in business and avoid the second solution which involves ramming the barrier by calling in the government. This latter method (explained in Chapter 12) requires your valuable time for paperwork and conferences and more paperwork. Of course in some instances you may wish to take both actions, that is, try a suitable business arrangement as well as call in the government.

This chapter deals with organizational and transactional arrangements that are not always a part of everyday international trade yet are valuable techniques used by businessmen and women to leap over non-tariff, as well as tariff barriers to get on with international business.

At first glance the discussion of Countertrade, Franchising, and United States Foreign Trade Zones in one chapter may seem diverse, but when you are considering how to vault a trade barrier, instead of ramming it, these concepts often become complementary. For instance an offset arrangement such as a licensing deal might require co-investing as well as the use of one of the sub-sets of countertrade called *counterpurchase* or *compensation*. Similarly co-investing could easily require the use of a Free Zone in order to meet minimum content requirements of the European union after 1992. Two forms of ingenious financing alternatives are discussed: "a forfait" and countertrade. In addition, you will learn how to market by direct mail, take advantage of Foreign Trade Zones, offsets (which includes licensing, co-investing, technology transfers); franchising, and marketing subsidiaries.

Production sharing, which also fits in the general category of offsets is developed in the next chapter.

You should think of these specialties as rooks or pawns on an international trade chessboard. Make the right moves and you will succeed in achieving your global profit strategy.

As an example, many firms are worried about the effect that the possible realization of a 1992 European Customs Union might have on their business. Companies are maneuvering to take the right action to have continued access to that market and be positioned for future profits. Executives are also considering what to do about the non-market countries. What if they become viable markets? By what means will you do business with consumers in those nations? While reading this chapter keep in mind these and other cases. First some background on Europe after 1992.

1992 EUROPEAN COMMUNITY (EC): Case study

Western Europe's most recent attempt to re-regulate toward economic unity has an excellent chance to meet its goals by the self imposed deadline of 1992. Three hundred measures have been compiled which, when adopted and passed into law, will unify the European market.

The Single European Act, initiated by Alteriero Spinelli, and adopted in July 1987 contains two features which auger for success of a single market by 1992. The first provides that most directives now need only a majority to become law. Secondly, the concept of mutual recognition means that the council may decide that what is legal in one country is considered legal in all member countries. Once it took ten years to change or write a single law and have it adopted, but now re-regulation is moving ahead at an aggressive pace. Approximately 120 of the 300 EC directives have already been passed and another 150 are under consideration with optimistic on-schedule adoption.

History Note: Originally, six countries—Germany, France, Italy, Belgium, the Netherlands, and Luxembourg—comprised the European Economic Community (EEC) when it was born in 1958 under the aegis of the Treaty of Rome. But, their first attempt to remove quotas and tariffs failed. Later, the Fouchet Plan of 1961 failed to establish a common European foreign policy. That was followed by the Werner Plan of 1970 which sought to establish an Economic and Monetary Union (EMU), but because it threatened national power it failed. In 1973, Great Britain, Ireland, and Denmark left the European Free Trade Association and joined the EEC. Greece joined in 1981, followed by Portugal and Spain in 1986, bringing the group to its current strength of twelve. (NOTE: Turkey has applied to become a member.) The name has changed to the more simple European Community (EC) to reflect goals that are now more than just economic. The group is considering closer collaboration on defense, developing a common system of government, creating an open market, and moving toward a monetary union. Of these various objectives, the one with least threat to national power and the one with the most support is an effort to create an open European market.

THE CHANGES

The intent of the unifying effort is to create a Europe without frontiers, where capital, services, products, and people can move freely. Major elements of the re-regulation effort are the establishment of a common tax law and the removal of internal barriers.

Common tax law

Value-added tax rates now vary among member nations from as little as 2 percent to as high as 33 percent. The Commission hopes to agree on a common tax rate, but as a minimum establish a workable method of setting rates within a few percentage points.

Internal barriers

Currently each member protects its local industries by imposing various handicaps to market entry. The commission would remove or restructure four major areas: financial services; transportation; technical standards, and government procurement.

Financial services. The intent of this re-regulation would be to allow freedom of capital movements, and the establishment of financial firms and services across borders.

Transportation. Deregulation of the transportation industry could be the most radical change. Currently, because of a complicated permit system and long waits at border crossings, the average speed of trucks crossing Europe is less than 15 miles per hour. The elimination of cumbersome paperwork and other border barriers could significantly reduce ground transportation costs in time and money. The airline industry is also targeted for changes related to fee splitting by binational carriers and customs checks.

Technical standards. Government regulations with regards to industrial standards and safety currently vary because some countries are not as advanced as others. By establishing a minimum level and a common proof or certification, it is expected there will be less protection and more equal access to markets.

Government procurement. By broadening the existing EC bidding process, closing loopholes, and improving the method of redress, the commission expects to open more industries to the competitive process.

POSITIONING FOR 1992

Is Europe, Inc. worth worrying about? In terms of population, the EC has 325 million in a space smaller than the United States—20 percent more than the United States and twice that of Japan. Europeans are the world's biggest traders with a 20 percent share of all trade and 50 percent of that is within the Community itself.

For American and other non-EC nation companies, the issue is how to position to fairly compete prior to and after the re-regulation. The post 1992 period could create opportunities, as well as problems for foreign companies and those that prepare for the change will benefit.

Mergers have already increased among companies already operating within the EC. Such things as changes to labeling, pricing, and distribution could require your firm to consider a continuous monitoring process in order to remain competitive. To guarantee entry and fair opportunity, non-EC firms that do not already have a foundation position have the option of franchising, licensing, co-venturing, or establishing a marketing subsidiary.

Using the ECs 1992 re-regulation as a case example, the remainder of this chapter examines the options your firm could use to successfully compete in a changing economic environment.

JOINT VENTURES

Joint ventures, or *co-investments*, is a foreign business arrangement wherein the foreign firm has sufficient equity to have a say in the management of the company to protect its interests. This method of entering foreign markets has swept the world in recent years. The advantages of co-investment are that it is more profitable than royalties from licensing; there is greater control; and very often better marketing results. On the other hand, the joint venture represents a greater commitment than either licensing or franchising and results in higher risks during political turmoil. Control is the vital element in the development of a joint venture and the agreement must be carefully structured.

Joint venture control tips

- ✎ Have the by-laws stipulate that the United States firm will select the management.
- ✎ Provide in the by-laws that the American firm has either a majority of stockholders or a third party, sympathetic to the United States, that provides the deciding vote.
- ✎ Spread the local 49 or 50 percent among many shareholders.

MARKETING SUBSIDIARIES

Marketing subsidiaries are either wholly owned or joint ventures organized to support direct exporting by providing information and a successful tactical entry and sales effort. Instead of exporting through a foreign importer, the establishment of a subsidiary represents a physical presence and a greater commitment. In other words, your home company exports to itself.

When using this technique, you should consider centrally positioning the foreign organization such that it remains in continual communication with the marketing department of the parent company. By this means it can pass on local experience and respond to market feedback with regard to image and protectionist maneuvers.

LICENSING

A licensing agreement offers the exporter the fastest entry into a foreign market without the logistical headaches of production pressures of exporting. Long run profits and control are exchanged for royalties. It at once reduces risk, circumvents import restrictions, and protects the product from patent, trademark, or copyright infringement by providing local monitoring.

Licensing is an arrangement wherein the licensor gives something of value to the licensee in exchange for certain performance and payments. Commercial licensing arrangements comprise one or more of the following:

- Know-how
- Patent rights
- Copyrights
- Trademark rights
- Technical advice including diagrams, feasibility studies, manuals and plans
- Architectural and engineering designs

In return the licensee agrees to do all or some of the following:

- Pay some amount usually a royalty related to sales volume;
- Produce the product; and/or
- Market the product in some specified sales territory.

Licensing is not only the fastest means of getting into a foreign market, it is also a means of establishing a foothold with little capital outlay. It provides valuable advantages for a small- or medium-sized company to gain market entry, most notable is the ability to gain some local knowledge before committing to its own operations. It also offers a shield against political risk in that by dealing through a local firm, expropriation is forestalled or minimized. From the foreign government's point of view licensing is often a preferred arrangement because it brings opportunities for technology transfer.

Licensing Tips

- ✎ Carefully select the licensee. Draw up a list of candidates then eliminate those who are less likely to provide that needed long-term relationship.
- ✎ Get expert assistance in drawing up the agreement.
- ✎ Retain control through a combination of equity in the licensee, and duration of the relationship.
- ✎ Retain know-how of key parts.
- ✎ Put a key person in charge of the arrangement—don't let it become a back-burner process.

Licensing by any company—particularly small- and medium-sized firms should be considered as a method of getting quickly into the market, but the structure of the license is critical and should be handled with the assistance of a consultant or an attorney. See Appendix H for a sample license agreement.

The principal elements of a modern comprehensive contractual agreement are:

☞ *Product coverage*. Often the products are listed in an annex to the main document. Define the rights and products broadly enough to take in all peripheral processes and apparatus on which you intend to receive royalties.

☞ *Rights*. Specify and identify by number, date of issue, and term, each patent, trademark, know-how, and copyright.

☞ *Territorial coverage*. Territorial scope may differ from distribution rights so be specific in the definition.

☞ *Term of contract*. Fix the tenure or period of the license.

☞ *Extension and renewal clauses*. Rights may be exclusive or nonexclusive and you should retain the right to extend or renew depending on the licensee's performance.

☞ *Protection of rights*. Care should be taken to retain, where appropriate, the action to proceed against infringement. In general, licensees should not be left to restrain such infringements for its own benefit.

FRANCHISING

More and more American firms are establishing franchises internationally. Fast-foods immediately come to mind because the big names have stores in London, Rome, Tokyo, and Paris, but there are many other examples such as rent-a-car, real estate, and druggists. The primary reason for using this method to enter distant markets is that foreign laws are usually not overly restrictive. In fact, franchising is encouraged by most countries because it tends to foster local ownership and increased employment.

The *franchise* is a system of vertical distribution. More important than that, it is a method of doing business that combines big business know-how with the dynamism of entrepreneurship. Franchising's strength comes from sharing goals and objectives.

Franchises produce new business opportunities, new jobs, and new entrepreneurs because they allow people with limited capital and experience to succeed in their own enterprise. In the United States, statistics show that about 95 percent of all franchises are still in business after five years compared to less than 20 percent of independently owned businesses.

John Naisbitt, in *The Future of Franchising* forecasts that by the year 2010, half of all retail sales will be by franchise. It isn't hard to figure out why so many firms, even many of America's corporate giants, have chosen franchising as a means to grow fast or lose a market. The franchiser doesn't have to spend money to open franchises, and it's immediately profitable because someone pays you to start one.

As the franchisor you will be expected to provide know-how, training, trademarks, tradenames, techniques, management expertise and market research assistance. But, the key to your overseas franchise success will be a strong relationship developed by a careful balance of good support programs and hands-off operation. Experience has shown that motivated franchisees most often manage their businesses better than your own employees.

But, there are hazards on both sides. Here are some of the things each side wants to ensure a successful partnership.

What the Franchisor wants:

- An operator who has local knowledge of the market
- Someone who has adequate business experience
- Someone who has sufficient funds to risk the capitalization costs and franchise fees and make it through the bad times
- A dedicated manager with a ''stake in the enterprise''
- A team player

What the Franchisee wants:

- An exclusive territory
- To be able to transfer the franchise
- To know if the franchisor will take the franchise back
- To know the background of the franchisor, is he a veteran or a beginner?
- To know who will pay for the training
- To know what kind of promotion the franchisor provides
- Financing

The elements of a franchise

Of course the laws of the country in which you franchise will govern, but fundamentally there are two elements to the process: (a) The Disclosure Statement, sometimes referred to as the Offering Circular or Sale Prospectus; and (b) The Franchise Agreement.

Disclosure statement. Prior to any sale, the franchisor should disclose the following information to a prospective operator:

☞ Franchisors identifying information

☞ Business experience of franchisor, the officers and the directors

☞ Any litigation history

- ☞ Any bankruptcy history
- ☞ Description of the franchise
- ☞ Initial funds required of the operator
- ☞ Recurring funds
- ☞ Obligations of the purchase
- ☞ Affiliated persons franchisor requires or advises to be used by the franchisee
- ☞ Financing arrangements
- ☞ Restrictions of sales
- ☞ Termination, cancellation, and renewal
- ☞ Site selection
- ☞ Training
- ☞ Financial information about the franchisor

Franchise agreement. This is fundamental to the relationship and should include:

- ☞ Franchise fee/royalties
- ☞ Location
- ☞ Trademarks/service marks/logo
- ☞ Advertising
- ☞ Training/business support
- ☞ Protection of trade secrets
- ☞ Maintenance and repairs
- ☞ Accounting and records
- ☞ The business system
- ☞ Allowable modifications to the business system
- ☞ Quality control and performance
- ☞ Insurance required
- ☞ Length of franchise
- ☞ Rights and duties of parties upon termination
- ☞ Business start-up
- ☞ Hours of operation
- ☞ Transferability of interest
- ☞ Franchisor's right of first refusal
- ☞ Disability or death of franchisee
- ☞ Taxes/permits/applicable laws

☑ Default, opportunity to cure

☑ Disclaimers

☑ Termination and renewal

Some say that franchising is the business phenomena of the 20th century and because of the success of such giants as McDonald's, Kentucky Fried Chicken, and Dunkin' Donuts franchising will become the expansion method of the 21st century. In any case, the process can be complicated and you should get sound advice.

DIRECT MAIL

Direct Mail is a medium of advertising and communicating through the mail. Marketing through the mail is fundamentally the same whether it be domestic or international. The process involves identifying the potential consumer universe within the target country and soliciting a response based on presentation of the written word through the postal system. This method has two techniques:

One-step: This method is designed to generate an immediate sale. A response from a qualified (interested) consumer is developed from either an advertising appeal which includes a purchase coupon, or a message sent through the postal system to a highly qualified segment of the population which also includes an order form.

Two-step: With this method an initial message either an advertisement or a message is used to generate a response from qualified (interested) consumers within a larger "unqualified" population. A second or subsequent appeal is then used to close the sale.

The key words are "response" and "qualified," because if the message does not generate a response from prospects that have a high degree of interest (qualified), the process has failed.

Almost any product or service can be sold by direct mail, but your results depend on these elements; the mailing list; the offer; and the package.

The mailing list is the most important element because in order to make sales you must send your offer to interested prospects. It is estimated that because of population mobility, most lists of names in the United States will deteriorate 20 to 25 percent in a given year due to bad addresses. Other countries are generally less mobile.

Next, make your offer simple and clear. Seldom do you get a second chance to explain your points when you are communicating by mail. No letter is too long if it tells the whole story and keeps the reader's attention. Make certain you write and re-write your message until anybody can understand what you're selling. In this regard, let a few disinterested people read the material before you mail it.

The package is the presentation of the material to the prospect. There are no hard and fast rules, but generally the package consists of a letter, a circular or catalog, an order form and a return envelope.

- The letter should clearly explain your offer and entice the buyer to move and not procrastinate
- The circular or catalog should be uncluttered and show and tell the products uses and qualities.
- The order form should be easy to fill out and return to you in the return envelope.

The dominant skills required for direct mail are the ability to write persuasive, compelling copy, and have an understanding of statistics. By its very nature, direct marketing is like fishing in a pond. First, the right pond must be selected. That is, the universe of interested, potential customers in the foreign country must be identified. Then the campaign must continually test the message including price, and description of the product until the right bait is offered that produces a sale. It cannot be overemphasized that just like fishing, this marketing tactic requires testing, over and over, until the right formula is found, and this can be measured statistically. The success of direct marketing is directly related to statistical analysis.

The start-up of a direct marketing campaign typically begins with test mailings that are no larger than that required to give a statistically measurable response.

A firm using this technique for the first time should not attempt to ''reinvent the wheel.'' An axiom of this method is: go where the competition has been; and use the techniques they have already pioneered. On the other hand, the fact that competitors are not using this method should not necessarily be a deterrent, but one should be suspicious.

There are a number of reasons why you would not use direct mail. The relative acceptance of direct mail varies among countries, just as does the sophistication of their postal systems. Media availability can also be a problem as can finding a pool of talented direct marketing personnel.

A successful direct mail campaign should:

- Be able to flourish on statistical percentages of as small as $1/2$ to 5 percent of a mail offering.
- Develop a technique to generate a current qualified mailing list.
- Create mailing pieces (message) based on precise information about the target universe.

- Run test mailings to verify the viability of the direct mail approach.
- Refine the mail package.
- Have sufficient resources (funds) to stay with a viable concept until the refinement can be evaluated.
- Expand the scale of the offerings once the right message, price point, product related appeals, and mailing lists are identified.

FINANCING ALTERNATIVES

After World War II, when an almost pure ''sellers market'' became a buyers market, there developed a demand for more ingenious financing mechanisms or face loss of a sale. You see, financial barriers are as real as tariff barriers and your ability to assist a potential buyer overcome this problem can make or break. Two of these methods particularly useful with the non-market as well as the debt ridden countries are ''a forfait'' and ''countertrade.''

FORFAIT FINANCING

A *forfait* is a French term and literally translates to surrendering rights. And that is the case for the classical *forfaiting transaction*, where the buyer gives up rights when purchasing a promissory note at discount from a seller (usually an exporter). This forfeiting of rights is signified by signing on the back of the note the words ''without recourse'' at the time of endorsement.

All of this may seem like complicated ''banker's talk'' to the average businessperson, but the method is growing. This is particularly true when doing business with developing nations who need capital equipment and place pressures on exporters to carry term paper in addition to government supported schemes such as countertrade and offsets (discussed next).

Strong export oriented countries, particularly European have used this method as a matter of course. Financing houses in Switzerland, United Kingdom and most other major banks in Europe handle these transactions as matter-of-factly as they would handle a Letter of Credit (L/C).

Why use forfaiting?

You use forfaiting to sell a balance sheet asset for liquidity. You might not have wanted to accept long term debt from your buyer in the first place, but you wanted to sell your products. Suppose through competitive pressures such as not losing out to another seller, you have been forced to accept a debt instrument from your buyer. Now you need cash for working capital or other internal business reasons. Or, you may just want the debt instrument removed from your balance sheet because of the country risk exposure it represents.

How it works

The manufacturer (exporter) who agrees to discount the promissory notes is quoted a fixed price by the forfaiter (buyer of note) which locks in an interest expense while receiving immediate cash for the transaction. The forfaiter is only involved in the financial part of the transaction and in no sense enters any part of the commercial agreement reached between buyer and seller of the merchandise. Thus, the integrity of all parties is of paramount importance.

Forfaiting is expensive, usually several points above prime plus front-end fees; however, keep in mind that the financial institution that buys the promissory note assumes not only the forfaiting risk but also the country risk exposure (in lieu of an insurance premium the exporter would otherwise pay separately).

COUNTERTRADE

Another creative alternative to sticky sales projects—which might not otherwise happen due to currency barriers—is countertrade. Out of necessity, global businesses from all nations are engaging in this practice. It is especially growing among capital equipment manufacturers, but has application for many interesting projects. For instance, Pierre Cardin agreed to serve as a consultant to China in exchange for silks and cashmeres. Coca Cola often uses countertrade. For instance, Coca Cola traded its syrup for: (a) cheese from a factory it built in the Soviet Union, (b) for oranges it planted in an orchard in Egypt, and (c) for tomato paste from a plant installed in Turkey.

Countertrade is an umbrella term for a variety of unconventional reciprocal trading arrangements, the basic forms of which are: counterpurchase, compensation, barter, buy-back, or swap. *Offset* and *Switch trade* are terms used to describe unique types of countertrade often encompassing one or more of the above forms.

In general, these processes involve the direct exchange of goods—technology or know how—for other goods, without use of money as the medium of exchange and often without involvement of a third party. They differ from each other with respect to the length of time to complete the transaction, the type of goods involved, and the financial arrangements involved.

Countertrade is still relatively new for many United States companies; as a result they often aren't familiar or comfortable with it. Nevertheless, the practice is growing and so is the expertise of American business people. In 1972 there were no more than 12 countries involved in countertrade. By 1985, more than 80 countries used the process. According to a recent report by the International Trade Commission, between two and three percent of all world trade is countertrade and in 1984, 5.6 percent or $7.1 billion of United States sales contracts involved the process.

U.S. government position

At the outset of any discussion of countertrade, you should understand why the United States government does not fully support this method of doing business. Countertrade and barter are viewed as inconsistent with an open, free trading system and not in the best long-term interest of the contracting parties. The point is, many foreign governments mandate countertrade, offsets, and other performance requirements and this is contrary to multilateral trade and payments principles, which all free-market countries support. On the other hand, the United States government is neutral about countertrade arrangements negotiated between private firms without government influence. In fact, under the heading of Support Services at the end of this section, you will learn how the United States government provides advisory services for export packages that might include countertrade requirements.

Reasons for countertrade

There are several reasons why businesses and countries use countertrade transactions.

1. *Credit Constraints*. Some countries have international debt problems that require them to manage their foreign currency very carefully. Getting dollars out of the country to pay an exporter is often determined by the national priority of the goods being traded. Through countertrade agreements, countries such as Brazil, Mexico and Peru, burdened by huge foreign debts and lacking capital of their own, can acquire the imports they need to keep their industry running and boost domestic growth.
2. *Creative Marketing and Financing*. Developing countries, wishing to minimize outlays of hard currency, use mixes of countertrade and soft currency. They often negotiate the establishment of cash-generating projects which are independent of the original transaction thus drawing new investments into the country.
3. *Dealing with Controlled (non-market) Economies*. Recent attitude changes by the United States and other Western nations toward controlled economies, such as the Soviet Union's, bodes well for an increase in countertrade. Countertrade can be used to overcome bilateral currency-clearing difficulties or transfers of technology.

Who uses countertrade?

Participation in countertrade is dominated by exchanges between developed and developing nations, but it also occurs between one developing nation and another. One such deal occurred in late 1985 when a group of Brazilian businessmen agreed to swap $600 million worth of goods instead of paying for them outright. Strapped for cash, Peru swapped non-ferrous metals such as silver, copper, and zinc, as well as agricultural and non-traditional export products for Brazilian soybeans, sugar, and diverse manufactured goods—tractors, trucks, etc.

Barter deals do occur between the United States and Europe, but not due to lack of currency. More often these trades are arranged as an easy way to unload surplus products. Third World countries also countertrade their surpluses. Nigeria for instance, has traded its oil for everything from chickens to automobiles, and Iran and Iraq have swapped oil for finished steel to rebuild as a result of their ongoing war.

United States aerospace companies have the most experience as they have been trading airplanes for goods for many years. One of the best stories is about McDonnell Douglas. When Yugoslavia sought to purchase $35 million worth of McDonnell Douglas' aircraft, the country had only $26 million available for the proposed purchase. Rather than miss the sale, Douglas suggested that Yugoslavia supply "Mac-Air" with parts for the aircraft equal in value to the missing $9 million. The arrangement succeeded and McDonnell Douglas Aircraft has been refining its countertrade techniques ever since.

Forms of countertrade

Countertrade is a reciprocal trading arrangement. Countertrade transactions include:

- *Counterpurchase* obligates the foreign supplier to purchase from the buyer goods and services unrelated to the goods and services sold, usually with a one-to-five-year period.

- *Reverse countertrade* contracts require the importer (a United States buyer of machine tools from Eastern Europe, for example) to export goods equivalent in value to a specified percentage of the value of the imported goods—an obligation that can be sold to an exporter in a third country.

- *Buyback arrangements* obligate the foreign supplier of plant, machinery, or technology to buy from the importer a portion of the resultant production during a 5-to-25-year period.

- *Clearing agreements* between two countries that agree to purchase specific amounts of each other's products over a long-term specific period of time, using a designated "clearing currency" or barter in the transactions.

- *"Switch" arrangements* that permit the sale of unpaid balance of a clearing account to be sold to a third party, usually at a discount, that may be used for producing goods in the country holding the balance;

- *Swap schemes* through which products from different locations are traded to save transportation costs (e.g., Soviet oil may be "swapped" for oil from a Latin American producer, so the Soviet oil is shipped to a country in South Asia, while the Latin American oil is shipped to Cuba).

- *Barter arrangements* through which two parties directly exchange goods deemed to be of approximately equivalent value without any flow of money taking place.

Counterpurchase

Companies in the industrialized countries seeking to sell their products in most Non-market (Communist) Economies (NME's) and Less Developed Countries (LDC's) often discover that the LDC's or NME's will not agree to purchase contracts, unless the exporting companies agree to buy or market products of the LDC or NME that are valued at less than those products in the original Western purchase contract. If the products offered by NME's or LDC's are unrelated to the products being sold by the company seeking to export (i.e., they do not result from the Western export plant, equipment, technology, or products), the agreement is referred to as a "counterpurchase" arrangement.

Compensation

Sometimes referred to as "buybacks," *compensation agreements* entail the sale of plant, equipment, and/or technology in return for resultant products once the facilities become functional. These types of arrangements, frequently shorter-term and involving the sale of a "turnkey" facility, became popular in the mid-1960s. Most early compensation deals involved the sale of technology and machinery for large-scale petrochemical facilities and mining operations. Compensation has two classifications:

1. *Direct*. This is a counterdelivery related directly to the product being sold. (Also known as *buyback*.)
2. *Indirect*. This includes all counterdelivery of products unrelated to the product being sold. (Also known as *counterpurchases*.)

Barter

Barter is the contractual direct exchange of goods or services (usually a short-term transaction) between principals without the use of money as a medium of exchange and without the involvement of a third party. In this type of arrangement, the two contracting parties decide the value of the products (or services) to be exchanged. When the volume of the exchange and delivery dates are agreed upon, each side fulfills its obligation and the deal is complete.

Switch

Switch trading, typically associated with East-West countertrade occurs after counterdeliveries of products begin. If the recipient of the countertrade products cannot dispose of the goods, the products are turned over to a Western trading house specializing in switch trade. A switch operation frequently involves a series of complicated transactions before a hard currency buyer is found. *Trading house experts*, or *switch traders*, maintain a self-developed network of companies and individuals that offer ready markets for discounted countertrade products. Many of these deals take more than one year to complete and most of the switch trading organizations are located in Western Europe and deal primarily in Eastern European goods. There are advantages and disadvantages in dealing with switch traders. Obviously a company can easily dispose of countertrade obligations to a switch trading house. This releases the companies own staff from the time-consuming tasks of marketing the goods. The disadvantage is that a switch trade is often looked on as an insincere attempt to establish a long-term trade relationship.

Offset

A final type of countertrade, the *offset agreement*, is mainly used for long-term defense-related sales, and other ''big ticket'' items. They are used by a country to help recover the hard currency drain resulting from the purchase. Offset arrangements can generally be classified into one of three categories:

1. *Direct offsets* include any business that relates directly to the product being sold. Generally, the foreign vendor seeks local contractors to joint venture or co-produce certain parts;
2. *Indirect offsets* include all business unrelated to the product being sold; generally the vendor is asked to buy a country's goods or invest in an unrelated business; or
3. A combination of direct and indirect offsets.

What does countertrade cost?

The variables for a countertrade deal are time, knowledge of how to dispose of a product, and volume. Some large firm's have established their own profit or cost centers to specialize in satisfying countertrade obligations, but most smaller companies deal through agents or trading companies. Twenty-five thousand dollars plus expenses up front is not unusual for a countertrade commission. That amount should be deducted later from a success or retainer fee. The trade-off is the cost of consultant commissions against developing your own in-house capability.

Another cost might be as a result of overvaluation of products on the part of producers. Care must be given that a negative cost factor isn't borne by one party or the other due to incorrect valuation. It is not unusual that products offered for countertrade are overvalued by the producer. If the products to be received in return are urgently needed, you might be able to negotiate a lower value. However, many countries rebel at these efforts, because they view it as an insult, lowering the prestige of the country and the producer. To avoid this type of loss, you might have to inflate the price of the primary goods to arrive at an accurate relative value.

Countertrade Risks

Countertrade is fraught with horror stories, so marketing in countries that barter is not a game for amateurs. Statistics show that 50 percent of all world countertrade deals lose money or only break even. You should be aware from the beginning that there have been cases where the result was a warehouse full of goods unsalable in an intended market.

Here is a list that a small- to medium-sized firm, relatively new to export, should know about dealing with countertrade:

- ☞ Know what goods are involved
- ☞ Who moves the goods
- ☞ What fees are involved
- ☞ Search out any hidden costs
- ☞ Know the countertrade liabilities
- ☞ Know the quality
- ☞ Know the market value of the product today
- ☞ Know the market value of the product in the future
- ☞ Know the exporting procedures and get agreement on when the countertrade is complete
- ☞ Expect to pre-sell the product in the United States or a third country
- ☞ Get the negotiations down on paper. Write the specifications, purchase orders, and letters of credit very precisely
- ☞ Countertrade is expensive in terms of time, and transportation, so negotiate the entire deal before moving anything

One solution would be to hire a countertrade specialist. Why? Primarily to understand the culture of the country in which you plan to deal. On the other hand, quality of the compensation product is often as important as cultural differences. A China specialist would analyze the existing industries in the Chinese province where the American product is to be built and match them with known United States markets. That specialist would also know that another factor in dealing with China, is that their bureaucrats are not good at coordinating between trade organizations. They don't always talk to each other. As a result the time factor is sometimes lost or forgotten, causing excessive delays in negotiations and closing deals.

Support Services

Few of even the larger United States manufacturers have developed their own in-house countertrade organizations. Most firms and especially the smaller-sized and product-specific firms need services from third parties such as banks, brokers, traders, some law firms, or specialized end users.

It's essential to know what goods can enter the United States. Many products offered in countertrade require the skills of specialized traders because the goods come from low-tech or low-growth industries. More important, the negotiator must know end user needs. American exporters should also be cautious because some foreign products often don't measure up to world standards.

An American manufacturer should expect the countertrade specialist to handle everything including the inventory and have the funds credited to their account. In other words, it should be hands-off from start to finish. Therefore, countertrade specialists should be present with representatives of the manufacturing company during countertrade negotiations.

A list of consultants can be obtained from the Department of Commerce, and the United States Chamber of Commerce. The Commerce Department provides assistance to United States firms that have countertrade options included in an exporting package, and they disseminate information about foreign practices.

American general trading companies have been in the countertrade business in Europe for several years and are experienced. Some of the new Export Trading Companies also have the know-how. Of course the involvement of these companies is determined by the products involved, their competence with those products, their required profit margins and risk criteria. See Chapter 7 for a partial list of firms that can handle your countertrade accounts.

Major commercial banks in the United States supplement their export related services with countertrade services. Most of this has been an advisory kind of service by matching bank clients; however some, particularly those that have formed trading companies under the Export Trading Company Act of 1982 will actually manage a client's countertrade transaction.

Guidelines for Countertrade:
- Get professional help.
- Let a consultant or a trading company act as principal and primary negotiator from the beginning.
- Get the consultant or trading company involved as far in advance as possible to survey the goods, conduct a feasibility study, and get a buyer.

FREE ZONES

Special zones for free trade, sometimes called *in-bond regions*, did not develop in any significant way until the 19th century. Some of the more notable zones worldwide are the port regions of Hamburg, Hong Kong, Koushieng in Taiwan, and Jurong Port in Singapore. Inland free zones also exist, most notable of which are the in-bond, free zones surrounding the Mexican Maquiladoras. Even the Soviet Union is establishing free zones to promote interchange of business with market economies.

Free zones, under legislation of the sovereign nation where they are located, are considered outside the customs territory of that country. The concept is an ancient one, dating back to Egyptian times. Goods entering the zone pay no tariff or other taxes, under a guarantee (bond) that they will not be entered into the domestic market. Should they enter the domestic market, all duties must be routinely paid. While in these free zones, typically goods can be altered, assembled, manufactured and manipulated. Thus they become areas where barriers to free trade are circumvented.

U.S. FOREIGN TRADE ZONES

Everywhere else in the world they are called free zones except in the United States, where they are called *Foreign Trade Zones* (FTZ). FTZs are, in the United States like elsewhere, restricted areas considered outside the Customs Territory under the supervision of the Customs Service. A list of American Foreign Trade Zones can be found in Appendix G.

Typically an FTZ is a large warehouse, fenced and alarmed for security reasons, which tenants lease in order to bring in merchandise, foreign or domestic, to be stored, exhibited, assembled, manufactured or processed in some way. They are usually located in or near customs ports of entry, usually in industrial parks or in terminal warehouse facilities. The usual customs entry procedures and payment of duties are not required on foreign merchandise in the zone unless it enters the customs territory for domestic consumption. The importer has a choice of paying duties either on the original foreign material or the finished product. Quota restrictions do not normally apply to foreign merchandise in a zone.

From the point of view of the local governments in the United States that build them, the purpose of a Foreign Trade Zone (FTZ) is to stimulate international trade and thus contribute to the economic growth of a region by creating jobs and income. But from the point of view of an import-exporter it's all about profits.

How to establish a Foreign Trade Zone

Under the law (FTZ Act of 1934, as amended (19 U.S.C. 81 a-u)), a Foreign Trade Zone can be approved for each port of entry, and for each city bounding on a water entry. There can be more than one site within a zone, and a zone may be authorized to have sub-zones. In fact, the only limit to the number of sites and sub-zones is imagination and economic viability, i.e., will the zone make a profit, or at least make a contribution to the economy.

The Act of 1934, created a Foreign Trade Zones Board to review and approve applications to establish, operate, and maintain zones. The Board consists of the Secretary of Commerce (Chairman), Secretary of the Army, and the Secretary of Treasury. Applications should conform to the provisions of the Act and be submitted in accordance with 15 CFR Part 400.

The United States Customs Service must approve activation of the zone before any merchandise is admitted under the Foreign Trade Zones Act.

History Note. The success of free zones like the "free port of Hamburg" stimulated American interest, which culminated in the passage of the Foreign Trade Zones Act of 1934 and its amendment in 1950. The early history of American Foreign Trade Zones (FTZ) is not glamorous. Growth was slow and profits modest. Until the early 1970s the number of Foreign Trade Zones authorized and in operation in the United States was less than twenty-five and that number had not changed appreciably since the enabling legislation was passed in 1934. However since 1975 the number of FTZs has grown at an almost exponential rate. At last count the number of authorized general purpose zones was more than 110 with 56 special sub-zones and 50 applications pending.

What are the advantages of using an FTZ?

Actually, perceived advantages are limitless, unfortunately there are many cases of firms who have begun operations in FTZs and lost money. Each operation in the zone must make business and profit sense and must be individually analyzed. Here is a list of the regulatory advantages:

1. Customs procedural requirements are minimal.
2. Merchandise may remain in a zone indefinitely, whether or not it is subject to duty.

3. Customs security requirements provide protection against theft.
4. Customs duty and internal revenue tax, if applicable, are paid when merchandise is transferred from a foreign trade zone to the customs territory for consumption.
5. While in a zone, merchandise is not subject to United States duty or excise tax. Tangible personal property is generally exempt from state and local ad valorem taxes.
6. Goods may be exported from a zone free of duty and tax.
7. The zone user who plans to enter merchandise for consumption in the customs territory may elect to pay either the duty and taxes on the foreign material placed in the zone or on the article transferred from the zone. The rate of duty and tax and the value of the merchandise may change as a result of manipulation or manufacture in the zone. Therefore, the importer may pay the lowest duty possible on the imported merchandise.
8. Merchandise under bond may be transferred to a foreign trade zone from the customs territory for the purpose of satisfying a legal requirement to export or destroy the merchandise. For instance, merchandise may be taken into a zone in order to satisfy any exportation requirement in the Tariff Act of 1930, or an exportation requirement of any other federal law insofar as the agency charged with its enforcement deems it advisable. Exportation or destruction may also fulfill requirements of certain state laws.

The role of the Customs Service

The District Customs Director's office is responsible for controlling the admission of merchandise into the FTZ, the handling and disposition of merchandise within the FTZ, and the removal of merchandise from it. Here are several specific responsibilities:

- The District Director is the local resident member of the FTZ Board
- Customs collects duty & taxes when foreign merchandise is brought into the zone
- Customs is responsible for controlling the admission of merchandise into the zone
- Customs is also responsible for the handling and disposition within the zone
- FTZ operations are supervised, inspected and/or audited by customs officers.

Foreign Trade Options

There are two basic ways that space in a Foreign Trade Zone (FTZ) may be leased and three general categories of zone users. These distinctions create different options for zone use.

The first choice for a tenant is to lease space in a zone on either a short or long-term basis. The second leasing choice is whether to use the public zone portion of the zone warehouse or the private portion of the facilities.

Short term tenants frequently use the zone for temporary storage of goods when the final destination has not been determined. Long-term tenants use it for various cost savings benefits which accrue from manipulations and manufacturing that require value added.

The public portion of a zone is most often used to take advantage of the high security an FTZ provides, to gain a financial advantage, or to store an inventory that has United States import quota restrictions (when the quota opens up, the product is already in the United States and can be moved into the market quickly). The private lease facilities are most often used by those firms that intend to manufacture or manipulate their product.

Categories of FTZ users

The first category user is the importer/exporter/re-exporter. This user admits domestic and foreign merchandise into the zone and exports the same or a modified product.

The second category of user is the non-manufacturing importer. This user is closely related to the category one user, except that in this case the importer is only interested in the space for the cost saving benefits.

Category three user is a manufacturer producing in a Foreign Trade Zone. In this case the user wishes to take advantage of inverted tariff choices (allowing duty to be set on the imported components or on the finished product) for cost savings.

What goods may be placed in an FTZ?

Any domestic goods or goods originating abroad that are not prohibited by law, whether dutiable or not, may be placed in an FTZ. Goods that may not be lawfully "imported" such as obscene and immoral films, pictures advocating treason or insurrection, and goods made by convicts or forced labor may not be entered into an FTZ. Goods that may not "enter the United States Customs territory, such as textiles for which the quota is closed, may be placed in an FTZ.

Of course, the Foreign Trade Zones Board reserves the right to exclude any merchandise it deems detrimental to the public interest, health and safety.

Merchandise that may enter come under certain "status" classifications:

Privileged foreign status. Prior to any manipulation or manufacture which would change its tariff classification, an importer may apply to the district director to have imported merchandise in the zone given privileged foreign status. The merchandise is classified and appraised and duties and taxes are determined as of the date the application is filed. Taxes and duties are payable, however, only when such merchandise or articles manipulated, manufactured or produced from such merchandise are transferred to the customs territory.

Domestic status. This status, which may be approved upon application to the district director, is available for merchandise which is (a) the growth, product, or manufacture of the United States on which all internal revenue taxes, if applicable, have been paid, (b) previously imported merchandise on which all internal revenue taxes have been paid, or (c) merchandise previously admitted free of duty. Domestic merchandise may be returned to the customs territory free of duty and taxes upon compliance with the customs regulations.

Zone restricted status. Merchandise transferred to a zone from the customs territory for storage or for the purpose of satisfying a legal requirement for exportation or destruction is considered exported and cannot be returned to the customs territory for consumption unless the Foreign Trade Zones Board rules specifically that its return is in the public interest. The status of merchandise transferred to a zone under these circumstances is "zone restricted." Zone restricted merchandise may not be manipulated, except to destroy it, or manufactured in a zone. As in the case of privileged status, the zone user must apply for zone restricted status on the appropriate foreign trade zones form.

Nonprivileged foreign status. Nonpriviliged foreign status is a residual category for merchandise that does not have privileged or zone restricted status. Articles composed entirely of or derived entirely from nonprivileged merchandise are classified and appraised in their condition at the time of legal transfer to the customs territory for consumption or for customs bonded warehousing.

Articles of mixed status. Because manipulation and manufacturer generally are permitted in a zone, articles transferred to the customs territory may be composed in part, of, or derived in part from, merchandise that is privileged and nonpriviledged, whether foreign and/or domestic. The articles are appraised according to the status of the merchandise of which they are composed or from which derived, as explained above.

Additionally, foreign merchandise, subject to specified customs controls and conditions, may be temporarily removed from a zone without formal entry for the performance of certain limited operations and therefore returned in the same zone status to the zone from which it is removed. This procedure is designed to remove unnecessary burdens on zone inventory and accounting procedures where, in so doing, there is no danger to the revenue.

What type of business would use an FTZ and what operation would they perform?

All businesses may not benefit from FTZ operations, and those contemplating it must analyze their market potential and economic potential. Some that might benefit are:

- Automotive Parts—repack, remark and distribute
- Clothing—cut and sew imported fabric for import and export
- Food stuffs—label, sample and repack for shipment
- Liquor—affix stamps, destroy broken bottles, defer duty
- Machinery—inspect, repair, clean and paint
- Office equipment—inspect and distribute
- Televisions and other electronics repackaged for shipment
- Sporting goods—sort and repackage for shipment

An FTZ is simply a way for a business to save money, no more and no less

A Foreign or "free" Trade Zone (FTZ) is one of the integral elements of a complete trading system and those who work in the international arena, particularly in finance, and marketing need to: (1) understand what a Foreign Trade Zone is designed to do; (2) become aware of its money saving advantages; and (3) begin planning for operations.

Money saving reasons to use an FTZ

The uses of a Foreign Trade Zone for money-saving reasons is only limited to the creativity of the user and the trade-off of the costs of leasing space in a Foreign Trade Zone versus storing goods in a commercial warehouse. Here are several standard reasons:

1. *Cost of Money.* Drawback is the recovery of duty already paid and is a costly and time-consuming process. The Treasury Department does not expedite the repayment of duties already paid, and if they finally do, they only pay 99 percent of the original amount, keeping 1 percent to cover administrative costs. If the duty had not been paid in the first place that sum of money could have been earning interest. The interest and administrative cost result in a cost of money that for companies with high inventories, could have avoided by using a Foreign Trade Zone.

2. *Cash Flow.* The money paid to the customs service under the tariff schedule is money no longer available for other uses, even if that money

is later recovered under drawback procedures. Using an FTZ to defer duty or taxes improves a cash flow position.

3. *Reclamation*. There are many examples of reclamation within an FTZ which can provide a cost savings, in fact the possibilities are limited only by the imagination of the user and the legality of the operation. Consider these examples: A computer manufacturer imports chips from offshore (Asia or Mexico). Before importing them into the United States the manufacturer conducts the Quality Assurance (QA) check within the FTZ. The firm reclaims the gold and other materials from the failed boards, sends the recovered material back to the offshore plant and imports only the chips that pass QA, thus avoiding duty on the failed units.

4. *Inverted Tariff*. A Foreign Trade Zone is the only method in United States law whereby an importer can choose between paying the duty rate of material parts or the rate of a finished product. The importer would of course make the choice that provided the greatest cost savings.

5. *Lower Insurance Costs*. A Foreign Trade Zone is required to be a secure area. It is fenced and alarmed and often guarded. For that reason and because the value of an inventory is not increased by the value added in the FTZ, the inventory stored within a zone is often charged at lower insurance rates.

6. *Transportation Time Savings*. Goods destined for a Foreign Trade Zone (FTZ) are not delayed on the dock for customs, but rather because they are considered in-bond, are usually given priority for pierside movement. Therefore, those items that have some manipulations, reclamation or need to be broken into smaller shipping amounts can be expelled by using the Foreign Trade Zone.

7. *Reduced Pierside Pilferage and/or Damage*. Because there are no dockside delays, there is less risk of theft, pilferage and damage to the incoming goods.

8. *Fine Avoidance*. Goods imported into the United States with improper or incorrect labels are subject to fines. By checking the labels within a Zone the fines can be avoided.

9. *Advantage over a Bonded Warehouse*. Avoid the cost of a bond—the zone operator buys the bond.

10. *Environmental Protection*. Reclamation activities within an FTZ are centered within an enclosed area, using special machines and can be carefully controlled.

11. *General System of Preferences (GSP)*. Combining the mix of content to gain the duty-free advantage of this multilateral trade agreement.

12. *Customs Item 9802.00.80503 (formerly 807)*. Duty reduction can be obtained through the use of this item of customs law related to offshore assembly. Relates to labor content.
13. *Customs Item 9801.00.10108 (formerly 800)*. This item offers duty-free treatment of United States origin goods improved or advanced in condition or value while abroad. Relates to packaging material content.
14. *State and Local Taxes*. Under federal law, tangible personal property imported into an FTZ, and tangible personal property produced in the United States and held in an FTZ for export, is exempt from state and local ad valorem taxes.
15. *Quota Allocations*. Duty and charges against quota allocations can be avoided if shipments are rejected.
16. *Eliminate* duty on merchandise re-exported or destroyed in the zone.
17. *Defer* duty on foreign goods until they leave the zone.
18. *Indefinite* storage awaiting a more receptive market or more favorable sales conditions.

Generalized System of Preferences (GSP). A concept developed within UNCTAD to encourage the expansion of manufactured and semi-manufactured exports from developing countries by making goods more competitive in developed country markets through tariff preferences. This multilateral trade agreement provides duty-free treatment of certain products of designated developing countries (including Mexico, but excluding Korea, Taiwan, Singapore and Hong Kong effective January 1, 1989). When eligible products originating in a GSP designated country are imported into the United States, they receive duty-free treatment if certain documentary, origin and other requirements are met. The most significant requirement is the 35 percent value criteria—to be eligible for duty-free treatment, the value of materials originating in the GSP country, plus direct costs of processing performed in the GSP country, must equal at least 35 percent of the total United States customs appraised value.

Item 9802.00.80503 (formerly 807.00). A provision of the United States Tariff Schedule which permits an exemption from dutiable value for components of United States origin contained in articles imported into the United States. This ad valorem duty reduction scheme applies only to those components incorporated into the imported article by means of assembly and operations incidental to assembly. This exemption technique is often used for goods produced using offshore production sharing like the Mexican Maquiladora Program. See Chapter 10 for a complete treatment of production sharing.

Item 9801.00.10108 (formerly 800.00). Under this provision of the tariff schedule of the United States, duty-free treatment may be permitted for United States origin goods returned to the United States that have not been improved in value while overseas. Items such as packing materials, tags, cartons, containers, etc., fit this situation.

Case studies that saved millions of dollars

Using a Foreign Trade Zone is not to the advantage of every business, but those that do not take the time to do some simple calculations might find that they are paying significantly higher costs than their competitor.

The case of the leather boot/roller skate. An importer found very high quality boots manufactured in China but the tariff at the time was too high. Cleverly, he shipped the boots into a Foreign Trade Zone, attached wheels to the bottoms and entered the boots as roller skates. Now at practically no duty, this businessperson made a lot of money.

The case of the maritime sub-zone. National Ship Building Company in San Diego, California discovered a quirk in United States import laws that says a vessel is "an intangible" and not subject to tariff. The company applied and received permission to become a sub-zone of the Long Beach Foreign Trade Zone. Foreign parts were brought into the zone duty free, incorporated into the hull of the vessel, then sailed away duty free. More than $1,000,000 was saved due to this clever use of the law.

Case of the computer chip. Computer chips were manufactured offshore in Singapore. Before they were entered into the customs territory of the United States they were brought into a Foreign Trade Zone for Quality Control (QA) inspection. Those found below standards were crushed, ground and sorted. The gold used in the chips was reclaimed, but never entered into the United States. It was shipped back to the plant in Singapore. The remainder of the waste materials were entered as trash, duty free. Only those chips that passed QA were entered for duty purposes. This firm avoided drawback, and thus kept their money working for the company, not Uncle Sam.

CUSTOMS BONDED WAREHOUSE

A bonded warehouse is a building or other secure area within the customs territory of the United States where dutiable foreign merchandise may be placed for a period up to five years without payment of duty. Only cleaning, repacking and sorting may take place. The owner of the bonded warehouse incurs liability and must post a bond with the United States Customs Service and abide by those regulations pertaining to control and declaration of tariffs for goods on departure. The liability is canceled when the goods are removed.

The law

Authority for establishing bonded warehouses is set forth in Title 19, United States Code (U.S.C.), section 1555.

Types of bonded warehouses

United States Customs Regulations authorizes eight different types of bonded warehouses:

1. Storage areas owned or leased by the United States Government to store merchandise undergoing customs inspection, under seizure, or unclaimed goods.
2. Privately owned warehouses used exclusively to store merchandise belonging or consigned to the proprietor.
3. Publicly bonded warehouses used exclusively to store imported goods.
4. Bonded yards or sheds used to store heavy and bulky imported merchandise, such as pens for animals—stables and corrals, and tanks for the storage of imported fluids.
5. Bonded grain storage bins or elevators.
6. Warehouses used for the manufacture in bond, solely for exportation, of imported articles.
7. Warehouses bonded for smelting and refining imported metal-bearing materials.
8. Bonded warehouses created for sorting, cleaning, repacking or otherwise changing the condition of imported merchandise, but not manufacturing.

How to establish a bonded warehouse

Your local Customs District Office has all the information you need to establish a Bonded Warehouse. In general, the following five items must be fulfilled:

☞ Submit an application to the district office giving the location and stating the class of warehouse to be established. Such application should describe the general character of the merchandise, the estimated maximum duties and taxes which could become due at any one time, and whether the warehouse will be used for private storage or treatment or as a public warehouse.

☞ A fee of $80.

☞ A certificate that the building is acceptable for fire insurance purposes.

☞ A blueprint of the building or space to be bonded.

☞ A bond of $5000 or greater on each building depending on the class of the bonded area.

Bonded warehouse or foreign trade zone?

Table 9-1 shows the advantages of a foreign trade zone over a bonded warehouse.

_____Table 9-1 Comparison of FTZ to Bonded Warehouse._____

Function	Bonded Warehouse	Zone
Customs Entry	A bonded warehouse is within U.S. Customs territory; therefore a Customs Entry must be filed to enter goods into the warehouse.	A Zone is not considered within Customs territory. Customs entry is, therefore, not required until removed from a Zone.
Permissible Cargo	Only foreign merchandise may be placed in a bonded warehouse.	All merchandise, whether domestic or foreign, may be placed in a Zone.
Customs Bonds	Each entry must be covered by either a single entry, term bond or general term bond.	No bond is required for merchandise in a Zone.
Payment of duty	Duties are due prior to release from bonded warehouses.	Duties are due only upon entry into U.S. territory.
Manufacture of goods	Manufacturing is prohibited.	Manufacturing is permitted with duty payable at the time the goods leave the Zone for U.S. consumption. Duty is payable on either the imported components or the finished product, whichever carries a lower rate.
Appraisal and Classification	Immediately.	Tariff rate and value may be determined either at the time of admission into a Zone or when goods leave a Zone, at your discretion.
Storage periods	Not to exceed 5 years.	Unlimited
Operations on merchandise destined for domestic consumption	Only cleaning, repackaging and sorting may take place and under Customs supervision.	Sort, destroy, clean, grade, mix with foreign or domestic goods, label, assemble, manufacture, exhibit, sell, repack.
Customs Entry Regulations	Apply fully.	Only applicable to goods actually removed from a Zone for U.S. consumption.

Being aware of all the possibilities is a vital part of competing and winning the trade game. Not every importer/exporter will need countertrade or make use of a foreign trade zone or a customs bonded warehouse, but proper and advanced planning is essential to take advantage of the subtleties of the trade laws. An appreciation of the capabilities of each of the business tools presented in this chapter could lead to the recognition of a winning opportunity.

The next chapter is about production sharing and uses the Mexican Maquiladora and Singapore Programs as excellent examples that demonstrate the many benefits this kind of international business arrangement offers.

10
Benefit from production sharing

COMPETING IN THE GLOBAL AGE OF INTERDEPENDENCE REQUIRES TAKING the output of production and vaulting that product into the international marketplace. But if price isn't competitive and quality isn't world class, nothing happens.

Many small- and medium-sized companies have products that are no longer at the cutting edge of technology. Facing flat domestic sales, they are interested in expanding overseas, but to sustain their competitiveness, cost adjustments are required.

If your product fits this montage, you would do well to analyze your plant processes and consider a different mix of the factors of production, capital, materials, know-how, and labor.

LOWER LABOR COSTS

Often the major cost driver is physical content. Some American firms move toward automation as a substitute for high labor costs, but many more have neither a product that lends itself to robotics nor the capital to invest. This chapter explains how to source lower worldwide labor costs and production sharing opportunities in order to make competitive adjustments.

THEORY AND HISTORY

The theory of production sharing is not new. Adam Smith in his book *The Wealth of Nations* (1776) spoke of the absolute advantage that one country might have over another in international trade due to its natural resources. David Ricardo in

1817, went further to develop a theory that nations might not only have an absolute advantage, but a relative one as well, product by product. The Swedish economists, Eli Heckscher and Bertil Ohlin revised the theory in the 1930s by suggesting that the real comparative advantage was in the mix of "factors endowments" (land, labor, and capital) leading to price differences among products.

Taking this theory into the practical world of business we see that some nations are better off in certain factors of production than others. Some have distinct advantages in the education of their people leading to a higher level of technology. Others have an abundance of labor leading to lower costs of value-added physical content in the production process.

Production sharing or value-added processing is as old as business itself. The Egyptians did it at various locations in Africa, the Romans did it when they went to the Middle East, and the British did it in India. Even the United States, while setting about to rebuild a war torn world after World War II, encouraged production sharing. Facilities quickly sprang up offering lower labor costs.

During the period of its early post-war growth, Japan was best known as one great big offshore assembly factory. Today the Japanese and many other industrialized foreign manufacturers have left their shores and are sharing production in the United States (for know-how) and Mexico (for labor) in order to exploit North American comparative advantages and to be close to the United States market.

AMERICA'S COMPARATIVE ADVANTAGES AND DISADVANTAGES

The ultimate goal of production sharing is to get the right inputs for the right output. The United States has capital; highly skilled (but relatively expensive) labor; high-technology innovation; sophisticated communications networks; and an excellent East-West transportation system linking superb seaports.

On the other hand, the United States has a huge trade deficit and needs to get its products into foreign markets. Many believe the international trade deficit is transitory and will automatically disappear when the high dollar problem is solved. However, the United States had a trade deficit long before the dollar became strong and will remain so after it has weakened unless businesses aggressively improve their world competitive positions. For that to happen, American businesses must find lower labor rates and take advantage of cheaper sources of raw materials. The name of the production sharing game for United States manufacturers is to transfer those processes that contain high physical content offshore. Thus, value is added to the product at less cost using lower labor rates and highly trainable foreign work forces.

Offshore production provides five advantages to the American company:

1. Production/assembly plants can be nearer the export market.

2. Lower costs of production make products more competitive in the domestic marketplace.
3. Products can be offered at more competitive prices for the export market.
4. A firm can add plant capacity without a large capital expenditure.
5. Value can be added to the product at less cost.

"A ROSE BY ANY OTHER NAME..."

Production sharing means manufacturing or assembling in a country or region, not the home base of the parent company, in order to take comparative advantage of production factors, principally to lower cost. Other names commonly used for this process are:

Captive plants	Complementary assembly facilities
Co-production	Export factories
Export platforms	Export processing zones
Global factories	Global production zones
In-bond programs	Maquiladoras
Off-border production	Offshore production
Non-captive plants	Twin-plants
Value-added processing	

THE COMMONALTIES

Most, if not all of the countries that offer production sharing are classified as developing or least-developed nations. Because the advantages for these countries are jobs, technology transfer, economic development, and foreign exchange income, attracting production sharing opportunities has become very competitive. The most obvious benefit to American companies is the surplus of labor that translates into relatively low wage rates. However, there are other constants, such as special tariff treatment under United States Customs laws.

Tariff treatment

Familiarity with the Harmonized Tariff Schedule is important when considering the best tactical advantages of production sharing.

General Systems of Preferences (GSP)

In order to stimulate their economic development, the United Nations General Systems of Preferences (GSP) has designated certain countries, territories and associations as "recipients" of special tariff treatment. Some 84 independent nations are eligible under the United States tariff schedule. Twenty-eight nonindependent and three associations of countries are also eligible. In order to qualify for duty-free entries under this program, it must be established that the sum of the direct cost of processing operations performed in the country, plus the materials produced in the country are more than 35 percent of the appraised value of the product at the time of its entry into the United States. Needless to say, Country of Origin Markings (explained later in this chapter) are required as an element of proof.

Special U.S. tariff programs

In addition to special treatment provided for by the United Nations, the United States has its own programs designed to stimulate trade and economic development with specific countries and groups of countries.

Caribbean Basin Initiative (CBI). Effective January 1, 1984, the Caribbean Basin Economic Recovery Act, provided for twelve years, a one-way free trade area consisting of 27 Caribbean Basin countries. Virtually all products exported from the included countries are eligible.

United States-Israel Free Trade Area. The United States-Israel Free Trade Act, an arrangement similar to the CBI, also provides for special no-duty treatment of most goods entering the United States from Israel.

Canadian Free Trade Agreement. This Act, agreed to in early 1989 between Canada and the United States, provides for the elimination of all tariffs between the countries by 1998, expansion of government procurement opportunities, the liberalization of laws and regulations related to services, and the continuance of a favorable investment climate.

United States Harmonized Tariff Schedule. Previously known as Articles 807, 806.30, and 806.20 these tariff provisions assess duty only on the value added in the foreign country. TSUSA (Harmonized) article 9802.00.80503 (formerly 807) is the provision that allows products assembled abroad, in whole or in part, which are United States made, to enter into the United States commercial system paying duty on only the value added.

Article 9802.00.60008 (formerly 806.30) refers to non-precious metals manufactured or subject to a manufacturing process in the United States.

Article 9802.00.50402 (formerly 806.20) are articles repaired or altered abroad.

Country of origin markings

Every article of foreign origin entering the United States must be legibly marked with the English name of the country of origin unless an exception from marking is provided for in the law. Basically, the law requires that the "ultimate purchaser'' or last person in the United States who receives the article in the form in which it was imported, be informed as to where the article was made.

In the case of production sharing, the parent company of the overseas organization is the ultimate consumer of the imported articles and requests a waiver from the marketing requirements. Waivers are granted when the imported article is substantially transformed into a new and different product in the United States wherein the imported article is not sold or offered for sale in its imported condition either over the counter or as a replacement part.

WHO ARE THE LABOR EXPORTERS?

Some say production sharing is the fastest growing industry in the world today. Mexico, closest to the vast United States domestic market, is the fastest growing of these offshore production sharing areas. As shown in Fig. 10-1, Mexico also has the greatest market share; followed by Singapore, Taiwan, Hong Kong and Malaysia.

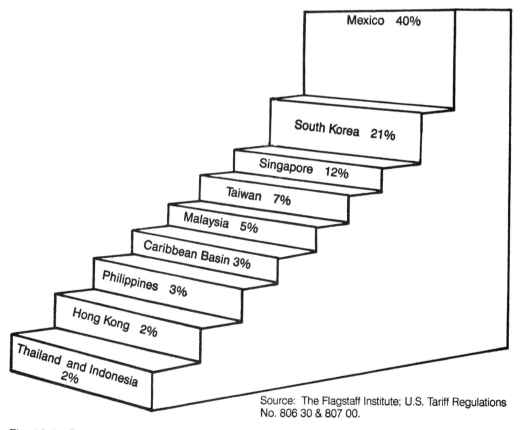

Source: The Flagstaff Institute; U.S. Tariff Regulations No. 806 30 & 807 00.

Fig. 10-1   Percentage of share in production sharing market—Developing countries participation in the Maquiladora industry.

Even the Soviet Union is moving into the production sharing business. Free economic zones have been authorized for areas ranging from Armenia and Estonia to the Port of Nakhodka in the Soviet Far East. The foreign investment incentives for these zones include: Duty-free export and import; a reduction in tax and lease payment discounts; labor policies governed by the local zones; and application for free market prices. Fifty percent of the production and assembly would be ordered by the state at state prices, the remainder at market prices.

THE DECISION

There are five major factors that an executive must consider when making the production sharing decision:

Suitability What is the suitability of my product for production sharing?

Location What are the relative advantages of the various production sharing locations for my product?

Method What method of production sharing? Invest (long term) or shelter (short term)?

Costs What are the comparative fully burdened costs at each location?

Control How much must we control the production process?

Product suitability

Do you make something or process something that has a great deal of labor content? Analyze your business. Are you operating on the edge of profitability because of high labor costs? If you reduced your manufacturing costs would your product be more competitive when exported to world markets?

Figure 10-2 shows that the electric and electronics sector has the greatest share of the value added market. This is principally because this industry has the advantage of a low ratio of weight and volume to value making it highly profitable to transport. Many other products lend themselves to low labor rate assembly: The criteria is labor content. Such things as coupon counting, sewing, and welding are among other possibilities.

Certainly offshore production deserves serious business consideration, but it is not for every firm.

Labor savings. It is not for the company with a product that has less than 25 percent content in the cost of goods sold.

Product maturity. It is an excellent method to achieve high volume assembly, but it is not for the company that does not have a mature product and market for that product. Don't try to make an offshore assembler of your engineering laboratory. An offshore location is not an efficient place to prototype or

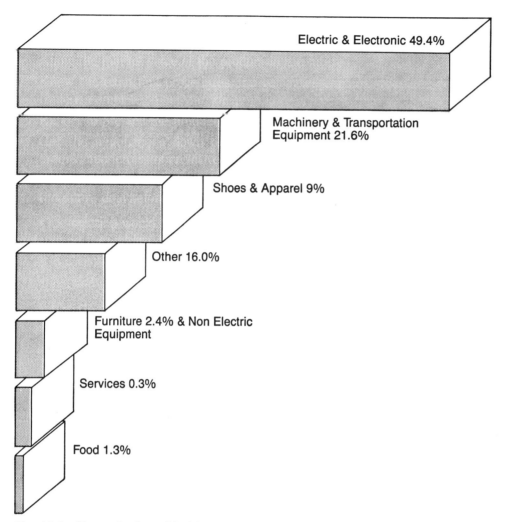

Fig. 10-2   Share of value added, by sector (1984).

do custom manufacturing. Do your Research and Development (R&D) work in the home plant, prototype and get the product into the market before you go offshore. Languages, distances, and cultures get in the way of engineering changes and before you know it you will be bogged down in production and not meeting sales goals. It just doesn't work.

Location

Figure 10-3 shows that compared with other offshore centers, the distances from Mexico to most marketplaces in the United States are shortest. While it usually takes from three to four weeks to transport goods from the Far East to the United States, it takes only three or four days from Mexico. The high cost of

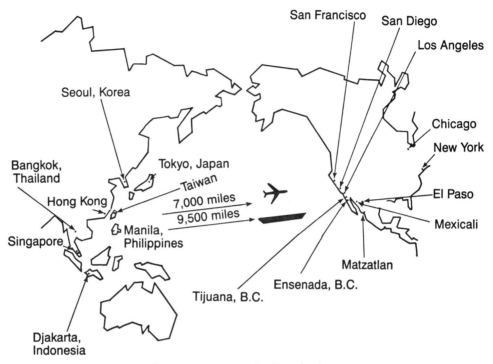

Fig. 10-3   Distance to and from overseas production sharing.

Pacific Ocean transportation stands between the labor intensive offshore production capability of Taiwan, China, India, and Malaysia.

On the other hand, Asian, West African, and Central American locations often provide advantages when the target market is Asia, Europe, or South America.

What about labor productivity? In some countries the high degree of manual dexterity, trainability and motivation to work often exceeds United States averages in unit output. Large populations together with substantial histories of manufacturing and impressive "soft" infrastructures of technical institutes, business schools, and universities provide a fertile technical environment in many less-developed lands.

Method

Nations with an abundance of lower cost labor, market their production sharing programs as "investment" opportunities, but investment is not the only method. Private companies have ingeniously developed processes that provide for the sheltering of risk of foreign companies by contracting through an intermediary to rent space and employees, or subcontract for piece rate assembly/production.

Investment

A foreign firm can invest in most production sharing countries. You can own and operate a plant, or enter into a joint venture to do so. In addition to low labor rates, each competing country offers significant investment incentives and concessions. Some of these include:

- Duty-free import of capital goods, equipment, and raw materials in one or more free zones.
- Tax holidays, i.e., exemptions from tax on profits.
- Rent-free land.
- Waivers of import licensing for imported capital goods and other production materials.
- One hundred percent ownership for export oriented enterprises.
- Free remittance of profits and dividends after payment of taxes.
- Personal tax exemptions.
- Accelerated depreciation.
- Investment tax credits.
- Increased deductions for business entertainment in connection with export sales.
- "Double deduction" of export promotion expenses.
- Special financial assistance, such as grants for research, feasibility studies, and export marketing development.
- Provisions for employee training.

Risk sheltering

Some of the countries that offer production sharing have unstable political systems and a history of nationalizing industries on a whim. Thus, the savings brought about by investment is often outweighed by reasons to shelter the risk.

Two sub-methods have sprung up over the years which allow firms to avoid the risk of overseas investment yet take advantage of lower labor rate opportunities.

Subcontracting. Driven by local investors who offer specialized assembly and manufacturing processes on a piece rate basis; this method has grown at a natural pace. The contractee can have the entire product manufactured or provide the molds, raw materials, and/or semi-assembled parts and the contractor returns the product to the United States having supplied only the labor.

Subleasing. This method, principally used for the Mexican Maquiladora Program, differs from subcontracting by offering space and employee rental computed at an average hourly rate instead of a per unit basis. With this method, the contractee usually provides the materials, machinery, equipment, and the management.

Control

Global factories can be characterized as "captive" or "non-captive." A *captive* facility would be one that is dedicated and controlled by a single parent company for assembly or production. A *non-captive* plant is typically owned by a native of the country where it may be located and operated to serve many foreign companies on a contractual basis.

Think of investment as a movement toward autarky (self sufficiency), with the plant at an overseas location. On the other hand, subcontracting is a movement away from vertical integration. Each has its advantages and disadvantages.

Table 10-1 provides a comparison of the methods in terms of costs and commitment to the offshore production country. Figure 10-4 shows pictorially how they function.

_____Table 10-1   **Comparison Chart of Production Sharing Methods.**_____

Method	Production Cost	Commitment	Investment Cost	Control
Own/Joint	Least	Most	Major	Complete
Sub-Cont.	Most	Least	None	Little
Sub-lease	Less	Less	Minor	Some

Fully burdened costs

Can offshore production add to profitability? Industrial estimates suggest that there is a range of between $15,000 to $22,000 per production line worker per year that can be saved when compared to United States salaries. However, make certain you compare apples to apples rather than apples to oranges. In your analysis don't calculate just the hourly labor rates. Be more interested in "fully burdened direct costs." For example, if the minimum wage of an unskilled worker is $.60 per hour in Mexico, the fully burdened rate for a wholly owned plant would be closer to $1.35 per hour including medical, insurance, taxes, etc. It might be as high as $4.00 or $5.00 per hour for a sub-contract operation. You should understand that in a competitive labor market a business can seldom get away with paying minimums to trained workers. For example, in the United States aerospace industry fully burdened rates can be as much as $25 to $30 per hour.

Table 10-2 offers typical burdened (including medical, insurance, taxes, overhead, etc.) hourly wage rates.

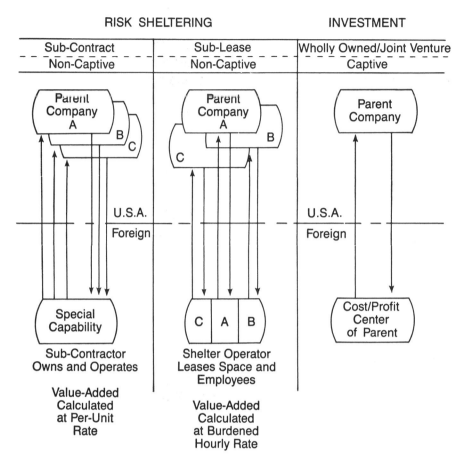

Fig. 10-4   Offshore assembly options.

Table 10-2   Typical Average Fully Burdened Direct Labor Rates/Hour (Unskilled).

United States	Mexico	Korea	Taiwan	Hong Kong	India
$10-13	$1.35	$3.95	$3.45	$2.05	$.80

COUNTRY CASE STUDY ANALYSIS

Obviously each company and product has its own special financial, marketing, production, and personnel considerations. To give you a framework to make a production sharing decision, the remainder of this chapter is dedicated to presenting two case studies of two different countries as examples of production sharing opportunities.

In sequence, the studies are: (1) Mexico, which is closest to the United States and has the largest share of the world offshore assembly market and, (2) Singapore, which has a very mature program. These countries represent extremes, in that Mexico's program is rather simple but very successful, and Singapore's program is complex, offering almost every incentive scheme possible.

Space and time prevent discussions of every competitive production sharing country. Indonesia, India, Taiwan, Thailand, Uruguay, as well as West Africa and many Central American countries such as El Salvador also offer excellent opportunities for certain products and should not be neglected in your analysis. A list of contacts is offered at the end of this chapter.

COUNTRY CASE STUDY #1: The Mexican Maquiladora

The only land border anywhere on the globe that lies between a third world country and an industrial democracy is the one between Mexico and the United States. It is logical, therefore, that production sharing between the two has grown.

BACKGROUND

Mexico, the northernmost country of Latin America, lies just south of the United States. The Rio Grande river forms about two-thirds of the boundary between the two countries. At virtually every border crossing extending from Tijuana on the west to El Paso then following the Rio Grande, assembly plants have been built which are known as *maquiladoras*. This is Mexico's co-production program, and it has become a shining star in the global industrial world.

The exact meaning of the word maquiladora is somewhat vague. Some say it originated from the Spanish word maquila, which in colonial times was the toll that millers collected for processing someone else's grain. Maybe the connection is threshing out profits? *Quien sabé?* Who Knows?

The original intent of the program was to mitigate unemployment on the Mexican border brought about by the discontinuance of the American farm labor program called "Brazero" and at the time was thought to be a temporary program. It is now here to stay.

Plant operations first began in 1959, but the program was not officially authorized by the government until 1965. By the end of 1966 there were 12 plants operating in Mexico with a total employment of 3,000.

In 1972, the program was expanded to include economically depressed areas throughout the interior of Mexico. This industry had a 65 percent employment increase between 1982 and 1985. At this time there are about 800 plants employing between 220,000 and 250,000 Mexican workers, and before 1990 the number employed is expected to be about one million.

Commonly called a "twin-plant" or complementary assembly facility for foreign (predominantly United States) manufacturing companies, these plants operate in-bond with special authorization from the Mexican government.

Maquiladoras perform a wide variety of production services, the most prominent of which are the manufacture and assembly of electronics. This is because electronics has a very high value to weigh relationship and therefore is less expensive to transport. They are also involved with automotive products, textiles, wearing apparel, toys, coupons, furniture and many others.

The program authorizes capital equipment and raw materials to enter duty free and there is no Mexican tax or tariff on the products exported from Mexico. Under United States Harmonized Tariff Schedule (TSUS) article 9802.00.60008 (formerly 806.30) and article 9802.00.80503 (formerly 807), American firms can operate subsidiary fabrication and assembly plants and return the output to their United States locations with only the value added by the non-United States materials and the process of transformation in the Mexican plant being charged duty in the exchange. Mexico is a United Nations "recipient" country, so if the product contains 35 percent or more of Mexican content, chances are that it will qualify for import to the United States under the Generalized System of Preferences (G.S.P.) free of duty. The Maquiladora was designed to be an export program and ordinarily all of the products from a maquila must be exported, but Mexican law allows 20 percent of the goods manufactured or assembled in the in-bond plants to be imported duty free into Mexico.

LABOR COSTS

The cost per hour for an unskilled Mexican worker is about $1.00 at the border, $.93 in Monterey, and $.82 further inland. This includes a 40 percent employee fringe benefit package and periodic increases in minimum salaries. Even though Mexican wage rates increase to keep up with inflation, the price of the peso has been falling, such that the effective wage rate has been constant. Table 10-3 offers a way of analyzing potential annual employee savings.

_____Table 10-3   Typical Annual Employee Savings (Maquiladora)._____

Average hourly earnings for U.S. Electrical/Electronic industries (1983)	$8.84
Average fringe benefits (@ 35% discount labor)	$3.09
Minimum savings due to reduction of overhead (@ 15% of direct labor)	$0.88
Total Direct labor cost per hour worked	$12.81
Average hourly rate for Mexican labor, fully burdened	$3.60
Hourly savings per employee	$9.21
Hours per Mexican work week	X 48
Weekly savings per employee	$442.08
Weeks worked annually	X 48
Annual savings per employee	$21,219.84

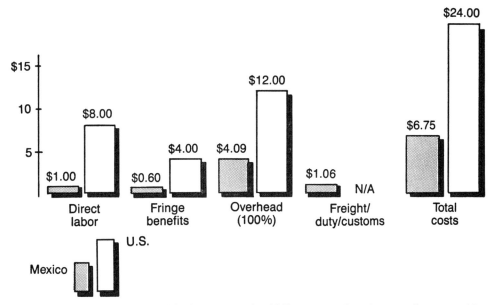

Fig. 10-5 Assembly costs: Mexico versus the U.S. average hourly costs for assembly operations.

Figure 10-5 offers another way of looking at the advantages of low cost labor inputs: Plants that are in-bond can be 100 percent foreign owned. These are called twin-plants or "captive plants" of the parent. Of course this means buying or leasing a building, hiring and training a work force, and putting a management team in place, all of which takes time and commitment. Joint venturing with a plant that already exists can lessen that start-up time.

Another way to get started is to contract with one of the many "shelter" companies that have sprung up along the border. This is attractive to the United States manufacturer who knows the product but doesn't yet understand doing business in Mexico. These shelter firms offer to take on the entire interface. They provide a service to lease a building, hire a work force, manage the operation, and take care of the nitty gritty of accounting, paying tariffs and coordinating transportation. The foreign firm essentially pays only a burdened hourly (value added) rate to the shelter company.

Subcontracting directly with a Mexican non-captive Maquiladora, one that is privately held, already has the existing production capability and is making similar products, is one way to avoid delays. These companies usually require the parent company to provide all materials and machinery and quote in terms of unit cost of assembling the product.

Maquiladoras generally are smaller than most United States companies: A small firm might have 14 or 15 employees; a medium-sized company, 100 to 120 employees; and a large one might have as many as 700 people, mostly women, working in several plants.

WHO USES MAQUILADORAS?

Who takes advantage of the program? No less than the major auto manufacturers—GM, Ford, and Chrysler. Giants such as General Electric and Hughes Aircraft and smaller firms like Elgar Corp. and AC/DC Electronics are also there. Most of the offshore work is done for American firms, but Canadians and even the Japanese, Koreans, and Chinese from Hong Kong are now using Mexican labor. As a result of their interest, production of manufactured goods by Maquiladoras showed a 28 percent increase in 1985. Table 10-4 shows a partial list of companies participating.

Table 10-4   Who Uses Maquiladoras?

AC/DC Electronics	Litton
American Hospital Supply	Matsushita
Aerojet General	Mattel Toys
Black and Decker	Mitsubishi
Chrysler	National Coil
Colgate Palmolive	Nipomex
Diablo Systems, Inc.	Nortronics
Digital	Samsonite
Dupont	Sanyo
Elgar	Texaco
Exxon	United Technology
Ford	Zenith
General Electric	General Motors
GTE	Honeywell
Hughes Aircraft	

ARE THERE PROBLEMS?

Maquiladoras are not without problems, but as they mature even these seem to be lessening. As the program has grown, plant size has increased. No longer is the "mega-maquiladora" (more than 1000 workers) an exception.

With growth there has been a definite increase in management complexity in running the in-bond plants. Process sophistication and competition has put pressure on the labor force as well as the technical and administrative staffs. Many of the workers are members of unions; however, strikes are rare because while the out-of-work employee in the United States receives unemployment benefits, their Mexican counterparts get nothing. In some areas there is a high turnover due to wage competition and skill shortages, but as one top manager stated, "the employees, most of whom are women, respond as much to modern management techniques, fair treatment and respect for cultural differences, as they do higher wage incentives."

Unsuccessful Maquiladoras have been, with few exceptions, the result of not doing adequate homework. For success, it is essential to be familiar with the laws, language and customs. Selection of a qualified counterpart is the most critical decision.

The Bill Ingram Success Story: William D. Ingram is a 32-year-old man who, in 1984, decided he wanted to be his own boss. Bill is not your run-of-the-mill entrepreneur. He is a 1979 Stanford Economics/Engineering graduate with a 1983 Harvard MBA, but he has the same "fire-in-the-belly" and grit that everyone must have who wants to be on their own. With his MBA in hand and $10,000 savings, Bill went to live in Tecate, Mexico and started his own Maquiladora. He rented a small building for $100.00 a month, hired 5 Mexican employees, then began a door-to-door sales effort to find his first contract.

Today, Bill's company is headquartered in San Diego and has operations in both San Diego and Tecate, employs 150 well trained personnel, and is doing about $2,000,000 volume annually. His goal is $10 million net in the next five years. Bill's company, KevTon, Inc. is a contract manufacturer for companies in the aerospace, electronics, and medical industries. KevTon is qualified to mil-spec soldering and inspection requirements and serves several United States Department of Defense contractors.

When asked his perspective on production sharing and the Mexican Maquiladora Program in particular, Bill answered, "The price is right, but that's only one reason why my clients come to me. Another major reason is the United States is at full employment and our plants are at almost 90 percent capacity. To avoid the high cost of capital investment for additional capacity, many firms are turning production and assembly operations over to sub-contractors like me."

Benefits for Mexico

As the program has grown, so has its value to Mexico. Maquiladoras have become Mexico's second largest source of foreign exchange, and are fast becoming a primary method to repay the more than $100 billion in international debts, much of which is held by American banks. In addition to becoming a major source of income, the program has also provided excellent opportunity for employee training, but more important for Mexico, it has provided jobs.

SUMMARY OF PRINCIPAL ADVANTAGES AND LAWS

The world's production sharing countries change their laws frequently to remain competitive within the industry. The following discussion was current as of March 1990.

Labor costs

As a result of the high rate of inflation, legal minimum wages in Mexico are being increased several times a year; however, the effect of these increases has been more than offset in terms of dollars, by the continuing devaluation of the Mexican peso.

Working conditions

The maximum work week is six 8-hour shifts, although a 44–45 hour work week is often practiced. Regular time for a night shift is seven hours and for a split shift seven and a half hours. Mexico's labor law requires payment for a full seven days per week, if all regular work time is worked.

Overtime. Double time must be paid for the first nine hours of overtime each week and triple pay if unusual circumstances require more than nine extra hours (the legal maximum). Triple pay is also provided for work on the seven legal holidays; and Sunday work entitles an employee to a premium of 25 percent of regular pay even if there was a day off during the week.

Vacation. Under the present law, each worker is entitled to six working days of vacation after the first year of employment. Vacation increases an additional two days for each of the first three subsequent years and for every five years of service after the fourth.

Fringe benefits. Most employers provide fringe benefits beyond the minimums required by Mexican law. Such things as company cafeterias, transportation allowances, day care centers, and bonuses based on attendance and production goals are not unusual.

Social Security. All employers are required to register with the Mexican Social Security Institute and to register all their employees, including foreigners working in Mexico. Insured employees and their dependents are provided medical attention, including medicines and hospitalization. Limited unemployment compensation in cases of illness, maternity, occupation disease and accidents, as well as day care centers and old age compensation is also provided.

Many companies furnish their white collar workers and executives with major medical and group life insurance in lieu of using the often overcrowded facilities of the Social Security Institute.

Termination of employment. Mexican labor law grants to permanent employees, the right to receive seniority premiums equal to twelve days' salary for each year of service whenever separated with or without just cause, or upon voluntary retirement after 15 years of service. Such compensation is payable upon the death of an employee, to his or her beneficiaries.

Proximity to the United States

Shipping time required to send materials from United States companies to processing plants is much less than to most other locations, excepting in some cases, the distance to Caribbean locations. Inventories in transit can be much lower.

Other advantages of the shorter distances is the reduction of travel time, and the ease with which United States technical and supervisory personnel can move back and forth.

Another excellent concept is that of a *twin plant*. Established on the United States side of the border, a small operation can coordinate projects and accomplish certain preparatory functions before materials are shipped to Mexico.

Private reimbursable entry

Because of the uniqueness of a common border between the highly industrialized American economy and Mexico, United States Customs and the government of Mexico have on a case-by-case basis authorized a special arrangement called the Private Reimbursable Entry. This amounts to a private port of entry managed under United States and Mexican Customs authority by a large foreign company exclusively for its own business purposes. Approval of this arrangement has taken place in El Paso and other locations along the border where adjacent industrial land on both sides of the border is available. Legal limited access roads and airports can be considered for land border cargo such as cattle importation, or airplane or automobile assembly.

Notice of such arrangements must be published in the United States *Federal Register* for a suitable period to allow protests prior to becoming operational. This type of arrangement is complex because it requires gaining approval from both government's State, Commerce and Treasury Departments. Do be careful to avoid running afoul of the ever present United States Foreign Corrupt Practices Act.

Ownership of land and buildings

Within 100 kilometers of the borders or 50 kilometers of the coastlines of Mexico, non-Mexicans are prohibited from holding title to real estate. However, Mexican banks can act as trustees to serve as the holders of title for a period of 30 years, thus allowing foreigners, as beneficiaries to hold all rights to such land and the buildings thereon. Such beneficial rights are fully transferable. In all other locations (other than border and coastline) foreigners can hold title to land.

Foreign ownership of corporations

Non-Mexicans can own 100 percent of the capital stock of Mexican corporations organized to operate as maquila companies. It is not necessary for foreign investors to obtain prior authorization to:

- Transfer capital stock or fixed assets between investors
- Purchase capital stock held by Mexicans
- Open new establishments and relocations
- Manufacture new lines of products (except for textiles)

Requirements to establish a maquila company

There are essentially only five basic requirements for the establishment of a maquila company:

☞ Approval of the charter of incorporation of the Mexican company, providing for operation as a maquiladora, by the Secretariat of Foreign Affairs, which is the incorporating agency of the Mexican government.

☞ Signature of the charter before a Mexican Notary Public.

☞ Registration of the company, its shares held by foreigners and its foreign shareholders in the National Register of Foreign Investment.

☞ Approval of a maquila program for export, by the specialized section of the Secretariat of Commerce and Industrial Development (SECOFI).

☞ Registration of the operating contract with the parent company with the Secretariat and the National Registry of Transfers of Technology. (When there is no charge for technical assistance or use of patents, this procedure is quite rapid.)

Incentives

The maquiladora program is an export oriented program and as such has been of great value to the Mexican government. Its success is attributable not only to low wages and its proximity to the United States, but also to the incentives offered to foreign firms that participate.

Duty-Free Imports. The principal incentive by the Mexican government to maquila operations is the right to import machinery, equipment and materials duty-free for export production. Temporary imports also are exempt of Mexico's value added tax (VAT).

A company that has obtained approval of their maquila export program may import:

1. Raw materials and components of all types, packaging materials, labels, etc., for production, for a period of up to six months (which may be extended upon request).

2. Machinery, equipment, tools, instruments, measuring and testing devices, parts, manuals and blueprints, as well as whatever is necessary for quality control and training, for as long as the maquila program remains in effect.

The importing company must post a bond with the Mexican Customs Department to cover the cost of the duties which would be paid if the items are not exported, or physically destroyed, within the time limits specified.

Tax incentives

Charges by the maquila companies for their services to foreign companies are not subject to the value added tax (VAT). They are considered taxable at zero percent, but any tax paid to its suppliers is refundable on the basis of monthly VAT returns.

Debt/equity swaps

Mexico's program for the favorable conversion of their external debt can be useful in the case of foreign owned maquila companies planning to invest in the construction or purchase of land and buildings. It works this way:

1. From a foreign bank, a foreign investor acquires the rights to collect debt owed by the Mexican government due in 1998 or later, currently at a discount of about 40 percent.
2. The foreign investor then transfers these rights to its Mexican subsidiary in payment of a subscription to an increase in the capital stock of the subsidiary.
3. The Mexican government, after review and approval of the investment plan, makes funds available to the Mexican company for the full face value of the foreign debt converted to pesos at the free market rate of exchange, less a discount usually equal to between 5 to 16 percent of the amount involved (depending on the use of the funds).
4. In exchange for the funds, the Mexican company issues shares of Qualified Capital Stock to the foreign investor. This stock may not be transferred to any Mexican resident or redeemed under specially favorable terms before 1998, or the date the government debt would have come due.

Sales within Mexico

For periods of 12 months, individual maquila companies may obtain a permit from SECOFI to import and sell up to 20 percent of their production within Mexico. The conditions of this importation are:

1. A sufficient supply of the products is not available in Mexico.
2. Existing Mexican suppliers of similar products will not be damaged.
3. Payment of Mexican import duties on the imported content of the products sold.

Foreign exchange control

Since 1982, Mexico has had a controlled exchange market coexisting with a completely free market. The controlled market rate is set daily, and has reflected a continuing devaluation of the Mexican peso, basically set to offset the continuing excess of the inflation rate in Mexico over that occurring in the United States.

Maquila companies are exempt from exchange control procedures applicable to general exporters, including the requirement to agree to convert the amounts of their invoices (which must be dominated in United States dollars or other convertible foreign currency) to Mexican pesos in the controlled market, except as follows:

1. Maquilas must convert sufficient foreign currency at the controlled rate to cover their locally incurred expenses, taxes and costs of goods purchased (except fixed assets).
2. Maquilas may use free market dollars to pay for imported merchandise and expenses outside Mexico, as well as obtain Mexican pesos to pay for local purchases of fixed assets.

Mexican profit taxation

Mexico's corporate tax rules are in transition because of a change to their tax law which became effective January 1, 1987. The principal changes during the transition period, which ends in 1991, provides for a gradual reduction of the flat rate from 42 to 35 percent when the annual taxable income exceeds a specified amount. On the other hand, the change drastically reduces the deductions for interest expense and exchange rate losses on foreign currency transactions.

Personal income tax

Residents are taxed on their worldwide personal income from all sources, but have a right to a foreign tax credit for foreign source income, and favorable treatment on capital gains from certain investments and business enterprises. A tax return is required to be filed by April 30 each year.

Foreign citizens who establish their home in Mexico and are not outside the country for more than 183 days of a calendar year, nonconsecutive or not, are considered residents for Mexican tax purposes.

Nonresidents are subject to a flat 30 percent of their remuneration for work performed in Mexico and paid by a Mexican company. Many nonresidents assigned to a Mexican maquila, take advantage of the twin plant concept and take their pay from the nonresident companion corporation with all or part of their salaries being absorbed by the American firm. American citizens who do pay personal income taxes can take a foreign tax credit for the Mexican tax withheld. Nonresident foreigners should obtain renewable six-month immigration permits.

Expatriate living conditions

Living in Mexico can be gracious and inexpensive; however, the country has not yet attained the standards found in the average American, Japanese, or European city. In addition, the language of administration and business is Mexican. For those maquilas operating in the interior there are usually small communities of expatriates and/or retired foreigners, but the infrastructure and lack of services such as telephone can prove frustrating. However, because most maquilas are located near the border, most nonresidents, particularly managers and executives, live on the United States side and commute.

COUNTRY CASE STUDY #2: Singapore

The country has no natural resources other than its harbor and its people, so in early 1961, the Government established an autonomous body called the Singapore Economic Development Board. This quasi-government organization's task was to spearhead the transformation of the country from a trading nation to a modern diversified economy with emphasis on manufacturing and services. In so doing, their thrust was development of capital intensive, highly skilled, export oriented manufacturing industries.

BACKGROUND

Singapore is an island located at the southern tip of the Straits of Malacca, about 137 kilometers north of the equator. The Republic of Singapore comprises the main island and 57 smaller ones with a total land area of approximately 600 square miles. It has a population of 2.6 million, half of whom are under age 30.

It is second only to Rotterdam in terms of tonnage moved through its port and is by far the busiest port in Asia. Known as the crossroads of the world, it is served by more than 500 shipping lines and is an important stopover in the networks of most international airlines.

Modern Singapore was founded in 1819 by Sir Stamford Raffles as a trading post for the East India company, and in 1867, along with Malacca and Penang, became a British colony. Following several organizational changes, during the 1950s and early 1960s, Singapore separated from Malaysia by mutual consent.

By the late 1960s, a rapid inflow of investments by multinational corporations (MNCs) from around the world brought a rapid industrialization, which today can support the manufacturing of such sophisticated products as computers, Winchester disk drives, facsimile machines, optics and other precision engineering products.

Under United States Tariff Schedules (Harmonized) 9802.00.80503 and 9802.00.60008 (formerly TSUS 807 and 806.30) American firms can operate subsidiary fabrication and assembly plants and return the output to their United States locations with only the value added by the non-United States materials and the process of transformation in the Singapore plant being charged duty in the exchange.

Like Mexico, Singapore is a United Nations "recipient" country, so if the product contains 35 percent or more of Singapore content, chances are that it will qualify for import to the United States with no duty under the Generalized System of Preferences (G.S.P.).

FORMS OF BUSINESS ORGANIZATION

Because of its small domestic market, most projects in Singapore must be export oriented.

Subcontract

As in most other production sharing countries, enterprising natives of Singapore have developed plants that provide a service for short-term assembly operations. Most of these companies keep offices or representatives in the major cities of developed countries to market their specialties to target industries. Contact can be made through embassies or the Singapore Economic Development Board (see addresses at end of chapter).

Investment

Most business is carried on in the form of sole trader or partnership. An *ordinary partnership* is one where the partners share equally the gains and losses. A *limited partnership* is one in which one or more partners are only liable to the extent of their capital contributions. Of course a limited partnership must have one or more general partners without limit for the firm's debts. All sole traders and partnerships must be registered under the Singapore Business Registration Act of 1973.

Foreign corporations

The most common form of business entity in Singapore is the limited liability company which may be private or public.

Private company. A private company can:

- Restrict the right to transfer shares
- Limit its numbers to fifty
- Prohibit public subscription of its shares
- Prohibit invitation of the public to deposit money with it
- Prohibit shares from being held directly or indirectly by a corporation

Formation procedures of a private company.

☞ Obtain written approval from the Registrar of Companies to use the name.

☞ If the proposed company has foreign participation, gain approval of the Trade Development Board in the case of trading company, or the Economic Development Board and Monetary Authority in the case of a manufacturing or finance company.

☞ Two or more persons subscribe their names to the articles of association.

☞ Submit an application with a copy of the company's memorandum and articles of association to the Registrar of companies.

☞ The company can commence business from the date the certificate of incorporation is issued.

Formation procedures of a public company. Although the procedures are almost exactly the same as that of a private company, a public company cannot begin business until it has filed a prospectus or statement in lieu of prospectus.

Branches of foreign corporations. A branch of a foreign corporation must submit to the Registrar of Companies:

☞ Copy of its certificate of incorporation

☞ Copy of its charter

☞ List of its directors

☞ Memorandum of appointment stating the names and addresses of two agents in Singapore

☞ Statutory declaration by the agents

☞ Notice of the situation of its registered office in Singapore

☞ Copy of annual accounts within two months after holding its annual meeting

SINGAPORE ADVANTAGES

The Singapore dollar is generally stable at about half the value of the United States dollar and worker's salaries are very competitive. Table 10-5 shows typical salaries of various employment groups.

_____Table 10-5   Typical Monthly Salaries (Singapore)._____

Occupation	Average monthly Basic wages (S$)
Basic unskilled labor	500 – 600
Office Clerk	750
Typist	750
Stenographic-typist	1,000
Steno-Secretary	1,500
Sales, Shop assistant	600
Production Supervisor	1,500
Architect, Engineer	2,600

Working conditions

The Singapore Employment Act regulates the working conditions for those whose monthly salaries do not exceed S$1,250 or about United States $600.00. The work week is fixed at 44 hours.

Overtime. Payment at one and a half times the hourly rate of pay for overtime and two thirds the hourly rate for holidays and normal week days off. Overtime is limited to 72 hours a month.

Vacation. Under the Act, there are 11 paid public holidays, seven days annual leave after one year's service and an additional one day's annual leave for every subsequent 12 months of continuous service with one employer. Sick leave, limited to 14 days, is paid after one year of service, but can be extended to as much as 60 days where hospitalization is involved. Retirement benefits may be payable after five years service.

Fringe benefits. Consideration of fair and reasonable modern benefits is a part of managing in Singapore. Such things as cafeterias, and day care are as much a part of business life in this country as in any throughout the world.

Social Security. The government social insurance program in this country is called the Central Provident Fund (CPF). All employees in the private sector are required to contribute and are augmented by their employers. The employer's contribution is 10 percent and the employee's is 25 percent, combining for the 35 percent of monthly wages subject to a ceiling of S$6,000 per month.

Amounts may be withdrawn in a lump sum on reaching the statutory retirement age of 55 years or prematurely in the event of permanent disablement or migration. The board also allows funds to be withdrawn prior to retirement to purchase a home and for certain approved securities.

Another fund called the Skills Development Fund (SDF) requires employers to pay one percent on employees earning up to S$750 a month. This fund is used to pay grants to employers and promote the training skills necessary to carry out Singapore's restructuring efforts.

Medisave is Singapore's National Health Plan. It is designed to meet the basic needs of the average citizen. The income for the program comes from CPF. Six percent (three percent employer and three percent employee) is set aside to help pay hospitalization bills of the immediate family.

Ownership of land and buildings

Most industrial land is owned by the State and is governed by Ground Leases controlled and managed by the Jurong Town Corporation at reasonable rents. Jurong, the town immediately surrounding the port has 25 industrial estates in which more than 3000 companies with 200,000 workers represent more than 70 percent of the nation's work force. Of this number, about 60 percent of the companies are foreign owned or joint ventures. Although there are other estates than those of Jurong in which many foreign companies are doing business, Jurong's popularity is its extensive infrastructure and support services including cargo handling at the Port and Marine Base.

Many industrialists prefer to buy or rent factories that are already built because they can begin production almost immediately. The various estates offer these standard factories at very competitive prices. Average rentals for upper floors are about S$0.65 per square foot per month and about S$0.95 per square foot for ground floor. Sale prices range from S$65 to S$175 per square foot

Leases on industrial land with or without building, are granted for an initial period of 30 years with options for an additional 30 years.

Incentives

Singapore's list of incentives is rivaled by few nations in the production sharing business. They are aggressive—Singapore wants your business. The country's incentives fall into two categories: 1) Economic expansion by income tax legislation, and 2) other non-fiscal expansion incentives.

Economic expansion by income tax relief. Economic expansion incentives are administered by the Economic Development Board. The board takes a very liberal approach to almost any product that brings technology to Singapore or creates jobs.

Pioneer industries. Pioneer industries are declared by the Minister of Finance to be in the economic interest of Singapore. These enterprises are exempt from company tax for five to ten years from the date they commence production.

Pioneer service companies. These are the following service related industries that receive an incentive tax relief period for five years or more, but not to exceed ten years:

- Any engineering or technical services, including laboratory, consultancy and research and development activities;
- Computer-based information and other computer related services;
- Development or production of any industrial design.

Expansion of established enterprise. A capital equipment expansion that exceeds S$10 million to improve an approved product, may be granted an expansion certificate. This exempts the holder from tax on the increased income resulting from the expansion for a period of up to five years.

Expanding service companies. Companies that expand as a Pioneer Service Company may apply for approval as an expanding service company. Once approved, the firm receives a tax exemption on the incremental profits made during a period not to exceed five years.

Export incentive. This incentive is designed to encourage manufactured exports. The normal period is five years, although it may be extended for up to fifteen years if the fixed capital expenditure exceeds S$150 million and half of the paid-up capital is held by permanent residents of Singapore. During this period 90 percent of the company's qualifying export profits are to be exempt from tax. To qualify, at least 20 percent of the value of total sales must be exports, and must amount to more than S$100,000 per year.

Investment allowance. This incentive is an alternative to pioneer status and export incentives. It is particularly beneficial for projects that might not generate profits early enough to benefit from fixed period tax holiday schemes. Profits are tax-exempt at various percentages for different projects and assets up to 50 percent of the actual investment on factory buildings and new productive equipment for an approved project.

Liberalized investment allowance. This provides for a wider range of activities than the investment allowance scheme, and fixes the exempt rate on profits at 30 percent of the qualifying expenditure on machinery and equipment.

Warehousing and servicing incentives. The intent of this incentive is to encourage the establishment of warehouses for manufactured goods which are to be sold and exported. Half of the companies qualifying export profits are exempt from tax for five years.

International consultancy services incentive. Intended to encourage overseas projects in management, design engineering, plant fabrication and computer processing services, this incentive exempts half of the qualifying export profits for five years.

International trade incentive. Trading companies that export non-traditional Singapore products (other than coconut oil, tin, natural rubber, etc.) may be exempt from paying tax on half of their export profits for five years. The qualification is limited to companies that have a minimum of S$10 million/year Singapore manufactured or domestic produced, or at least S$20 million in non-traditional commodities.

Product development assistance. This scheme provides cash grants to encourage local design, development, and indigenous technical know-how. It is only available to companies that have at least 31 percent ownership by Singapore citizens of permanent residents. The maximum grant is limited to $5000, but can be applied to 50 percent of the cost feasibility studies, as well as the costs of product development.

Tax exemption on interest on approved loans. The idea behind this incentive is to encourage foreign loans for capital investments. A tax exemption may be granted on interest withholding tax provided the consequence is lower cost to the borrower.

Approved royalties, fees and development contributions. Application can be made for a reduced rate of tax or exemption altogether on payments of royalties, fees and development contributions.

New technology companies. This incentive scheme is to encourage ventures into new technology and applies to holding companies that are at least 50 percent owned by Singapore citizens or permanent residents. It provides tax allowances for losses made by a technology company.

Operational headquarters. To encourage multinational corporations to set up their headquarters in Singapore, a concessionary tax of only 10 percent on their service income is available for up to 10 years.

Accelerated depreciation allowance. Singapore's Income Tax Act offers a normal depreciation of plant and machinery; however, an accelerated method allows most equipment to be written off over a period of three years, and computers, industrial robots and office automation in one year.

Research and development expenditure. In addition to investment and depreciation allowances, Singapore offers several other incentive schemes to stimulate quality industries and to promote research and development.

- Double deduction of R&D expenditures other than on buildings and equipment.
- Extension of allowances on industrial buildings
- A tax exempt reserve of 20 percent of their taxable income for R&D to be used within three years.

Shipping profits of Singapore ships. To encourage ship owners to register their ships in Singapore, profits of those that fly the country's flag are exempt from tax.

Other non-fiscal expansion incentives. These are an array of financing programs aimed at stimulating business development, particularly research and marketing for export.

Small industries finance scheme. This is a program that provides financial assistance in the form of low interest loans to small local businesses (less than S$3 million in fixed productive assets. It is available to both manufacturing and service companies, including exporters.

Small Industries Technical Assistance Scheme (SITAS). To encourage the use of external experts to upgrade business operations, the Economic Development Board will reimburse up to 90 percent of the cost of engaging a consultant.

Skills training grants. Assistance is available through this scheme to encourage existing operations to mechanize their operations. Training facilities and assistance is available to upgrade employee skills for the new equipment.

Interest grants for mechanization. This scheme is intended to reduce the cost of financing the cost of mechanization of existing manual operations.

Development consultancy. This scheme provides for grants paid to consultants to assist local Singapore businesses improve operations and training plans.

Small Enterprise Development Bureau

The Small Enterprise Development Bureau acts as a one-stop assistance supermarket with six different programs available to stimulate the growth of small business.

Capital Assistance Scheme (CAS). This is for investors who wish to apply for capital in the form of equity or fixed or floating rate loans which range from 5 to 15 years.

Product Development Assistance Scheme (PDAS). To encourage local company's product design and development, this scheme offers a grant equal to 50 percent of the approved development costs.

Initiatives in New Technology (INTECH). This is an encouragement scheme for local manufacturers and service companies for investments and manpower development in the application of new technology. Grants are provided equal to 30 to 50 percent of approved costs of the project.

Market Development Assistance Scheme (MDAS). Provides financial and other assistance to companies marketing Singapore-made goods and services overseas. Must be a Singapore registered company with at least 30 percent local equity.

Research and Development Assistance Scheme (RDAS). This is an incentive which provides seed-money for industrial undertakings of R&D that a firm would not pursue because of insufficient resources of high risk.

Venture Capital Scheme. Under this scheme, an overseas investor is allowed to deduct from income up to 100 percent of the equity in an approved project that assists local companies to acquire or diversify into new technology industries.

Personal income tax

Income earned in Singapore is taxable whether or not the individual is a resident in Singapore for tax purposes. Personal income tax is charged on a sliding scale ranging from as little as 3.5 percent to 33 percent after deductions. A resident is one who is physically present in Singapore for 183 days or more in a year.

Non-resident income is not taxed if it does not exceed 60 days in a calendar year. Employment of greater than 60 days, but less than 183 days is taxed at 15 percent.

EXPATRIATE LIVING CONDITIONS

Living conditions in this country are among the best, and except for the cost of housing and automobiles, is the same or lower than in the United States. Accommodations are expensive and there is a 150 percent duty levied on the pre-tax value of a new car. As a result of these high costs, allowances are usually provided by employers.

On the other hand, household help in the form of amahs, gardeners, and drivers are very reasonable, thus allowing increased time for social activities. Singapore abounds with private social and sports clubs for expatriates such as the American Association, the American Club, and the Singapore American Community Action Council (SACAC).

Singapore's restaurants are famous for their quality, and the food selection ranges from the best of Asian to every Western delicacy.

Children's schooling

American schools are well established in Singapore offering preparation for the ACT and SAT college entrance examinations. Other schools for Dutch, English, French, German, Swiss and Japanese are available.

All foreign nationals attending school in this country must have a student pass issued by the Singapore Ministry of Education.

Medical and health

This country has excellent dentists, doctors, and surgeons serving in well equipped government and private hospitals. Non-Singapore citizens must pay for treatment in government hospitals but the costs are reasonable. Many companies provide for private medical assistance for expatriate employees and their families.

HOW TO MAKE CONTACT

Many nations offer production sharing programs and each focuses their promotion on the benefits and differences between their incentives and their competitors. The following is a list of some of the offices that you can contact to find out about the current offerings:

Trade Development Authority of India

Head Office
Bank of Baroda
16 Parliament Street
New Delhi 110001

Ministry of Industry
Udyog Bhawan
New Delhi 110011

New York Office
445 Park Avenue, 18th Floor
New York, NY 10022

Frankfurt Office
Wilhelm-Leuschner-Str. 93
6000 Frankfurt/Main 1
Federal Republic of Germany

Tokyo Office
Atagoyamo Bengoshi Bldg.
Room No. 302-303
6-7, Atago Cho
1-Chome, Minato-Ku
Tokyo, Japan

Indonesia

Home Office
The Investment Coordinating Board
Badan Koordinasi Penanaman Modal (BKPM)
Jalan Gatot Subroto No. 6
P.O. Box 3186
Jakarta, Indonesia

New York Office
Indonesia Trade Promotion Center
4 East 54th Street
New York, NY 10022

Trade Commission of Mexico

Head Office
Camino Santa Teresa #1679
Jardines del Pedregal
Mexico, DS 01900

New York Office
655 Madison Ave., 16th Floor
New York, NY 10021

Los Angeles Office
8484 Wilshire Blvd., Ste. 808
Beverly Hills, CA 90211

Singapore Economic Development Board

Head Office
250 North Bridge Road
#24-00 Raffles City Tower
Singapore 0617

New York Office
55 East 59th Street
New York, NY 10022

Frankfurt Office
6000 Frankfurt/Main
Untermainanlage 7
Federal Republic of Germany

Tokyo Office
The Imperial Tower, 8th Floor
1-1 Uchisaiwaicho 1-Chome
Chiyoda-ku, Tokyo 100

Thailand

Home Office
Office of the Board of Investment
16th-17th Floors, Thai Farmers Bank Building
400 Phaholyothin Road
Bangkok 10400 Thailand

New York Office
Thailand Board of Investment
Five World Trade Center, Suite 3443
New York, NY 10048

Frankfurt Office
Thai Trade and Investment Center
Bethmann Strasse 58
6000 Frankfurt Am Main
Federal Republic of Germany

Tokyo Office
Thailand Board of Investment
3rd Floor, Akasaka Brighton Building
1-5-2 Akasaka, Minato-ku
Tokyo 107

Uruguayan Government Trade Bureau

Head Office
Ministerio de Industria y Energia (Ministry of Industry)
Rincon 747

U.S. Office
747 Third Ave., 37th Floor
New York, NY 10017

El Salvador

FUSADES
Salvadoran Foundation for Economic
and Social Development
Alameda Roosevelt 3107
Edificiode La Centroamericana, Sexto Piso
San Salvadore, El Salvador
Central America

The next chapter explains the current practices and methods of doing business with non-market (communist) countries.

11

Develop business with non-market countries

IF, AS DR. CLAYTON YEUTTER, SECRETARY OF AGRICULTURE AND FORMER United States Trade Representative once said, "trade is the currency of peace," then expanding trade with non-market (Communist) countries is in the best interest of all nations.

Recently, as a result of *perestroika* (restructuring), *glasnost* (openness), and fresh, foreword-thinking international leadership there appears to be a movement toward freer markets in most controlled countries. These winds of change portend increased trade volume and opportunities for small- and medium-sized businesses.

This chapter is designed to provide a starting point and a method to bridge the market/non-market trade mechanism should you find that these business opportunities are for you.

WHO ARE THE NON-MARKET COUNTRIES?

Albania, Bulgaria, Czechoslovakia, German Democratic Republic (East Germany), Hungary, Poland, Rumania, and Yugoslavia are the satellite economies within the Union of Soviet Socialist Republics's (Russia) Eastern Europe trading arena. Algeria, Cambodia, Cuba, North Korea, and Vietnam represent other major markets which are associated yet maintain a detached trade focus. The People's Republic of China (PRC) is also Communist but trade relations with the West re-established in the early 1970s have brought excellent results in spite of setbacks, such as the Tiananmen Square massacre. Smaller markets such as

Namibia, Estonia, Latvia and Lithuania are additional Communist countries struggling to break into the changing trade scenario.

NOTE: The year 1989 saw the most dramatic changes on the European Continent since the end of World War II. From the June elections in Poland to the crumbling of the Berlin Wall, the world has witnessed the steady march toward democracy, freedom, and the revolutionary swing to market oriented economies across Central and Eastern Europe.

Bulgaria, East Germany, Poland, Hungary, Czechoslovakia, Rumania, Yugoslavia as well as the Soviet states of Latvia, Estonia and Lithuania are in various states of change.

Businesspeople should understand that the movement toward privatization will not happen overnight and the suggestions offered in this chapter will remain valid during the transition period, which could take as much as ten years.

ECONOMIC BACKGROUND

One can, in very rudimentary terms picture the economic methods of Communist countries, as being the "flip-side" of most free-market economic systems. For instance, in a market economy, the dominant share of productive activity is conducted by private businesses. Fettered only by regulations that have been determined by the government to be good for the majority, such as public safety, their products are distributed according to competitive commercial markets. A smaller segment of production, such as social services, utilities and infrastructure (roads, electricity and water), and the government organizations themselves are centrally planned and organized. For instance, the United States Federal budget is centrally planned in time periods not unlike the five-year plans found in socialist countries.

On the other side of the mirror, production and distribution in the non-market economies is centrally planned and controlled, usually in five-year increments. Operations are conducted by state or worker owned organizations called combines, which are made up of from 20 to 40 individual enterprises with total work forces in each combine varying from 60,000 to 250,000 employees. The products of these combines are then distributed according to the five-year plan. A very small portion of the production effort in communist countries is held in private hands and distributed according to market allocation and commercial competition.

POTENTIAL TO INTERACT

Most companies in non-market countries, except in perhaps some export oriented segments of the economy, have no experience in marketing or shopping for equipment in the West.

On the other hand, private free-market companies already know how to deal with government controlled enterprises. For instance, to win a contract to build roads or sell a product to local, state, or central government organizations in the United States or Japan, private companies must learn to submit proposals and make bids. It follows then that many free-market companies already know a great deal about how to do business with non-market organizations—it just means adjusting to a different language and bureaucratic procedures.

Understanding the non-market method

John Pfeiffer, a specialist in doing business in the Soviet Union described the system as follows: "The non-market method denies consumer needs. For instance, factory manager A makes only one kind of shoes, but in various sizes. Factory manager B makes mattresses, but only one size. In a given year, both managers try to produce exactly the number decided by the central planning group. Factory A is in the East and Factory B is 3000 miles away in the West. Therefore, there is no way for the factory managers to know the needs of the people at the other end of the country. So, picture a Russian lady walking into a local consumer store. She wants two pairs of shoes, but of slightly different styles, for her daughters—sorry, only one style and one pair per customer! Then she asks for a larger mattress—sorry, no have—'they' only planned for one size, besides you bought your allocation last year, none this year! Does she get angry? Wouldn't you? On the other hand, it is just as likely that the Soviet mother could have found bare shelves—nothing in stock because the planners didn't plan correctly or the factory workers didn't meet goals. On paper Marxist theory looks good—utopia, but in truth no one works without profit. Medals don't work—patriotism only works in the short run."

TRADE PROSPECTS

As early as the mid-1970s, French President Valery Giscard d'Estaing said, "The idea (of communism) is dead. The real question now is, will communism survive? It's a dramatic change no one could have foreseen even a decade ago."

Many object to Mr. d'Estaing's prophesy calling it extremely premature. Nevertheless, from a business point of view, there are signs that the non-market nations will at least test the mixing of market economics with their Marxism policies of the past. In fact, such experimentation has been going on for over a decade in Yugoslavia, Hungary, and China.

The outlook for increased business with the People's Republic of China is always full ahead, but keep your hand on the throttle. China has a heritage of private commerce and thirty years of harsh tactics under Marxist rule isn't even a tick mark on the time line of generation after generation of people who made their living by free markets. However, Western businessmen must always keep in mind the fits and starts since 1949: The "Great Leap Forward" in 1958 was followed by a deep recession in 1961. Then came Cultural Revolution #1 (1963–1965), and Cultural Revolution #2 (1966–1970) which included another recession in 1967. There was the Retrenchment of 1976, and more recently the ruthless events of the Tiananmen Square massacre on June 4th of 1989. Nevertheless, China has maintained one of the fastest growth rates in the world, and the debate in China today is not whether to reform, but how to reform and how quickly. An even greater issue for Chinese intellectuals is whether to embrace the entire free-market theory or only parts of it.

Russia is another story. From the point of view of doing business, the Soviet Union is a "babe-in-the-woods." That country has practically no residual history of individual economic enterprise. Most memories of what went before have been erased by 70 years and several generations of socialistic thinking since the communist revolution. In addition, for all intents Russia was, at one point, conquered and put into slavery during World War II. That's not to say capitalism and free enterprise can't be learned—when you're hungry, you learn to hustle.

That's also not to say there hasn't been East-West trade in the past. Some American companies such as Continental Grain, Cargill, Caterpillar, Occidental Petroleum, Philip Morris, Monsanto, and Dresser have been doing business with the Union of Soviet Socialist Republics almost continuously, hot or cold war, it made little difference. Similarly, Finland, France, Italy, and West Germany have bridged the barriers on a continuing basis. However, for the rest of the free-market world, trade relations has been a moving target. What currency? Who do we contact? Will the politicians let us trade this year? The markets and mechanisms are not in place. To do business in Russia, Western businesses might have to invest as much in training and teaching as they do in operational hardware. In many cases such training is negotiable and paid for by the Russians.

NOTE: According to a Wednesday, April 5, 1989 Wall Street Journal article, the first class of about 50 Russian MBA candidates will begin their studies in April 1990. The Khabarovsk Institute of National Economy, located more than 4000 miles east of Moscow will offer the first masters degree program under the tutelage of Professors from Portland State University in Oregon. According to the director of the institute, the program is expected to become widely copied throughout the Soviet Union. In the past the Soviet Union has sent many bright students to such schools as Harvard, MIT, and Princeton to obtain graduate business degrees.

Yugoslavia, Hungary, and East Germany are further ahead than the Soviet Union when it comes to trade with the West. Yugoslavia seems to have taken pages right out of the Japanese play book and are already marketing in the United States. The number of Hungarian companies enjoying the right to conduct foreign trade activities on their own doubled between 1980 and 1987, and at the moment some 350 enterprises are allowed to export and import directly.

Regardless of the experience or lack of it in doing business with the West, one thing remains a constant in all non-market countries. The state run monopolies that currently handle international trade are hopelessly inefficient. For instance, if a factory needs a new machine, the first step is to search within the country for that machine. Given that it is not available from within, foreign currency must be allocated for an international purchase. The total search time, the approval for currency allocation, and finally the purchase by the foreign trade organization often takes as long as two years. So, be prepared for a certain amount of frustration.

U.S. EAST-WEST FOREIGN TRADE POLICY

In the past, like two sisters vying for the handsome prince, trade relations between East and West since World War II have vacillated. On a geopolitical level, each wanted to impress the undecided third world prize that their philosophy was best for mankind. Yet, on an economic basis, each wanted to remain friendly so they might have access to the populations and the markets of the other. After all, Russia is a trillion dollar market—second in the world only to the United States.

Today, with the exceptions of Cuba, Vietnam, North Korea, and Cambodia for foreign policy reasons, there is currently a general normalization of trade relationships with non-market countries.

Since 1972 when President Nixon went to China and the subsequent full normalization of diplomatic relations in 1979, that relationship has spawned excellent two-way trade.

The question of increasing East-West trade has not been relationship problems as much as it has been the market difficulties and the regulatory difficulties. The United States, as a member of the Multilateral Coordinating Committee (COCOM) (not to be confused with COMECON or CMEA), which consists of the North Atlantic Treaty Organization (NATO) and Japan, adheres to a strict program of technology control (explained later in this chapter). These restrictions tend to dampen the sale of the very kinds of consumer products most needed in the non-market countries.

In spite of recent changes in the Eastern block and overtures by the Soviet Union, the truth about trade relations is that they remain uncertain, but uncertainty is the magic of free enterprise and competition. Those who create the magic become the big business winners.

FOREIGN TRADE ORGANIZATIONS

Foreign trade by non-market countries is conducted by state trade organizations within the overall plans and guidelines established by the relevant economic policymaking bodies such as state economic, financial, and planning commissions.

These foreign trade offices are responsible for the uniform management, planning, organization and control of trade on the basis of each country's legislation and economic plans. Doing business with these trade organizations is very much like doing business with Western governments. It means struggling to understand the bureaucratic rules and meeting rigidly defined procedures.

As members of the Council for Mutual Economic Assistance (COMECON or CMEA) the various trade monopolies also have responsibility to cooperate with other centralized state organs to prepare and carry out measures that deepen socialist economic integration. However, in practice, with more and more government approval, each country is on its own and recently each has been expanding its share of trade with developing and industrialized capitalistic countries. It is this expansion that provides the opportunity for Western businesses.

Council for Mutual Economic Assistance (COMECON or CMEA). An intergovernmental organization established in 1949 to coordinate the economies of member states and now consisting of the Soviet Union, Bulgaria, Czechoslovakia, the German Democratic Republic (''East Germany''), Hungary, Mongolia, Poland, Rumania, Cuba and Vietnam. The purpose of the Council, according to its charter, is to improve economic cooperation among participating countries and to accelerate their economic and technological progress.

As an example, since 1985, Yugoslavia has had as close to a free enterprise system as can be visualized and yet be a socialist country. Yugoslavians are free to come and go abroad to increase their knowledge and return with hard currency. Their new foreign trade and foreign exchange system is based on the concept of a market oriented socialist economy. These laws proclaim free trade as the general basis for their foreign trade system and the convertibility of the dinar is one of the country's goals. Foreign trade transactions can be carried out by any business organization that can show it can meet turnover targets, employ qualified personnel for performing foreign trade, and possesses the capacity to finance foreign trade transactions.

Starting April 1, 1989, Russian companies were able to trade directly with foreign firms rather than having to work through the handful of state-run intermediaries. The state operated import-export structure will continue to function, but this new free-market method is a breakthrough in Soviet trade policy and means increased business for enterprising Western firms.

Unfortunately, most Western firms don't know what factories in the nonmarket countries need or what they are allowed to sell. Lists of the companies registered to do business with the West are available through appropriate government offices and the various private consulting businesses that are already springing up to fill the experience void.

RESEARCHING A MARKET

Prior to approaching non-market trade organizations, exporters should analyze the potential market for their goods and services and importers should test the salability of products to be purchased from these countries.

Unfortunately, the amount and completeness of market information varies from country to country and most do not issue requests for global tenders. The process of gaining market information can be difficult and frustrating.

For the export process, the starting point should always be your nearest United States Commerce Department district office; however, it is likely you will find more and better information by dealing with the country desk officer who specializes in your country of interest at Commerce headquarters in Washington, DC. From there one should make direct contact with the United States Foreign Commercial Service Officer (FCS) at the nearest American embassy.

Many non-market countries have just begun to publish detailed information about their past economic performance and little is offered about their future economic and trade plans. Nevertheless, your nearest major library that has been designated a repository of United States Government information should provide, as a minimum, a baseline of what is already known in the United States.

For the import process, most non-market countries maintain Commercial Officers in their foreign embassies and many have developed excellent booklets and pamphlets which contain some helpful information about who to contact for product information.

Based upon your research and using the same rules outlined in Chapter 3, you should develop a market plan which will be sufficiently detailed to reach the decision-making units (DMUs) of your target non-market country.

CONTACTS AND INFORMATION

China, Hungary, Yugoslavia, and the German Democratic Republic (GDR) are the most aggressive in responding to inquiries and marketing their nation's needs and products. At a minimum, most other countries, through their overseas embassies offer lists of current addresses to whom you may send for information. In some cases, non-profit organizations are popping up in the United States to act as conduits for information and contacts for firms who are interested in doing business with a specific country. Most of these are headquartered in Washington, DC.

The following is a partial list of addresses you might find useful for getting started.

Soviet Union

U.S. DEPARTMENT OF COMMERCE
International Trade Administration
Jack Brougher, Director U.S.S.R. Division
14th and Constitution Ave., NW
Washington, DC
(202) 377-4655

U.S. COMMERCIAL OFFICE (USCO)
c/o The American Embassy
APO New York 09862
Tel: 225-48-47; Telex: 871-7805 US-COMM SU.

TRADE REPRESENTATIVE OF THE U.S.S.R.
2001 Connecticut Ave., NW
Washington, DC 20008
(202) 232-0975

TRADE REPRESENTATIVE OF THE U.S.S.R.
2790 Green St.
San Francisco, CA 94123
(415) 922-6642

U.S.-U.S.S.R. TRADE AND ECONOMIC COUNCIL
805 Third Ave.
New York, NY 10022
Tel: (202) 644-4550

U.S.S.R. CHAMBER OF COMMERCE AND INDUSTRY
U.S.S.R., 10100
Ulitsa Kuibysheva, 6
Moscow, U.S.S.R.
Tel: 923-43-23, Telex: 411126

China

U.S. DEPARTMENT OF COMMERCE
International Trade Administration
Office of the PRC and Hong Kong
Room H2317
14th and Constitution Ave., NW
Washington, DC 20230
Tel: (202) 377-3583

U.S. EMBASSY
3 Xiushui Bej Jie
Jianguomenwai
Beijing, PRC
Tel: 532-3831, Telex: 22701 Amemb CN, Fax: (011-86-1) 532-3297

U.S. CONSULATE GENERAL
China Hotel Office Tower
Room 1262-64
Liu Hua Lu
Guangzhou, PRC
Tel: 677842 ext. 1293/4, Telex: 44888 GZDFH CN, Fax: (011-86-20)
66-6409

U.S. CONSULATE GENERAL
1469 Huaihai Zhong Lu
Shanghai, PRC
Tel: 379-880, Tel: 33383 USCG CN, Fax: (011-86-21) 33-4122

U.S.-CHINA BUSINESS COUNCIL
1818 N Street, NW
Suite 500
Washington, DC 20036
(202) 429-0340

EMBASSY OF THE PEOPLE'S REPUBLIC OF CHINA
2300 Connecticut Ave., NW
Washington, DC 20008
(202) 328-2520

German Democratic Republic (GDR)

U.S. DEPARTMENT OF COMMERCE
International Trade Administration
Office of GDR Division
14th and Constitution Ave., NW
Washington, DC 20230
(202)377-4901

EMBASSY OF THE GERMAN DEMOCRATIC REPUBLIC
1717 Massachusetts Ave., NW
Washington, DC 20036
(202) 232-3134

MINISTRY OF FOREIGN TRADE OF THE GDR
Unter den Linden 44/60
Berlin/DDR - 1080
Tel: 230, Telex: 1152361

CHAMBER OF FOREIGN TRADE OF THE GDR
Schonholzer Strasse 10/11
Berlin/DDR 1100
Tel: 48220, Telex: 114840 inter dd

LEIPZIG TRADE FAIR OFFICE
Markt 11/15
Leipzig/DDR - 7010
Tel: 71810, Telex: 0512294

Hungary

U.S. DEPARTMENT OF COMMERCE
International Trade Administration
Office of Hungary Division
14th and Constitution Ave., NW
Washington, DC 20230
(202)377-4901

EMBASSY OF THE HUNGARIAN PEOPLE'S REPUBLIC
2401 Calvert Street, NW
Suite 1021
Washington, DC 20008
Tel: (202) 387-3140, Telex: 440236 hungex

EMBASSY OF THE HUNGARIAN PEOPLE'S REPUBLIC
Office of the Commercial Counsellor
150 East 58th Street, 33rd Floor
New York, NY 10022
Tel: (212) 752-3060, Telex: 422438 HEBO UI

Yugoslavia

U.S. DEPARTMENT OF COMMERCE
International Trade Administration
Office of Hungary Division
14th and Constitution Ave., NW
Washington, DC 20230
(202) 377-4901

U.S. FOREIGN COMMERCIAL SERVICE
U.S. Embassy
Kneza Milosa 50
11000 Belgrade, Yugoslavia
Tel: (11) 645-655
Telex: 11529 AMEMBA YU

BUSINESS REPRESENTATIVE
Yugoslavian Embassy
2410 California Street, NW
Washington, DC 20008

U.S.-YUGOSLAV ECONOMIC COUNCIL, INC.
818, 18th Street, NW, Suite 818
Washington, DC 20006
Tel: (202) 857-0170

YUGOSLAV CHAMBER OF ECONOMY
767 Third Ave., 24th Floor
New York, NY 10017

YUGOSLAV CHAMBER OF ECONOMY
Terazije 23
11011 Belgrade, Yugoslavia
Tel: (11) 339-461
Telex: 11638 YU YUGOKOM

PREPARING PROPOSALS

Ideally, as a result of your market research and knowledge of the individual country's institutions and organizations, your proposal will be tailored and targeted to meet specific requirements or abilities for the kind of business you write about.

Initial proposal

The form of your initial proposal to a trade monopoly or a private company is important. Above all it should be straightforward and in simple language. Initial proposals should contain a basic introduction of your company, an explanation of the areas you have in mind that would interest the country, and specific proposals and products or services to get the relationship started.

Your initial correspondence should have a cover letter of no more than three pages which explains the objective of your proposal and asks for a response. You should include a brief description of your company, but don't confuse them with a laundry list of all your products. Colorful graphic material helps to show your technological advantages. It is a good idea to translate the cover letter into the language of the country. This is not essential if you are doing business with one of the central trade monopolies because they usually have language experts on their staffs. Translation is a must if you are writing to any entity other than foreign trade organizations or central ministries. There is no way to estimate how long it would take a small company in a rural area to respond, if ever, if the initial letter is not in the appropriate foreign language.

Proposals should concentrate on a small number of products or product lines you wish the foreign organization to consider. To maximize your success, you should prepare separate proposals for each major product or service you are offering.

Follow-up communications

Be patient about your initial proposal. It's doubtful you will get a response in less than a month. By its very nature, international trade takes time, and establishing a relationship with an organization in a non-market country could take even longer than usual. However, once you have received a sentiment of interest the real work and fun begins.

Do keep in mind that establishing the relationship is the first order of business. Mistrust is spelled ''doom'' when care is not taken to know the parties involved and develop a respectful understanding.

Many firms pause at this point to introduce key team members to intercultural and background information about the target non-market country.

Firms intending to import from a non-market country

Most foreign organizations prefer to meet with prospective importers in person before proceeding to detailed commercial negotiations. Therefore, you should solicit an invitation to go to the country to get acquainted with the foreign companies and their product lines. The best time for your visit is at the same time major trade fairs are taking place in that country and other nearby countries. Make your trip serve multi-purposes.

Firms intending to export to a non-market country

One of the most popular and fruitful methods of presenting your company and its products is to hold a technical seminar. Remember, it is the higher technology that the non-market countries are interested in, so emphasize your most advanced products. Do keep in mind United States export control laws that limit the kind of technology you can discuss and offer for sale.

For these seminars, it is best that you use a team approach. That is, in addition to your best technical personnel who will discuss the technologies in detail, also have marketing and financial members of your staff attend.

NEGOTIATING THE CONTRACT

In spite of recent reforms, the economies of all non-market countries remain highly centralized; therefore you should expect negotiations to be bureaucratic, complicated, and slow-moving.

During presentations of products and services you must first convince end users of the effectiveness of your product. In some cases you might find the non-market ministry has called in scientific advisory groups who will have a great deal of influence about the technical aspects of the product. End users must then convince the appropriate central planning or economic commissions that there is a need for the product. Then, even though the end user initiated the negotiations, Foreign Trade Organizations might become involved in a wide range of contract matters concerning arbitration, shipping, financing, inspection, and packaging.

Of course, the time required to hammer out a contract will vary from country to country, but in general, for the bureaucracy to work their magic, you should be prepared for periodic breaks in the negotiations.

Technical negotiations

In general, companies are first invited to provide the technical characteristics of their products. Unfortunately, your initial description may not lead to immediate commercial negotiations, because the non-market countries have bigger eyes for modern technology than the purse required to pay for it. On the other hand, the organizations who review your technological presentations might not have the authority, experience or qualifications to conduct negotiations.

Obtaining modern technology is the name of the game for all countries, market or non-market. It must be assumed that your presentations will gain interest if for no other reason than to compare with what already exists in the reviewing country. Businessmen in non-market countries will take as much as you are willing to give away, on the other hand they also know that private companies cannot reveal proprietary technology for free. You should be up-front with your policies. They will understand so long as the policies are stated in advance and are clear.

Commercial negotiations

Don't assume that just because non-market countries have been operating with central planning and under socialistic rules that no one knows how to negotiate. On the contrary, hard-nosed, tough-minded businesspeople exist in every corner of the globe. Most negotiations with non-market countries can be characterized as requiring great patience and attention to detail. Americans are often ready to stop negotiations at the second digit after the whole dollar ($100.00), non-market negotiators are more likely to count to the fourth or fifth digit ($100.00000). The Chinese in particular have a reputation for taking their time. If you cannot leave your "Wall Street" clock behind and if you are not prepared to wait it out, then don't go.

CHINESE CASE STUDY

Before going to China, the youthful chief executive of a small but aggressive manufacturing company in Southern California had the impression his visit would be for only two or three days. After all, the Chinese, who had been out of the mainstream for more than a decade during the 1950s, would be less than astute in international business.

The truth is China has two thousand years of trading history, and by nature the Chinese people are capitalists, gamblers, and understand how to bargain. The People's Republic of China (PRC) has a surplus of foreign exchange, but as this American businessman quickly learned, they often prefer to countertrade (CT) instead of spending their hard currency.

More than two weeks later the young executive had learned the hard way the reality of China. He sat in the anteroom of the Shandong Branch of the China National Machinery and Equipment Import and Export Corporation. In front of him was a contract painstakingly developed by his staff. The American had come prepared for a joint venture in which his firm would provide the know-how to build a machine known to be at the cutting edge of high-technology. It was the technology the Chinese wanted, and he expected to come away with dollars up-front and a percentage of the profits.

Instead he was offered a buy-back, or as the Chinese call it, a *direct compensation arrangement*. By this method a factory in China would manufacture parts to be exported to the United States for assembly into the American machine.

The company President and his small staff team discussed this offer in private. The Americans were suspicious of the quality of the Chinese parts. They were also worried about how they would handle complicated engineering changes with officials who were five thousand miles away.

When they met again with their counterparts and declined the deal, pressing instead for hard currency, the Americans learned why "Mai Mai," the Mandarin word for business, literally means buy-sell.

The Chinese can be oblique, clever traders. They often use broad general language, leaving options open for themselves. In the early years after the Nixon visit in 1972, they may have had little understanding of profits and revenues and even less understanding of the concept of margins. In those days countertrade was lucrative. Now they price on the world market and cut a tough bargain. Getting "cheap" out of China is a thing of the past.

The interpreter suggested an alternative. Would they consider *trade compensation*? This calls for the foreign firm to sell one product and receive another in payment. The equivalent American term is "countertrade."

The young executive's visit to China represented a milestone for the American company. It was their first venture into international trade and they didn't want to go home empty-handed. So, he said, "why not?" Even though he had no idea how to handle trade compensation. But, before he signed the contract, he went back to school to learn about countertrade.

CONTRACTUAL CLAUSES

Most non-market negotiators interpret contracts literally, so you should exclude anything you can't live with, but argue strongly for inclusion of those things you find important, even though it may be considered so customary that it might not be included in other international contracts.

Often, you will be presented with standardized sales or purchase contracts from which you will revise, lengthen, and generally carve into the final document. In other words, everything is negotiable.

Payment

Currency is the major issue in doing business with non-market countries. Most will resist denominating contracts in foreign currencies, and very few of their currencies are freely convertible. Nevertheless, the central banks of most of these countries do have international banking relationships and do have foreign currency accounts. Some, like China, have established exchange rates and forward contracts in their currency which are available at the customary costs of about 5 percent for a 6-month contract and about 1.2 percent for a 1-month contract.

More and more contracts can be denominated in United States dollars and most sales and purchase transactions call for payment by irrevocable Letters of Credit (L/C) against presentation of sight draft and shipping documents.

Letters of Credit are negotiated on the non-market side by the central bank, usually headquartered in that country's capital city.

Delivery

For goods purchased from non-market countries, you should negotiate specific delivery dates with penalty clauses at a fixed percentage of the contract price for each week of delay up to a maximum, at which time you should retain the right to cancel the contract. Above all, be certain you have found a buyer before accepting such a contract (see how to countertrade in Chapter 9). As an exporter, you should expect that non-market negotiators will require the same.

Negotiations of extensions on delivery are not unusual; nevertheless, don't expect the non-market country to automatically concede. In fact, there are numerous cases where there has been unrelenting insistence that penalties be paid.

Force majeure

Force majeure is the title of a standard clause in contracts that exempts the parties from fulfillment of their obligations as a result of conditions such as earthquakes, floods, labor disputes, or war that are beyond their control.

Some non-market countries have, for ideological reasons, resisted attempts by foreign companies to define acts of God or labor unrest as acceptable instances of force majeure. Nevertheless, the willingness to do so is becoming more commonplace.

If you are exporting sophisticated equipment or technology always insist on a force majeure that takes into account approval by the United States government in the form of a validated license. Export licenses are not granted automatically, and will remain closely controlled for the long term.

Arbitration

Friendly negotiations between contracting parties remains the preferred method of settling disputes. In fact, many businesses perceive formal arbitration only slightly less an unfriendly act than settling in the courts and also believe that both undermine the development of long-term relationships. Nevertheless, an arbitration clause should be a part of every contract. The clause may specify arbitration before the non-market country's arbitration commission, if they have one, or before a third country organization. Typically Den Hague, Switzerland, Sweden, Canada or Singapore have been called out as third country negotiators.

Any of three arbitration rules are recommended:

1. Convention on the Recognition and Enforcement of Foreign Arbitral Awards (New York Convention).
2. United Nations Commission on International Trade Law.
3. Those of the International Chamber of Commerce.

Amicable dispute settlement between the two parties involved is often costly, time-consuming, and frustrating; nevertheless, it remains the best method. One way to resolve sticky issues is to adjust product or service performance of future contracts.

Claims, seller's guarantees and inspections

Clauses authorizing inspection and quality control before goods leave a non-market country can be negotiated, even though many of these countries insist that their own inspection system be used. For imports into these countries you should expect that products, particularly modern technology products, will be inspected prior to acceptance. Many non-market purchasing contracts will even insist on inspection, at-plant, prior to shipment.

Trademarks, invention, patents and copyrights

Protection for proprietary and patent rights is only a recent change. In the past, intellectual property belonged to the state. It was only as late as October 1983 that the GDR passed a Patent Act, and it was not until 1985 that China's patent law came into effect.

Today, most non-market countries are members of the World Organization for Intellectual Property and signatory to the most important international conventions linked to the United Nations.

For example, Yugoslavia is a signatory to the Paris Convention, the World Intellectual Property Organization (WIPO), the Madrid Agreement, the Nice Agreement, the Locarno Agreement and has signed the Patent Cooperation Treaty.

Some countries, like China, have bilateral agreements with their trading partners which require both parties to protect the patents, trademarks, and copyrights belonging to the citizens of the other.

Nevertheless, it is good business for companies to back up these changes by means of contractual assurances to protect technology and patents and limit its use in the country. Each country is different, so in addition to appropriate clauses in your contracts, you should research and register your intellectual property in each country where you intend to do business.

Shipping

By importing on an f.o.b. (free on board) basis and exporting c.i.f. (cost, insurance, and freight) many non-market countries are able to book transport in both directions through their state owned freight forwarders and ocean shipping lines. These lines have, in the past, operated principally on routes connecting socialist and developing nation trading partners, but it would be expected these would be expanded to more Western ports as that trade grows. Many of these lines have adopted intermodalism including roll-on/roll-off and container technology and are fully compatible with modern Western port facilities.

Not withstanding a non-market country's preference for its own ocean line, normalization of trade has brought with it many bilateral agreements which afford equal opportunity for United States flag vessels to carry sea cargoes to non-market ports. Facilities in non-market ports vary from some that have very inefficient cargo-handling procedures, such as China, to the most modern, such as the GDR's deep-sea port of Rostock.

Air carrier service has been increasing worldwide. Carriers such as Flying Tiger, United, and Northwest have scheduled services between many of these countries. Courier service is also provided by companies such as DHL, Airborne Express, and United Parcel Service.

Inland shipping is a different story. Foreign companies are generally not allowed to engage in freight forwarding within non-market countries. However, several large Western freight forwarders have formed joint ventures for land transportation and intermodal services.

Insurance

Insurance is also a centrally controlled function in non-market countries and that explains another reason why most prefer to buy on f.o.b. basis and sell c.i.f. In this way they preserve foreign exchange and retain the insurance business.

Insurance, whether arranged through a Western company or from the non-market organization, can provide ocean marine cargo coverage for both imports and exports, hull and voyage, and coverage against war risks. Coverage is also available for:

- Compensatory trade
- Goods processed through the country in question
- Engineering projects and the installation of foreign equipment
- Property insurance for joint ventures
- Liability for foreign exhibitions
- Accident for foreign nationals working in the countries.

The United States Overseas Private Insurance Corporation (OPIC) has signed agreements with many of the non-market countries to make ''Political Risk Insurance'' and other programs available for United States traders and investors.

Finance

The financial policies of most prominent non-market countries have been extremely conservative. They want currency, although in recent years some have willingly accepted export credits. Those that are members of the International Monetary Fund and the World Bank are taking advantage of those programs.

The United States Export-Import Bank has a continuing and current status of the financial policies of these countries and should be contacted early-on in any project effort.

MARKETING

As a result of your research, your market plan should include an analysis of the tactics necessary to reach the appropriate decision-making unit (DMUs) in your non-market country, whether it be at the consumer level or at the government level.

Advertising

Advertising under the socialist system was once considered inappropriate, but that position has been reconsidered and is now generally looked upon as a method of keeping the people informed about the products and services of a modern society.

Like many other functions in non-market countries, most advertising is also centrally controlled. Your message, including the acceptability of content and the product for the people of the country involved will be judged by the government approved organization. That does not mean that your work will be heavily censored, nor does it mean that you should resist doing business in this manner based on principal. In fact, many of these state organizations provide services that can assist you in cultural focusing, composition, and printing. The same channels for mass advertising exist in all non-market countries as in the West, and assuming the message is well thought-out and aimed, it can find its way into magazines, newspapers, television, and radio stations.

Ads on TV by western firms is a recent change in the Union of Soviet Socialist Republics. Arrangements can be made through Vneshtorg-Reklama.

Direct mail is a growing back-up method of advertising and personally informing potential clients. Most government advertising agencies keep stocks of addresses from all spheres of the economy.

Trade exhibits

International fairs continue to be the most important trade events. Several, such as the GDR's Leipzig Fair, and the Chinese Guangzhou Export Commodities Fair are held twice a year and are premier shows.

In recent years, in addition to the major industrial fairs, mini-fairs also are being held in most non-market countries.

Information about fairs in your target non-market country can be obtained through the United States Department of Commerce, the targeted foreign country, or the associated Chamber of Commerce.

Consultants

A large number of consulting firms have established offices to provide assistance to foreign firms seeking to expand their commercial relationships.

Because of the lack of accurate, up-to-date information about the latest policies and business methods, difficulty in delivering business proposals to the correct organization, and the high cost of maintaining offices in countries such as the Soviet Union and China, these consultants continue to be advantageous for many companies.

Most have the capability to make appointments with senior officials and assist in the negotiation of contracts. Needless to say, it is important to establish your own corporate identity in the eyes of your non-market counterparts and the selection of the appropriate consultant is vital in this regard. When used, the consultant's purpose should be only to bring the parties closer together more quickly, never to stand between the parties.

Science and technology

Besides general improvement of their economy, the goal of every non-market country is to systematically and comprehensively upgrade their scientific and technological establishment. There is an almost insatiable appetite for journals, seminars, and technical documents. In many cases these countries are interested in the purchasing of complete turnkey facilities.

Even though industrial know-how and modern technology ranks high in terms of release of foreign currency from central banks, many countries prefer to negotiate for counterpurchases and co-venture arrangements instead of an outright purchase.

U.S. REGULATIONS

Because of national security the United States has very stringent rules with regard to the exportation of goods, services, and know-how to non-market countries. Great care should be exercised before releasing documents, journals, or proprietary technology.

The following treatment is offered to help you comply with this most serious aspect of doing business with these countries. The penalties can be significant. Prison, large fines, or both can result from non-compliance. However, with the expansion of trade with non-market countries it is expected that these controls will be reviewed with the intent to increase the economic development opportunities and free enterprise through increased trade opportunities.

The Export Administration Act of 1979 (Act) lists three general guidelines for the use of export controls which are further explained in the Export Administration Regulations (Regs).

First, controls are applied to exports which according to the Act, "would make a significant contribution to the military potential of any other country or combination of countries which would prove detrimental to the national security of the United States."

Second, controls are used "where necessary to further signify the foreign policy of the United States or to fulfill its declared international obligations."

Third, controls are also used "where necessary to protect the domestic economy from the excessive drain of scarce materials and to reduce the serious inflationary impact on foreign demand."

The first step is to find out whether your shipment requires a validated license or whether you may export under one of the General License authorizations that are defined in Part 371 of the Regulations.

To comply with the controls regarding trade with non-market countries, you must refer to the Commodity Control List (CCL), Supplement No. 1 to para 399.1 of the Regulations, to find out if the commodity you intend to export is classified as falling into the "strategic," "short supply," "any other," or "unpublished" technical data category.

You probably will have to apply for a validated export license if your product falls into those four categories in the CCL:

Strategic: Commodities to any destination; or, in a few cases, only to a destination to which exports are restricted for national security purposes, e.g., certain communist destinations. These are considered significant to the design, manufacture, or utilization of military hardware.

Short supply: A product which is considered to be in short supply in the United States, is wanted abroad, and would cause an excessive drain on United States supplies and a serious inflationary impact on the United States economy.

Other: Any other commodity to a destination for which there are foreign policy concerns.

Unpublished: This refers to technical data or information to certain destinations related to design, production, or use of a product, that is not available to the public. It is not described in detail in books, magazines, or pamphlets nor is it taught in colleges or universities. It is know-how that a person will not release without charging for it.

If in doubt about licensing your product for export, contact your nearest Department of Commerce District Office.

TRAVEL

The most convenient way to enter the eastern European non-market countries, including the Soviet Union is through major European cities, e.g., Paris via Air France, Zurich via Swiss Air, Frankfurt via Lufthansa or on United States airlines such as United or Pan Am. To make your way to China, Northwest, United Airlines, Japan Airlines and CAAC, the Chinese airline, fly from the United States via Tokyo.

Entry/exit requirements

A valid passport and entry/exit business visas are required for travel in Russia and China and most other non-market countries. To obtain a visa you must take it in two steps:

Step one: Obtaining visa sponsorship. Each traveler including spouses must receive "visa support" from a sponsoring non-market organization. Send a telex to your sponsor and include a copy of the telex with your visa application. Applications can be obtained from consulates.

Step two: The application. Visas are issued by embassies and consulates in the United States only to business travelers who are invited by authorized non-market organizations. Prior to submission of your application, you must first make your travel arrangements, well in advance. Then submit the visa application along with three identical $1^1/_2$-inch by $1^3/_4$-inch photos and photocopies of pages two and three of your United States passport to your nearest consulate. Allow at least one month lead time before your day of departure. Remember you must leave on or before the date on your departure visa, therefore, if there is a chance that you will need more time, extend your dates early-on. It's easier to leave early than to stay longer than indicated. There are exceptions to this. For instance, visas for Yugoslavia are good for one year, and in Hungary you can get a visa on arrival at the airport.

Customs

Customs declarations are required by non-market countries upon entry and must be retained for presentation to the customs inspector upon departure. It is a record of the valuables in your possession when you enter the country. You might be asked to produce items such as cameras, watches, and electronic devices to prove you are re-exporting them. Certain matter, such as books, periodicals, films, and tapes, considered political in nature or as casting aspersions on the nation involved, may be confiscated.

Money matters

Remember, the currency of most non-market countries may not be brought into or taken out of the country, except for a few as souvenirs. Exchange your currency in small amounts at authorized exchange institutions (banks or exchange offices).

Credit cards such as MasterCard, American Express, Carte Blanche, Eurocard, and Visa are generally accepted as are traveler's checks.

Time

Keep in mind that time, as it is in any travel situation, is reckoned from Greenwich, England, and you should plan, in advance, the local time of your visits. Except for a brief period in the fall when Moscow switches back to standard time before the United States does, Moscow time is eight hours ahead of the United States Eastern Time.

Electrical current

In most countries you will find 110, 127, and 220 volts, A.C., 50-cycle power. Converters and transformers are needed for all electrical equipment, i.e., razors, hair dryers, etc., but be sure to buy the converter before you leave the United States—it is unlikely they will be readily available otherwise.

Holidays

See the Appendix for a listing of holidays for the country you are visiting.

Availability of Western goods

In recent years, a small number of Western goods have been placed on sale at "dollar stores" near tourist centers and major hotels, but to be on the safe side take along all personal hygiene supplies and medicines that might be needed. You should take particular care to take refills of prescriptions and if you wear glasses or contact lenses, take an extra pair along. Kodak film for both 35mm and 110 cameras is available in most large cities.

Telephones

The telephone system in most major cities is automatic dial for local calls and is relatively inexpensive. Be sure to obtain necessary telephone numbers from your business contacts before you leave since directories might not be available. As an example, in Russia the telephone directory is published once every seventeen years. Since in many hotels there is no central hotel switchboard, soon after your arrival in the country, find out your hotel room telephone number and give it to your contacts.

The quality of long distance connections is often poor, it can take as much as 8 to 12 hours to make a call. Compared to the United States, non-market prices are very expensive, so it is wise to have offices in the United States place calls to you or reverse the charges.

Health care

Check with the United States Public Health Service, Foreign Immunization Clinic, well in advance of your trip to determine what vaccinations and inoculations are required and/or recommended for travel at a particular time to the countries where you intend to do business. Take care of your health before and during your stay, but if you should become hospitalized, notify the American Embassy at once.

Miscellaneous

As a nice courtesy, but not essential initially, it is a good idea to take along sufficient business cards both in English and in the language of the country where you expect to do business.

Foreign trade practices

Use the Chinese Case Study given earlier as your model for doing business in non-market countries and beware that any method of doing business may be offered. Trade compensation, joint ventures, or offers to set up plants in a Special Economic Zone may be put on the table. Be ready to negotiate.

The next chapter will explain how the United States government trade negotiating and remedy system works.

12

Level the playing field

"BUT SMALL- AND MEDIUM-SIZED BUSINESSES CAN ONLY DO SO MUCH. THE government has to help!" you say.

You're right.

In Chapter 1 you were challenged to press on in spite of the regulated world of international trade. You were told it was your duty as a businessperson to defeat the barriers and obstacles by finding ways to accommodate, circumvent, or avoid. You were told that there was very little you could do about the interstate controls and structural barriers that "tilt" the playing field and prevent free trade. Therefore, to this point, the book has been about business tactics—the proactive things you can do to win the trade game.

MAKE YOUR "BEEF" KNOWN

However, when all else fails, even the most independent entrepreneurial American businessperson will squeal for help. In international business matters that recourse is the comfort that your government will stand behind you, if you've done your homework.

Competition in price, quality, delivery and service is something you deal with every day. It's the American way!

But where do you go to get relief on those matters beyond your control?

There are illegal or unfair practices by foreign companies that affect your ability to compete in your own domestic market. They are the same practices that can be used by domestic American firms except the remedies are more difficult because the parties involved are on the other side of an international border, in other sovereign lands. In addition there are barriers, visible and invisible, that block your competitiveness in foreign markets. In some cases your only remedy is to take action on your own, in the courts; however, in other situations your government will help.

This chapter explains the grounds, related to unfair trade, that warrant government intervention; who to contact to make your "beef" known; and how to present the proper documentation. It also explains the various organizations, both United States and international that are involved in monitoring and negotiating illegal or unfair trade practices and interstate controls.

Can you understand the United States trade remedy system? Yes, you bet you can!

This area of international trade can be complex because it includes such matters as balance of payments, the maneuverings of politicians, and negotiations between sovereign nations. Nevertheless, small- and medium-sized businesses can have an impact by making their positions known to the right people in government. In fact, the United States Congress has an office called the Trade Remedy Assistance Office to help smaller businesses. The address and telephone number is provided at the end of this chapter.

Do you need a lawyer to do something about these activities? The answer is yes and no. As the manager/leader of the business, your job is to keep your eye on the donut—to know where the business is going and how to keep the entire organization pulling together. It is impossible for anyone to know all the domestic, international and foreign laws involved in a given business project. You could probably research these matters as well as anyone, but your time is better spent looking after your business. An attorney or other consultant that specializes in international trade matters is a valuable resource and every business should include such a contact on its international trade team.

WHAT ARE THE BARRIERS?

One of the premises of this book, as capsulated in the thoughts of Richard Whalen and presented in Chapter 1 is that international trade is a "game." To reiterate, Whalen said, "the international struggle is actually a little understood contest [game] among governing elites testing relative ingenuity and skill in devising new political and economic arrangements to offset mounting social and cultural obstacles to productivity."

Whether we agree or disagree precisely with the premise, it is clear that nations do erect barriers, visible and invisible (Chapter 9) for many reasons. Each sovereign state, to one degree or another, controls the flow of funds, people, thought, and goods across its territorial boundaries and therefore, controls competition by foreign companies.

The application of appropriate measures to reduce or counter the effects of those barriers requires continual diagnosis by both private and public sectors. What are the interstate controls applied by various states?

The visibles

The visible tariffs are the ones you can see. They are the taxes or duties that you pay to import a product into another nation. They are written in the tariff schedule of each country and vary from nation to nation depending on the comparative advantage or disadvantage that nation might have in relation to other countries. Quotas and excise taxes are other kinds of visible barriers to free trade.

The invisibles

The invisible tariffs are those you can't find on the customs books. They include:

- Restrictions on government procurement
- Domestic subsidies
- Restrictive customs, procedures, and valuations
- Import licensing
- Technical standards
- Antidumping practices
- Control over foreign investment
- Discriminatory foreign exchange rates
- Manipulation of public health and administrative rules
- Limiting trade only through State Trading Companies (Non-market)
- Institutional processes such as multi-tiered distribution, language criteria, or overly rigid qualifications that penalize foreigners

---

An excellent discussion of barriers, in detail by country can be found in the book titled *Foreign Trade Barriers*. Order through your nearest government bookstore or the United States Government Printing Office, S/N 041-001-00326-6.

WHO CAN HELP?

There are many staff offices and governmental organizations waiting to help you. For instance, the Commerce Department's office on GATT related matters alone has as many as 25 – 30 people who investigate and write staff papers. The International Trade Commission has a staff of more than 450 to respond to problems brought to them by Commerce, Congress, and the President. You should become familiar with the following government organizations.

International Trade Administration (ITA)

As the trade unit of the United States Department of Commerce, ITA carries out the United States Government's nonagricultural foreign trade activities. It encourages and promotes United States exports of manufactured goods, administers United States statutes and agreements dealing with foreign trade, and advises on United States international trade and commercial policy.

U.S. Department of Agriculture (USDA)

Carries out the United States Government's agricultural trade activities. It encourages and promotes United States exports of agricultural products, administers United States statutes and agreements dealing with foreign trade of agricultural products, and advises on United States international agricultural trade policy.

U.S. International Trade Commission (USITC)

USITC, formerly the United States Tariff Commission, was created in 1916 by an Act of Congress. Its mandate was broadened and its name changed by the Trade Act of 1974. It is a quasi-judicial, independent, bipartisan fact-finding agency of the United States Government that studies the effects of tariffs and other restraints to trade on the United States economy. In its adjudicative role, the USITC makes determinations of injury and threat of injury by imports on United States industry. It conducts public hearings to assist in determining whether particular United States industries are injured or threatened with injury by dumping, export subsidies in other countries, or rapidly rising imports. It also studies the probable economic impact on specific United States industries of proposed reductions in United States tariffs and non-tariff barriers to imports. Its six members are appointed by the President with the advice and consent of the United States Senate for nine-year terms (six-year terms prior to 1974).

United States Trade Representative (USTR)

This is a cabinet-level official with the rank of Ambassador who is the principal advisor to the President on international trade policy. The United States Trade Representative is concerned with the expansion of United States exports, United States participation in GATT, commodity issues, East-West and North-South trade, and direct investment related to trade. As Chairman of the United States Trade Policy Committee, he or she is also the primary official responsible for United States participation in all international trade negotiations. Prior to the Trade Agreements Act of 1979, which created the Office of the United States Trade Representative, the comparable official was known as the President's Special Representative for Trade Negotiations (STR), a position first established by the Trade Expansion Act of 1982. Since the passage of Public Law 100-418 known as The Omnibus Trade and Competitiveness Act of 1988, some authority has been transferred from the President to the USTR to defend United States rights in international trade, particularly under section 301 of the Trade Act of 1974.

INTERNATIONAL ORGANIZATIONS

In addition to taking unfair trade matters directly (bilateral) to the culprit country under United States trade laws, several organizations exist that are constantly working on taking the "game" out of international trade.

The General Agreement on Tariffs and Trade (GATT)

This is a multilateral trade agreement, referred to as the "General Agreement" in this chapter, aimed at expanding international trade as a means of raising global welfare. GATT rules reduce uncertainty in connection with commercial transactions across national borders. Ninety-four countries accounting for approximately 80 percent of world trade are Contracting Parties to the General Agreement, and some 30 additional countries associated with it benefit from the application of its provisions to their trade. The designation "GATT" also refers to the organization headquartered at Geneva through which the General Agreement is enforced. This organization provides a framework within with multilateral negotiations—known as "Rounds"—are conducted to lower tariffs and other barriers to trade, and a consultative mechanism that may be invoked by governments seeking to protect their trade interests.

A *round*, in the context of the GATT, means a conference or continuing series of negotiations. The first five rounds are referred to as: Geneva 1947, Annecy (France) 1949, Torquay (England) 1951, Geneva 1956, and the Dillon Round (Geneva) 1960–1962. These five rounds focused principally on reducing tariff rates following procedures developed by the United States in negotiating its reciprocal trade agreements during the 1930s and early 1940s.

The sixth round, called the Kennedy Round 1964–1967 was again concerned with multilateral tariff cuts, but was also the first time that negotiations addressed certain non-tariff barriers.

The seventh GATT round—the Tokyo Round 1973–1979, in addition to tariff reductions, produced a series of detailed "codes" or rules (explained more fully later in this chapter) on the use of non-tariff measures by governments.

In September 1986, representatives of 92 countries met in Punta del Este, Uruguay to set the agenda for the eighth round called the Uruguay Round. During this multilateral negotiating period the members again took up "Standstill/rollback" of tariffs, but also began work on the new issues of trade in services, intellectual property rights, and trade-related investment.

The United Nations Conference on Trade and Development (UNCTAD)

This is a subsidiary organ of the United Nations General Assembly that seeks to promote international trade and particularly to focus international attention on economic measures that might accelerate Third World development. Now with 168 member States, it has become a principal instrument of the General Assembly for deliberation and negotiation in the field of international trade and related issues of international economic co-operation.

Conferences are held every four years in different capitals of member States. The first Conference was convened (UNCTAD-I) in Geneva in 1964. Between conferences, the continuing work of the organization is carried out by the Trade and Development Board together with its various committees and subsidiary bodies.

This organization's primary responsibility is the negotiation and re-negotiation of international commodity agreements; therefore, additional conferences are convened for this purpose as required.

World Intellectual Property Organization (WIPO)

A specialized agency of the United Nations system that seeks to promote international cooperation in the protection of intellectual property. WIPO administers the International Union for the Protection of Industrial Property (the "Paris Union"), which was founded in 1883 to reduce discrimination in national patent practices; the International Union for the Protection of Literary and Artistic Works (the "Bern Union"), which was founded in 1886 to provide analogous functions with respect to copyrights; and other treaties, conventions and agreements concerned with intellectual property.

The Multi-Fibre Arrangement

The Multi-Fibre Arrangement (MFA) is an international agreement originally designed to expand trade in textile products, particularly exports from developing countries. Over its history the MFA has developed into an arrangement sanctioning bilateral quotas and restrictions on textile imports. Its informal origin, in 1961, was as a Short-Term Arrangement. However, in 1974 the United States, along with 42 other countries formalized it by signing and putting into effect a three-year agreement. Subsequently there have been three extensions.

The latest extension, in 1986, called MFA IV expanded coverage to include virtually all known and conceivable fibers that may be used to manufacture textile or apparel products.

RECOURSE

There are only two levels of recourse. Legal disputes related to competition can arise company-to-company, or industry-to-government. Industry-to-government must eventually have enough substance to end up government-to-government to be handled either bi-laterally or multi-laterally.

Company-to-company

At the outset you should understand that commercial law having to do with the settling of transactional disputes between companies over such things as non-payment, quality, delivery, or contracts is beyond the scope of this book. Company-to-company legal disputes are yours to fight.

Transaction disputes

In this regard, you should be aware that there is no body of international law to which all foreign trade is subject. International law, at best, is a collection of treaties referred to as Friendship, Commerce and Navigation (FCN), which are conventions and agreements between nations that have, more or less, the force of law.

Don't be confused by the existence of the World Court at the Hague and the International Court of Justice, the principal judicial organ of the United Nations. These courts apply only to disputes between sovereign nations, not between private citizens or companies.

In reality, each country has its own body of law. Most are based in the three major bodies of law—Common, Code, or Islamic—but there are many other minor codes of law found in various smaller states. *Common law* is derived from English law and found in England, United States, Canada and other countries that have come under the influence of England. *Code law* is derived from Roman law and is found in the majority of all other nations of the world. *Islamic law* (Shari'a), as its name implies, is found in those Muslim nations who practice the teachings of the prophet Muhammad. Common law has its basis in tradition, past practices, and legal precedent. Code law is, in general, based on a system of written rules (codes) of law. Islamic law gains its basis in historical sources. In spite of their apparent complexities, the three legal systems are not dramatically different insofar as business is concerned.

Litigation between citizens of different countries is expensive, frustrating and takes far longer than any other legal matter. Most experienced international businesspeople suggest these three steps: (1) placate the injured party; (2) if that doesn't work, arbitrate, and (3) only when every other method has failed, litigate. The best advice is to always seek a settlement through arbitration, rather than sue. Always include a jurisdictional and arbitration clause in contracts.

Beyond the transaction

Situations not related to a transaction, but which affect your ability to compete on an international basis include patent, copyright, or trademark infringement, violations of United States antitrust laws, misappropriation of trade secrets, and false advertising. It if affects only your own company and your opportunity to compete in your own country, then you are on your own to bring suit under United States commercial laws just as you would if it were another domestic company.

If the theft of intellectual rights or false advertising affects your ability to compete in another country, you are obligated to bring suit in that country.

Industry-to-government

It is unlikely that your government will help you fight your individual legal battles with another government. However, they often will assist with those things that affect an entire industry. And most of those kinds of problems are brought before government bodies by industry associations. That is not to say that your individual problem cannot be brought before one of the government organizations. It just means that you should have exhausted other means and have built a very strong case.

If the problem affects other companies or an entire industry then your government might become involved. The only way this can be known is if you bring your problem to the attention of the Commerce Department and the ITC.

If the Commerce Department's preliminary investigation shows ''less than fair value,'' then there are two directions to go. If it is a *defensive* matter, i.e., it is related to imports, the matter is passed to the United States International Trade Commission for investigation ''of injury'' and appropriate action. If it is an *offensive* matter, that is it relates to exports, the matter goes to the United States International Trade Representative for negotiation, and if that fails the ITC can take counter-action.

SEEKING REMEDIES

At the outset you should understand that the government-to-government remedy system is cumbersome and takes time. This is primarily because, as a member of the General Agreement, the United States is obligated, with exceptions, to provide advance written notice of impending unilateral action and give the parties an opportunity for consultation. This is often the case even though action could be taken under existing United States laws.

Before explaining here the specific actions available, a review of how the current remedy system came about is in order.

Recall in the prolog to this book there was a discussion of the disastrous period of trade history between World War I and World War II when nations used cut-throat, beggar-thy-neighbor policies to protect their industries and the welfare of their people. The United States even got into that dangerous business when the Smoot-Hawley Act of 1930 was passed. That law, with an average rate of 53 percent on dutiable imports, provoked retaliatory tariff increases by other countries and the result was a worldwide round of ever increasing escalation of trade restrictions. Chaos is the only word for the result. It led to a sharp decline in world trade and the Great Depression. Some say it was the primary cause of World War II.

Sanity was restored when Secretary of State Cordell Hull conceived of the Reciprocal Trade Agreements Act of 1934. Under that act, the President of the United States was given authority to enter into reciprocal trade agreements with foreign governments to reduce tariffs without the necessity of ratification by the Senate. This Act also incorporated the Most-Favored-Nation (MFN) principle, which has served as the cornerstone of the United States trading system ever since. Under the MFN principle, the benefits of any bilateral tariff reductions negotiated by the United States are expended to all MFN countries. The idea is that by making such concessions other nations might give similar treatment to United States exports in their country. Eventually this bilateral approach developed into the multilateral method of trade negotiations.

One result of World War II, and possibly the only important notion, was that economic cooperation was essential to maintain peace. With this truism in mind, the United States, after consultation with the British, proposed an international trade organization to expand world trade and employment.

The long and short of it was that even though the United States thought of the idea, Congress refused, in 1950, to ratify the proposed International Trade Organization (ITO), also known as the Havana Charter, which was to be formed as a Specialized Agency of the United Nations system, similar to the International Monetary Fund and the World Bank. However, it so happened that during one point of the three years of negotiations, the drafters of the ITO saw a need for another organization which would keep the records of the various tariff negotiations so that one concession would not be undercut by other, newer trade measures. They called this the General Agreement and it was never intended to become the international trade organization. However, over time the GATT assumed, as a result of a series of amendments, the commercial policy provisions of the Havana Charter and became the founding document for the international trade institution. For the United States, the GATT came into existence as an executive agreement, which, under the United States Constitution, does not require Senate ratification.

GATT was signed in 1947, as an interim agreement, and since then it has been the internationally recognized institution concerned with international trade negotiations. The Interim Commission of the ITO (ICITO), which was established to facilitate the creation of the ITO, subsequently became the GATT Secretariat. The guiding principles of the GATT include:

- The Most-Favored-Nation (MFN) clause (Article I of the General Agreement) which became its cornerstone.
- Reliance on tariffs as opposed to other commercial measures (e.g., quantitative restrictions).
- Provision of a stable and predictable basis for trade through negotiated "bindings" of tariffs at fixed maximum levels.
- Settlements of disputes through consultation, conciliation and, as a last resort, dispute settlement procedures.
- Part Four of the General Agreement (Articles XXXVI, XXXVII, and XXXVIII), adopted in 1965, contains explicit commitments to ensure appropriate recognition of the development needs of developing country Contracting Parties.

Contracting parties to the GATT agree to abide by these basic principles. However, the GATT recognizes that it might be necessary in certain circumstances to suspend some of the rules. Believing it unrealistic to expect every country to completely open its economy to foreign competition, a provision is included that allows countries to temporarily, but legally depart from the rules and establish quotas for balance-of-payments or infant industry reasons.

THE LAWS AND THEIR APPLICATION

Most international trade agreements (principally the GATT rules and codes) provide for a variety of procedures that allow a signatory to take protective or compensatory measures when there is unfair competitive trade practices that cause or threaten injury to its commercial or other interests.

In the same sense, there are corresponding United States domestic laws—some antedating the international agreement, some enacted to implement the foreign agreement. Therefore, more than one law or rule often applies.

Your first step is to specifically identify the illegal or unfair activity in terms of its injury to your firm and if possible, its possible injury to your industry. In every instance, proof must be made that the injury is "material."

Material injury is defined as harm that is not inconsequential, immaterial, or unimportant.

The second step is to determine if the activity is an import which is affecting your domestic market or an activity which is affecting your ability to export/do business overseas.

Having done that, link the injury to one or more existing United States laws, Friendship, Commerce and Navigation (FCN) agreements, or GATT rules you feel have been violated. In many cases more than one law, agreement, or rule will apply. You might not know all the legal implications, unilateral trade agreements and rules that are applicable, and you need not—that is what government investigators are paid to do.

Next, submit your grievance, in the form of a letter of petition for relief to your congressman, the ITC, and The Secretary of Commerce. From a professional point of view, make certain you send copies of each letter to the other. Even though everyone will want to help, no one likes surprises or to be put in a squeeze between government agencies. Figure 12-1 shows graphically the procedure.

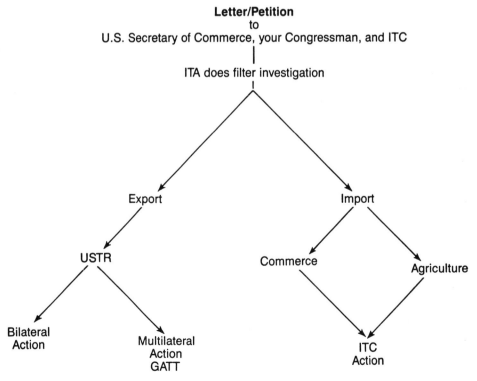

Fig. 12-1   Grievance submission procedure.

RECOURSE FROM UNFAIR IMPORTING PRACTICES

Unfair imports are products that enter the Commerce of the United States and unfairly affect domestic business. Remedies for these situations come under the purview of the International Trade Administration (ITA) of the Department of Commerce and the United States International Trade Commission (ITC). Petitions on these matters should be filed simultaneously with both agencies.

Selective export subsidies (countervailing duty)

Suppose a subsidy is provided by a foreign country, or person or organization of that country to certain merchandise which is then exported to the United States. If the result of the subsidy can be shown to materially injure or threaten material injury by reason of imports of that merchandise into the United States, you may ask for help from the United States Government. You may also seek assistance if you believe the introduction of the merchandise might also materially threaten the establishment of an industry for that merchandise.

Applicable laws. Three separate provisions of United States law are operative in this case:

The first applies to imports from countries that are members of GATT. In these cases the law that applies is Title VII, Subtitle A of the Tariff Act of 1930, as added by the Trade Agreements Act of 1979 (19 U.S.C. 1671) and amended by the Trade and Tariff Act of 1984, Pub. 2. 98-573. This law requires a test for injury and various other procedural steps before a remedy is applied.

The second provision is for all other countries who do not accept GATT responsibilities. For these the law that applies is Section 303 of the Tariff Act of 1930 (19 U.S.C. 1303), as amended by the Trade Agreements Act of 1979. This older law does not require the test for injury before action is taken.

The third is P.L. 100-418 (The Omnibus Trade and Competitiveness Act of 1988) which expands earlier laws by providing for the monitoring of imports of *"downstream" products*, (products that contain the components subject to a countervailing order or other remedy).

The GATT rules that apply are Articles VI, XVI and XXIII.

Remedy. A countervailing United States duty equal to the foreign subsidy on the articles in question would cancel out the advantage of that merchandise. This is the remedy that can be imposed by the United States International Trade Commission after determination of the existence and amount of subsidization, and an injury test (in those cases where required). The remedies authorized individually or in conjunction with any other are: (1) increase tariff duty, (2) impose a tariff-rate quota, or (3) impose a quantitative restriction. For major exporting countries "orderly marketing agreements" may be negotiated either bilaterally or through multilateral action.

Antidumping practices

This is the practice of penetrating United States markets to gain rapid market share through the technique of pricing goods under fair value such as below the price charged for the same or like product in their home market or below its cost of production. Again, material injury or threat of material injury must be established.

Applicable laws. The United States laws that apply in this case are Title VII, Subtitle B of the Tariff Act of 1930, as added by the Trade Agreements Act of 1979 (19 U.S.C. 1673–1673i) and P.L. 100-418.

GATT deals with this matter under Article VI (Antidumping and Countervailing Duties) and in the more detailed "GATT Agreement on Implementation of Article VI" known as the Antidumping Code which was formulated in 1979.

Remedy. Antidumping investigations are carried out simultaneously by the ITA to determine "less than fair value" and if so, the margin of dumping, and the U.S.I.T.C. to determine whether the injury criteria have been met. If both tests are met, an antidumping order is automatically issued by the United States International Trade Commission (ITC) which requires antidumping duties be paid by the offender and remains in effect as long as the product continues to be dumped.

Impact of P.L. 100-418. Expands earlier laws by providing for the monitoring of imports of "downstream" products (products that contain the components subject to an antidumping order or other remedy).

Investigations of costs of production

Assume you manufacture a product for x amount of dollars and country A manufactures and imports that same product into the United States for $x - 50$ percent. In this situation, the foreign manufacturer's price is not artificial, as was the case with dumping, but by reason of wages and other factors of production the costs of production cause material injury to your company in the United States market.

Applicable laws. In this case, the United States law that applies is Section 336 (a) of the Tariff Act of 1930.

Remedy. The ITC can increase the statutory rate of duty on the imported item as necessary to equalize the differences in costs of production (not to exceed certain statutory limits).

Illegal practices

Earlier in the chapter there was mention of the action necessary to remedy such matters as: patent, copyright, trademark infringement, violation of antitrust laws, misappropriation of trade secrets, and false advertising. In addition to taking your own legal action you may petition the United States Government for assistance.

An example of a recent problem were allegations that certain foreign companies were infringing on the patents of Erasable Programmable Read-only memories (EPROM) made by a United States domestic company. That company brought the matter to the ITC under Section 337 of the Tariff Act of 1930 and it subsequently has been brought before an administrative law judge for determination.

Applicable laws. The above cited Section 337 of the United States code declares unlawful unfair methods of competition and unfair acts in the importation of articles into the United States, the effect of which is (1) to destroy or substantially injure an industry, or (2) to prevent the establishment of such an industry, or (3) to restrain or monopolize trade and commerce in the United States. With the enactment of P.L. 100-418, Section 337 is enhanced from the point of view of injured firms.

Remedy. The ITC's remedy is to direct that the foreign articles be excluded from entry into the United States. Any party that persists in violation of the commission's order could be subject to a civil penalty of up to the greater of $10,000 per day or the domestic value of the articles entered or sold on such day in violation of the order. The majority of these cases have alleged unfair importation of an article using technology of a valid, unexpired United States patent.

Impact of P.L. 100-418. The section of this law which applies to intellectual property rights protection approaches the problem in three ways: (1) It makes it easier for firms to obtain remedies against pirated products imported into the United States. (2) Defines the lack of intellectual property rights protection as an unfair trade practice under Section 337. (3) Allows patent holders to seek damages from violators in federal court.

Investigations of injury from increased imports

This is the case where articles are imported in such increased quantities as to be a substantial cause of serious injury, or the threat thereof, to the domestic industry producing an article like or directly competitive with the imported article.

Applicable laws. The United States laws that apply in this case are Section 201 (b) of the Trade Act of 1974 (19 U.S.C. 2251 (b)), and P.L. 100-418 (The Omnibus Trade and Competitiveness Act of 1988).

Remedy. If the Commission makes an affirmative injury determination and recommends import relief, the President may impose (1) higher tariffs, (2) a tariff-rate quota system, (3) quantitative restrictions, or (4) some combination thereof.

Impact of P.L. 100-418. Prior to enactment, in 1988 of P.L. 100-418, the purpose of import relief under Section 201, as amended, was "to prevent or remedy serious injury or the treatment thereof" to an industry and "to facilitate the orderly adjustment to new competitive conditions."

The new law addresses responsiveness on the part of the ITC and the President to enact relief to the injured firms by setting or tightening deadlines to act. It also strengthens and focuses on the adjustment objective by defining "positive adjustment" as the encouragement of industries to submit a plan with their petition for remedy that outlines the steps they are prepared to make. These positive adjustments are:

1. Explanation of how the affected domestic industry will compete after the relief has been terminated or the transfer of resources to other productive endeavors.
2. Methods of transferring dislocated workers to productive pursuits.

General investigations of trade and tariff matters

Think of the situation where you believe and have evidence that a United States Customs law or the relationship between the United States and a foreign country relative to tariffs, bounties, preferential treatment and almost any other trade matter has gone amuck and you want it investigated by the International Trade Commission.

Applicable laws. The United States law under which the ITC conducts investigations is Section 332 of the Tariff Act of 1930 (19 U.S.C. 1332).

Remedy. This is purely an investigative action by the ITC. You should not expect any specific action; however, the result could be action in conjunction with several of the other laws explained in this or the next part.

Escape clause/import relief

As a rule the *escape clause* is a provision included in all international trade agreements. It permits a party to the agreement to withdraw or modify a previously agreed trade concession.

In this instance you are aware that the United States and another nation has incurred an obligation as signatories to GATT or other agreement; nevertheless, products of a company(s) from that nation are causing "substantial cause of serious" injury or threat of injury to producers of a like or directly competitive product.

Applicable laws. Since 1975, the United States law that pertains to these cases are Sections 201-203 of the Trade Act of 1974 (19 U.S.C. 2251-2253).

This procedure involves a determination by the U.S.I.T.C. with regard to injury or threat of injury followed by remedial action as recommended to the President by the ITC, his own remedial action, or no action at all. Should the President elect not to act, Congress can enact by joint resolution (if done within 90 days) using what is known as "fast-track" procedures.

The GATT article that applies is XIX (Emergency Action on Imports of Particular Products).

Remedy. The prerequisite for action under the "escape clause" is advance written notice to the culprit country and the opportunity for consultation. Three unilateral remedies may be taken: imposition of an increased tariff duty; imposition of tariff-rate quotas; or modification of quantitative restrictions. An orderly market agreement also can be negotiated. Import relief provided under this procedure generally may not remain in effect more than five years and must be scaled down after the third year.

Investigations of market disruption by imports from communist countries

In this instance you have determined that an import from a communist country is causing a distortion of the market with respect to a domestically produced article. In this case, the term "communist country" means any country dominated or controlled by communism.

Applicable law. The United States law that applies is Section 406 (a) of the Trade Act of 1974 (19 U.S.C. 2436 (a)).

Remedy. The International Trade Commission (ITC) conducts an investigation at the request of the President or the U.S.T.R., upon resolution of either the Committee on Ways and Means of the House of Representatives or the Committee on Finance of the Senate, on its own motion, or upon the filing of a petition by an entity, including a trade association, firm, certified or recognized union, or group of workers, which represent an industry. If the Commission finds that market disruption exists it must recommend appropriate relief. Such relief can range from an increase in, or imposition of, rates of duty to quantitative restrictions.

Investigations under the Agricultural Adjustment Act

This is a situation in which the Secretary of Agriculture believes an article or articles are being imported into the United States under such conditions and in such quantities as to render ineffective, or materially interfere with, any program or operation undertaken by the United States Department of Agriculture (USDA), or to reduce substantially the amount of any product being processed in the United States from any agricultural commodity covered by a USDA program.

Applicable law. Section 22 of the Agricultural Act, (7 U.S.C. 624).

Remedy. The President without waiting for the results of the ITC investigation may impose either an import quota or an appropriate import fee (not in excess of 50 percent ad valorem) to alleviate the difficulty.

RELIEF FROM EXPORT BARRIERS

Export barriers are interstate (government) controls that impede, block or otherwise restrict your ability to fairly compete in a foreign market. The remedies for these activities come under the purview of the United States Trade Representative (USTR). They are the activities that must be negotiated under GATT or other trade agreements.

Enforcement of U.S. trade-agreements rights and response to foreign unfair trade practices

You expect companies from other countries to respect bilateral or multilateral agreements entered into in good faith. Suppose however, in attempting to market in a foreign country you find a trade practice that does not give the same fair business opportunity that the United States provides under the same agreement. You want the trade agreement enforced or a United States response to that foreign practice which restricts or discriminates.

Applicable laws. Chapter 1 of Title III of the Trade Act of 1974 (19 U.S.C. 2411), as revised by Title IX of the Trade Agreements Act of 1979; Section 301 as well as 303-306 of the Trade Act of 1974 as amended by the Trade Agreement Act of 1979, and P.L. 100-418 also apply.

GATT Articles VI (Antidumping), XVI (Subsidies/Countervailing), and XXIII (Nullification or Impairment) offer a vehicle for pursuing remedial action with respect to measures by another country.

Remedy. Under these provisions the president, upon determining a foreign violation, shall take action as appropriate to enforce such United States rights or eliminate unfair foreign practices.

The President of the United States can take action on his own motivation, or any interested person may file a petition with the USTR requesting the President to do something about the violation. The USTR reviews the allegations of the petition and, not later than 45 days after the date on which he received the petition determines whether to initiate an investigation with the aim of formulating a recommendation for the President.

The action may be applied to all countries or solely against the products or services of the specific foreign country involved. The President may suspend or withdraw trade-agreement concessions for the country involved or impose duties and other restrictions on imports of, and fees and restrictions on the services of, the country involved. The USTR may request the views of the ITC regarding the probable impact on the United States economy if action is taken.

Impact of P.L. 100-418
(The Omnibus Trade and Competitiveness Act of 1988)

In the recent past, some critics of United States trade policy have charged that the President had not used his Section 301 authority sufficiently and that our trade partners had been able to block United States exports with impunity.

As a result, Public Law 100-418, in part, was designed to increase the use of Section 301, i.e., go on the offensive to open foreign markets by:

- Transferring responsibility from the President to the USTR the authority to determine if a foreign trade practice meets Section 301 criteria for action, thereby reducing the influence of non-trade Presidential advisors. (Inasmuch as the USTR is a Presidential appointee, these matters remain subject to the President's direction).

- Limiting the discretion of the Administration by requiring Section 301 investigations of certain "unjustifiable practices" and countries and by setting time limits on action.

- Adding "Super-301," which is the part that established "priority practices" and "priority foreign countries" for action.

- Expanding the coverage of unreasonable trade practices. This section expands the coverage of Section 301 to include certain foreign government practices.

Unjustifiable trade practices. Under this section of the new law (P.L. 100-418) the USTR must take measures against a country violating a United States right established under a treaty, such as GATT, or conducting other "unjustifiable" trade practices. Such measures would have to be equal in value to the burden of the foreign practice and would end after four years, unless the United States industry petitioned successfully for continuation.

Super-301. This new portion of P.L. 100-418 expands the coverage of 301 to include certain government and business practices. Super-301 refers to the provision whereby the USTR may initiate priority action against "priority practices" and "priority foreign countries." A priority practice is one that if eliminated could result in the greatest increase in United States exports. This new approach permits "generic" or "bundling" of foreign practices for purposes of applying a remedy.

During the investigation into a priority country, the USTR must negotiate over a three-year period with that country for the reduction of its practice. If during that period a successful agreement is negotiated the case is terminated, if not retaliation may be taken.

Unreasonable trade practices. P.L. 100-418 also specifies certain "unreasonable" trade practices and therefore subject to Section 301 action:

- Export targeting. A government measure that gives a domestic industry an unfair competitive advantage in trade.
- Denial of worker rights such as collective bargaining and the right to strike.
- Denial of market opportunities because of foreign government toleration of anti-competitive activities.

THE TOKYO ROUND CODES

A major outcome of the sixth round of GATT multilateral negotiations was a set of six codes for non-tariff measures and one agreement on trade in civil aircraft. The codes established new rules on government procurement, technical barriers to trade, customs valuation, import licensing, antidumping, and subsidies and countervailing measures.

Domestic subsidies

Ship building is an industry which provides an example of how subsidies are used to protect a domestic industry. As an example, Japan, Brazil, and Denmark provide low-cost financing for a substantial portion of a ship's cost, repayable over a long period of time at a low interest rate. West Germany, Spain, and the Netherlands, on the other hand, prefer direct construction subsidies to shipyards for a percentage of the contract price.

Applicable laws. Section 301 of the Trade Act of 1974 as amended by the Trade Agreement Act of 1979, and P.L. 100-814. The GATT Agreement on Subsidies and Countervailing Measures is the international ruling arrangement.

Remedy. The United States government takes up claims on the behalf of private parties those practices which are inconsistent with the GATT Code. In addition, Section 301 and P.L. 100-418 gives the right to a private party to file a formal petition with the USTR against any act, policy, or practice of a foreign government that is inconsistent under the Code. If the results of dispute settlement consultations required by the Code are unsatisfactory, the President may impose a range of options including import restrictions, countervailing duty, fees, or restrictions.

Restrictive customs procedures and valuations

The Customs Valuation Code addresses the rules and procedures used by national customs authorities to determine a value for goods entering their jurisdiction. Prior to the Tokyo Round, determinations of value varied greatly between countries, as customs officials used different national laws and regulations. Dutiable values were in some case substantially inflated through the use of arbitrary methods. The code specifies that transaction value, the price actually paid or payable for the goods, is the basic value to be used for customs purposes. Adjustments are allowed in specific cases where price actually paid does not cover all costs. A sequence of other valuation methods are provided when transaction value is unknown.

Applicable laws. The Agreement on Implementation of Article VII of the GATT (Customs Valuation Agreement); Section 310 of the Trade Act of 1974, as amended by Section 901 of the Trade Agreements Act of 1979; and P.L. 100-418.

Remedy. The President after due consultations, and recommendations from the USTR may impose import restrictions on the products of the foreign country involved in the case.

Import licensing

Various countries maintain licensing systems under which importers are required to obtain a license before they can import a particular product into the country. The Agreement on Import Licensing Procedures (The Licensing Code) recognizes that there are acceptable uses for licensing procedures. It therefore deals only with the procedures and not with the existence or extent of such systems. The intent is to bring visibility (make information more open), simplify, clarify, and minimize the administrative requirements.

Applicable laws. The GATT Agreement on Import Licensing Procedures (The Licensing Code); Section 310 of the Trade Act of 1974, as amended by Section 901 of the Trade Agreements Act of 1979; and P.L. 100-418.

Remedy. The President after due consultations, and recommendations from the USTR may impose import restrictions on the products of the foreign country involved in the case.

Technical standards

Differences between nations' standards, testing and approval procedures, and certification systems often have hindered the free flow of international commerce. The GATT Agreement on Technical Barriers to Trade (The Standards Code) does not attempt to create standards for individual products, nor to set up specific testing and certification systems. Rather it is designed to eliminate the use of standards and certification systems as a barrier to international trade by establishing a framework of common rules. The Code applies to all products, both agricultural and industrial. It does not apply to standards involving services; technical specifications included in government procurement contracts; nor standards established by private companies for their own use.

Applicable laws. The GATT Agreement on Technical Barriers to Trade (The Standards Code); Section 310 of the Trade Act of 1974, as amended by Section 901 of the Trade Agreements Act of 1979; and P.L. 100-418.

Remedy. On the behalf of private parties, the United States government takes up claims of practices which are inconsistent with the GATT Code. In addition, Section 301 and P.L. 100-418 gives the right to a private party to file a formal petition with the USTR against any act, policy, or practice of a foreign government that is inconsistent under the Code. If the results of dispute settlements consultations required by the Code are unsatisfactory, the President is required to take all appropriate action to obtain elimination of the policy or practice including import restrictions on the products of the foreign country involved in the case.

Government procurement

Prior to the Tokyo Round, government purchases were for the most part closed to foreign suppliers. The GATT Government Procurement Code seeks to open up these transactions to international competition by obligating signatories not to discriminate against the products of other signatories in purchases of goods by government entities (agencies) that are covered by the Code. The Code only applies to specified federal agencies, not state, provincial or other local agencies, and to purchases valued above approximately $150,000. It does not apply to service or construction contracts.

Applicable laws. GATT Agreement on Government Procurement; Title III, section 901 of the Trade Agreements Act of 1979; Section 301 of the Trade Act of 1974; and P.L. 100-418.

Remedy. Even though the Agreement can only be invoked by a signatory government, a private party can informally raise, with both the USTR and the Department of Commerce, a foreign practice that is or appears to be inconsistent with the agreement. In addition, under Section 301 and 901 a private party has the right to file a formal petition. The United States has always taken up such claims on behalf of private parties. The President, after due consultations and recommendations from the USTR may suspend trade agreement concessions and impose duties or fees and restrictions on the goods and services of the foreign country.

Antidumping

The implications of this Code were discussed earlier under the heading "Imports that Affect United States Domestic Business."

Trade in civil aircraft

The difference between the Agreement on Trade in Civil Aircraft (The Aircraft Agreement) and other Codes is that it is the first multilateral sectorial trading arrangement designed to expand upon trade liberalization as provided in the general GATT trading rules. This Code establishes rules on both tariff and non-tariff measures. Although military aircraft are excluded from agreement coverage, the signatories agree to eliminate tariffs on over 95 percent of the trade in civil aircraft including parts, components, assemblies of civil aircraft, and ground flight simulators. In addition, signatories agreed to apply the Standards Code to operating and maintenance procedures.

Applicable laws. GATT Agreement on Trade in Civil Aircraft (The Aircraft Agreement); Title III, section 901 of the Trade Agreements Act of 1979; Section 301 of the Trade Act of 1974; and P.L. 100-418.

Remedy. The President after due consultations, and recommendations from the USTR may impose import restrictions on the products of the foreign country involved in the case.

REMEDIES NOT DIRECTLY RELATED TO THE PRIVATE SECTOR

Of interest to private companies and industry in general are a number of matters that have a growing impact on the United States economy as a whole. This section reviews the laws that apply and the actions available to the President and other sectors of the government to obtain relief from these practices.

Discriminatory foreign exchange rates

Prior to 1985, the United States had a laissez-faire policy toward the dollar, i.e., let the market determine exchange rate values. However, relative currency fluctuations are widely viewed as an important factor in trade flows and a major cause of the large current account deficit. As a result, stability has become a major policy goal.

Since 1985, the administration has been coordinating policies with other countries multilaterally and negotiating bilaterally with Taiwan and South Korea regarding their exchange rates.

Applicable laws. P.L. 100-418 requires that negotiations be continued and places reporting requirements on the Executive Branch.

Remedies. This new law affects the conduct of United States exchange rate policy in the following ways:

- *Multilateral Negotiations.* The President of the United States is required to achieve better macroeconomic policy coordination, more appropriate current account balances and exchange rates, and to develop a program to improve existing mechanisms for coordination and long-term exchange rate stability through negotiation.

- *Bilateral Negotiations.* The Secretary of the Treasury is required to determine annually, in consultation with the International Monetary Fund (IMF): (a) which countries manipulate their exchange rates relative to the dollar; and (b) initiate bilateral negotiations with those countries that do manipulate, have large global current account surpluses, and have significant bilateral trade surpluses with the United States.

Imports threatening national security

This activity needs little explanation. There is a remedy for those goods introduced into the United States which threaten national security.

Applicable laws. Section 232 of the Trade Expansion Act of 1962 (Safeguarding National Security); 19 U.S.C. 1862; P.L. 100-418; and GATT Article XXII (Security Exceptions) all apply.

Remedy. Under the GATT agreement any signatory may take ''any action which it considers necessary for the protection of its essential security interests.'' United States law requires the President, after investigation and advice by the Secretary of Commerce, to ''take such action, and for such time, as he deems necessary to adjust the imports'' of a product so that they will not threaten to impair the national security. Specific action under 301 has been by means of bilateral Voluntary Restraint Agreements (VRA).

Impact of P.L. 100-418. Shortens the time limit currently allowed the Secretary of Commerce's investigation under Section 232 from one year to 270 days (about 9 months). It also enhances the role of the Secretary of Defense.

Controls over foreign investment

There has been an explosion of foreign direct investment in United States businesses and assets since 1980 and that sharp increase has become a major concern of the Congress, particularly as it affects national security interests. Previous legislation barred foreign direct investment in such industries as maritime, aircraft, banking, resources and power. Generally, those sectors are closed; however, certain domestic production including availability of human resources, products, technology, materials, and other supplies and services have been somewhat overlooked.

Applicable laws. P.L. 100-418 extends the term national security and interprets it broadly without limitation to a particular industry.

Remedy. Given credible evidence that foreign direct investment or impending investment would impair the national security, the President is expected to take action he considers ''appropriate'' to suspend or prohibit foreign acquisitions, mergers, or takeovers.

Action to protect the balance of payments

As a matter of general interest, the United States has on the books a law which authorizes the President to proclaim, in specific circumstances and under specific conditions, temporary measures ''to deal with large and serious United States balance-of-payments deficits.''

Applicable laws. Section 122 (Balance-of-Payments Authority) of the Trade Act of 1974 (19 U.S.C. 2132).

GATT Article XII (Restrictions to Safeguard the Balance of Payments), and Article XI (Quantitative Restrictions).

Remedy. The President of the United States may impose a surcharge, not to exceed 15 percent ad valorem, and/or import quotas.

WHO TO CONTACT

General Assistance

TRADE REMEDY ASSISTANCE OFFICE
U.S. International Trade Commission
500 E St., S.W.
Washington, DC 20436
Phone 1-(800) 343-9822 or (202) 252-2200

TRADE ADVISORY CENTER
Office of the Deputy Assistant Secretary
for Trade Agreements
Room 3036
U.S. Department of Commerce
Washington, DC 20230
(202) 377-3268

TRADE ADVISORY CENTER
Office of the Deputy Assistant
Secretary for Industry Projects
Room 1015-C
U.S. Department of Commerce
Washington, DC 20230
Phone: (202) 377-3268

United States Department of Commerce also has a number of offices that specialize in remedy assistance:

SMALL BUSINESS ASSISTANCE, ITA
(202) 379-3176

OFFICE OF INVESTIGATIONS, ITA
(202) 377-5497

DUMPING, ITA
(202) 377-1779

COUNTERVAILING, ITA
(202) 377-5414

COUNTRY DESK OFFICE ASSISTANCE
(202) 377-3022 (Ask for a list)

STANDARDS INFORMATION CENTER
Technology Building, Room B-166
National Bureau of Standards
Washington, DC 20234
Phone: (301) 921-2092

Agricultural assistance

DIRECTOR OF MULTILATERAL TRADE POLICY AFFAIRS
Room 5530, Administration Bldg.
U.S. Department of Agriculture
Washington, DC 20250
Phone: (202) 382-1312
        also
TRADE AND ASSISTANCE & PLANNING OFFICE
USDA
(202) 447-8502

The Multilateral Subsidies Code

OFFICE OF THE GENERAL COUNSEL
Office of the United States Trade Representative
600 17th St., N.W.
Washington, DC 20506
Phone: (202) 395-3432

Action under Section 301

CHAIRMAN, SECTION 301 COMMITTEE
Office of the United States Trade Representative
600 17th St., N.W.
Washington, DC 20506
Phone: (202) 395-3432

Countervailing duty investigations and the subsidies information

OFFICE OF POLICY
Office of the Deputy Assistant
Secretary for Import Administration
Room 2800, 14th St. & Constitution, N.W.
U.S. Department of Commerce
Washington, DC 20230
Phone: (202) 377-1780

Material injury investigations in U.S. countervailing duty actions

OFFICE OF INVESTIGATIONS
Room 615
U.S. International Trade Commission
500 E Street, S.W.
Washington, DC 20436
Phone: (202) 252-1161

The Government Procurement Code

TRADE NEGOTIATIONS AND AGREEMENTS DIVISION
Office of Trade Policy
Room 3031
U.S. Department of Commerce
Washington, DC 20230
Phone: (202) 377-3681

GATT Affairs Staff

OFFICE OF THE U.S. TRADE REPRESENTATIVE
Room 507
600 17th Street, N.W.
Washington, DC 20506
Phone: (202) 395-3063

Foreign government standards

For Industrial:
TRADE NEGOTIATIONS AND AGREEMENTS DIVISION
Office of Trade Policy
Same as above.

For Agricultural:
USDA TECHNICAL OFFICE
Room 5528
South Agricultural Building
14th St. & Independence Ave., S.W.
Washington, DC 20250
Phone: (202) 382-1318

The Antidumping Code

OFFICE OF POLICY
Import Administration
Room 3716
U.S. Department of Commerce
Washington, DC 20230
Phone: (202) 377-3716

OFFICE OF THE GENERAL COUNSEL
Office of the United States Trade Representative
600 17th Street, N.W.
Washington, DC 20506
(202) 395-3150

Antidumping investigations

OFFICE OF INVESTIGATIONS
Import Administration
Room 3087, 14th St. & Constitution Ave., N.W.
U.S. Department of Commerce
Washington, DC 20436
Phone: (202) 377-5497

Material injury investigations in the U.S. antidumping investigations

OFFICE OF INVESTIGATIONS
U.S. International Trade Commission
500 E Street, S.W.
Washington, DC 20436
(202) 252-1161

Compliance with antidumping duty orders

OFFICE OF COMPLIANCE
Import Administration
Room 3067
U.S. Department of Commerce
Washington, DC 20230
Phone: (202) 377-5253
          also
CUSTOMS SERVICE
Office of Trade Operations
Other Agency Enforcement
(202) 566-8651

The Licensing Code

GATT AFFAIRS DIVISION
Office of Multilateral Affairs
International Trade Administration
U.S. Department of Commerce
Room 3515
Washington, DC 20230
Phone: (202) 377-3681

OFFICE GATT AFFAIRS
Office of the U.S. Trade Representative
Room 503
600 17th Street, N.W.
Washington, DC 20506
Phone: (202) 395-3063

Trade in civil aircraft

COORDINATOR OF AEROSPACE TRADE POLICY
Office of the U.S. Trade Representative
600 17th Street, N.W.
Washington, DC 20506
(202) 396-4510

INDUSTRY SPECIALIST, AIRCRAFT
Office of Trade Policy
International Trade Administration
U.S. Department of Commerce
Washington, DC 20230
(202) 377-3703

Throughout this book the author has proposed an offensive strategy with focus on the positive business applications (tactics) that are already on the books. By making maximum use of these various activities, American businesses can expand their international presence, and continue to win the trade game.

Appendix A
World Commercial Holidays

THERE ARE HUNDREDS OF HOLIDAYS AND OTHER PERIODS WHEN BUSINESS IS discouraged in particular countries; therefore, when planning your business travel it is wise to consult the following list of commercial holidays.

Keep in mind that this list of calendar dates, arranged alphabetically by country around the world, is intended only as a working guide. It may vary by several days due to calendar changes year-to-year, and in the case of the Moslem world, by lunar sightings. Before scheduling final business arrangements, corroboration of specific days is suggested.

Abu Dhabi Jan. 1 (New Year's), March 16* (Ascension), May 17–19* (Eid ul Fitr), July 24–26* (Eid al Adha), Aug. 6 (Sh. Zayed Accession), Aug 25* (Islamic New Year's), Oct 21* (Prophet's Birthday), Dec. 2 (UAE National Day).

*Exact dates of these religious holidays depend upon sighting of the moon, and are announced shortly before they occur.

Afghanistan Jan 2–5 est. (Id-e-Adha), Feb. 2 (Tenth of Moharram), March 21 (Nawroz), April 5 (Milad-e-Nawi), May 27 (Independence Day), July 17–probable (Republic Day), Aug 22–25 est. (Jeshyn-i-Istenlal), Aug. 31 (Pushtunistan Day), Sept. 9 (Parliament Day), Sept. 18 est. (First of Ramazan), Oct. 15 (Deliverance Day), Oct 17–19, (Id-e-Fitr).

The regular weekend holiday is from Thursday noon through Friday. Saturday and Sunday are regular workdays.

Due to the recent establishment of a new regime, some of the strictly government holidays listed above may be changed.

Algeria Jan. 1 (New Year's), Jan. 4–5 (Aid el Adha), Jan. 25 (Moharem), Feb. 3 (Achaoura), April 5 (Mouloud), June 19 (Anniversary of 19th June), July 5 (Independence), Oct. 18–19 (Aid el Fitr), Nov. 1 (Anniversary of the start of the Revolution).

Angola Jan. 1 (New Year's), June 13 (Corpus Christi), Aug. 15 (Restoration Day), Oct. 5 (Republic Day), Nov. 1 (All Saints), Dec. 1 (Independence), Dec. 8 (Immaculate Conception), Dec. 25 (Christmas).

Argentina Jan. 6 (Twelfth Night), Feb. 25–26 (Carnival), April 11–14 (Easter), May 1 (Labor Day), May 25 (Revolution Day), June 10 (Sovereignty Day), June 13 (Corpus Christi), June 20 (Flag Day), July 9 (Independence Day), Aug. 15 (Assumption), Aug. 17 (Death of San Martin), Oct. 12 (Columbus Day), Nov. 1 (All Saints), Nov. 11 (San Martin de Tours), Dec. 8 (Immaculate Conception), Dec. 25 (Christmas).

Aruba Jan. 1 (New Year's), Feb. 15 (Carnival Monday), March 18 (Flag Day), April 1 (Good Friday), April 4 (Easter Monday), April 30 (Queen's Birthday), May 1 (Labor Day), May 12 (Ascension), Dec. 25 (Christmas), Dec. 26 (Boxing Day).

Australia   Jan. 1 (New Year's), Jan. 28 (Australia Day), April 12 – 15 (Easter), April 25 (ANZAC Day), Dec. 25 (Christmas), Dec. 26 (Boxing Day).

REGIONAL HOLIDAYS: March 4 (Eight Hour Day), *Tasmania*, (Labor Day), *Western Australia*; March 11 (Labor Day), *Victoria*; March 12 (Canberra Day), *Canberra*; May 6 (Labor Day), *Queensland*; May 13 (Adelaide Cup Day), *South Australia*; June 3 (Foundation Day), *Western Australia*; June 17 (Queen's Birthday), all States except Western Australia; Aug. 14 (Exhibition Day), *Queensland*; Sept. 25 (Show Day), *Western Australia*; Sept. 26 (Melbourne Show Day), *Melbourne*; Oct. 7 (Labor Day), *Australian Capital Territory* and *New South Wales*; Oct. 14 (Labor Day), *South Australia*; (Queen's Birthday), *Western Australia*; Nov. 4 (Bank Holiday), *Tasmania*; Nov. 5 (Melbourne Cup Day), *Melbourne*.

Austria   Jan. 1 (New Year's), April 12 – 15 (Easter), May 1 (Labor Day), May 23 (Ascension), June 3 (Whit Monday), June 13 (Corpus Christi), Aug. 15 (Assumption), Oct. 26 (National Holiday), Dec. 25 (Christmas), Dec. 26 (St. Stephen's), Dec. 31 (Bank Holiday).

REGIONAL HOLIDAYS: March 19 (St. Joseph), *Carinthia, Styria, Tyrol, Vorarlbery*; Sept. 24 (St. Rupert), *Salzburg*; Oct. 10 (Plebiscite Anniversary), *Carinthia*; Nov. 11 (St. Leopold) *Lower Austria, Upper Austria, Vienna*.

Regional holidays are mainly observed by schools and farmers. Some public offices and a few business enterprises might also be closed but their number is decreasing from year to year.

Also, many businesses will be closed on the following days, which are part of long weekends: May 24, June 14, Aug. 16, Dec. 27.

Bahamas   Jan. 1 (New Year's), April 12 – 15 (Easter), June 3 (Whit Monday), June 7 (Labor Day), July 10 (Independence Day), Aug. 5 (Emancipation Day), Oct. 12 (Discovery Day), Dec. 25 – 26 (Christmas).

Bahrain   Jan. 1 (New Year's), Jan. 3 – 5 (Eid al-Adha), Jan. 23 (Islamic New Year), Jan. 31 – Feb. 1 (Ashura), Apr. 3 (Birthday of the Prophet), Oct. 16 – 18 (Eid al-Fitr), Dec. 16 (Bahrain National Day), Dec. 23 – 25 (Eid al-Adha).

The religious holidays are subject to a shift of one day in either direction. Almost all businesses observe a six-day work week with Friday off.

Bangladesh   Jan. 6 – 8 ext. (Eid-ul-Azha), Feb. 4 ext. (Muharram), Feb. 21 (National Mourning Day), March 26 (Independence Day), April 14 (Bengali New Year's), April 6 ext. (Eid-i-Milad-un-Nabi), May 1 (May Day), last week in May, est. (Buddha Purnima), Sept. 2 est. (Shab-i-Barat), last week in Sept. to the first week in Oct., est. (Durga Fuja), Oct. 15 est. (Shab-i-Qadr), Oct. 16 (Jamat-ul-Wida), Oct 17 – 19 est. (Eid-ul-Fitr), Dec. 16 (Victory Day), Dec. 25 (Christmas). Muslim religious holidays are dependent on the sighting of the moon and may move several days in either direction.

In addition to these holidays, there will be a number of national and optional holidays, the dates of which are not yet known. Option holidays may or may not be observed by commercial firms.

In most cities in Bangladesh, for most firms Saturdays are half-days and Sundays are fully closed days.

Barbados Jan. 1 (New Year's), April 12 (Good Friday), April 15 (Easter Bank Holiday), May 1 (May Day), June 3 (Whit Monday), Aug. 5 (Bank Holiday), Oct. 7 (Clerk's Day), Nov. 30 (Independence Day), Dec. 25 (Christmas), Dec. 26 (Boxing Day).

Belgium Jan. 1 (New Year's), April 15 (Easter Monday), May 1 (Labor Day), May 23 (Ascension), June 3 (Whit Monday), July 11 (Flemish Holiday), July 21 (Independence Day), Aug. 15 (Assumption), Nov. 1 (All Saints), Nov. 2 (All Souls), Nov. 11 (Veterans Day), Nov. 15 (Dynasty Day), Dec. 25 (Christmas), Dec. 26 (Boxing Day).

When official Belgian holidays fall on Saturday or Sunday, they are taken either on the previous Friday or on the following Monday.

Belize (formerly British Honduras) Jan. 1 (New Year's), March 9 (Baron Bliss Day), April 12 – 15 (Easter), April 24 (Queen's Birthday), May 1 (Labor Day), May 24 (Commonwealth Day), Sept. 10 (National Day), Oct. 12 (Columbus Day—Northern Districts Only), Nov. 14 (Prince Charles' Birthday), Nov. 19 (Carib. Settlement Day—Southern Districts Only), Dec. 25 (Christmas), Dec. 26 (Boxing Day).

Benin Jan. 16 (Martyr's Day), April 1 (Youth Day), May 1 (Labor Day), Oct. 26 (Armed Forces Day), Nov. 30 (National Day), Dec. 23 (Women's Day), Dec. 31 (Production Day).

Although they are not included on the official list, Benin holidays also include Christmas Day, New Year's Day, and two Moslem holidays whose dates vary according to the lunar calendar.

Bermuda Jan. 1 (New Year's), April 12 (Good Friday), May 24 (Empire Day), June 17 (Queen's Birthday), Aug. 1 (Cup Match), Aug. 2 (Somers Day), Nov. 11 (Remembrance Day), Dec. 25 (Christmas), Dec. 26 (Boxing Day).

Bolivia Jan. 1 (New Year's), Feb. 25 – 26 (Carnival), March 23 (Abaron Day), April 11 – 14 (Easter), May 1 (Labor Day), June 1 (Corpus Christi), July 16 (La Paz Day), Aug. 5 – 7 (Independence Days), Oct. 12 (Dia de la Raza), Nov. 2 (All Souls), Dec. 25 (Christmas).

Botswana Jan. 1 (New Year's), April 12 – 15 (Easter), May 23 (Ascension), May 27 (President's Day), June 3 (Whit Monday), June 10 (Commonwealth Day), Aug. 5 (First Monday in August), Sept. 30 (Botswana Day), Oct. 24 (United Nations Day), Dec. 25 (Christmas), Dec. 26 (Boxing Day).

Brazil Jan. 1 (New Year's), Jan. 25 (Sao Paulo anniversary), *Sao Paulo only*; Jan. 26 (Santos anniversary), *Santos only*; Feb. 2 (Nossa Senhora dos Navegantes), *Porto Alegre only*; Feb. 25 – 26 (Carnival); April 12 (Good Friday); April 21 (Tiradentes); May 1 (Labor Day); Sept. 7 (Independence); Oct. 12 (Nossa Senhora Aparecida), *Brasilia, Cuiaba and Goiania only*; Nov. 2 (All Souls Day); Nov. 15 (Proclamation of the Republic); Dec. 8 (Immaculate Conception), *not observed in Rio de Janeiro and Sao Paulo*; Dec. 25 (Christmas).

Additional holidays may be observed when declared by presidential proclamation.

Brunei Jan. 1 (New Year's), Feb. 17 (Chinese New Year's), Feb. 23 (Brunei National Day), March 16 (Israk Meraj), April 18* (First Day of Ramadan), May 4* (Anniversary of the Revelation of the Koran), May 18 – 19* (Hari Raya Puasa), May 31 (Royal Brunei

Armed Forces Day), July 15 (Sultan's Birthday), July 25* (Hari Raya Haji), Aug. 15* (First of Hijrah), Oct. 4* (Prophet Mohammad's Birthday), Dec. 26 (Christmas Holiday).

*Exact dates of these religious holidays depend upon sighting of the moon, and will be announced shortly before they occur.

Bulgaria   Jan. 1 – 2 (New Year's), May 1 – 2 (Labor Day), May 24 (Education Day), Sept. 9 – 10 (Liberation Day), Nov. 7 (Oct. Revolution Day).

The day preceding an official holiday is only a half-day.

Burma   Jan. 4 (Independence Day), Feb. 12 (Union Day), March 2 (Peasants' Day), March 7 (Full moon of Tabaung), March 27 (Resistance Day), April 14 – 16 (Thingyan-Water Festival), April 17 (Burmese New Year), May 1 (Worker's Day), May 5 (Full moon of Kasen), July 19 (Martyr's Day), Aug. 2 (Full moon of Waso—Beginning of Buddhist Lent), Oct. 30 (Full moon of Thadingyut—End of Buddhist Lent), Nov. 28 (Full moon of Tazaungmon—Tazaungdaing Festival), Dec. 8 (National Day), Dec. 25 (Christmas).

Burundi   Jan. 1 (New Year's), April 15 (Easter Monday), May 1 (Labor Day), May 23 (Ascension), June 3 (Pentecost Monday), July 1 (Independence Day), Aug. 15 (Assumption), Sept. 15 (Victory of Uprona Party), Oct. 13 (Assassination of National Hero), Nov. 1 (All Saints), Nov. 28 (Republic Day), Dec. 25 (Christmas).

Cameroon   Jan. 1 (Independence Day), Jan. 15 est. (Feast of the Lamb—Muslim), Feb. 11 (Youth Day), April 12 – 15 (Easter), May 1 (Labor Day), May 20 (National Day), June 3 (Monday after Pentecost), Aug. 15 (Assumption), Oct. 1 (Reunification Day), Oct. 25 – 30 est. (End of Muslim Fasting Month—Ramadan), Nov. 1 (All Saints), Dec. 10 (Human Rights Day), Dec. 25 (Christmas).

Canada   Jan. 1 (New Year's), April 12 – 15 (Easter), May 20 (Victoria Day), July 1 (Dominion Day), Aug. 5 (Civic Holiday—*Ontario, Alberta, British Columbia and Manitoba only*), Sept. 2 (Labor Day), Oct. 14 (Thanksgiving), Nov. 11 (Remembrance Day), Dec. 25 (Christmas), Dec. 26 (Boxing Day).

Central African Republic   Jan. 1 (New Year's), March 29 (Anniversary of Boganda's Death), April 15 (Easter Monday), May 1 (Labor Day), May 14 (Anniversary of the Installation of the first African Government), May 23 (Ascension), June 3 (Pentecost), Aug. 13 (Independence Day), Aug. 15 (Assumption), Nov. 11 (Anniversary of the Election of Deputy Boganda to the French National Assembly), Dec. 2 (Republic Day), Dec. 25 (Christmas).

Chad   Jan. 1 (New Year's), Jan. 8 (Aid al Kabir—70 days after end of Ramadan), Jan. 11 (National Day), March 20 (Mouloud al Nabi), April 15 (Easter Monday), May 1 (Labor Day), May 23 (Ascension), May 25 (African Continent Liberation Day), June 2 – 3 (Pentecost), Aug. 11 (Independence Day), Aug. 15 (Assumption), Oct. 24 (Aid as Saguir—end of Ramadan), Nov. 1 (All Saints), Nov. 28 (Proclamation of the Republic), Dec. 25 (Christmas).

Chile   Jan. 12 (New Year's), April 12 (Good Friday), May 1 (Labor Day), May 21 (Battle of Iquique), Aug. 15 (Assumption), Sept. 18 – 19 (Independence), Oct. 12 (Columbus Day), Nov. 1 (All Saints), Dec. 8 (Immaculate Conception), Dec. 25 (Christmas).

China   Jan. 1 (New Year's), Feb. 17–19 (Spring Festival), May 1 (Labor Day), Oct. 1–2 (Chinese National Day).

Colombia   Jan. 1 (New Year's), Jan. 6 (Epiphany), March 19 (St. Joseph's Day), April 11–14 (Easter), May 1 (Labor Day), May 23 (Ascension), June 3 (Corpus Christi), June 21 (Feast of the Sacred Heart), June 29 (SS. Peter and Paul), July 20 (Independence Day), Aug. 7 (Battle of Boyaca), Aug. 15 (Assumption), Oct. 12 (Columbus Day), Dec. 8 (Feast of the Immaculate Conception), Dec. 25 (Christmas).

Congo   Jan. 1 (New Year's), May 1 (Labor Day), July 31 (Readjustment of the Revolution), Aug. 15 (The Three Glorious Days), Nov. 1 (All Souls), Dec. 25 (Children's Day), Dec. 31 (Proclamation of the Republic).

Costa Rica   Jan. 1 (New Year's), March 19 (St. Joseph's Day), April 11 (Juan Santamaria), April 11–14 (Easter), May 1 (Labor Day), June 13 (Corpus Christi), June 29 (SS. Peter and Paul), July 25 (Annexation of Guanacaste), Aug. 2 (Feast of Our Assumption), Sept. 15 (Independence), Oct. 12 (Columbus Day), Dec. 8 (Immaculate Conception), Dec. 25 (Christmas).
   Little business is carried on Dec. 15–Jan. 10.

Cyprus   Jan. 1 (New Year's), Jan. 4 (Kurban Bayram), Jan. 6 (Epiphany Day), Jan. 19 (Arch. Makarios Name Day), Feb. 25 (Green Monday), March 25 (Greek Independence Day), April 1 (EOKA Day), April 5 (Birthday of the Prophet), April 12–15 (Easter), April 23 (Opening of the Turkish Grand Natl. Assembly), May 19 (Turkish Youth Day), Aug. 15 (Assumption of the Blessed Virgin), Aug. 30 (Turkish Victory Day), Oct. 17 (Ramazan Bayram), Oct. 28 (OHI Day), Oct. 29 (Turkish Republic Day), Dec. 24 (Kurban Bayrami), Dec. 25 (Christmas), Dec. 26 (Boxing Day).

Czechoslovakia   Jan. 1 (New Year's), April 15 (Easter Monday), May 1 (May Day), May 9 (National Day), Oct. 28 (State Holiday), Dec. 24–25 (Christmas).

Dahomey   Jan. 1 (New Year's), sometime in Feb. (El Kabir), April 26 (Id el Mulud), May 1 (May Day), May 31 (Ascension), June 11 (Pentecost Monday), Aug. 1 (Independence Day), Aug. 15 (Assumption), Nov. 1 (All Saints), Dec. 25 (Christmas).

Denmark   Jan. 1 (New Year's), April 11–15 (Easter), May 10 (Prayer Day), May 23 (Ascension), June 3 (Whit Monday), Dec. 25–26 (Christmas).
   Most industries and banks are closed on May 1 and June 5.

Dominica   Jan. 1 (New Year's), Feb. 15–16 (Carnival), April 1 (Good Friday), April 4 (Easter), May 2 (May Day), May 23 (Whit Monday), Aug. 1 (August Monday), Nov. 3 (Independence Day), Nov. 4 (Community Day), Dec. 26 (Christmas Holiday), Dec. 27 (Boxing Day).

Dominican Republic   Jan. 1 (New Year's), Jan. 21 (Nuestra Sra. de la Altagracia), Jan. 26 (Juan Pablo Duarte), Feb. 27 (Independence Day), April 12 (Good Friday), May 1 (Labor Day), June 13 (Feast of Corpus Christi), Aug. 16 (Dominican Restoration), Sept. 24 (Nuestra Sra. de las Mercedes), Dec. 25 (Christmas).

Ecuador   Jan. 1 (New Year's), Feb. 25–26 (Carnival), April 12 (Good Friday), May 1 (Labor Day), May 24 (Quito Independence), July 24 (Simon Bolivar's Birthday), Aug. 10

(Independence), Oct. 9 (Guayaquil Independence), Oct. 12 (Columbus Day), Nov. 2 (All Souls), Nov. 3 (Independence of Cuenca), Dec. 6 (Founding of Quito—local), Dec. 25 (Christmas).

Holidays that fall on Tuesdays will be observed on the preceding Monday and holidays that fall on Wednesday and Thursday will be observed on Friday. Exceptions are Jan. 1, May 1, Nov. 2, and Dec. 25.

Egypt Jan. 3–6 est. (Id al-Adha), Jan. 23 est. (Islamic New Year), April 3 est. (Prophet's Birthday), April 30 (Sham el Nassim), June 18 (Evacuation Day), July 23 (Egyptian National or Revolution Day), Oct. 14–16 est. (Id al-Fitr), Dec. 20–23 est. (Id al-Adha).

El Salvador Jan. 1–2 (New Year's), April 10–14 (Easter Week), May 1 (Labor Day), Aug. 1–6 (August holidays), Sept. 15 (Independence Day), Oct. 12 (Columbus Day), Nov. 2 (All Souls), Nov. 5 (1st call to Independence), Dec. 25 (Christmas).

Government offices in El Salvador are closed April 8–15, April 27, June 22 and Dec. 24–31. Banks are closed June 29–30 and Dec. 29–30.

Equatorial Guinea Variable Date (Good Friday), Variable Date (Corpus Christi—60 days after Easter Sunday), May 1 (Labor Day), June 5 (President's Birthday), Aug. 3 (Armed Forces Day), Aug. 15 (Constitution Day), Oct. 12 (Independence Day), Dec. 8 (Immaculate Conception), Dec. 25 (Christmas).

Ethiopia Jan. 7 (Ethiopian Christmas), Feb. 19 (Martyrs of Yekatit), Aug. 22 (Assumption), Sept. 11 (Ethiopian New Year), Sept. 27 (Maskal).

Dates of Christmas and Easter holidays vary from those listed for other countries because Ethiopian calendar differs from Gregorian.

Fiji Jan. 1 (New Year's), April 8 (Prophet's Birthday), April 12–13 (Easter), June 17 (Queen's Birthday), Oct. 7 (Fiji Day), Nov. 11 (Prince Charles' Birthday), Nov. 13 (Diwali Festival), Dec. 25 (Christmas), Dec. 26 (Boxing Day).

Finland Jan. 1 (New Year's), Jan. 12 (Epiphany), April 12–15 (Easter), May 1 (May Day), May 18 (Ascension), June 1 (Whitsun Eve), June 22 (Midsummer's Day), Nov. 2 (All Saints), Dec. 6 (Independence Day), Dec. 25–26 (Christmas).

Many offices and shops are closed the afternoon of the workday immediately preceding a Finnish holiday. In addition, banks are closed the afternoon of Dec. 31 and April 11 and all day Dec. 24 and June 21.

France Jan. 1 (New Year's), April 15 (Easter Monday), May 1 (Labor Day), May 23 (Ascension), June 3 (Whit Monday), July 14 (Bastille Day), Aug. 15 (Assumption), Nov. 1 (All Saints), Nov. 11 (Veterans Day), Dec. 25 (Christmas).

August is regarded in France as a poor month for conducting business, as most firms are closed for vacation.

Gabon Jan. 1 (New Year's), March 12 (Renovation Day), April 15 (Easter Monday), May 1 (Labor Day), May 23 (Ascension Day), June 3 (Pentecost), Aug. 17 (National Day), Nov. 1 (All Saints), Dec. 4 (death of Leon M'Ba), Dec. 25 (Christmas).

Gambia Jan. 1 (New Year's), Feb. 13 (National Day), April 12–15 (Easter), Aug. 15 (Assumption), Dec. 25 (Christmas), Dec. 26 (Boxing Day).

The days of Id-El-Kabir and Id-El-Fitr will depend on the lunar calendar.

West Germany   Jan. 1 (New Year's), April 12 – 15 (Easter), May 1 (Labor Day), May 23 (Ascension), June 3 (Whit Monday), June 17 (Day of German Unity), Nov. 20 (Repentance Day), Dec. 24 half-day (Christmas Eve), Dec. 25 – 26 (Christmas).

REGIONAL HOLIDAYS: Jan 6 (Epiphany), *Baden-Wuerttemberg, Bavaria*; Feb. 25 (Rose Monday), *Bonn, Cologne, Duesseldorf, Mainz, and other Catholic areas celebrating Carnival*; June 13 (Corpus Christi), *Hesse, North Rhine-Westphalia, Rhineland-Palatinate, Saarland, Baden-Wuerttemberg and Catholic areas of Bavaria*; Aug. 15 (Assumption), *Saarland, Catholic areas of Bavaria*; Nov. 1 (All Saint's), *Baden-Wuerttemberg, North Rhine-Westphalia, Rhineland-Palatinate, Saarland, Catholic areas of Bavaria*.

East Germany   Jan. 1 (New Year's), April 12 – 14 (Easter), May 1 (Labor Day), June 3 (Whit Monday), Oct. 7 (Anniversary of Founding of the GDR), Dec. 25 – 26 (Christmas).

Ghana   Jan. 1 (New Year's), Jan. 1 (National Redemption Day), March 6 (Easter), Aug. 5 (Bank Holiday), Dec. 25 (Christmas), Dec. 26 (Boxing Day).

Greece   Jan. 1 (New Year's), Feb. 25 (Kathara Deftera), March 25 (Independence), April 12 – 15 (Easter), May 1 (May Day), Aug. 15 (Assumption), Oct. 28 (OXI Day), Dec. 25 (Christmas).

REGIONAL HOLIDAYS: March 7 (Dodeconese Accession Day), observed only in *Rhodes*; Oct. 4 (Liberation of Nanthi), only in *Xanthi*; Oct. 26 (St. Dimitrios), only in *Thessaloniki*; Nov. 30 (St. Andrea's), only in *Patras*.

Grenada   Jan. 1 – 2 (New Year's), Feb. 7 (Independence Day), April 1 (Good Friday), April 4 (Easter Monday), May 1 (Labor Day), May 23 (Whit Monday), June 2 (Corpus Christi), Aug. 1 – 2 (Emancipation Day), Probably Aug. 8 (Carnival), Oct. 25 (Thanksgiving Day), Dec. 25 (Christmas), Dec. 26 (Boxing Day).

Guatemala   Jan. 1 (New Year's), April 11 – 14 (Easter), May 1 (Labor Day), June 30 (Army Day), Aug. 15 (Assumption), Sept. 15 (Independence), Oct. 20 (Revolution Day), Nov. 1 (All Saints), Dec. 24 – 25 (Christmas), Dec. 31 (New Year's Eve).

Banks also will be closed April 10, July 1, Oct. 12, Sept. 16, and Oct. 21.

Guinea   Jan. 1 (New Year's), Jan. 15 est. (Tabaski), May 1 (Labor Day), May 14 (Anniversary of Parti Democratique de Guinee), Sept. 28 (Referendum Day), Oct. 2 (Independence), Nov. 9 est. (End of Ramadan), Nov. 22 (Anniversary of Defeat of the Invasion of Guinea), Dec. 25 (Christmas).

Holidays may be added on short notice.

Guyana   Jan. 1 (New Year's), sometime in Jan. (Eid-Ul-Azha), Feb. 23 (Republic Day), sometime in March (Phagwah), sometimes in April (Youman Naubi), April 12 – 15 (Easter), May 1 (Labor Day), Aug. 5 (Commonwealth Day), Oct. 24 (United Nations Day), sometime in Oct. (Deepavali), Dec. 25 (Christmas), Dec. 26 (Boxing Day).

Haiti   Jan. 1 (New Year's and Independence Day), Jan. 2 (Ancestor's Day), Feb. 26 (Mardi Gras), April 11 – 14 (Easter), May 1 (Agriculture and Labor Day), May 18 (Flag and University Day), May 22 (National Sovereignty Day), May 23 (Ascension), June 13

(Corpus Christi), June 22 (Presidence a Vie), Aug. 15 (Assumption), Oct. 17 (Anniversary of Death of Dessalines), Oct. 24 (United Nations Day), Nov. 1 (All Saints), Nov. 2 (All Souls), Nov. 18 (Anniversary of Battle of Vertieres and Haitian Armed Forces), Dec. 5 (Anniversary of Discovery of Haiti), Dec. 25 (Christmas).

Holidays may be added on short notice.

Honduras   Jan. 1 (New Year's), April 11–14 (Easter), May 1 (Dia del Trabajo), Sept. 15 (Proclamacion de la Independencia de Centro America), Oct. 3 (Nacimento del General Francisco Morazan), Oct. 12 (Descubrimiento de America), Oct. 21 (Dias de las Fuerzas Armadas de Honduras), Dec. 25 (Christmas).

Hong Kong   Jan. 1 (first weekday in Jan.), Jan 23–25 (Chinese New Year), April 5 (Ching Ming Festival), April 12–15 (Easter), April 25 (Queen's Birthday), June 24 (Tuen Ng Festival), July 1 (first weekday in July), Aug. 5 (Liberation Day), Oct. 1 (day following Chinese Mid-Autumn Festival), Oct. 23 (Chung Yeung Festival), Dec. 25–26 (Christmas).

Hungary   Jan. 1 (New Year's), April 4 (Liberation Day), April 15 (Easter Monday), May 1 (Labor Day), Aug. 20 (Constitution Day), Nov. 7 (October Revolution Day), Dec. 25 (Christmas), Dec. 26 (Boxing Day).

Iceland   Jan. 1 (New Year's), April 11–15 (Easter), April 25 (First Day of Summer), May 1 (Labor Day), May 23 (Ascension), June 3 (Whit Monday), Aug. 5 (Bank Holiday), Dec. 24 (Christmas Eve, half-day), Dec. 25 (Christmas), Dec. 26 (Boxing Day), Dec. 31 (New Year's Eve, half-day).

India   Jan. 1 (New Year's), Jan. 5 (Id-ul-Zhua), Jan. 26 (Republic Day), Feb. 10 (Mahasivarntri), March 8 (Holi), April 1 (Ramanavami), April 5 (Mahavir Jayanti), April 12 (Good Friday), May 6 (Buddha Purnima), Aug. 15 (Independence Day), Oct. 2 (Id-ul-Fitr), Oct. 24–25 (Dussehrn), Nov. 13 (Diwali), Nov. 29 (Guru Nanak's Birthday), Dec. 25 (Christmas).

Indonesia   Jan. 1 (New Year's), Jan. 4 est. (Id-ul-Adha), Jan. 25 est. (1st Muharam), April 5 (Prophet's Birthday), April 12 (Good Friday), May 23 (Ascension of Jesus Christ), Aug. 12 (Ascension of Prophet Muhammad), Aug. 17–18 (Id-ul-Fitr), Dec. 24 est (Id-ul-Adha), Dec. 25 (Christmas).

Iran   Jan. 4 (Ed-e-Ghorban), Jan. 12 (Id-e-Ghadir), Feb. (Ashura), March 21–22 (No-Ruz—Iranian New Year), March 23 (Death of the Prophet and Death of Imam Hassan), April 2 (Sizdah), April 11 (Birthday of the Prophet and Birthday of Imam Jaafar Sadegh), Aug. 5 (Constitution Day), Aug. 16 (Mabas), Sept. 3 (Birthday of the 12th Imam), Oct. 8 (Death of Imam Ali), Oct. 17 (Id-e-Fetr), Nov. 10 (Death of Imam Jaafar Sadegh), Nov. 26 (Birthday of Imam Reza), Dec. 24 (Id-e-Ghorban).

Iraq   Jan. 1 (New Year's), Jan. 2–5 est. (Id al-Adha), Jan. 6 (Army Day), Jan. 23 est. (Islamic New Year), Feb. 3 est. (Ashura), April 3 est. (Prophet's Birthday), May (Labor Day), July 14 (Declaration of the Republic), July 17 (Revolution Day), Oct. 16–18 est. (Id al-Fitr), Dec. 24–27 est. (Id al-Adha).

Ireland   Jan. 1 (banks only), March 17–18 (St. Patrick's Day), April 12–15 (Easter),

June 3 (bank holiday), Aug. 5 (bank holiday), Dec. 25 (Christmas), Dec. 26 (St. Stephen).

Israel   April 7 (Passover, first day), April 13 (Passover, last day), April 25 (Israel Independence Day), May 27 (Pentecost), Sept. 17–18 (Rosh Hashana—New Year), Sept. 26 (Yom Kippur—Day of Atonement), Oct. 1 (First Day of Tabernacles), Oct. 8 (last day of Tabernacles).

On Fridays, and days preceding holidays, businesses close at 1 P.M. Sundays are working days in Israel and on Saturdays all businesses are closed.

Banks are closed March 8 (Purim) and July 28 (Commemoration of the Destruction of the Temple).

Italy   Jan. 1 (New Year's), Jan. 6 (Epiphany), March 19 (Feast of St. Joseph), April 15 (Easter Monday), April 25 (Liberation Day), May 1 (Labor Day), May 23 (Ascension), June 2 (Founding of the Republic), June 13 (Corpus Christi), Aug. 15 (Assumption), Nov. 1 (All Saints), Nov. 4 (National Unity Day), Dec. 8 (Immaculate Conception), Dec. 25 (Christmas), Dec. 26 (St. Stephen's).

REGIONAL HOLIDAYS: June 24 (St. John's Day), celebrated only in *Turin, Florence* and *Genoa*; June 29 (SS. Peter and Paul) celebrated in *Rome* only; July 15 (Feast of St. Rosalia) celebrated in *Palermo* only; Sept. 19 (Feast of St. Gennaro) celebrated in *Naples* only; Nov. 3 (Feast of St. Giusto), celebrated in *Trieste* only; Dec. 7 (Feast of St. Ambrose) celebrated in *Milan* only.

The month of August is a poor business period as many firms are closed for vacations.

Ivory Coast   Jan. 1 (New Year's), April 15 (Easter Monday), May 1 (Labor Day), May 23 (Ascension), June 3 (Pentecost), Aug. 7 (Independence), Aug. 15 (Assumption), sometime in Sept. (End of Ramadan), Nov. 1 (All Saints), sometime in Nov. (Tabaski), Dec. 25 (Christmas).

Jamaica   Jan. 1 (New Year's), Feb. 27 (Ash Wednesday), April 12–15 (Easter), May 23 (Labor Day), Aug. 5 (Independence Day), Oct. 21 (National Heroes Day), Dec. 25 (Christmas), Dec. 26 (Boxing Day).

Japan   Jan. 1 (New Year's), Jan. 15 (Adult's Day), Feb. 11 (Nat'l Foundation Day), March 21 (Vernal Equinox Day), April 29 (Emperor's Birthday), May 3 (Constitution Day), May 5–6 (Children's Day), Sept. 15–16 (Respect for the Aged Day), Sept. 23 (Autumnal Equinox Day), Oct. 10 (Sports Day), Nov. 3–4 (Culture Day), Nov. 23 (Thanksgiving Day).

Many firms will also be closed Dec. 31 and Jan. 2–4.

Jordan   Jan. 2 est. (Id al Adha), Jan. 22 est. (Islamic New Year), Feb. 27 est. (Prophet's Birthday), May 25 (Independence), Aug. 11 (King Hussein's Accession to Throne), Oct. 13 est. (Id al Fitr), Nov. 14 (King Hussein's Birthday).

In addition, government institutions and some commercial and financial establishments close on the following days: Jan. 15 (Arbor Day), March 3 (Coronation of King Faisal), March 22 (Arab League Day), May 1 (Labor Day).

Many Moslem and Christian establishments close on Fridays, Christian businesses on Sundays.

Kenya   Jan. 1 (New Year's), April 12–15 (Easter), May (Labor Day), June 1 (Madaraka Day), Oct. 21 (Kenyatta Day), sometime in Oct. (Id-Ul-Fitr), Dec. 11–13 (Independence Days), Dec. 25 (Christmas), Dec. 26 (Boxing Day).

Korea   Jan. 1–3 (New Year's), March 1 (Independence Movement Day), April 5 (Arbor Day), June 6 (Memorial Day), July 17 (Constitution Day), Aug. 15 (Independence), Sept. 30 (Thanksgiving), Oct. 3 (National Day), Dec. 25 (Christmas).

Kuwait   Jan. 1 (New Year's), Jan. 2–5 est. (Waqfa and Adha), Jan. 24 est. (Islamic New Year), Feb. 25 (National Day), April 3 est. (Birth of the Prophet), Aug. 14 est. (Ascension of the Prophet), Oct. 16–18 est. (Al-Fitr Eid), Dec. 23–25 est. (Waqfa and Adha).

Laos   Jan. 1 (International New Year), Feb. 7 (Makhabouxa—Buddhist holiday), March 1 (National Day of Support for Veterans and War Victims), March 23 (Armed Forces Day), April 13–16 (Laos New Year), May 1 (Labor Day), May 6 (Vixakhabouxa—Buddhist holiday), May 7 (Rocket Festival), May 11 (Constitution Day), July 19 (Independence), Aug. 17 (Day of the Dead—Buddhist holiday), Sept. 1 (Ho Khao Salak—Buddhist holiday), Oct. 1 (End of Buddhist Lent), Oct. 2 (Boat Races), Oct. 24 (United Nations Day), Oct. 28 (Wat Simouang Festival), Oct. 29–31 (That Luang Festival).

Lebanon   Jan. 1 (New Year's), Jan. 3 est. (Al-Adha), Jan. 25 est. (Moslem New Year), Feb. 2 est. (Ashoura), Feb. 9 (Saint Maron's Day), March 22 (Arab League Day), Apr. 4 est. (Prophet's Birthday), Apr. 12–15 (Easter), Apr. 19–23 (Easter—Greek Orthodox), May 1 (Labor Day), May 6 (Martyr's Day), May 23 (Ascension), May 30 (Ascension—Greek Orthodox), Aug. 15 (Assumption), Oct. 17 est. (Ramadan), Nov. 1 (All Saints), Nov. 22 (Independence), Dec. 25 (Christmas and Al Adha).

Lesotho   Jan. 1 (New Year's), March 12 (Moshoeshoe's Day), April 12–15 (Easter), May 2 (King's Birthday), May 23 (Ascension), May 24 (Commonwealth Day), Aug. 5 (National Tree Planting Day), Oct. 4 (Independence), Oct. 7 (National Sport Day), Dec. 25 (Christmas), Dec. 26 (Boxing Day).

Liberia   Jan. 1 (New Year's), Jan. 7 (Pioneer's Day), Feb. 11 (Armed Forces Day), March 13 (Decoration Day), March 15 (J. J. Roberts Day), April 12 (Day of Fasting and Prayer), May 14 (Unification Day), May 25 (Africa Liberation Day), July 26 (Independence), Aug. 24 (Flag Day), Nov. 7 (Thanksgiving Day), Nov. 29 (Former President William V.S. Tubman's Birthday), Dec. 1 (Matilda Newport Day), Dec. 25 (Christmas).
Most offices will be closed Dec. 25 through Jan. 10.

Libya   Jan. 2–3 est. (Id al Adha), Jan. 23–24 est. (Hijra New Year), Feb. 10–11 est. (Ashura Day), March 8 (Syrian National Day), March 28 (Evacuation Day), April 12 est. (Prophet's Birthday), May 25 (Africa Day), June 11 (Evacuation Day), July 23 (Egyptian National Day), Aug. 11 est. (Al-Isra'wa al-Ma'raj), Aug. 29 est. (Niaf Sha'ban), Sept. 1 (Libya Revolution Day), Oct. 7 (Evacuation Day), Oct. 12–13 est. (Id al Fitr), Dec. 21–22 est. (Id al-Adha).

Liechtenstein   Jan. 1 (New Year's), Jan. 6 (Epiphany), Feb. 2 (Candlemas), March 19 (St. Joseph's), Aug. 15 (Assumption), Sept. 8 (Nativity), Nov. 1 (All Saints), Dec. 3 (St. Luke's Day), Dec. 8 (Immaculate Conception), Dec. 25–26 (Christmas).

Luxembourg   Jan. 1 (New Year's), April 15 (Easter Monday), May 1 (Labor Day), May 23 (Ascension), June 3 (Whit Monday), June 23 (Grand Duke's Birthday), Aug. 15 (Assumption), Nov. 1 (All Saints), Nov. 2 (All Souls), Dec. 25–26 (Christmas).

Madagascar   Jan. 1 (New Year's), March 29 (Day Commemorating the Martyrs of the Malagasay Revolution), April 4 (Easter Monday), May 1 (Labor Day), May 12 (Ascension), May 23 (Whit Monday), June 26 (Independence Day), Aug. 15 (Assumption), Dec. 30 (Anniversary of the Democratic Republic of Madagascar.

Malagasy Republic   Jan. 1 (New Year's), March 29 (Commemoration of the 1947 Revolt), April 15 (Easter Monday), May 1 (Labor Day), May 23 (Ascension), June 3 (Whit Monday), June 26 (Independence Day), Aug. 15 (Assumption), Nov. 1 (All Saints), Dec. 25 (Christmas).
   Holidays listed for Malagasy Republic are estimates and may change.

Malawi   Jan. 1 (New Year's), March 3 (Martyr's Day), April 12–15 (Easter), May 14 (Kamuzu Day), July 6 (Republic Day), Aug. 5 (Bank Holiday), Oct. 17 (Mother's Day), Dec. 25 (Christmas), Dec. 26 (Boxing Day).

Malaysia   Jan. 1 (New Year's), Jan. 4 (Hari Raya Haji), Jan 23–24 (Chinese New Year), Jan. 25 (First Day of Muharram), April 5 (Birthday of Prophet), May 1 (Labor Day), June 5 (Birthday of H.M. Yang di-Pertuan Agong), Aug. 31 (National Day), Oct. 17–18 (Hari Raya Puasa), Dec. 24 (Hari Raya Haji), Dec. 25 (Christmas).
   REGIONAL HOLIDAYS: Feb. 6 (Thaipusam), *Penang*; March 8 (Birthday of H.R.H. Sultan of Selangor), *Selangor*; April 12–15 (Easter), *Sabah, Sarawak*; May 6 (Wesak Day), *West Malaysia*; June 1–2 (Dayak Festival), *Sarawak*; July 1 (Birthday of H.E. Governor of Sarawak), *Sarawak*; Nov. 13 (Doepavali), *West Malaysia*; Dec. 26 (Boxing Day), *Sabah, Sarawak*.

Mali   Jan. 1 (New Year's), sometime in Jan. (Tabaski), Jan. 20 (Army Day), April 15 (Easter Monday), May 1 (Labor Day), May 25 (Day of Africa), Sept. 22 (Independence), sometime in Oct. or Nov. (Ramadan), Nov. 19 (Liberation), Dec. 25 (Christmas), sometime around Christmas (Mouloud).

Malta   Jan. 1 (New Year's), Jan. 6 (Epiphany), Feb. 10 (St. Paul's Shipwreck), March 19 (St. Joseph), April (Good Friday), May 1 (St. Joseph the Worker), May 23 (Ascension), June 13 (Corpus Christi), June 29 (SS. Peter and Paul), Aug. 15 (Assumption), Sept. 8 (National Day), Nov. 1 (All Saints), Dec. 8 (Immaculate Conception), Dec. 25 (Christmas).
   Business will be moderate May 11–14 (Carnival).

Martinique   Jan. 1 (New Year's), Feb. 15–17 (Carnival), April 1 (Good Friday), April 4 (Easter Monday), May 12 (Ascension), May 23 (Pentecost), July 14 (Bastille Day), Aug. 15 (Assumption), Oct. 10 (Columbus Day), Nov. 1–2 (All Saints Day), Dec. 25 (Christmas).

Mauritania   Jan. 1 (New Year's), Mid-Jan. est. (Id el Adha), Mid-April est. (Id el Mouloud), May 1 (Labor Day), May 25 (OAU Day), Oct. 17 (Id el Fitr), Nov. 28 (Independence).

Mauritius   Jan. 1–2 (New Year's), Jan. 23 est. (Id el Adha), Jan. 29 est. (Cavadee), Feb. 8 est. (Chinese Spring Festival), Feb. 27 est. (Maha Shivara-tree), March 12 (Independence), April 15 (Easter Monday), April 20 est. (Yaum-Un-Nabl), May 1 (Labor Day), Aug. 15 (Assumption), Sept. 5 est. (Ganesh Chaturthi), Sept. 16 est. (Mid-Autumn Festival), Oct. 3 est. (Id-El-Fitr), Oct. 24 (United Nations Day), Oct. 30 est. (Divali), Nov. 1 (All Saints), Nov. 8 est. (Gangam Asnam), Dec. 25 (Christmas), Dec. 26 (Boxing Day).

Mexico   Jan. 1 (New Year's), Feb. 8 (Anniversary of Mexican Constitution), March 21 (Juarez' Birthday), April 12 (Good Friday), May 1 (Labor Day), May 5 (Anniversary of The Battle of Puebla), Sept. 1 (President's Annual State of the Union Address), Sept. 16 (Anniversary of Proclamation of Mexican Independence), Oct. 12 (Columbus Day), Nov. 2 (All Souls), Nov. 20 (Revolution Day), Dec. 25 (Christmas).

Monaco   Jan. 1 (New Year's), Jan. 27 (Sainte Devote), March 5 est. (Mi-Careme), April 15 (Easter Monday), May 1 (May Day), May 23 (Ascension), June 3 (Pentecost Monday), Aug. 15 (Assumption), Nov. 1 (All Saints), Nov. 19 (National Holiday), Dec. 8 (Immaculate Conception), Dec. 25 (Christmas).

Morocco   Jan. 1 (New Year's), Jan 4 est. (Aid El Kebir), Jan. 24 est. (Moslem New Year), March 3 (Throne Day), April 5 est. (Mouloud), April 7 (Passover), April 15 (Easter Monday), May 1 (Labor Day), May 23 (Ascension), June 3 (Whit Monday), Aug. 15 (Assumption), Sept. 17 (Rosh Hashana), Sept. 26 (Yom Kippur), Oct. 17 est. (Aid El Fitr), Nov. 1 (All Saints), Dec. 25 (Christmas).

During the Moslem month of Ramadan, about Sept. 17 – Oct. 16, banks are open from 9:30 A.M. to 2 P.M., Moroccan Gov't offices, 9 A.M. to 2 P.M. In addition to Moslem holidays, the above list includes Christian and Jewish holidays that are not observed by all businesses or government agencies.

Mozambique   Jan. 1 (New Year's), June 10 (Day of Portugal), June 13 (Corpus Christi), July 24 (Lourenco Marques City Day), Aug. 15 (Assumption), Aug. 20 (Beira City Day), Oct. 5 (Day of Republican Regime), Nov. 1 (All Saints), Dec. 1 (Independence Restoration Day), Dec. 8 (Immaculate Conception), Dec. 25 (Christmas).

Nepal   Jan. 11 (Prithvi Jayanti), Jan. 29 half-day (Martyr's Day), Jan. 28 (Basant Panchami), Feb. 18 (Tribhuvan Jayanti and Democracy Day), Feb. 20 (Shivaratri), March 8 (Fagu), March 31 (Chaitra Ashtami), April 1 (Ram Nawami), April 14 (New Year's), May 6 (Buddha Jayanti), Oct. 16 (Ghatasthapana), Oct. 22 – 31 (Dashain), Dec. 16 (Mahendra Jayanti and Constitution Day), Dec. 29 (King Birendra's Birthday).

Sept. 18 (Tij), and Nov. 7 (Queen Aishwarya's Birthday) are holidays for women only.

Aug. 4 (Gai Jatra), and Sept. 30 (Indra Jatra) are half-holidays in Kathmandu Valley only.

All dates after April 14 are tentative.

Netherlands   Jan. 1 (New Year's), April 12 (Easter), April 30 (Queen's Birthday),

May 23 (Ascension), June 3 (Whit Monday), Afternoon of Dec. 5 (St. Nicholas Eve), Dec. 25–26 (Christmas).

June 29–July 13 is summer vacation for the metalworking industry. July 13–27 is summer vacation for the building and textile industry.

Netherlands Antilles   Jan. 1 (New Year's), April 12–15 (Easter), April 30 (Queen's Birthday), May 1 (Labor Day), May 23 (Ascension), June 3 (Whit Monday), Dec. 15 (Statute Day), Dec. 25 (Christmas), Dec. 26 (Boxing Day).

New Zealand   Jan. 1 (New Year's), April 12–15 (Easter), April 25 (ANZAC Day), June 3 (Queen's Birthday), Oct. 28 (Labor Day), Dec. 25 (Christmas), Dec. 26 (Boxing Day).

REGIONAL HOLIDAYS: Jan. 21 (Anniversary Day), *Wellington* only; Jan. 28 (Anniversary Day), *Auckland* only.

Nicaragua   Jan. 1 (New Year's), April 11 (Holy Thursday), April 12 (Holy Friday), May 1 (Labor Day), July 14 (Day of National Dignity), Sept. 14 (Battle of San Jacinto), Sept. 15 (Independence), Oct. 12 (Columbus Day), Dec. 25 (Christmas).

REGIONAL HOLIDAYS: Aug. 1 and Aug. 10 are *Managua* local holidays (Patron Saint) from noon on.

Niger   Jan. 1 (New Year's), Second week in Jan. est. (Tabaski), April 15 (Easter Monday), May 1 (Labor Day), Second week in May est. (Mouloud), May 23 (Ascension), June 3 (Pentecost Monday), Aug. 3 (Independence), Aug. 12 (Assumption), First Week in Nov. est. (Korite), Nov. 1 (All Saints), Nov. 18 (Republic Day), Dec. 25 (Christmas).

Nigeria   Jan. 1 (New Year's), Jan. 2–4 (Id-el-Kabir), April 4 (Id-el-Maulaud), April 12–15 (Easter), Oct. 1 (National Day), Oct. 16–17 (Id-el-Fitr), Dec. 23–24 (Id-el-Kabir), Dec. 25 (Christmas), Dec. 26 (Boxing Day).

Norway   Jan. 1 (New Year's), April 12–15 (Easter), May 1 (Labor Day), May 17 (Constitution Day), May 23 (Ascension), June 3 (Whit Monday), Dec. 25–26 (Christmas).

Oman   3–7 (Eid-al-Adha al-Mubarak), Jan. 23 est. (Moslem New Year, First of Mohram), April 5 est. (Prophet's Birthday), July 16 est. (Ascension Night of the Prophet), Oct. 18–24 est. (Eid-al-Fitr al-Mubarak), Nov. 8–19 (National Day), Dec. 25–29 est. (Eid al-Adha al-Mubarak).

Pakistan   Jan. 4–5 (Eid-ul-Azha), Feb. 3 (Muharram), March 23 (Pakistan Day), April 5 (Eid-i-Milad-un-Nabi), May 1 (May Day), Aug. 14 (Independence), Sept 6 (Defense of Pakistan Day), Sept. 11 (Death Anniversary of Quaid-i-Azam), Oct. 11 (Eid-ul-Fitr), Dec. 24–25 (Eid-ul-Azha, Birthday of Quaid-i-Azam and Christmas).

July 1 and Dec. 31 are holidays for banks only.

Panama   Jan. 1 (New Year's), Jan. 9 (Day of Mourning), Feb. 26 (Mardi Gras), April 12 (Easter), May 1 (Labor Day), Oct. 11 (Revolution Day), Nov. 3–4 (Independence), Dec. 8–9 (Mother's Day), Dec. 25 (Christmas).

In addition, the following limited holiday observances are usually scheduled: Jan. 2 (Mourning for President Remon), Aug. 15 (Founding of Panama City) observed only in *District of Panama*, Nov. 1 (Flag and Soldiers Day), Nov. 5 (Founding of City of Colon) observed only in *District of Colon*, Nov. 10 (Cry of Independence) observed in *Los Santos*.

In addition, most stores and offices may be closed Feb. 23–26.

Papua New Guinea   Jan. 1 (New Year's), April 1 (Good Friday), April 2 (Easter Saturday), April 4 (Easter Monday), June 13 (Queen's Birthday), July 23 (Remembrance Day), Sept. 16 (Independence Day), Dec. 26 (Boxing Day), Dec. 27 (Christmas).

Paraguay   Jan. 1 (New Year's), Feb. 3 (St. Bias Day), March 1 (Heroe's Day), April 11 (Holy Thursday), April 13 (Good Friday), May 1 (Labor Day), May 14–15 (Independence), June 12 (Peace of Chaco), June 13 (Corpus Christi), Aug. 15 (Founding of Ascuncion), Aug. 25 (Constitution Day), Sept. 29 (Victory of Boqueron), Oct. 12 (Columbus Day), Nov. 1 (All Saints), Dec. 8 (Our Lady of Caacupe), Dec. 25 (Christmas).

People's Republic of China   Jan. 1 (New Year's), January–February (Spring Festival, Chinese New Year—varies but shuts down virtually all business for 3 days), May 1 (Labor Day), Oct. 1–2 (China's National Day).

Peru   Jan. 1 (New Year's), April 11 half-day (Holy Thursday), April 12 (Good Friday), May 1 (Labor Day), June 29 (SS. Peter and Paul), July 28–29 (Independence), Aug. 30 (St. Rose of Lima), Oct. 9 (National Day), Nov. 1 (All Saints), Dec. 8 (Immaculate Conception), Dec. 25 (Christmas).

Philippines   Jan. 1 (New Year's), April 9 (Bataan Day), April 11–14 (Easter), May 1 (Labor Day), June 12 (Independence), July 4 (Philippine-American Friendship Day), Nov. 1 (All Saints), Nov. 30 (Bonifacio Day), Dec. 25 (Christmas), Dec. 30 (Rizal Day).

June 24 (Manila Day), is observed in *Manila* only.

Poland   Jan. 1 (New Year's), April (Easter Monday), May 1 (Worker's Day), June 13 (Corpus Christi), July 22 (National Day), Nov. 1 (All Saints), Dec. 25–26 (Christmas).

Portugal   Jan. 1 (New Year's), Feb. 26 (Carnival), April 12–13 (Easter), June 10 (Portugal Day), June 13 (Corpus Christi), Aug. 15 (Assumption), Oct. 5 (Proclamation of Portuguese Republic), Nov. 1 (All Saints), Dec. 1 (Restoration of Portuguese Independence), Dec. 8 (Immaculate Conception), Dec. 24–25 (Christmas)

June 24 (St. John's Day) is a holiday in *Oporto*.

Romania   Jan. 1–2 (New Year's), May 1–2 (Labor Day), Aug. 23–24 (National Day).

Rwanda   Jan. 1 (New Year's), April 15 (Easter Monday), May 1 (Labor Day), May 23 (Ascension), June 3 (Pentecost), July 1 (National Day), July 5 (Peace and National Unity Day), Aug. 15 (Assumption), Sept. 25 (Referendum Day), Oct. 26 (Armed Forces Day), Nov. 1 (All Saints), Dec. 25 (Christmas).

Saudi Arabia   Jan. 1–8 est. (Id al-Adha), April 3 est. (Birthday of the Prophet), Aug. 14 est. (Ascension of the Prophet), Oct. 12–19 est. (Id al-Fitr).

In addition, the normal pace of business and official activity will be interrupted during the entire month of Ramadan (beginning around Sept. 16) immediately preceding Id al-Fitr and for about a month beginning around Nov. 22 during the pilgrimage season.

Senegal   Jan. 1 (New Year's), Jan. 4 est. (Tabaski), April 4 (Independence), April 15 est. (Mouloud), April 15 (Easter Monday), May 1 (Labor Day), May 23 (Ascension), June 3 (Pentecost), July 14 (African Community Day), Aug. 15 (Assumption), Oct. 18 est. (Korite), Nov. 1 (All Saints), Dec. 25 (Christmas).

Sierra Leone Jan. 1 (New Year's), sometime in Jan. (Eid Ul Ahla), sometime in April (Moulid un Nabi), April 19 (Independence), April 11 – 14 (Easter), June 3 (Whit Monday), Aug. 5 (Bank Holiday), sometime in Oct. (Eid ul Fitri), Dec. 25 (Christmas), Dec. 26 (Boxing Day).

Singapore Jan. 1 (New Year's), Jan. 4 est. (Hari Raya Haji), Jan. 23 – 24 (Chinese New Year), April 12 (Good Friday), May 1 (Labor Day), May 6 (Vesak Day), Aug. 9 (National Day), Oct. 18 (Hari Raya Puasa), Nov. 13 est. (Deepavali), Dec. 24 est. (Hari Raya Haji), Dec. 25 (Christmas).

Solomon Islands Jan. 1 (New Year's), April 1 (Good Friday), April 2 (Holy Saturday), April 4 (Easter Monday), May 23 (Whit Monday), June 10 (Queen's Birthday), July 7 (Independence Day), Dec. 25 (Christmas), Dec. 26 (National Day of Thanksgiving).

Somalia Jan. 4 – 5 est. (Id-el-Adha), April 5 est. (Prophet's Birthday), May 1 (Labor Day), June 26 (Independence Day—northern region), July 1 (Independence Day), Oct. 21 (Revolution Day), Dec. 23 – 24 est. (Id-el-Fitr).

All businesses are closed on Fridays.

South Africa Jan. 1 (New Year's), April 12 – 15 (Easter), May 23 (Ascension), May 31 (Republic Ay), Sept. 2 (Settler's Day), Oct. 10 (Kruger Day), Dec. 16 (Day of the Covenant), Dec. 25 (Christmas), Dec. 26 (Family Day).

Spain Jan. 1 (New Year's), Jan. 6 (Epiphany), March 19 (St. Joseph), April 11 – 14 (Easter), May 1 (Labor Day), May 23 (Ascension), June 13 (Corpus Christi), June 29 (SS. Peter and Paul), July 18 (National Uprising Day), July 25 (Santiago Day), Aug. 15 (Assumption), Oct. 1 (Day of Caudillo, Government holiday only), Oct. 12 (Columbus Day), Nov. 1 (All Saints), Dec. 8 (Immaculate Conception), Dec. 25 (Christmas).

LOCAL HOLIDAYS: May 15 (St. Isidro) is celebrated in *Madrid* only; April 15 (Easter Monday), June 24 (St. John the Baptist), Sept. 24 (Our Lady of Mercy) are celebrated in *Barcelona* only; June 19 (Liberation Day), are observed only in *Bilbao*.

Saturdays, until 2 P.M. is a work day in Spain.

Sri Lanka Jan. 5 (Haj Festival), Jan. 8 (Poya), Jan. 14 (Thai Pongal), Feb. 6 (Poya), Feb. 20 (Maha Sivarathri), March 7 (Poya), April 6 (Poya and Prophet's Birthday), April 12 (Good Friday), April 13 – 14 (Sinhala and Tamil New Year's), May 1 (May Day), May 6 (Poya), Sept. 7 (Poya), Sept. 26 (Bandaranaike Commemoration Day), Sept. 30 (Poya), Oct. 17 (Ramazan Festival Day), Oct. 30 (Poya), Nov. 13 (Deepavali), Nov. 20 (Poya), Dec. 25 (Christmas and Haj Festival Day), Dec. 28 (Poya).

June 30 and Dec. 31 are bank holidays.

St. Lucia Jan. 1 – 2 (New Year's), Feb. 22 (Independence Day), April 1 (Good Friday), April 4 (Easter), May 2 (May Day), Aug. 1 (August Bank Holiday), Oct. 3 (Thanksgiving), Dec. 13 (National Day), Dec. 26 (Christmas Holiday).

St. Vincent Jan. 1 (New Year's), Jan. 22 (Discovery Day), April 1 (Good Friday), April

4 (Easter), May 2 (May Day), May 23 (Whit Monday), July 4 (Caricom Day), July 5 (Carnival), Aug. 1 (August Monday), Oct. 27 (Independence Day), Dec. 26 (Christmas Holiday).

Sudan Jan. 1 (New Year's and Independence Day), Jan. 4 – 7 est. (Kurban Bairam), Jan. 24 est. (Moslem New Year's), March 3 (Southern Accord Anniversary), April 5 est. (Sham al Naseem), May 25 (May Revolution), Oct. 12 (Inauguration Day), Oct. 17 – 19 est. (Ramadan Bairam), Dec. 24 – 27 est. (Kurban Bairam).

Businesses are closed on Fridays.

Suriname Jan. 1 (New Year's), March 9 est. (Holi Phagwa), April 12 – 15 (Easter), April 30 (Queen's Birthday), May 1 (Labor Day), July 1 (Emancipation Day), Oct. 18 est. (Id ul Fitre), Dec. 25 (Christmas), Dec. 26 (Boxing Day).

Swaziland Jan. 1 (New Year's), Jan. 12 (Inewala), April 12 – 15 (Easter), April 25 (Flag Day), May 23 (Ascension), June 10 (Commonwealth Day), July 22 (King's Birthday), Aug. 26 (Reed Dance), Sept. 6 (Independence), Oct. 24 (United Nation's Day), Dec. 25 (Christmas), Dec. 26 (Boxing Day).

Sweden Jan. 1 (New Year's), Jan. 6 (Epiphany), April 12 – 15 (Easter), May 1 (Labor Day), May 23 (Ascension), June 3 (Whit Monday), June 21 – 22 (Mid-Summer), Nov. 2 (All Saints), Dec. 24 – 26 (Christmas).

Banks, offices and government and commercial institutions will close early on Jan. 5, May 22, Nov. 1 and Dec. 31.

Switzerland Jan. 1 (New Year's), Jan. 2 (Barzelistag), April 12 – 15 (Easter), May 23 (Ascension), June 3 (Whit Monday), Aug. 1 (National Day), Dec. 24 (Christmas Eve, half-day), Dec. 25 (Christmas), Dec. 26 (St. Stephen's).

REGIONAL HOLIDAYS: Thirty other holidays are observed locally, of which the following are noteworthy for major business centers: March 4 – 6 (Carnival), *Basel*; April 22 (Sechselauten), *Zurich*; May 1 (Labor Day afternoon), *major cities*; Sept. 5 (Thanksgiving), *Geneva*; Sept. 9 (Knabenschiessen), *Zurich*; Dec. 31 (Restoration Day), *Geneva*.

Syria Jan. 1 (New Year's), Jan. 2 – 5 est. (Id al-Adha), Jan. 23 est. (Islamic New Year), Feb. 22 (National Unity Day), April 3 est. (Prophet's Birthday), April 18 (Independence), May 1 (Labor Day), Oct. 16 – 18 est. (Id al-Fitr), Dec. 24 – 27 est. (Id al-Adha).

Taiwan Jan. 1 – 2 (New Year's), Jan. 22 (Chinese New Year's Eve half-day), Jan. 23 – 24 (Chinese New Year/Spring Festival), March 29 (Youth Day), April 5 (Festival of the Sweeping Tombs), June 24 (afternoon only, Dragon Boat Festival), Sept. 28 (Confucius' Birthday/Teachers Day), Sept. 30 (Moon Festival), Oct. 10 (Double Ten Day), Oct. 25 (Taiwan Restoration Day), Nov. 12 (Dr. Sun Yat-sen's Birthday), Dec. 25 (Constitution Day).

In addition, many non-official and religious holidays are celebrated by various segments of the population. While businesses are not closed, businessmen may not be available.

Tanzania Jan. 4 est. (Id-el-Haj), Jan. 12 (Zanzibar Revolution Day), Feb. 5 (Birthday of Zanzibar Afro Shirazi Party), April 4 est. (Maulid), April 12 – 15 (Easter), April 26

(Union Day), May 1 (Worker's Day), July 7 (Saba Saba Day), Oct. 17 est. (Id-el-Fitr), Dec. 9 (Independence/Republic Day), Dec. 23 (Id-el-Haj), Dec. 25 (Christmas).

Thailand Jan. 1 (New Year's), April 6 (Chakri), April 13 (Songkran), May 5 (Coronation Day), May 6 (Wisaka Bucha), July 4 (Asalaha Bucha), July 5 (Buddhist Lent), Aug. 12 (Queen's Birthday), Oct. 23 (Chulalongkorn), Dec. 5 (King's Birthday), Dec. 10 (Constitution), Dec. 31 (New Year's Eve).

Togo Jan. 1 (New Year's), Jan. 13 (National Liberation Day), April 15 (Easter Monday), April 27 (Independence), May 1 (Labor Day), May 23 (Ascension), June 3 (Whit Monday), Aug. 15 (Assumption), Nov. 1 (All Saints), Dec. 25 (Christmas).

Trinidad & Tobago Jan. 1 (New Year's), April 12 – 15 (Easter), June 3 (Whit Monday), June 13 (Corpus Christi), June 19 (Labor Day), Aug. 5 (Discovery Day), Aug. 31 (Independence), Oct. 25 est. (Divali), Oct. 29 est. (Eid-ul-Fitr), Dec. 25 (Christmas), Dec. 16 (Boxing Day).

Little business is conducted during the National Carnival, Feb. 25 – 26.

Tunisia Jan. 1 (New Year's), Jan. 3 (Aid El Kebir), Jan. 18 (Remembrance Day), Jan. 24 (Ras El Am El Hijri), March 20 (Independence), April 5 (Mouled), April 9 (Martyr's Day), May 1 (Labor Day), June 1 – 2 (Victory Day), July 25 (Republic Day), Aug. 3 (President's Birthday), Aug. 13 (Women's Day), Sept. 3 (Commemoration Day), Oct. 15 (Evacuation of Bizerte), Oct. 16 – 17 (Aid Seghir), Dec. 25 (Aid El Kibir).

Turkey Jan. 1 (New Year's), Jan. 4 – 7 (Feast of Sacrifice), April 23 (National Sovereignty and Children's Day), May 1 (Spring Day), May 27 (Freedom and Constitution Day), Aug. 30 – 31 (Victory Day), Oct. 18 – 20 (Feast of Sugar), Oct. 29 (Independence), Dec. 24 – 27 (Feast of the Sacrifice).

United Arab Emirates Jan. 1 (New Year's), Jan. 3 est. (Waqfa), Jan. 4 – 7 est. (Eid al-Adha), Jan. 25 est. (Islamic New Year), April 4 est. (Birthday of the Prophet), Aug. 6 (Accession Day), Aug. 15 est. (Eid al-Fitr), Dec. 2 (UAE National Day).

Where a Friday falls within the projected holiday period, an additional day, either before or after the period stated, is normally added.

Although Christmas is not an official holiday, some merchants close.

United Kingdom (Includes England, Wales, Scotland, Northern Ireland, and The Channel Islands Jan. 1 (New Year's), throughout U.K.; March 18 (St. Patrick's Day), *Northern Ireland only*; April 12 – 15 (Easter), throughout U.K., May 27 (Spring Bank Holiday) *excluding Scotland, but including Channel Islands*; Aug. 5 (Scottish Bank Holiday), *Scotland only*; Aug. 26 (Late Summer Holiday), *excluding Scotland, but including Channel Islands*; Dec. 25 (Christmas), *throughout U.K.*; Dec. 26 (Boxing Day), *excluding Scotland and Channel Islands*.

Upper Volta Jan. 1 (New Year's), Jan. 3 (Revolution Day), Jan. 4 est. (Tabaski), April 15 (Easter Monday), April 5 est. (Mouloud), May 1 (Labor Day), May 23 (Ascension), June 3 (Whit Monday), Aug. 15 (Assumption), Oct. 18 est. (Ramadan), Nov. 1 (All Saints and Army Day), Dec. 11 (National Day), Dec. 25 (Christmas).

Uruguay Jan. 1 (New Year's), Jan. 6 (Epiphany), Feb. 25 – 26 (Carnival), April 11 – 12 (Holy Week—some businesses may close the entire week), May 1 (Labor Day), May 18

(Battle of Las Piedras), June 19 (Artigas' Birthday), July 18 (Constitution), Aug. 25 (Independence), Oct. 12 (Columbus Day), Nov. 2 (All Souls), Dec. 8 (Day of the Beaches), Dec. 25 (Christmas).

U.S.S.R.   Jan. 1 (New Year's), Feb. 23 (Soviet Army Day), March 8 (International Women's Day), May 1–2 (May Day/International Labor Day), May 9 (Victory Day 1945), Oct. 7 (Constitution Day), Nov. 7–8 (Anniversary of the Great October Socialist Revolution 1917).

Vanuatu   Jan. 1 (New Year's), March 5 (Custom Chief's Day), April 1 (Good Friday), April 4 (Easter Monday), May 1–2 (Labor Day), May 12 (Holy Thursday), July 29–30 (Independence Day), Aug. 15 (Assumption), Nov. 29 (Unity Day), Dec. 25 (Christmas), Dec. 26 (Family Day), Dec. 27 (Public Holiday).

Venezuela   Jan. 1 (New Year's), Jan. 6 (Epiphany), Feb. 25–26 (Carnival), March 19 (St. Joseph's), April 11–15 (Easter), April 19 (Declaration of Independence), May 1 (Labor Day), May 23 (Ascension), June 13 (Corpus Christi), June 24 (Battle of Carabobo) June 29 (SS. Peter and Paul), July 5 (Independence), July 24 (Bolivar's Birthday), Aug. 15 (Assumption), Oct. 12 (Columbus Day), Nov. 1 (All Saints), Dec. 8 (Immaculate Conception), Dec. 24 half-day (Christmas Eve), Dec. 25 (Christmas), Dec. 31 half-day (New Year's Eve).

REGIONAL HOLIDAYS: Feb. 3 (Sucre's Birthday), *Cumana, State of Sucre*; March 10 (Vargas' Day), *La Guaira*; Nov. 18 (Chiguinauira Day), *Maracaibo, State of Zulia*.

Religious holidays falling on Tuesday, Wednesday, Thursday or Friday will be automatically transferred to Monday of the following week.

Vietnam   Jan. 1 (New Year's), Jan. 22–25 (Tet-Lunar New Year), April 2 (Anniversary of King Hung Vuong), April 14 (Easter), May 1 (Labor Day), May 6 (Buddha's Birthday), Nov. 1 (National Day), Dec. 25 (Christmas).

Yemen Arab Republic   May 16–22 (Eid al-Fitr), July 23–28 (Eid al-Adha), Aug. 13 (Islamic New Year's), Sept. 26 (YAR Revolution Day), Oct. 14 (South Yemen Revolution Day—not a regular working day; some government and business employees may take off Saturday, Oct. 15), Oct. 24 (Prophet's Birthday).

Yugoslavia   Jan. 1–2 (New Year's), May 1–2 (May Day), July 4 (Fighter's Day), Nov. 29–30 (Republic Day).

REGIONAL HOLIDAYS: July 7 (Serbia Uprising Day), only in *Serbia*; July 27 (Croatian Uprising Day), only in *Croatia*.

Zaire   Jan. 1 (New Year's), Jan. 4 (Martyrs of Independence), May 1 (Labor Day), May 20 (National Party Day), June 30 (Independence), Oct. 27 (Anniversary of Changing Country's Name), Nov. 17 (Armed Forces Day), Nov. 24 (Anniversary of New Regime), Dec. 25 (Christmas).

Zambia   Jan. 1 (New Year's), March 19 (Youth Day), April 1 (Good Friday), April 2 (Holy Saturday), April 12–15 (Easter), May 1 (Labor Day), May 25 (African Freedom Day), June 3 (Whit Monday), July 1 (Heroes' Day), July 2 (Unity Day), August 1 (Farmers' Day), Aug. 12 (Youth Day), Oct. 24 (Independence), Dec. 25 (Christmas), Dec. 26 (Boxing Day).

Zimbabwe   Jan. 1 (New Year's), April 1 (Good Friday), April 4 (Easter Monday), April 18 (Independence Day), April 19 (Defense Forces National Day), May 2 (Workers' Day—public holiday), May 25 (Africa Day), August 11 – 12 (Heroes' Day), Dec. 26 – 27 (Public Holiday).

Appendix B
Foreign Currencies

Country	Currency Name	Symbol
Afghanistan	Afghani	Af.
Albania	Lek	L.
Algeria	Dinar	DA.
Argentina	Peso	$a
Australia	Dollar	$A
Austria	Schilling	S
Bangladesh	Taka	TK
Belgium	Franc	BF
Bolivia	Peso	$b
Brazil	Cruzerio	Cr$
Bulgaria	Lev	LW
Burma	Kyat	K
Canada	Dollar	CAN$
CFA	Franc	CFAF
Chile	Escudo/Peso	E
Chinese Republic	Yuan	RMBY
Colombia	Peso	Col$
Costa Rica	Colon	C
Cuba	Peso	Po
Cyprus	Pound	FC
Czechoslovakia	Koruna	K
Denmark	Krone	Dkr
Dominican Republic	Peso	RD$
Ecuador	Sucre	S/
Egypt	Pound	LE
El Salvador	Colon	C
Ethiopia	Dollar	Eth$
Finland	Franc	Fmk
France	Franc	F
Ger. (Dem. Rep.)	Mark	M
Ger. (Fed. Rep.)	Mark	DM

Country	Currency Name	Symbol
Ghana	Cedi	nC
Greece	Drachma	Dr
Guatemala	Quetzal	Q
Guinea	Syli	GF
Haiti	Gourde	G
Honduras	Lempira	L
Hong Kong	Dollar	HK$
Hungary	Forint	Ft
Iceland	Krona	Ikr
India	Rupee	Re
Indonesia	Rupiah	Rp
Iran	Rial	Rl
Iraq	Dinar	ID
Ireland	Pound	LIr
Israel	Pound	IL
Italy	Lira	Lit
Japan	Yen	Y
Jordan	Dinar	JD
Kenya	Shilling	KSh
Khmer	Riel	CR
Korea (North)	Won	WN
Korea (South)	Won	W
Kuwait	Dinar	KD
Laos	Kip	K
Lebanon	Pound	LL
Liberia	Dollar	$
Libya	Dinar	LD
Malawi	Kwacha	MK
Malaysia	Dollar/Ringgit	M$
Mali	Franc	MF
Mauritania	Ouguiya	UM
Mexico	Peso	Mex$
Mongolia	Tughrik	Tug
Morocco	Dirhan	DH
Nepal	Rupee	NRe
Netherlands Ant.	Guilder	Ant.f.

Country	Currency Name	Symbol
Netherlands	Guilder	f
New Zealand	Dollar	$NZ
Nicaragua	Cordoba	C$
Nigeria	Naira	N
Norway	Krone	NKr
Pakistan	Rupee	PRe
Panama	Balboa	B
Paraguay	Guarani	G/
Peru	Sol	Sl
Philippines	Peso	P
Poland	Zloty	zy
Portugal	Escudo	ESc
Qatar	Riyal	QR
Rhodesia	Dollar	R$
Romania	Leu	L
Saudi	Riyal	SRl
Singapore	Dollar	S$
South Africa	Rand	R
Spain	Peseta	Ptas
Sri Lanka	Rupee	SLRe
Sudan	Pound	Lsd
Surinam	Guilder	Sur.F.
Sweden	Krona	SKr
Switzerland	Franc	SWF
Syria	Pound	LS
Taiwan	(new) Dollar	NT$
Tanzania	Shilling	Tsh
Thailand	Baht	B
Tunisia	Dinar	D
Turkey	Lira	LT
Uganda	Shilling	USh
U.S.S.R.	Ruble	R
United Arab Emir.	Dirham	DL
United Kingdom	Pound Sterling	L
United States	Dollar	$
Uraguay	Peso/New Peso	UR$

Country	Currency Name	Symbol
Venezuela	Bolivar	Bs
Viet Nam	Dong	VND
Yugoslavia	Dinar	Din
Zaire	Zaire	z
Zambia	Kwacha	K

Appendix C
Foreign Management Titles

Foreign Term	Abbreviations	English Translations
French		
Administrateur	Adm.	Member of the board of directors
Administrateur-delegue or Administrateur-directeu	Adm.-digue. or Adm.-dir.	Similar to above (examples: Werksleiter, works-manager; Einkaufsleiter, purchasing agent)
Chef	—	Head of a department (example: chef du service technique, chef technician; chief d'ateleir, shop superintendent; ingenier en chef, chief engineer; chef du service des achate, purchasing agent)
Directeur	Dir.	Manager (example: Directeur de l'usine, works manager; directeur technique, technical director)
Directeur General	Dir. Gen.	General manager
Fonde de pouvoirs	—	Management person holding legal authority to sign as delegate of top management
Gerant	Ger.	Top managerial function in some small limited companies
President	Pres.	Chairman of the board of directors who is generally chief executive
Secretaire General	Sec. Gen.	Administrative head, whose function may include public relations and publicity
German		
Aufseher	—	Chief engineer
Aufsichtsratsmitglid	Aufsichtsratsmtgd	Member of board of directors
Direktor	Dir.	Manager (example: Technischer direktor, technical mgr., etc.)
Generaldirektor	Gen. Dir.	General manager, generally the executive head of a company
Ingenieur	Ing.	Engineer
Inhaber	Inh.	Owner
Leitender Ingenieur	Ltr. Eng.	Chief engineer
Leiter	Ltr.	Similar to above (examples: Werksleiter, works-manager; Einkaufsleiter, purchasing agent)
Prokurist	Prok.	Middle-manager, who holds authority to sign as a legal delegate of top management

Foreign Term	Abbreviations	English Translations
Spanish		
Consejero or miembro	Cons. or miemb.	Member of board of directors
junta directora	del la junta dir.	—
Director General or Gerente General	Dir. Gen. or Grte. Gen.	General manager
Director or Gerente	Dir. or Grte.	Manager (examples: Director tecnico, technical director; de la fabrica, plant manager)
Gerente	Ger.	Top manager in some small limited companies
Jefe	Jef.	Head (examples: Jefe de fabricacion, production manager; ingenerio jefe, chief engineer; metalurgista jefe, chief metallurgist; jefe de fabrica, works manager; jefe or agente de compras, purchasing agent)
Presidente	Prte.	President or board chairman
Socio-Gerente	Socio-Grte.	Partner-manager
Superintendents	Superintd.	Head (examples: Jefe de fabricacion, production manager; ingenerio jefe, chief engineer; metalurgista jefe, chief metallurgist; jefe de fabrica, works manager; jefe or agente de compras, purchasing agent)

Appendix D
Foreign Business Titles

Abbreviation	Language	Foreign Term	English Translation
A/B	Swedish	Aktiebolaget	Joint Stock Company
A. en P.	Spanish	Associacion en Participacion	Association in Participation
A.G.	German	Aktiengesellschaft	Joint Stock Company
A/S	Danish	Aktieselskabet	Joint Stock Company
A/S	Norwegian	Aktieselskapet	Joint Stock Company
Br.	Swedish	Broderna	Brothers
BR.	Danish and Norwegian	Broderne	Brothers
Ca.	Italian	Compagnia	Company
Cia.	Portuguese	Companhia	Company
Cia.	Spanish	Compania	Company
Cie.	French	Compagnie	Company
Com.	Spanish	Comanditario	Partner (silent)
Com.	Spanish	Comisionista	Commission Merchant
C. por A.	Spanish	Compania por Acciones	Stock Company
Estabs.	French	Establissements	Establishments
Eftf.	Norwegian	Efterfolger	Successor
Eftf.	Swedish	Eftertradare	Successor
Frs.	French	Freres	Brothers
Fgo.	Italian	Figlio, Figli	Son, Sons
Flo.	Portuguese	Filho	Son
Fls.	French	Fils	Son, Sons
F-lli.	Italian	Frateli	Brothers
F-llo.	Italian	Fratello	Brother
Ges.	German	Gesellschaft	Company
Gm.b.H.	German	Gesellschaft mit beschranker Haftung	Limited Liability Company
G.K.	Japanese	Gomei Kaisha	Unlimited Partnership
Gebr.	German	Gebruder	Brothers
Hers.	French	Heritiers	Heirs
H/B	Swedish	Handelsbolaget	Trading Company
H.mij.	Dutch	Handelmaatschappij	Trading Company
Handelsges.	German	Handelsgesellschaft	Trading Company
Hno.	Spanish	Hermano	Brother
Hnos.	Spanish	Hermanos	Brothers
Hers.	Portuguese	Herdeiros	Heirs
Hereds.	Spanish	Herederos	Heirs
Hnos. en Liq.	Spanish	Hermanos en Liquidacion	Brothers in Liquidation

Abbreviation	Language	Foreign Term	English Translation
Ims.	Portuguese	Irmaos	Brothers
K.G.	German	Kommanditgesellschaft	Limited Silent Partnership
K.B.	Swedish	Kommanditbolaget	Limited Silent Partnership
K.S.	Danish	Kommanditselskabet	Limited Silent Partnership
K.K.	Japanese	Kabushiki Kaisha	Joint Stock Company
K.G.K.	Japanese	Kabushiki Goshi Kaisha	Joint Stock Limited Partnership
K.	Japanese	Kaisha	Company
K.	Danish	Kompaniet	Company
Ka.	Japanese	Kokeisha	Successors
Kai.	Japanese	Kyodai	Brothers
Ltd.		Limited	
Ltda.	Spanish	Limitada	Limited
Lda.	Portuguese	Limitada	Limited
Mo.	Japanese	Musoko	Sons
Mij.	Dutch	Maatschappij	Company
Mn.	French	Maison	House (or store)
Nachf.	German	Nachfolger	Successor
N/V	Dutch	Namlooze Vennootschap	Stock Company
O/YO	Finnish	Osakeythic	Stock Company
Pty.	S. African, Australian	Proprietary	Corporation
Pty. Ltd.	S. African, Australian	Proprietary Limited	Limited Liability Company
Soc.Anon.	Spanish	Sociedad Anonima	Corporation
S.A.	Portuguese	Sociedade Anonima	Corporation
S.A.	French	Societe Anonyme	Corporation
S.A.	Italian	Societa Anonyma	Corporation
S.Acc.	Italian	Societa Accomandita	Limited Partnership
S.A. de C.V.	Spanish	Sociedad Anonima de	Stock Company of Variable Capital
S.A.R.L.	French	Societe a Responsabilite Limitee	Limited Liability Company
S. en C.	Spanish	Sociedad en Comandita	Limited Silent Partnership
S. en C	Portuguese	Sociedad en Commandita	Limited Silent Partnership
S. en C.	French	Societe en Commandite	Limited Silent Partnership
S. en C. por A.	Spanish	Sociedad en Comandita por Acciones	Limited Partnership by Shares
S. en N.C.	Spanish	Sociedad en Nombre Colectivo	Collective Partnership
S. en N.C.	French	Societe en Nom Collectif	Joint Stock Company
S.P.R.L.		Societe de Personnes de Responsibilite Limitee	
S.P.R.L.	Spanish	Societe en Participacion de Responsabilidad Limitda	Firm in Participation with Limited Liability
Skn	Japanese	Shoyuken	Proprietorship

Abbreviation	Language	Foreign Term	English Translation
S.p.A.	Italian	Stock Company	Societa per Azioni
S. por A.	Spanish	Stock Company	Sociedad por Acciones
Soc.	Spanish	Partnership or Company	Sociedad
Soc.	Portuguese	Partnership or Company	Sociedade
Soc.	French	Partnership or Company	Societe
Sn.	German	Son	Sohn
Sucs.	Spanish	Successors	Sucesores
Sucs.	Portuguese	Successors	Successores
Succs.	French	Successors	Successeurs
Suc.	Spanish	Branch	Sucursal
Test. de	Spanish	Estate of	Testamentaria de
Ver.	Dutch	Association	Vereeniging
Zn.	Dutch	Son	Zoon
Zen.	Dutch	Sons	Zoonen

Appendix E
U.S. Chambers of Commerce Abroad

(Source U.S. Chamber of Commerce, Washington DC, updated as of March 1, 1989)

Argentina
The American Chamber of Commerce in
    Argentina
Av. R. Saenz Pena 567
1352 Buenos Aires, Argentina
Phone: (541) 331-3436, Cable: USCHAMB-
    COM, Telex: (390) 211 39 BOS BK AR
FAX: (541) 30-7303

Australia
The American Chamber of Commerce in
    Australia
3rd Floor, 50 Pitt Street
Sydney, N.S.W. 2000, Australia
Phone: (612) 241-1907
Cable: AMCHAM SYDNEY, Telex: 72729
    ATTIAU
FAX: 011-61-2-251-5220

Austria
The American Chamber of Commerce in Austria
Turkenstrasse 9
A-1090 Vienna, Austria
Phone: (222) 31 57 51/2
Cable: USACHAMBER
FAX: (222) 31-01-632

Belgium
The American Chamber of Commerce in
    Belgium
Avenue des Arts 50, bte 5, B-1040
Brussels, Belgium
Phone: (02) 513 67 70/9
Telex: 64913 AMCHAM B
FAX: (2) 513 79 28

Bolivia
American Chamber of Commerce of Bolivia
Casilla de Correo 8268 Avda. Arce #2071. of. 2
La Paz, Bolivia
Phone: (5912)34-2523
Telex: (336) 3424 AMCHAM BV

Brazil: Rio de Janeiro
American Chamber of Commerce of
    Brazil-Rio de Janeiro, Avenida Rio
P.O. Box 916, Praco Pio X-15, 5th Fl.
Rio de Janeiro, Brazil
Phone: (5521) 203-2477
Cable: AMERCHACOM
Telex: (391) 213 4084 AMCH BR

Chile
Chamber of Commerce of the U.S.A. in the
    Republic of Chile
Av. Americao Vespucio Sur 80, 9 Piso,
    P.O. Box 4131
Santiago, Chile
Phone: (562) 484140
Cable: AMCHAMBER
Telex: (392) 340260 PBVTR CK

Colombia
Colombian-American Chamber of Commerce
Apartado Aereo 8008, Calle 35 No. 6-16
Bogota, Colombia
Phone: (571) 285-7800
Cable: CAMCOLAM BOGOTA
Telex: (396) 43326 and 45411 CAMC CO

Costa Rica

American Chamber of Commerce of Costa Rica
Calle 3, Avenidas 1 y 3, 20 piso, Apartado
    Postal 4946
San Jose, Costa Rica
Phone: (506) 33-21-33
Cable: AMCHAM
Telex: (323) 2186 POZUELO CR

Dominican Republic

American Chamber of Commerce of the
    Dominican Republic
P.O. Box 95-2, Hotel Santo Domingo
Dominican Republic
Phone: (809) 533-7292
Cable: AMCHAM
Telex: (346) 0415 TREISA

Ecuador

Ecuadorian-American Chamber of Commerce
Imbabura 214 y Panama, Piso 2, P.O. Box 11305
Guayaquil, Ecuador
Phone: (5934) 312760
Cable: EACH
Telex: (393) 43851 CAECAM ED

Egypt

American Chamber of Commerce in Egypt
Cairo Marriott Hotel, Ste. 1537, P.O. Box 33
Zamalek, Cairo Egypt
Phone: (202) 340-8883
Telex: 20870

El Salvador

American Chamber of Commerce of El Salvador
Apartado Postal (05) 9, Apt. ''A,'' 9th Floor,
    Condominio Los Heroes Blvd. Los Heroes
San Salvador, El Salvador
Phone: (503) 23-2419
Telex: (301) 20768 VERITATEM

France

The American Chamber of Commerce in France
21 Avenue George V
75008 Paris, France
Phone: (1) 47-23-70-28
Cable: AMCHAM
FAX: (1) 47 20 18 62

Germany

The American Chamber of Commerce in
    Germany
Rossmarkt 12, Postfach 100 162
D-6000 Frankfurt/Main 1, West Germany
Phone: (69) 28-34-01
Cable: AMECOC
Telex: 4189679 ACCD
FAX: (69) 28 56 32

Guam

Guam Chamber of Commerce
107 Ada Plaza Center, P.O. Box 283
Agana, Guam
Phone: (671) 472-6311
Telex: 7216160 BOOTH GM
Cable: CHAMAGANA

Guatemala

The American Chamber of Commerce in
    Guatemala
Apartado Postal 832, 7 Ave., 14-44, Zona 9 Edi-
    ficio la Galeria nivel 2, Oficina 19
Guatemala City, Guatemala
Phone: (5022) 31-22-35
Cable: AMCHAM GUTEMALA CITY
Telex: (305) 5379 PROVAR GU

Haiti

The Haitian-American Chamber of Commerce &
    Industry
Delmas P.O. Box 13486
Port-au-Prince, Haiti
Phone: (5091) 6-3164
Cable: HAMCHAM
Telex: (329) 2030001 (include address)

Honduras

Honduran-American Chamber of Commerce
Hotel Honduras Maya, Apartado Postal 1838
Tegucigalpa, Honduras
Phone: (504) 32-31-91 ext. 1056
Telex: (311) 1145 MAYA HO

Hong Kong

The American Chamber of Commerce in
  Hong Kong
1030 Swire House
Hong Kong
Phone: (852) 5-260165
Cable: AMCHAM
Telex: 83664 Amcc Hx
FAX: 011-852-5-810-1289

Indonesia

American Chamber of Commerce in Indonesia
The Landmark Centre, 22nd floor-Suite 2204,
  J1. Jendral Sudirman 1
Jakarta, Indonesia
Phone: 011-62-21-578-0656
Telex: 62822 IMARK IA
FAX: 011-62-21-578-2437

Ireland

The U.S. Chamber of Commerce in Ireland
20 College Green
Dublin 2, Ireland
Phone: (353) 1-79-37-33
Cable: AMCHAM DUBLIN
Telex: 31187 UCIL EI

Israel

Israel-American Chamber of Commerce &
  Industry
35 Shaul Hemelech Blvd., P.O. Box 33174
Tel Aviv, Israel
Phone: (3) 25 23 41/2
Telex: 32129 BETAM IL
FAX: (3) 25 12 72

Italy

The American Chamber of Commerce in Italy
Via Cantu 1, 20123
Milan, Italy
Phone: (2) 86-90-661
Cable: AMERCAM
Telex: 352128 AMCHAM I
FAX: (2) 80 57 737

Jamaica

American Chamber of Commerce of Jamaica
The Wyndham Hotel, 77 Knutsford Blvd.
Kingston 5, Jamaica
Phone: (809) 926-5430
Telex: (381) 2409 WYNDOTEL JA

Japan

The American Chamber of Commerce in Japan
Fukide Building, No. 2, 4-1-21 Toranomon,
  Minato-ku, Tokyo 105 Japan
Phone: (03) 433-5381
Cable: AMCHAM TOKYO
Telex: 2425104 KYLE J
FAX: 81-3-436-1446

Korea

The American Chamber of Commerce in Korea
Room 307, Chosun Hotel
Seoul, Korea
Phone: (822) 753-6471
Cable: AMCHAMBER
Telex: 28432 Chosun
FAX: 011-82-2-755-6577

Malaysia

American Chamber of Commerce in Malaysia
15.01, 15th Floor, Amoda, Jalan Imbi
55100 Kuala Lumpur, Malaysia
Phone: (603) 248-2407
Telex: MA 32388 AIA
FAX: 011-60-3-243-7682

Mexico

American Chamber of Commerce in Mexico
Lucerna 78-4, Mexico 6
D.F., Mexico
Phone: (905) 677-1039
Cable: AMCHAMMEX
Telex: (383) 1777609, 1771300 ACHAME

Morocco
The American Chamber of Commerce in
  Morocco
Immeuble "Xerox" 30, Avenue des Forces
  Armees Royales
Casablanca, Morocco
Phone: 22-14-49
Cable: AMCHAM
Telex: 24852 XEROX M

Netherlands
The American Chamber of Commerce in
  Netherlands
Carneigieplein 5
2517 KJ The Hague, The Netherlands
Phone: (70) 65-98-08/9
Cable: AMCHAM
Telex: 31058 AMCOC NL
FAX: (70) 64-69-92

New Zealand
The American Chamber of Commerce in
  New Zealand
P.O. Box 3408
Wellington, New Zealand
Phone: (04) 767081-J.L. Gordon
Telex: 3514 INBUSMAC NZ
FAX: 011-64-4-712-153

Nicaragua
The American Chamber of Commerce in
  Nicaragua
Apartado 202
Managua, Nicaragua
Phone: (5052) 62-486
Cable: AMCHAM
Telex: (302) 1255 VIRGIL

Pakistan
American Business Council of Pakistan
Shaheen Commercial Complex, 3rd Floor, M.R.
  Kayani Road, GPO Box 1322
Karachi Pakistan
Phone: (92) 21-526-436
Telex: 25620 CHASE PK

Panama
American Chamber of Commerce and Industry
  of Panama
Apdo. 168, Estafeta Balboa
Panama City, Panama
Phone: (507) 69-3881
Telex: (328) 3232 (ITT) BOSTONBK PA

Paraguay
Paraguayan-American Chamber of Commerce
Ntra. Senora de la Asuncion 719, Piso 8
Asuncion, Paraguay
Phone: (59521) 95-125
Telex: (399) 638 PY LAWYERS

Peru
American Chamber of Commerce of Peru
Av. Ricardo Palma 846, Miraflores
Lima 18, Peru
Phone: (5114) 47-9349
Cable: MACHAM PERU
Telex: (394) 21265 BANKAMER PE

Philippines
The American Chamber of Commerce of the
  Philippines
P.O. Box 1578, MCC
Manila, the Philippines
Phone: 818-7911
Cable: AMCHAMCOM
Telex: (ITT): 45181 AMCHAM PH
FAX: 011-632-817-6582

Portugal
American Chamber of Commerce in Portugal
Rua de D. Estefania, 155, 5Q-E
Lisbon 1000, Portugal
Phone: (1) 57 25 61
Telex: 42356 AMCHAM P

Saudi Arabia: Jeddah
The American Businessmen of Jeddah
P.O. Box 12264
Jeddah, Saudi Arabia
Phone: (966) 2-651-9068
Telex: 604697 SJ
FAX: (966) 265-11-464

Singapore
American Business Council of Singapore
Scotts Road, #16-07 Shaw Center
Singapore 0922
Phone: (65) 235-0077
Telex: 50296 ABC SIN
FAX: 011-65 732-5917

South Africa
The American Chamber of Commerce in South
Africa
P.O. Box 62280
Johannesburg, South Africa
Phone: (27) 11-788-0265
Telex: 4-29883 SA

Spain
The American Chamber of Commerce in Spain
Avenida Diagonal 477, 08036
Barcelona, Spain
Phone: (3) 321 81 95/6
Cable: AMCHAM SPAIN
FAX: (3) 321 81 97

Switzerland
Swiss-American Chamber of Commerce
Talacker 41
8001 Zurich, Switzerland
Phone: (01) 211 24 54
Cable: AMCHAMBER
Telex: 813448 IPCO CH
FAX: (1) 211-95-72

Taiwan
The American Chamber of Commerce in Taiwan
P.O. Box 17-277
Taipei, Taiwan 10419
Phone: (886) 2-551-2515
Cable: AMCHAM TAIPEI
Telex: 27841 AMCHAM
FAX: 011-886-1-542-3376

Thailand
The American Chamber of Commerce in
Thailand
P.O. Box 11-1095
Bangkok, Thailand
Phone: (662) 251-9266

Cable: AMERCHAM
Telex: 82827 KGCOM TH
FAX: 011-66-2-253-7388

Turkey
Turkish-American Businessmen's Association
Barbaros Bulvari No. 24/8, Balmumcu 80700
Istanbul, Turkey
Phone: (1) 175 16 88
Telex: 27450 MERM TR
FAX: (1) 166 23 41

United Arab Emirates
The American Business Council of Dubai
International Trade Center
Suite 1610, P.O. Box 9281
Dubai-United Arab Emirates
Phone: (971) 4 3777735
Telex: 48244 SERVE EM

United Kingdom
The American Chamber of Commerce (United
Kingdom)
75 Brook Street
London WIY 2EB, England
Phone: 01-493-0381
Cable: AMCHAM LONDON WI
Telex: 23675 AMCHAM
FAX: (1) 493 23 94

Uruguay
Chamber of Commerce of the U.S.A. in
Uruguay
Calle Bartolome Mitre 1337, Casilla de Correo
809
Montevideo, Uruguay
Phone: (5982) 95-90-59
Cable: AMCHAM
Telex: (398) 26674 BAPEN UY

Venezuela
Venezuelan-American Chamber of Commerce &
Industry
Torre Credival, Piso 10 2da Avenida de Campo
alegre, Apartado 5181
Caracas, 1010-A Venezuela
Phone: (582) 32-49-76
Cable: MABERCO
Telex: (395) 28399 CAVEA VC

Appendix F
Agent/Distributor Agreement Elements

I. Basic Component
   1. Parties to the agreement.
   2. Statement that contract supersedes all previous agreements.
   3. Fixing the duration (perhaps after a three- to six-month trial agreement).
   4. Territory:
      a) exclusive.
      b) non-exclusive.
      c) manufacturer's right to sell direct at reduced or no commission to local government and old customers.
   5. Products covered.
   6. Expression of intent to comply with government regulations.
   7. Clause limiting sales forbidden by United States Export Control Act.

II. Manufacturer's Rights
   1. Arbitration:
      a) if possible in manufacturer's country.
      b) if not, before International Arbitration Association.
      c) define rules to be applied (e.g., in selecting arbitrational panel).
      d) make sure award will be binding in distributor's country.
   2. Jurisdiction should be that of manufacturer's country (e.g., complete the signing at home).
   3. Termination conditions (e.g., manufacturer need not indemnify if contract is cancelled after due notice).
   4. Clarification of tax liabilities.
   5. Payment and discount terms.
   6. Conditions for delivery of goods.
   7. Non-liability for late delivery beyond manufacturer's reasonable control.
   8. Limitation on manufacturer's responsibility to provide information.
   9. Waiver of manufacturer's responsibility to keep lines manufactured outside the U.S. (e.g., by licensees) outside of covered territory.
  10. Right to change prices, terms, and conditions at any time.
  11. Right of manufacturer or his agent to visit territory and inspect books.
  12. Right to repurchase stock.
  13. Option to refuse or alter distributor's orders.
  14. Training of distributor personnel in U.S. subject to:
      a) practicability.
      b) costs to be paid by the distributor.
      c) waiver of manufacturer's responsibility for U.S. immigration approval.

III. Distributor's Limitations and Duties
   1. No disclosure of confidential information.
   2. Limitation of distributor's right to assign contract.
   3. Limitation on distributor's position as legal agent of manufacturer.
   4. Penalty clause for late payment.
   5. Limitation on right to handle competing lines.
   6. Placing responsibility for obtaining customs clearance.
   7. Distributor to publicize his designation as authorized representative in defined area.
   8. Requirement to remove all signs or evidence identifying him with manufacturer if relationship ends.
   9. Acknowledgment by distributor of manufacturer's ownership of trademark, trade names, patents.
   10. Information to be supplied by distributor:
       a) sales reports.
       b) names of active prospects.
       c) government regulations dealing with imports.
       d) competitive products and competitor's activities.
       e) price at which goods are sold.
       f) complete data on other lines carried on request.
   11. Information to be supplied by distributor on purchasers.
   12. Accounting methods to be used by distributor.
   13. Requirement to display products appropriately.
   14. Duties concerning advertising and promotion.
   15. Limitation on distributor's right to grant unapproved warranties, make excessive claims.
   16. Clarification of responsibility arising from claims and warranties.
   17. Responsibility of distributor to provide repair and other services.
   18. Responsibility to maintain suitable place of business.
   19. Responsibility to supply all prospective customers.
   20. Requirement that certain sales approaches and literature be approved by manufacturer.
   21. Prohibition of manufacture or alteration of products.
   22. Requirement to maintain adequate stock, spare parts.
   23. Requirement that inventory be surrendered in event of a dispute that is pending in court.

Appendix G
U.S. Foreign Trade Zones

Alabama

Zone No. 82, Mobile
OPERATOR: Mobile Airport Authority
Bldg. 11, Brookley Complex
Mobile, AL 36615
(205) 438-7334
GRANTEE: City of Mobile

Zone No. 83, Huntsville, Alabama
GRANTEE/OPERATOR: Huntsville-Madison
   County Airport Authority
P.O. Box 6006
Huntsville, AL 35806
(205) 772-9395

Zone No. 98, Birmingham, Alabama
GRANTEE/OPERATOR: City of Birmingham
Mayor's Office, City of Birmingham
Birmingham City Hall
Birmingham, AL 35203
(205) 254-2277

Alaska

Zone No. 108, Valdez, Alaska
GRANTEE: The City of Valdez, Alaska
Port of Valdez 200 S.W. Market St.
Suite 985
Portland, OR 97201-5713
(503) 227-4567

Arizona

Zone No. 48, Tucson, Arizona
GRANTEE/OPERATOR: Papago-Tiscon FTZ
   Corp.
San Xavier Community Center
P.O. Box 11246, Mission Station
Tucson, AZ 85734
(602) 881-0439

Zone No. 60, Nogales, Arizona
OPERATOR: Rivas Realty
3450 Tucson-Nogales Highway
Nogales, AZ 85621
(602) 287-3411
GRANTEE: Border Industrial Development, Inc.

Zone No. 75, Phoenix
GRANTEE: City of Phoenix
Community & Economic Dev. Adm., Suite D
920 E. Madison St.
Phoenix, AZ 85034
(602) 261-8707

Zone No. 139, Sierra Vista, Arizona
GRANTEE: Sierra Vista Economic Development
   Foundation, Inc.
P.O. Box 2380
Sierra Vista, AZ 85636
(602) 459-6070

Arkansas

Zone No. 14, Little Rock
OPERATOR: Little Rock Port Authority
7500 Lindsey Rd.
Little Rock, AR 72206
(501) 490-1468
GRANTEE: Arkansas Dept. of Industrial
   Development

California

Zone No. 3, San Francisco
OPERATOR: Foreign Trade Services, Inc.
Pier 23
San Francisco, CA 94111
(415) 391-0176
GRANTEE: San Francisco Port Commission

Zone No. 18, San Jose, California
GRANTEE: City of San Jose
801 North First St.
Rm. 408, City Hall
San Jose, CA 95110
(408) 277-5823

Zone No. 50, Long Beach, California
GRANTEE: Board of Harbor Commissioners of
the Port of Long Beach
P.O. Box 570
Long Beach, CA 90801-0570
(213) 590-4104

Zone No. 56, Oakland, California
OPERATOR: Oakland International Trade
Center, Inc.
633 Hegenberger Rd.
Oakland, CA 94621
(415) 639-7405
GRANTEE: City of Oakland

Zone No. 143, West Sacramento, California
GRANTEE: Sacramento-Yolo Port District
World Trade Center
West Sacramento, CA 95691
(916) 371-8000

Zone No. 153, San Diego, California
GRANTEE: City of San Diego
Economic Development Division, Security
Pacific Plaza
1200 Third Avenue, Suite 1620
San Diego, CA 92101
(619) 236-6550

Colorado

Zone No. 112, Colorado Springs, Colorado
OPERATOR: Front Range Foreign-Trade Zone,
Inc.
4675 Aerospace Boulevard
Colorado Springs, CO 80925
(303) 390-5666
GRANTEE: Colorado Springs Foreign-Trade
Zone, Inc.

Zone No. 123, Denver, Colorado
OPERATOR: Aspen Distribution
5401 Oswego St.
P.O. Box 39108
Denver, CO 80239
(303) 371-2511
GRANTEE: City and County of Denver

Connecticut

Zone No. 71, Windsor Locks, Connecticut
GRANTEE: Industrial Development Commission
of Windsor Locks
Town Office Building
50 Church Street
P.O. Box L
Windsor Locks, CT 06096
(203) 627-1444

Zone No. 76, Bridgeport, Connecticut
GRANTEE/OPERATOR: City of Bridgeport
City Hall
45 Lyon Terrace
Bridgeport, CT 06604
(203) 576-7135

Delaware

Zone No. 99, Wilmington, Delaware
GRANTEE/OPERATOR: State of Delaware
Delaware Development Office
Dover, DE 19901
(302) 736-4271

Florida

Zone No. 25, Port Everglades, Florida
GRANTEE/OPERATOR: Port Everglades Port
Authority
P.O. Box 13136
Port Everglades, FL 33316
(305) 523-3404

Zone No. 32, Miami
GRANTEE: Greater Miami Foreign Trade
Zone, Inc.
1601 Biscayne Blvd.
Miami, FL 33132
(305) 350-7700

Zone No. 42, Orlando
GRANTEE/OPERATOR: Greater Orlando Aviation
 Authority
9055 Tradeport Drive
Orlando, FL 32827
(407) 859-9485

Zone No. 64, Jacksonville, Florida
GRANTEE: Jacksonville Port Authority
P.O. Box 3005
Jacksonville, FL 32206
(904) 630-3070

Zone No. 65, Panama City, Florida
GRANTEE/OPERATOR: Panama City Port
 Authority
P.O. Box 15095
Panama City, FL 32406
(904) 763-8471

Zone No. 79, Tampa
GRANTEE: City of Tampa
Office of Urban Dev., City Hall
315 E. Kennedy Blvd.
Tampa, FL 33602
(813) 223-8381

Zone No. 135, Palm Beach County, Florida
GRANTEE: Port of Palm Beach District
P.O. Box 761
Palm Beach, FL 33480
(305) 832-4556

Zone No. 136, Brevard County, Florida
GRANTEE: Canaveral Port Authority
P.O. Box 267
Port Canaveral Station
Cape Canaveral, FL 32920
(407) 783-7831

Georgia

Zone No. 26, Shenandoah, Georgia
GRANTEE: Georgia Foreign-Trade Zone, Inc.
2100 RiverEdge Parkway
Suite 600
Atlanta, GA 30328
(404) 955-2100

Zone No. 104, Savannah, Georgia
GRANTEE/OPERATOR: Savannah Airport
 Commission
P.O. Box 2723
Savannah, GA 31402-2723
(912) 964-0904 or 964-0514

Zone No. 144, Brunswick, Georgia
GRANTEE: Brunswick Foreign-Trade Zone, Inc.
P.O. Box 2336
Brunswick, GA 31521
(912) 265-6900

Hawaii

Zone No. 9, Honolulu
GRANTEE/OPERATOR: State of Hawaii
Pier 2
Honolulu, HI 96813
(808) 548-5435

Illinois

Zone No. 22, Chicago
GRANTEE: Illinois International Port District
12700 Butler Drive
Lake Calumet Harbor
Chicago, IL 60633
(312) 646-4400

Zone No. 31, Granite City, Illinois
GRANTEE/OPERATOR: Tri-City Regional Port
 District
2801 Rocky Road
Granite City, IL 62040
(618) 877-8444

Zone No. 114, Peoria, Illinois
GRANTEE: Economic Development Council,
 Inc.
124 S.W. Adams, Suite 300
Peoria, IL 61602-1388
(309) 676-0755

Zone No. 133, Quad-City, Iowa/Illinois
GRANTEE: Quad-City Foreign-Trade Zone, Inc.
First National Bank of the Quad-Cities, Suite
 406
Quad-City, IL 61201
(309) 788-7436 or (319) 326-1005

Zone No. 146, Lawrence County, Illinois
GRANTEE: Bi-State Authority, Lawrenceville
Vincennes Airport
Route 4, Box 195
Lawrenceville, IL 62439
(618) 943-5733

Indiana

Zone No. 72, Indianapolis
OPERATOR: Indianapolis Economic Development
  Corporation
FTZ No. 72
P.O. Box 51681
Indianapolis, IN 46251
(317) 247-1181
GRANTEE: Indianapolis Airport Authority

Zone No. 125, South Bend, Indiana
OPERATOR: Material Trans Action
2741 N. Foundation Dr.
South Bend, IN 46634-1877
(219) 233-2666
GRANTEE: St. Joseph County Airport Authority

Zone No. 152, Burns Harbor, Indiana
GRANTEE: The Indiana Port Commission
6600 U.S. Highway 12
Portage, IN 46368
(219) 787-8636

Iowa

Zone No. 107, Des Moines, Iowa
OPERATOR: Centennial Warehouse Corporation
10400 Hickman Rd.
Des Moines, IA 50322
(515) 278-9517
GRANTEE: The Iowa Foreign-Trade Zone
  Corporation

Zone No. 133, Quad-City, Iowa/Illinois
GRANTEE: Quad-City Foreign-Trade Zone, Inc.
First National Bank of the Quad-Cities, Suite
  406
Quad-City, IL 61201
(309) 788-7436 or (319) 326-1005

Kansas

Zone No. 17, Kansas City, Kansas
GRANTEE/OPERATOR: Greater Kansas City
  FTZ, Inc.
920 Main Street, Suite 230
Kansas City, MO 64105
(816) 421-7666

Kentucky

Zone No. 29, Louisville
GRANTEE/OPERATOR: Louisville & Jefferson
  County
Riverport Authority
6219 Cane Run Road
Louisville, KY 40258
(502) 935-6024

Zone No. 47, Campbell County, Kentucky
GRANTEE/OPERATOR: Greater Cincinnati FTZ,
  Inc.
120 W. 5th Street
Cincinnati, OH 45202
(513) 579-3143

Louisiana

Zone No. 2, New Orleans
GRANTEE/OPERATOR: Board of Commissioners
  of the Port of New Orleans
P.O. Box 60046
New Orleans, LA 70160
(504) 897-0189

Zone No. 87, Lake Charles, Louisiana
GRANTEE/OPERATOR: Lake Charles Harbor &
  Terminal District
P.O. Box AAA
Lake Charles, LA 70602
(318) 439-3661

Zone No. 124, Gramercy Louisiana
GRANTEE: South Louisiana Port Commission
P.O. Drawer K
La Place, LA 70068-1109
(504) 652-9278

Zone No. 145, Shreveport, Louisiana
GRANTEE: Caddo-Bossier Parishes Port
   Commission
P.O. Box 1983
Shreveport, LA 71166
(318) 636-7266

Zone No. 154, Baton Rouge, Louisiana
GRANTEE: Greater Baton Rouge Port
   Commission
P.O. Box 380
Port Allen, LA 70767-0380
(504) 387-4207

Maine

Zone No. 58, Bangor, Maine
GRANTEE/OPERATOR: City of Bangor
Economic Dept., City Hall
Bangor, ME 04401
(207) 947-0341

Maryland

Zone No. 63, Prince George's County, Maryland
GRANTEE: Prince George's County Government
The Collington Center, Suite 104
16201 Trade Zone Ave.
Upper Marlboro, MD 20772
(310) 390-8123

Zone No. 73, Baltimore/Washington Int'l Airport
OPERATOR: All Cargo Expediting Services, Inc.
P.O. Box 28673
BWI Airport, MD 21240
(301) 859-4449
GRANTEE: Maryland Dept. of Transportation

Zone No. 74, Baltimore
GRANTEE: City of Baltimore
c/o Baltimore Economic Development Corp.
36 South Charles St.
Baltimore, MD 21201
(301) 837-9305

Massachusetts

Zone No. 27, Boston
GRANTEE: Massachusetts Port Authority
10 Park Plaza
Boston, MA 02116
(617) 973-5500

Zone No. 28, New Bedford, Massachusetts
GRANTEE/OPERATOR: City of New Bedford
Mayor's Office of Community Development,
   Rm. 215
133 William St.
New Bedford, MA 02740
(617) 999-2391 Ext. 309

Michigan

Zone No. 16, Sault Ste. Marie, Michigan
GRANTEE/OPERATOR: Economic Development
   Corp. of Sault Ste. Marie
1301 W. Easterday
Saulte Ste. Marie, MI 49783
(906) 635-9131

Zone No. 43, Battle Creek, Michigan
GRANTEE/OPERATOR: BC/CAL/KAL Inland
   Port
   Authority of S. Central Michigan Development
   Corp.
P.O. Box 1438
Battle Creek, MI 49016
(616) 968-8197

Zone No. 70, Detroit
GRANTEE/OPERATOR: Greater Detroit Foreign-
   Trade Zone, Inc.
200 Renaissance Ctr., Suite 650
Detroit, MI 48243
(313) 259-8077

Zone No. 140, Flint, Michigan
GRANTEE: Coty of Flint
Bishop International Airport
G-3425 West Bristol Road
Flint, MI 48507
(313) 766-8620

Minnesota

Zone No. 51, Duluth, Minnesota
GRANTEE/OPERATOR: Seaway Port Authority of
  Duluth
1200 Port Terminal Drive
P.O. Box 18677
Duluth, MN 55816-0877
(218) 727-8525

Zone No. 119, Minneapolis-St. Paul, Minnesota
GRANTEE: Greater Metropolitan Areaa FTZ
  Commission
1450 Minnesota World Trade Center
30 E. Seventh St.
St. Paul, MN 55101
(612) 297-4811

Mississippi

Zone No. 92, Harrison County, Mississippi
GRANTEE: Greater Gulfport/Biloxi Foreign-
  Trade Zone, Inc.
3825 Ridgewood Rd.
Jackson, MS 39211-6453
(601) 359-3038

Missouri

Zone No. 15, Kansas City, Missouri
GRANTEE/OPERATOR: Greater Kansas City
  FTZ, Inc.
920 Main Street, Suite 230
Kansas City, MO 64105
(816) 421-7666

Zone No. 102, St. Louis
GRANTEE/OPERATOR: St. Louis County Port
  Authority
130 South Bemiston
Clayton, MO 63105
(314) 721-0900

Montana

Zone No. 88, Great Falls, Montana
GRANTEE/OPERATOR: Economic Growth
  Council of Great Falls

P.O. Box 1273
Great Falls, MT 59403
(406) 761-5037

Nebraska

Zone No. 19, Omaha, Nebraska
GRANTEE/OPERATOR: Dock Board of the City
  of Omaha
Omaha-Douglas Civic Center
1819 Farnam St., Rm. 701
Omaha, NE 68183
(402) 444-5173

Zone No. 59, Lincoln, Nebraska
GRANTEE/OPERATOR: Lincoln Chamber of
  Commerce
1221 North Street, Suite 606
Lincoln, NE 68508
(402) 476-7511

Nevada

Zone No. 89, Clark County, Nevada
GRANTEE/OPERATOR: Nevada Development
  Authority
3900 Paradise Road, Suite 155
Las Vegas, NV 89109
(702) 739-8222

Zone No. 126, Sparks, Nevada
GRANTEE: Nevada Development Authority
  Nevada Foreign-Trade Zone
P.O. Box 11710
Reno, NV 89510
(702) 784-3844

New Hampshire

Zone No. 81, Portsmouth, New Hampshire
GRANTEE/OPERATOR: New Hampshire State
  Port Authority
555 Market Street
P.O. Box 506
Portsmouth, NH 03801
(603) 436-8500

New Jersey

Zone No. 44, Morris County, New Jersey
GRANTEE: N.J. Dept. of Commerce &
  Economic Dev.
Office of Int'l Trade
744 Broad St.
Newark, NJ 07102
(210) 648-3518

Zone No. 49, Newark/Elizabeth, New Jersey
GRANTEE/OPERATOR: Port Authority of NY and
  NJ
One World Trade Center, Rm. 64 West
New York, NY 10048
(212) 466-7985

Zone No. 142, Salem, New Jersey
GRANTEE: City of Salem Port Authority
62 Front Street
Salem, NJ 08709
(609) 935-6380

New Mexico

Zone No. 110, Albuquerque, New Mexico
OPERATOR: Foreign-Trade Zone of New Mexico
  FTZ Operators, Inc.
1617 Broadway N.E.
P.O. Box 26928
Albuquerque, NM 87125
(505) 842-0088
GRANTEE: The City of Albuquerque

New York

Zone No. 1, New York City
OPERATOR: S & F Warehouse, Inc.
Brooklyn Navy Yard, Bldg. 77
Brooklyn, NY 11205
(718) 834-0400
GRANTEE: City of New York

Zone No. 23, Buffalo
GRANTEE: County of Erie
Erie County Industrial Development Agency
Suite 300, Liberty Bldg.
424 Main St.
Buffalo, NY 14202
(716) 856-6525

Zone No. 34, Niagara County, New York
GRANTEE/OPERATOR: County of Niagara
County Office Bldg.
59 Park Ave.
Lockport, NY 14094
(716) 439-6033

Zone No. 37, Orange County, New York
OPERATOR: Wings Distribution, Inc.
72 Rt. 9W
New Windsor, NY 12550
(914) 562-1101
GRANTEE: County of Orange

Zone No. 52, Suffolk County, New York
GRANTEE/OPERATOR: County of Suffolk
1 Trade Zone Drive
Ronkonkoma, NY 11779
(516) 588-5757

Zone No. 54, Clinton County, New York
GRANTEE/OPERATOR: Clinton County
  Area Dev. Corp.
P.O. Box 19
Plattsburgh, NY 12901
(518) 563-3100

Zone No. 90, Onondaga, New York
GRANTEE: County of Onondaga
c/o Greater Syracuse Chamber of Commerce
100 E. Onondaga Street
Syracuse, NY 13202
(315) 470-1334

Zone No. 109, Watertown, New York
GRANTEE: The County of Jefferson
c/o Jefferson Industrial Dev. Agency
175 Arsenal St.
Watertown, NY 13601
(315) 785-3226

*Zone No. 111, JFK International Airport, New
  York*
OPERATOR: Port Authority of New York and
  New Jersey
64 N. One World Trade Center
New York, NY 10048
(212) 466-7516
GRANTEE: The City of New York

Zone No. 118, Ogdensburg, New York
GRANTEE: Ogdensburg Bridge and Port Authority
Ogdensburg, NY 13669
(315) 393-4080

Zone No. 121, Albany, New York
GRANTEE: Capital District Regional Planning Commission
214 Canal Square, 2nd Floor
Schenectady, NY 12305
(518) 393-1715

Zone No. 141, Monroe County, New York
GRANTEE: County of Monroe, New York
Monroe County Foreign-Trade Zone
110 County Office Bldg.
Rochester, NY 14614
(716) 428-5321

North Carolina

Zone No. 57, Mecklenburg County, North Carolina
OPERATOR: Piedmont Distribution Center
P.O. Box 7123
Charlotte, NC 28217
(704) 588-2868
GRANTEE: North Carolina Department of Commerce

Zone No. 66, Wilmington, North Carolina
OPERATOR: N.C. State Port Authority
2202 Burnett Blvd.
Wilmington, NC 28402
(919) 763-1621
GRANTEE: North Carolina Dept. of Commerce

Zone No. 67, Morehead City, North Carolina
OPERATOR: N.C. State Port Authority
2202 Burnett Blvd.
Wilmington, NC 28402
(919) 763-1621
GRANTEE: North Carolina Dept. of Commerce

Zone No. 93, Raleigh/Durham, North Carolina
GRANTEE: Triangle J Council of Governments
100 Park Drive, P.O. Box 12276
Research Triangle Park, NC 27709
(919) 549-0551

North Dakota

Zone No. 103, Grand Forks, North Dakota
GRANTEE/OPERATOR: Grand Forks Dev. Foundation
P.O. Box 1177
202 North 3rd
Grand Forks, ND 58206-1177
(701) 772-7271

Ohio

Zone No. 8, Toledo
GRANTEE: Toledo-Lucas County Port Authority
One Maritime Plaza
Toledo, OH 43604-1866
(419) 243-8251

Zone No. 40, Cleveland
GRANTEE: Cleveland Port Authority
101 Erieside Avenue
Cleveland, OH 44114
(216) 241-8004

Zone No. 46, Cincinnati
GRANTEE/OPERATOR: Greater Cincinnati FTZ, Inc.
120 W. 5th Street
Cincinnati, OH 45202
(513) 579-3143

Zone No. 100, Dayton, Ohio
GRANTEE/OPERATOR: Greater Dayton Foreign-Trade Zone, Inc.
1880 Kettering Tower
Dayton, OH 45423-1880
(513) 226-1444

Zone No. 101, Clinton County, Ohio
GRANTEE/OPERATOR: Airborne FTZ, Inc.
145 Hunter Drive
Wilmington, OH 45177
(513) 382-5591

Zone No. 138, Franklin County, Ohio
GRANTEE: Rickenbacker Port Authority
375 South High Street, 17th Floor
Columbus, OH 43215
(614) 461-9046

Zone No. 151, Findlay, Ohio
GRANTEE: Community Dev. Foundation
Municipal Bldg., Room 310
Findlay, OH 45840
(419) 424-7095

Oklahoma

Zone No. 53, Rogers County, Oklahoma
GRANTEE/OPERATOR: City of Tulsa-Rogers
  Cty. Port Auth.
Tulsa Port of Catoosa
5350 Cimarron Road
Catoosa, OK 74105
(918) 266-2291

Zone No. 106, Oklahoma City, Oklahoma
GRANTEE: The City of Oklahoma City
c/o Community Dev. Dept.
200 N. Walker, 4th Floor
Oklahoma City, OK 73102
(405) 231-2583

Oregon

Zone No. 45, Portland, Oregon
GRANTEE/OPERATOR: Port of Portland
P.O. Box 3529
Portland, OR 97208
(503) 231-5000 x220

Zone No. 132, Coos County, Oregon
GRANTEE: International Port of Coos Bay
  Commission
Oregon Int'l Port of Coos Bay
Port Bldg., Front & Market St.
Coos Bay, OR 97420
(503) 267-7678

Pennsylvania

Zone No. 24, Pittston, Pennsylvania
GRANTEE/OPERATOR: Econ. Dev. Council of N.
  Eastern Penn.
1151 Oak Street
Pittston, PA 18640-3795
(717) 655-5581

Zone No. 33, Pittsburgh
GRANTEE: Regional Industrial Dev. Corp of
  Southwestern Pennsylvania
Frick Building, Suite 1220
Pittsburgh, PA 15219
(412) 471 3939

Zone No. 35, Philadelphia
OPERATOR: Trans Freight Systems, Inc.
8415 Envoy Avenue
Philadelphia, PA 19153
(215) 365-7777
GRANTEE: The Philadelphia Port Corporation

Zone No. 147, Reading, Pennsylvania
GRANTEE: Foreign-Trade Zone Corporation of
  Southeastern Pennsylvania
645 Penn Street
Reading, PA 19601
(215) 376-6766

Puerto Rico

Zone No. 7, Mayaguez, Puerto Rico
GRANTEE/OPERATOR: Puerto Rico
  Industrial Dev. Co.
G.P.O. Box 2350
San Juan, PR 00936
(809) 764-1175

Zone No. 61, San Juan, Puerto Rico
GRANTEE/OPERATOR: Puerto Rico Commercial
  Dev. Co.
Commonwealth of Puerto Rico
G.P.O. Box 4943
San Juan, PR 00936
(809) 793-3090

Rhode Island

Zone No. 105, Providence and North Kingstown,
  Rhode Island
GRANTEE: Rhode Island Department of
  Economic Dev.
7 Jackson Walkway
Providence, RI 02903
(401) 277-3134

South Carolina

Zone No. 21, Dorchester County, South Carolina
OPERATOR: Carolina Trade Zone
2725 W. 5th North St.
Summerville, SC 29483
A.M. Quattlebaum (803) 871-4870
GRANTEE: South Carolina State Ports Authority

Zone No. 38, Spartanburg County, South Carolina
OPERATOR: Carolina Trade Zone
2725 W. 5th North St.
Summerville, SC 29483
(803) 871-4870
GRANTEE: South Carolina Ports Authority

Zone No. 127, West Columbia, South Carolina
GRANTEE/OPERATOR: Richland-Lexington
  Airport
  District
Columbia Metropolitan Airport
3000 Aviation Way
W. Columbia, SC 29169-2190
(803) 794-3427

Tennessee

Zone No. 77, Memphis
OPERATOR: Mid-South Terminals Company,
  Ltd.
P.O. Box 13286
Memphis, TN 38113
(901) 774-4889
GRANTEE: The City of Memphis

Zone No. 78, Nashville
GRANTEE: Metropolitan Nashville-Davidson
County Port Authority
172 Second Ave. North, Suite 212
Nashville, TN 37201
(615) 259-7468

Zone No. 134, Chattanooga, Tennessee
GRANTEE: Partners for Economic Progress,
  Inc.
1001 Market Street
Chattanooga, TN 37402
(615) 756-2121

Zone No. 148, Knoxville, Tennessee
GRANTEE: Industrial Dev. Board of Blount
  County
309 South Washington Street
Maryville, TN 37801-5095
(615) 983-7715

Texas

Zone No. 12, McAllen, Texas
GRANTEE/OPERATOR: McAllen Econ. Dev.
  Corp.
6401 S. 33rd Street
McAllen, TX 78501
(512) 682-4306

Zone No. 36, Galveston
OPERATOR: Port of Galveston
Galveston Wharves, P.O. Box 328
Galveston, TX 77553
(409) 766-6120
GRANTEE: City of Galveston

Zone No. 39, Dallas/Fort Worth
GRANTEE: Dallas/Fort Worth Regional
  Airport Board
P.O. Drawer DFW
Dallas/Fort Worth Airport, TX 75261
(214) 574-3121

Zone No. 62, Brownsville, Texas
GRANTEE/OPERATOR: Brownsville Navigation
  District Port of Brownsville
P.O. Box 3070
Brownsville, TX 78520
(512) 831-4592

Zone No. 68, El Paso, Texas
OPERATOR: El Paso International Airport
El Paso, TX 79925
(915) 772-4271
GRANTEE: City of El Paso

Zone No. 80, San Antonio
GRANTEE: City of Antonio
P.O. Box 9066
San Antonio, TX 78285
(512) 299-8080

Zone No. 84, Harris County, Texas
GRANTEE: Port of Houston Authority
P.O. Box 2562
Houston, TX 77252
(713) 670-2400

Zone No. 94, Laredo, Texas
OPERATOR: Laredo International Airport
Operator of Foreign-Trade Zone No. 94
518 Flightline, Building #132
Laredo, TX 78041
(512) 722-4933
GRANTEE: City of Laredo

Zone No. 95, Starr County, Texas
GRANTEE/OPERATOR: Starr County Industrial
  Foundation
P.O. Drawer H
Rio Grande City, TX 78582
(512) 487-5606

Zone No. 96, Eagle Pass, Texas
OPERATOR: Maverick Co. Dev. Corp.
P.O. Box 1188
Eagle Pass, TX 78853
(512) 773-3224
GRANTEE: City of Eagle Pass

Zone No. 97, Del Rio, Texas
GRANTEE/OPERATOR: City of Del Rio
City Manager's Office
P.O. Drawer DD
Del Rio, TX 78840
(512) 774-2781

Zone No. 113, Ellis County, Texas
OPERATOR: Trade Zone Operations, Inc.
100 Center Drive
Midlothian, TX 76065
(214) 299-6301
GRANTEE: Midlothian Chamber of Commerce

Zone No. 115, Beaumont, Texas
GRANTEE: Foreign-Trade Zone of Southeast
  Texas, Inc.
M-Bank Port Arthur
8200 Hwy. 69, Suite 403
Port Arthur, TX 77640
(409) 722-7831

Zone No. 116, Port Arthur, Texas
GRANTEE: Foreign-Trade Zone of Southeast
  Texas, Inc.
M-Bank Port Arthur
8200 Hwy. 69, Suite 403
Port Arthur, TX 77640
(409) 722-7831

Zone No. 117, Orange, Texas
GRANTEE: Foreign-Trade Zone of Southeast
  Texas, Inc.
M-Bank Port Arthur
8200 Hwy. 69, Suite 403
Port Arthur, TX 77640
(409) 722-7831

Zone No. 122, Corpus Christi, Texas
GRANTEE/OPERATOR: Port of Corpus Christi
  Authority
P.O. Box 1541
Corpus Christi, TX 78403
(512) 882-5633

Zone No. 155, Calhoun/Victoria Counties, Texas
GRANTEE: Calhoun-Victoria Foreign-Trade
  Zone, Inc.
2206 N. Highway 35 Bypass
Port Lavaca, TX 77979
(512) 552-3237

Zone No. 156, Weslaco, Texas
GRANTEE: City of Weslaco
500 South Kansas
Weslaco, TX 78596
(512) 968-3181 ext. 224

Zone No. 149, Freeport, Texas
GRANTEE: Port of Freeport
P.O. Box 615
Freeport, TX 77541
(409) 233-2667

Zone No. 150, El Paso, Texas
GRANTEE: Westport Econ. Dev. Corp.
#3 Butterfield Trail Blvd.
El Paso, TX 79906
(915) 775-1411

Utah

Zone No. 30, Salt Lake City
GRANTEE: Redevelopment Agency of Salt Lake
  City
285 West North Temple, Suite 200
Salt Lake City, UT 84103
(810) 328-3211

Vermont

Zone No. 55, Burlington, Vermont
GRANTEE/OPERATOR: Greater Burlington
  Industrial Corp.
P.O. Box 786
Burlington, VT 05402
(802) 863-5726

Zone No. 91, Newport, Vermont
GRANTEE/OPERATOR: Northeastern Vermont
  Dev.
  Assoc.
44 Main Street
St. Johnsbury, VT 05819
(802) 748-5181

Virginia

Zone No. 20, Suffolk, Virginia
GRANTEE: Virginia Port Authority
600 World Trade Center
Norfolk, VA 23510
(804) 683-8050

Zone No. 137, Washington Dulles Int'l Airport,
  Virginia
GRANTEE: Washington Dulles Foreign-Trade
  Zone
P.O. Box 17349
Washington Dulles Int'l Airport
Washington, DC 20041
(703) 661-8040

Washington

Zone No. 5, Seattle
GRANTEE/OPERATOR: Port of Seattle Commis-
  sion
P.O. Box 1209

Seattle, WA 98111
(206) 382-3257

Zone No. 85, Everett, Washington
GRANTEE: Puget Sound Foreign-Trade Zone
  Association
c/o Economic Development Partnership for
  Washington
18000 Pacific Highway South, Suite 400
Seattle, WA 98188
(206) 433-1629

Zone No. 86, Tacoma, Washington
GRANTEE: Puget Sound Foreign-Trade Zone
  Association
c/o Economic Development Partnership for
  Washington
18000 Pacific Highway South, Suite 400
Seattle, WA 98188
(206) 433-1629

Zone No. 120, Cowlitz County, Washington
GRANTEE: Cowlitz Economic Development
  Council
1338 Commerce, Suite 211
Longview, WA 98632
(206) 423-9921

Zone No. 128, Whatcom County, Washington
GRANTEE: Lummi Indian Business Council
2616 Kwina
Bellingham, WA 98266
(206) 734-8180

Zone No. 129, Bellingham, Washington
GRANTEE: Port of Bellingham
P.O. Box 1737
Bellingham, WA 98227-1737
(206) 676-2500

Zone No. 130, Blaine, Washington
GRANTEE: Port of Bellingham
P.O. Box 1737
Bellingham, WA 98227-1737
(206) 676-2500

Zone No. 131, Sumas, Washington
GRANTEE: Port of Bellingham
P.O. Box 1737
Bellingham, WA 98227-1737
(206) 676-2500

Wisconsin

Zone No. 41, Milwaukee
GRANTEE: Foreign Trade Zone of Wisconsin,
  Ltd.
2150 E. College Avenue
Cudahy, WI 53110
(414) 764-2111

Wyoming

Zone No. 157, Casper, Wyoming
GRANTEE: Natrona County International
  Airport
Casper, Wyoming 82604
(307) 472-6688

Appendix H
International Licensing Agreement

This agreement, made on this ___ day of _____, 19 ___, by and between ABC Corporation, a [state] corporation having its principal place of business at [city], [state], United States of America ("Licensor"), and XYZ Corporation, a [state] corporation having its principal place of business at [city], [state] ("Licensee");

WITNESSETH THAT:

Whereas Licensor is now and has been in the business of manufacturing and selling [product] identified as models [alpha/numerics], all of which are referred to hereinafter as "Licensor [product]"; and Whereas Licensor possesses engineering data and technical information on all of the Licensor [product] that he is willing to release to Licensee so that Licensee may itself manufacture and operate such [product]; and Whereas Licensor is the owner of certain Letters Patent in the licensed territory pertaining to certain of said Licensor [product], which patents are listed and identified in Exhibit "A" hereto attached; and Whereas Licensee is desirous of profiting from Licensor's information and data, entering into this agreement for the manufacture, use, and sale of the Licensor [product], and securing a license under said Letters Patent in the territory hereinafter specified.

NOW, THEREFORE:

In consideration of the premises and of the mutual covenants of the parties to be faithfully performed, the parties hereby covenant and agree as follows:

Section 1. Term

This agreement shall be effective for a period of [   ] years computed from the data of its execution.

Section 2. Grant

Licensor hereby grants to Licensee the exclusive right to manufacture, sell, and use Licensor [product] on the terms and conditions hereinafter set forth. The right to manufacture that is granted applies only to models [alpha/numerics]. Licensor agrees not to license third parties to manufacture, use, and sell embodiments of the above mentioned patents in the licensed territories so long as Licensee's license to manufacture, use, and sell the Licensor [product] is in full force and effect. The license granted shall include a license to manufacture, use, and sell the Licensor [product] under any applicable patent listed in Exhibit "A" and any additional patent of the licensed territory issued to Licensor during the term hereof.

Section 3. Territory

The license to manufacture, use, and sell granted in Section 2 shall be exclusive as to the countries listed in Exhibit "B" hereof, except when noted in said Exhibit as nonexclusive.

Section 4. Terms of payment

In consideration of the furnishing by Licensor to Licensee of the technical know-how, information, and data, Licensee hereby agrees to pay Licensor as a fixed royalty a total sum of [XXXX] thousand dollars ($XXX,XXX) in lawful currency of the United States of America, in addition to periodic royalties as hereinafter specified. This sum of [XXXX] thousand dollars ($XXX,XXX) shall be payable by Licensee to Licensor as follows:

a. [XXXX] thousand dollars ($XXX,XXX) within thirty (30) days following the execution of this agreement;

b. [XX] thousand dollars ($XX,XXX) at the end of the first twelve (12) months following the execution of this agreement;

c. [XX] thousand dollars ($XX,XXX) at the end of twenty-four (24) months following the execution of this agreement.

The initial payment provided herein shall be made before Licensor supplies Licensee with any technical information concerning the Licensor [product].

Section 5. Obligations of Licensor

a. Immediately following the first payment required in Section 4, Licensor shall supply Licensee with drawings and technical information, including, to the extent available, all drawings necessary for the production of the Licensor [product], including drawings of each part, drawings of assembled products, and drawings of jigs, tools, and testing and inspection apparatus, and data necessary for working, including processes, bills of material, working hours, and tolerances, in accordance with the following schedule, subject, however, to the continuation of payments by Licensee to Licensor as herein provided:

Model [alpha/numerics]—on or before _____
Model [alpha/numerics]—on or before _____
Model [alpha/numerics]—on or before _____
Model [alpha/numerics]—on or before _____

It is understood and agreed that these drawings and technical data shall be furnished by Licensor to Licensee in accordance with the foregoing schedule and without further payments to Licensor other than those herein specified.

b. Until Licensee shall be able to manufacture and supply the demand for Licensor [product] within the licensed territory, Licensor agrees that, at the request of Licensee, Licensor [product] shall be sold by Licensor to Licensee, in completed or "knocked down" form, in accordance with the attached Exhibit "C", subject to the maximum discounts listed therein. Payment for these Licensor [product] shall be by irrevocable letter of credit.

c. In the event any improvement of the Licensor [product], in relation to their manufacture or use, is made by either of the parties, technical information with respect thereto shall be furnished to the other party without payment. These improvements, if made by Licensee and if patentable, shall be filled and registered as patents under the joint ownership of both parties, and may be used by either party for any machine other than the Licensor [product] even after the termination of this agreement.

d. In furtherance of the program for the development of the Licensor [product] by Licensee, Licensor grants to Licensee permission at any time to send to Licensor's plant, at Licensee's expense, a reasonable supply to enable Licensee to manufacture the Licensor [product]. If requested by Licensee, Licensor will send to Licensee's plant at Licensee's expense one of Licensor's technicians at such time and for such period as may be agreed. Also upon the request of Licensee, Licensor will help and cooperate, at Licensee's expense, in Licensee's purchase of any parts necessary for the production of the Licensor [product]. The cost of these parts and their testing shall be at the expense of Licensee.

e. Licensor will furnish literature, mats of art work advertising, films, slides, and other promotional and training materials to Licensee at cost.

Section 6. Obligations of Licensee

a. Licensee agrees to bear all costs and expenses necessary to change the specification and drawings from American units to Metric units, when necessary.

b. Licensee agrees to use its best efforts to exploit and promote the increasing demand for Licensor [product] to the greatest extent possible throughout the licensed territory. To this end, Licensee agrees to maintain a competent sales, engineering, and service organization, satisfactory manufacturing facilities, and adequate factory space in good repair.

c. Licensee agrees to apply to every licensed Licensor Machine, whether manufactured to Licensor's or Licensee's specifications, the trademark "ABC" in the following manner: "ABC-XYZ." Licensee agrees that, upon termination of this Agreement, it will cease using the trademark "ABC" in any way except on [product] manufactured by it prior to such termination, and that it will voluntarily cancel any registration of any trademark, including the mark "ABC," which it may have secured during the life of this agreement.

d. Licensee agrees to permit Licensor to send a technician to Licensee's plant at any time to ascertain that the Licensor [product] are manufactured strictly in accordance with the specifications of Licensor. The cost of that inspection shall be borne by Licensor. While Licensor represents that it has made and sold commercially acceptable models of the Licensor [product], it is understood and agreed that, despite such inspections by Licensor, the operability, workmanship, and material of the licensed [product] shall be the sole responsibility of Licensee, and Licensor shall not be responsible for any damage caused by faulty or improper operation of the Licensor [product].

e. Licensee agrees that it will not do or permit any act or thing that would endanger any proprietary rights to use any trademark, trade name, or design of Licensor, and that it will not claim any proprietary interest in the trademark "ABC" except as a licensee under that mark, and then only during the life of this Agreement and subject to the control by Licensor of the nature and quality of the Licensor [product]. Licensee will, if required at any time, assign to Licensor any registration of the trademark "ABC" that it may acquire within the licensed territory, and execute any and all proper papers necessary to the protection of the trademark.

f. Licensee agrees to keep strictly confidential all technical information, drawings, specifications, manufacturing instructions, and other information relating to the Licensor [product], whether furnished by Licensor or developed or in any way acquired by Licensee in connection with the exploitation of the Licensor [product]. Licensee will not, without first obtaining the written consent of Licensor, communicate this confidential information and matters to anyone other than its employees, agents, or representatives, and then only to the extent necessary for the proper exploitation of the Licensor [product] in accordance with the provisions of this agreement.

Section 7. Royalties, minimum royalties, and reporting procedures

a. In consideration of the license herein granted and in addition to the fixed royalty payments specified in Section 4, Licensee further agrees to pay Licensor periodic royalties at the rate of four percent (4%) of Licensee's ex-factory price on each of the Licensor [product] or variations of the said models manufactured and sold hereunder. The same percentage rate shall apply on Licensee's ex-factory price for replacement parts and accessories manufactured and sold by Licensee. [Product], replacement parts, and accessories are considered sold when they are either billed out, shipped, or delivered, whichever is earliest. The ex-factory price does not include transportation, packing, insurance, service, and optional costs.

b. Periodic royalties due and accrued hereunder shall be paid by Licensee to Licensor within sixty (60) days after the close of each fiscal quarterly period of each fiscal year of this Agreement, the term "fiscal year" being defined as the twelve (12) month period following the execution of this Agreement.

c. Royalties and minimum royalties shall be payable to Licensor in United States dollars at its address in [city], [state].

d. Licensee agrees that at all times during the existence of this Agreement, it will keep accurate books of account and other records that shall contain all details relating to the manufacture and sale of the Licensor [product] and parts thereof, including the names and addresses of each purchaser of each Licensor Machine. Licensee agrees that these books of account and other records shall be kept in accordance with the legal regulations in existence in Germany and carefully preserved for at least ten (10) years.

e. Licensee agrees that it will furnish Licensor with a written statement within thirty (30) days following the close of each fiscal quarterly period showing the amount of periodic royalties due for that period. The statement shall show in detail sales of the Licensor [product] and accessories and parts therefore and the names and addresses of the customers to whom they were made. Licensee further agrees to pay Licensor within sixty (60) days after the close of each fiscal quarterly period the amount shown to be due according to the statement.

f. Licensee hereby grants to Licensor or its duly accredited representative, including any accredited certified public accountant, the right to inspect and make copies of the books of account of Licensee for the purpose of ascertaining or confirming the accuracy of the statements rendered hereunder. The cost of these inspections shall be borne by Licensor.

g. Licensee hereby agrees to pay Licensor royalties in the minimum amount of [XXXX] thousand dollars ($XX,XXX) per year beginning eighteen (18) months after the execution of this agreement. It is understood and agreed that the minimum royalties shall be paid by Licensee to Licensor within sixty (60) days following the end of the fiscal year, it being further understood and agreed that credit may be taken by Licensee against the minimum due for actual royalties already paid during the previous fiscal quarters of the year.

h. When the royalties paid by Licensee to Licensor during a particular year, calculated as hereinabove provided, exceed the minimum guaranteed yearly royalty, then the excess earned royalty of that year may be applied to one or both of two succeeding fiscal years in which the earned royalty did not amount to the guaranteed yearly minimum royalty for that particular year.

i. The total amount of royalties to be paid to Licensor by Licensee shall be calculated for each fiscal year as hereinabove defined as of the first day of the fiscal year until the last day of that fiscal year, and when the period of accounting does not reach one year, the minimum royalty shall be calculated at a daily rate as prorated according to the amounts due.

   j. Licensee shall withhold from the payments required to be remitted to Licensor the proper amount of [Country] income tax applicable thereto as required by the [Country] Government at the time of payment.

Section 8. Patent rights

Licensor makes no representation or warranty that the Licensor [product] licensed herein are free from any charge of infringement of any patent reasonable modifications in its specifications suggested to it by Licensee for the purpose of avoiding any charge of infringement that may be made.

Section 9. Termination

   a. If either party breaches any of the provisions of this Agreement, the other party may give notice of the default by registered air mail to the other party at the address stated hereinafter. If the defaulting party does not cure the breach or default within ninety (90) days from the date of receipt of the notice, then this Agreement shall terminate, subject to the terms and conditions hereinafter set forth.

   b. A party shall not be deemed to be in breach or default of any provision of this Agreement by reason of delay or failure in performance due to force majeure. However, if performance becomes impossible for more than one twelve (12) month period by reason thereof, the injured party may terminate this Agreement by giving notice as provided above.

   c. This Agreement shall terminate automatically in the event that Licensee is adjudicated to be or becomes bankrupt or places any of its property in liquidation for the purpose of meeting claims of its creditors.

   d. In the event that either party undergoes an important change in managing operations tending to alter or decrease the benefits of this Agreement to it, the period of the Agreement provided in Section 1 may be changed by mutual consent.

Section 10. Cessation of operations on termination

Upon termination or expiration of this Agreement, Licensee agrees to cease all manufacture and sale of the Licensor [product] and to return to Licensor drawings, designs, literature, and written technical information relating to the Licensor [product]. Licensee further agrees to prepare immediately upon termination or expiration of this Agreement a final accounting, which shall include all the Licensor [product] in process that Licensee shall be licensed thereafter to sell, providing royalties in respect thereto then due and payable are immediately paid. Upon termination or expiration of this Agreement, Licensee will make no further use of any technical information, drawings, specifications, manufacturing instructions, or other information relating to the Licensor [product], whether furnished by Licensor or developed or in any way acquired by Licensee in connection with the exploitation of the Licensor [product].

Section 11. Arbitration

Should there be any difference of opinion between the parties or if any dispute arises as to any of the matters provided for herein, the parties shall endeavor to settle the differences or dispute in an amicable manner through mutual consultation. In case the difference or dispute cannot be mutually settled, the matter shall be submitted for arbitration to the [Country] Commercial Arbitration Association, whose award shall be final and binding upon both parties.

Section 12. Applicable law

The law applicable to this agreement shall be the law of [Country].

Section 13. Notices

a. Notice required to be given under this Agreement shall be sent by registered air mail and addressed as follows:

ABC Corporation

_____

_____

_____

XYZ Corporation

_____

_____

_____

b. Notice of any change of mailing address of either party shall be given promptly to the other by registered air mail.

Section 14. Force majeure

No party to this Agreement shall be responsible to the other party for nonperformance or delay in performance of any terms or conditions of this Agreement due to the acts of God, acts of governments, wars, riots, strikes, accidents in transportation, or other causes beyond the control of the parties.

Section 15. Renewal

This Agreement is subject to renewal on mutually agreeable terms. A declaration of intent to renew shall be given by either Licensor or Licensee to the other party no later than one hundred and eighty (180) days prior to the expiration of this Agreement.

Section 16. Severability

Should any part or portion of this Agreement be held invalid, illegal, or void, the remainder of the Agreement shall continue in full force and effect as if the void, illegal, or invalid provision had been deleted or never included.

Section 17. Benefits

This Agreement and all rights granted pursuant to its terms shall be personal to the parties and shall be incapable of assignment, sublicense, or transfer without consent, however, shall not be withheld unreasonably.

In Witness Whereof, the parties hereto have caused this Agreement to be executed by their proper officers, duly authorized, on this _____ day of _____, 19 _____.

ABC Corporation (Licensor)
By _____
Its

Attest:

_____

Its Secretary

XYZ Corporation (Licensee)
By _____
Its

Attest:

_____

Its

Appendix I
Export Trade Certificate of Review Application

CERTIFICATIONS		
I certify that the applicant named in ITEM 1 above has authorized me to submit this application and the attachments, and to represent the applicant in seeking an export trade certificate of review.		
TYPED OR PRINTED NAME	SIGNATURE *(sign in ink)*	DATE

I certify that to the best of my knowledge and belief the information submitted in this application and the attachments is true and correct and fully responds to all items in the application.		
TYPED OR PRINTED NAME	SIGNATURE *(sign in ink)*	DATE

ITA-4093P (5-83)

USCOMM DC-83-21616

ITEM 1: Applicant/Organizer Information

Name of Applicant: _____

Principal Address: _____
Street   Room or Suite

_____
City   State   Zip

Name of Applicant's Controlling Entity, if any (if none enter "none"): _____

Principal Address: _____
Street   Room or Suite

_____
City   State   Zip

Individuals(s) authorized by the applicant to submit application and to whom all correspondence should be addressed:

Name: _____

Title: _____

Address: _____
Street   Room or Suite

_____
City   State   Zip

Telephone: _____

Relationship to Applicant: _____

ITEM 2: Name and principal address of each member, and of each member's controlling entity, if any:
(Attach to this application, clearly identifying attachment as response to ITEM 2.)

ITEM 3: Copy of any legal instrument under which the applicant is organized or will operate. Include copies, as appropriate, of its corporate charter, bylaws, partnership, joint venture, membership or other agreements or contracts under which the applicant is organized.
(Attach to this application, clearly identifying attachment as response to ITEM 3.)

ITEM 4: A brief description, preferably in the form of a chart or table, of the organization of the export-related operations of the applicant.
(Attach to this application, clearly identifying attachment as response to ITEM 4.)

ITEM 5(A) A copy of the applicant's most recent annual report, if any, and that of its controlling entity, if any.
(Attach to this application, clearly identifying attachment as response to ITEM 5(A).)

ITEM 5(B) To the extent the information is not included in the annual report, or in other documents submitted in connection with this application, attach a brief description of the applicant's operations, including:
(a) The nature of its business;
(b) The types of products or services with which it deals;
(c) The places where it does business.
(Attach this information to this application, clearly identifying attachment as response to ITEM 5(B).)

ITEM 6(A) A copy of each member's most recent annual report, if any, and that of its controlling entity, if any:
(Attach to this application, clearly identifying attachment as response to ITEM 6(A).)

ITEM 6(B) To the extent the information is not included in the annual report, or in other documents submitted in connection with this application, attach a brief description of each members operations, including:
(a) The nature of its business;
(b) The types of products or services with which it deals;
(c) The places where it does business.
(Attach this information to this application, clearly identifying attachment as response to ITEM 6(B).)

OMB Approved: 0625-0125

FORM ITA-4093P (5-83)	U.S. DEPARTMENT OF COMMERCE INTERNATIONAL TRADE ADMINISTRATION	SPECIAL ACTION:
No export trade certificate may be issued unless a completed application form has been received (15 USC 4011-4021).	**APPLICATION FOR AN EXPORT TRADE CERTIFICATE OF REVIEW**	☐ Application for Amendment ☐ Request for Expedited Review

DEPARTMENT OF COMMERCE USE ONLY		
Name of Applicant	Date Received	Date Deemed Submitted
Tracking System Number	Monitor	

CONFIDENTIALITY OF APPLICATION

Information submitted by any person in connection with the issuance, amendment, or revocation of a certificate of review is exempt from disclosure under the Freedom of Information Act, section 552, title 5, United States Code.

Except as provided under section 309(b)(2) of the Export Trading Company Act ("Act") and section 325.14(b)(3) of the regulations (15 CFR 325.14(b)(3), no officer or employee of the United States shall disclose commercial or financial information submitted pursuant to the Act if the information is privileged or confidential and if disclosure of the information would cause harm to the person who submitted the information.

NOTE: The exchange among competitors of competitively sensitive information may, in some circumstances, create risks that competition among the firms will be lessened and antitrust questions raised. The exchange of information about recent or future prices, production, sales or confidential business plans is especially sensitive. As a general matter, the danger that such exchanges will have anticompetitive effects is less when the firms involved have a small share of the market and greater if they have a substantial share.

Applicants may consider seeking the advice of legal counsel on whether any steps would be advisable in the applicant's particular circumstances to avoid issues of this nature. One possible step that the applicant may consider in preparing the application is to compile and submit these types of information through an unrelated third party, such as an attorney or consultant.

INSTRUCTIONS

The Department of Commerce urges applicants to read title III of the Export Trading Company Act (Pub. L. 97-290, Sections 4011-4021, title 15, United States Code) and the accompanying regulations (Volume 15, Code of Federal Regulations, Part 325) and the guidelines before completing this application form. These documents and additional information and guidance on the certification program are available free from:

Office of Export Trading Company Affairs
International Trade Administration
U.S. Department of Commerce
Washington, D.C. 20230
Telephone (202) 377-5131

Space is provided on the attached form for some of the information requested. In most cases you are being asked to supply additional information on supplemental sheets or attachments. Please include the name of the applicant on each supplement or attachment, and specifically identify the item number to which the attachment refers. The two certifying statements on the last page of this form MUST be completed before your application will be deemed submitted.

A person submitting information shall designate the documents or information which it considers privileged or confidential and disclosure of which would cause harm to the person submitting it.

File an original and two copies of the completed application either by first class mail, registered mail or by personal delivery during business hours to:

Office of Export Trading Company Affairs
International Trade Administration, Room 5626
U.S. Department of Commerce
Washington, D.C. 20230

Some information, in particular the identification of goods or services that the applicant exports or proposes to export, is requested in a certain form (standard industrial classification (SIC) numbers) if reasonably available. Where information does not exist in this form, an applicant is not required to create it, and may satisfy the request for information by providing it in some other convenient form.

If an applicant is unable to provide any of the information requested or if the applicant believes that any of the information requested would be burdensome to obtain and unnecessary for a determination on the application, the applicant should state that the information is not being provided or is being provided in lesser detail, and explain why.

Appendix J
International Trade Organizations

Agency for International Development (AID). The unit within the United States government responsible for the administration of United States bilateral development assistance programs. AID also participates actively in the development of other United States policies and programs related to Third World economic development.

Coordinating Committee for Multilateral Export Controls (COCOM). A committee established in 1951 by NATO member countries to coordinate their policies relating to the restriction of exports of products and technical data of potential strategic value to the Soviet Union and certain other countries. To date, it consists of NATO countries plus Japan, minus Iceland.

Council for Mutual Economic Assistance (COMECON or CMEA). An intergovernmental organization established in 1949 to coordinate the economies of member states and now consisting of the Soviet Union, Bulgaria, Czechoslovakia, the German Democratic Republic ("East Germany"), Hungary, Mongolia, Poland, Romania, Cuba, and Vietnam. The purpose of the Council, according to its charter, is to improve economic cooperation among participating countries and to accelerate their economic and technological progress.

Customs Cooperation Council (CCC). An intergovernmental organization created in 1953 and headquartered in Brussels, through which customs officials of participating countries seek to simply, standardize and conciliate customs procedures. The Council has sponsored a standardized product classification, a set of definitions of commodities for customs purposes, a standardized definition of value and a number of recommendations designed to facilitate customs procedures.

European Community (EC). A popular term for the European Communities that resulted from the 1967 "Treaty of Fusion" that merged the secretariat (the "Commission") and the intergovernmental executive body (the "Council") of the older European Economic Community (EEC) with those of the European Coat and Steel Community (ECSC) and the European Atomic Energy Community ("EURATOM"), which was established to develop nuclear fuel and power for civilian purposes.

The EEC first came into operation on Jan. 1, 1958, based on the Treaty of Rome, with six participating member states—France, Italy, the Federal Republic of Germany, Belgium, the Netherlands, and Luxembourg. From the beginning, a principal objective of the Community was the establishment of a customs union, other forms of economic integration, and political cooperation among member countries. The Treaty of Rome provided for the gradual elimination of customs duties and other internal trade barriers, the establishment of a common external tariff, and guarantees of free movement of labor and capital within the Community. The United Kingdom, Denmark and Ireland joined the Community in 1973, Greece in 1981, and Spain and Portugal in 1986. The Community is headquartered in Brussels.

The Council meets several times a year at the Foreign Ministere level, and occasionally at the Heads of State level. Technical experts from Community capitals meet regularly to deal with specialized issues in such areas as agriculture, transportation or trade policy.

European Free Trade Association (EFTA). A regional grouping established in 1960 by the Stockholm Convention, headquartered in Geneva, now comprising Austria, Iceland, Norway, Sweden, and Switzerland. Finland is an Associate Member. Denmark and the United Kingdom were formerly members, but they withdrew from EFTA when they joined the European Community in 1973. Portugal, also a former member, withdrew from EFTA in 1986 when it joined the EC.

EFTA member countries have gradually eliminated tariffs of manufactured goods originating and traded within EFTA. Agricultural products, for the most part, are not included on the EFTA schedule for internal tariff reductions. Each member country maintains its own external tariff schedule and each has concluded a trade agreement with the European Community that provides for the mutual elimination of tariffs for most manufactured goods except for a few sensitive products. As a result, the European Community and EFTA form a de facto free trade area.

Export-Import Bank of the United States (Eximbank). A public corporation created by executive order of the President in 1934 and given a statutory basis in 1945. The Bank makes guarantees and insures loans to help finance United States exports, particularly for equipment to be used in capital improvement projects. The Bank also provides short-term insurance for both commercial and political risks, either directly or in cooperation with United States commercial banks.

Foreign Credit Insurance Association (FCIA). An agency established in the United States in 1961 to offer insurance facilities in partnership with the Export-Import Bank of the United States for United States exporters.

General Agreement on Tariffs and Trade (GATT). A multilateral trade agreement aimed at expanding international trade as a means of raising world welfare. GATT rules reduce uncertainty in connection with commercial transactions across national borders. Ninety-two countries accounting for approximately 80 percent of world trade are Contracting Parties to GATT, and some 30 additional countries associated with it benefit from the application of its provisions to their trade.

The designation ''GATT'' also refers to the organization headquartered at Geneva through which the General Agreement is enforced. This organization provides a framework within which international negotiations—known as ''Rounds''—are conducted to lower tariffs and other barriers to trade, and a consultative mechanism that may be invoked by governments seeking to protect their trade interests.

The GATT was signed in 1947, as an interim agreement. It has been internationally recognized as the key international institution concerned with international trade negotiations since it became clear that the United States would not ratify the Havana Charter of 1948, which would have created an International Trade Organization (ITO) as a Specialized Agency of the United Nations system, similar to the International Monetary Fund and the World Bank. The Interim Commission of the ITO (ICITO), which was established to facilitate the creation of the ITO, subsequently became the GATT Secretariat.

The cornerstone of the GATT is the Most-Favored-Nation clause (Article I of the General Agreement). For the United States, the GATT came into existence as an executive agreement, which, under the United States Constitution, does not require Senate ratification. Part Four of the General Agreement (Articles XXXVI, XXXVII, and XXX-VIII), adopted in 1965, contains explicit commitments to ensure appropriate recognition of the development needs of developing country Contracting Parties.

International Monetary Fund (IMF). An international financial institution proposed at the 1944 Bretton Woods Conference and established in 1946 that seeks to stabilize the international monetary system as a sound basis for the orderly expansion of international trade. Specifically, among other things, the Fund monitors exchange rate policies of member countries, lends them foreign exchange resources to support their adjustment policies when they experience balance of payments difficulties, and provides them financial assistance through a special "compensatory financing facility" when they experience temporary shortfalls in commodity export earnings.

International Trade Administration (ITA). The trade unit of the United States Department of Commerce, ITA carries out the United States government's nonagricultural foreign trade activities. It encourages and promotes United States exports of manufactured goods, administers United States statutes and agreements dealing with foreign trade, and advises on United States international trade and commercial policy.

Organization for Economic Cooperation and Development (OECD). An organization based in Paris with a membership of the 24 developed countries. Their basic aims are: to achieve the highest sustainable economic growth and employment while maintaining financial stability; and to contribute to sound economic expansion worldwide and to the expansion of world trade on a multilateral, non-discriminatory basis. The OECD succeeded the Organization for European Economic Cooperation (OEEC) in 1961, after the post-World War II economic reconstruction of Europe had been largely accomplished.

Organization of Petroleum Exporting Countries (OPEC). A cartel composed of 13 leading oil producing countries that seek to coordinate oil production and pricing policies.

United Nations Conference on Trade and Development (UNCTAD). A subsidiary organ of the United States General Assembly that seeks to focus international attention on economic measures that might accelerate Third World development. The Conference was first convened (UNCTAD-I) in Geneva in 1964.

United States International Trade Commission (USITC). Formerly the United States Tariff Commission, which was created in 1916 by an Act of Congress. Its mandate was broadened and its name changed by the Trade Act of 1974. It is an independent fact-finding agency of the United States Government that studies the effects of tariffs and other restraints to trade on the United States economy. It conducts public hearings to assist in determining whether particular United States industries are injured or threatened with injury by dumping, export subsidies in other countries, or rapidly rising imports. It also studies the probable economic impact on specific United States industries of proposed reductions in United States tariffs and non-tariff barriers to imports. Its six members are appointed by the President with the advice and consent of the United States Senate for nine-year terms (six-year terms prior to 1974).

United States Trade Representative (USTR). A cabinet-level official with the rank of Ambassador who is the principal advisor to the United States President on international trade policy. The United States Trade Representative is concerned with the expansion of United States exports, United States participation in GATT, commodity issues, East-West and North-South trade, and direct investment related to trade. As Chairman of the United States Trade Policy Committee, he is also the primary official responsible for United States participation in all international trade negotiations. Prior to the Trade Agreements Act of 1979, which created the Office of the United States Trade Representative, the comparable official was known as the President's Special Representative for Trade Negotiations (STR), a position first established by the Trade Expansion Act of 1962.

World Bank. The International Bank for Reconstruction and Development (IBRD), commonly referred to as the World Bank, is an intergovernmental financial institution located in Washington, DC. Its objectives are to help raise productivity and incomes and reduce poverty in developing countries.

The World Bank was established in December 1945 on the basis of a plan developed at the Bretton Woods Conference of 1944. The Bank loans financial resources to credit worthy developing countries. It raises most of its funds by selling bonds in the world's major capital markets. Its bonds have, over the years, earned a quality rating enjoyed only by sound governments and leading corporations. Projects supported by the World Bank normally receive high priority within recipient governments and are usually well planned and supervised. The World Bank earns a profit, which is plowed back into its capital.

World Intellectual Property Organization (WIPO). A specialized agency of the United Nations system that seeks to promote international cooperation in the protection of intellectual property. WIPO administers the International Union for the Protection of Industrial Property (the "Paris Union"), which was founded in 1883 to reduce discrimination in national patent practices, the International Union for the Protection of Literary and Artistic Works (the "Bern Union"), which was founded in 1886 to provide analogous functions with respect to copyrights, and other treaties, conventions and agreements concerned with intellectual property.

Glossary

Ad Valorem Tariff A tariff calculated as percentage of the value of goods cleared through customs, e.g., 15 percent ad valorem means 15 percent of the value.

Adjustment Assistance Financial, training and reemployment technical assistance to workers and technical assistance to firms and industries to help them cope with adjustment difficulties arising from increased import competition. The objective of the assistance is usually to help an industry become more competitive in the same line of production, or to move into other economic activities. The aid to workers can take the form of training (to qualify the affected individuals for employment in new or expanding industries), relocation allowances (to help them move from areas characterized by high unemployment to areas where employment may be available, or unemployment compensation (to tide them over while they are searching for new jobs). The aid to firms can take the form of technical assistance through Trade Adjustment Assistance Centers located throughout the United States. Industry-wide technical assistance also is available through the Trade Adjustment Assistance Program. The benefits of increased trade to an importing country generally exceed the costs of adjustment, but the benefits are widely shared and the adjustment costs are sometimes narrowly—and some would say unfairly—concentrated on a few domestic producers and communities. Both import restraints and adjustment can be designed to reduce these hardships but adjustment assistance—unlike import restraints—allows the economy to enjoy the full benefits of lower-cost imported goods. Adjustment assistance also can be designed to facilitate structural shifts of resources from less productive to more productive industries.

ATA Carnet An international customs document that is recognized as an internationally valid guarantee and may be used in lieu of national customs documents and as security for import duties and taxes to cover the temporary admission of goods and sometimes the transit of goods. The ATA ("Admission Temporaire—Temporary Admission") Convention of 1961 authorized the ATA Carnet to replace the ECS ("Echantillons Commerciaux—Commercial Sample") Carnet that was created by a 1956 convention. ATA Carnets are issued by National Chambers of Commerce affiliated with the International Chamber of Commerce, which also guarantees payment of duties in the event of failure to re-export. A carnet does not replace an export license.

381

Balance of Payments   A tabulation of a country's credit and debit transactions with other countries and international institutions. These transactions are divided into two broad groups: *Current Account* and *Capital Account*. The *Current Account* includes exports and imports of goods, services (including investment income), and unilateral transfers. The *Capital Account* includes financial flows related to international direct investment, investment in government and private securities, international bank transactions, and changes in official gold holdings and foreign exchange reserves.

Balance of Trade   A component of the balance of payments, or the surplus or deficit that results from comparing a country's expenditures on merchandise imports and receipts derived from its merchandise exports.

Beggar-Thy-Neighbor Policy   A course of action whereby a country tries to reduce unemployment and increase domestic output by raising tariffs and instituting non-tariff barriers that impede imports, or by imposing competitive devaluation. Countries that pursued such policies in the early 1930's found that other countries retaliated by raising their own barriers against imports, which, by reducing export markets, tended to worsen the economic difficulties that precipitated the initial protectionist action; i.e., The Smoot-Hawley Tariff Act of 1930.

Bilateral Trade Agreement   A formal or informal agreement involving commerce between two countries. Such agreements sometimes list the quantities of specific goods that may be exchanged between participating countries within a given period.

Bounties or Grants   Payments by governments to producers of goods, often to strengthen their competitive position.

chonghap-mooyeok-sangsa   The Korean, term for a general trading company.

c.i.f.   An abbreviation used in some international sales contracts, when the selling price includes all "costs, insurance and freight" for the goods sold ("charge in full"), meaning that the seller arranges and pays for all relevant expenses involved in shipping goods from their point of exportation to a given point of importation. In import statistics, "c.i.f. value" means that all figures are calculated on this basis, regardless of the nature of individual transactions.

Codes of Conduct   International instruments that indicate standards of behavior by nation states or multinational corporations deemed desirable by the international community. Several codes of conduct were negotiated during the Tokyo Round that liberalized and harmonized domestic measures that might impede trade, and these are considered legally binding for the countries that choose to adhere to them. Each code is monitored by a special committee that meets under the auspices of GATT and encourages consultations and the settlement of disputes arising under the code. Countries that are not Contracting Parties to GATT may adhere to these codes. GATT Articles III and XXIII also contain commercial policy provisions that have been described as GATT's code of good conduct in trade matters. The United Nations also has encouraged several "voluntary" codes of conduct, including one that seeks to specify the rights and obligations of trans-national corporations and of governments.

Commodity   Broadly defined, any article exchanged in trade, but most commonly used to refer to raw materials, including such minerals as tin, copper and manganese, and bulk-produced agricultural products such as coffee, tea and rubber.

Common External Tariff (CXT)   A tariff rate uniformly applied by a common market or customs union, such as the European Community, to imports from countries outside the union. For example, the European Common Market is based on the principle of a free internal trade area with a common external tariff (also referred to in French as the *Tarif Exterieur Commun*—TEC) applied to products imported from non-member countries. "Free trade areas" do not always have common external tariffs.

Comparative Advantage   A central concept in international trade theory that holds that a country or a region should specialize in the production and export of those goods and services that it can produce relatively more efficiently than other goods and services, and import those goods and services in which it has a comparative disadvantage. This theory was first propounded by David Ricardo in 1817 as a basis for increasing the economic welfare of a population through international trade. The comparative advantage theory normally favors specialized production in a country based on intensive utilization of those factors of production in which the country is relatively well endowed (such as raw materials, fertile land or skilled labor), and perhaps also the accumulation of physical capital and the pace of research.

Countertrade   A reciprocal trading arrangement Countertrade transactions include:

Counterpurchase obligates the foreign supplier to purchase from the buyer goods and services unrelated to the goods and services sold, usually within a one- to five-year period.

Reverse countertrade contracts require the importer (a United States buyer of machine tools from Eastern Europe, for example) to export goods equivalent in value to a specified percentage of the value of the imported goods—an obligation that can be sold to an exporter in a third country.

Buyback arrangements obligate the foreign supplier of plant, machinery, or technology to buy from the importer a portion of the resultant production during a 5- to 25-year period.

Clearing agreements are made between two countries that agree to purchase specific amounts of each other's products over a specific period of time, using a designated "clearing currency" in the transactions.

"Switch" arrangements permit the sale of unpaid balance of a clearing account to be sold to a third party, usually at a discount, that may be used for producing goods in the country holding the balance.

Swap schemes are devised so products from different locations can be traded to save transportation costs (e.g. Soviet oil may be "swapped" for oil from a Latin American producer, so the Soviet oil is shipped to a country in South Asia, while the Latin American oil is shipped to Cuba).

Barter arrangements are made when two parties directly exchange goods deemed to be of approximately equivalent value without any flow of money taking place.

Countervailing Duties   Special duties imposed on imports to offset the benefits of subsidies to producers or exports in the exporting country. GATT Article VI permits the use of such duties. The Executive Branch of the United States government has been legally empowered since the 1890s to impose countervailing duties in amounts equal to any "bounties" or "grants" reflected in products imported into the United States. Under United States law and the Tokyo Round Agreement on Subsidies and

Countervailing Duties, a wide range of practices are recognized as constituting subsidies that may be offset through the imposition of countervailing duties.

Current Account That portion of a country's balance of payments that records current (as opposed to capital) transactions, including visible trade (exports and imports), invisible trade (income and expenditures for services), profits earned from foreign operations, interest and transfer payments.

Customs Classification The particular category in a tariff nomenclature in which a product is classified for tariff purposes, or the procedure for determining the appropriate tariff category in a country's nomenclature system used for the classification, coding and description of internationally traded goods. Most important trading nations—except for the United States, Canada, and the Soviet Union—classify imported goods in conformity with the Customs Cooperation Council Nomenclature (CCCN), formerly known as the Brussels Tariff Nomenclature (BTN).

Customs Harmonization International efforts to increase the uniformity of customs nomenclatures and procedures in cooperating countries. The Customs Cooperation Council has been seeking since 1970 to develop an up-to-date and internationally accepted "Harmonized Commodity Coding and Description System" for classifying goods for customs, statistical and other purposes. The Council hopes most of the major trading countries will implement the system by 1987.

Devaluation The lowering of the value of a national currency in terms of the currency of another nation. Devaluation tends to reduce domestic demand for imports in a country by raising their prices in terms of the devalued currency and to raise foreign demand for the country's exports by reducing their prices in terms of foreign currencies. Devaluation can therefore help to correct a balance of payments deficit and sometimes provide a short-term basis for economic adjustment of a national economy.

Developed Countries A term used to distinguish the more industrialized nations—including all OECD member countries as well as the Soviet Union and most of the socialist countries of Eastern Europe—from "Developing"—or less developed—countries. The developed countries are sometimes collectively designated as the "North," because most of them are in the Northern Hemisphere.

Developing Countries (LCDs) A broad range of countries that generally lack a high degree of industrialization, infrastructure and other capital investment, sophisticated technology, widespread literacy, and advanced living standards among their populations as a whole. Developing countries are sometimes collectively designated as the "South," because a large number of them are in the southern hemisphere. All of the countries of Africa (except South Africa), Asia and Oceania (except Australia, Japan and New Zealand), Latin America, and the Middle East are generally considered developing countries, as are a few European countries (Cyprus, Malta, Turkey and Yugoslavia, for example). Some experts define four subcategories of developing countries which have different economic needs and interest:

1. A few relatively wealthy OPEC countries—sometimes referred to as oil exporting developing countries—share a particular interest in a financially sound international economy and open capital markets
2. Newly Industrializing Countries (NIC's) have a growing stake in an open international trading system

3. A number of middle income countries—principally commodity exporters—have shown a particular interest in commodity stabilization schemes

4. More than 30 very poor countries (*least developed countries*) are predominantly agricultural, have sharply limited development prospects during the near future, and tend to be heavily dependent on official development assistance.

Dispute Settlement   Resolution of conflict, usually through a compromise between opposing claims, sometimes facilitated through the efforts of an intermediary. GATT Articles XXII and XXIII set out consultation procedures a Contracting Party may follow to obtain legal redress if it believes its benefits under GATT are impaired.

Domestic International Sales Corporation   (Interest Charge DISC). A special United States corporation authorized by the United States Revenue Act of 1971, as amended by the Tax Reform Act of 1984, to borrow from the United States Treasury at the average one-year Treasury bill interest rate to the extent of income tax liable on 94 percent of its annual corporate income. To qualify, the corporation must derive 95 percent of its income from United States exports; also, at least 95 percent of its gross assets, such as working capital, inventories, building and equipment, must be export-related. Such a corporation can buy and sell independently, or can operate as a subsidiary of another corporation. It can maintain sales and service facilities outside the United States to promote and market its goods.

Dumping   Under United States law, the sale of an imported commodity in the United States at "less than fair value," usually considered to be a price lower than that at which it is sold within the exporting country or to third countries. "Fair value" can also be the constructed value of the merchandise, which includes a mandatory 8 percent profit margin plus cost of production. Dumping is generally recognized as an unfair trade practice that can disrupt markets and injure producers of competitive products in the importing country. Article VI of GATT permits the imposition of special antidumping duties against "dumped" goods equal to the difference between their export price and their normal value in the exporting country.

Drawback   Import duties or taxes repaid by a government, in whole or in part, when the imported goods are re-exported or used in the manufacture of exported goods.

Embargo   Prohibition upon exports or imports, either with respect to specific products or specific countries. Embargoes have been ordered most frequently in time of war, but they may also be applied for political, economic or sanitary purposes. Embargoes imposed against an individual country by the United Nations—or a group of nations—in an effort to influence its conduct or its policies are sometimes called *sanctions*.

Escape Clause   A provision in a bilateral or multilateral commercial agreement permitting a signatory nation to suspend tariff or other concessions when imports threaten serious harm to the producers of competitive domestic goods. GATT Article XIX sanctions such "safeguard" provisions to help firms and workers adversely affected by a relatively sudden surge of imports adjust to the rising level of import competition. Section 201 of the United States Trade Act of 1974 requires the United States International Trade Commission to investigate complaints formally known as "petitions" filed by domestic industries or workers claiming that they have been injured or are threatened with injury as a consequence of rapidly rising imports and to complete any such investigation within six months. Section 203 of the Act provides that if the Commission finds that a domestic industry has been seriously injured or threatened with serious injury, it may recommend that the president grant relief to the industry in the form of adjustment assistance or temporary import restrictions in the form of tariffs, quotas, or tariff quotas. The president must then take action pursuant to the Commission's recommendations within 60 days, but he may accept, modify or reject them, according to his assessment of the national interest. The Congress can, through majority vote in both the Senate and the House of Representatives within 90 legislative days, override a presidential decision not to implement the Commission's recommendations. The president may impose import restrictions for an initial period of five years and to extend them for a maximum additional period of three years.

Exchange Controls The rationing of foreign currencies, bank drafts, and other instruments for settling international financial obligations by countries seeking to ameliorate acute balance of payments difficulties. When such measures are imposed, importers must apply for prior authorization from the government to obtain the foreign currency required to bring in designated amounts and types of goods. Because such measures restrict imports, they are considered non-tariff barriers to trade.

Exchange Rate The price (or rate) at which one currency is exchanged for another currency, for gold, or for Special Drawing Rights (SDR's).

Excise Tax A selective tax—sometimes called a *consumption tax*—on certain goods produced within, or imported into a country.

Export Quotas Specific restrictions or ceilings imposed by an exporting country on the value or volume of certain imports, designated to protect domestic producers and consumers from temporary shortages of the goods affected or to bolster their prices in world markets. Some International Commodity Agreements explicitly indicate when producers should apply such restraints. Export quotas are also often applied in Orderly Marketing Agreements and Voluntary Restraint Agreements, and to promote domestic processing of raw materials in countries that produce them.

Export Restraints Quantitative restrictions imposed by exporting countries to limit exports to specified foreign markets, usually pursuant to a formal or informal agreement concluded at the request of the importing countries.

Export Subsidies Government payments or other financially quantifiable benefits provided to domestic producers or exporters contingent on the export of their goods or services. GATT Article XVI recognizes that subsidies in general, and especially export subsidies, distort normal commercial activities and hinder the achievement of GATT objectives. An Agreement on Subsidies and Countervailing Duties negotiated during the Tokyo Round strengthened the GATT rules on export subsidies and provided for an outright prohibition of export subsidies by developed countries for manufactured and semi-manufactured products. The Agreement also established a special committee, serviced by signatories. Under certain conditions, the Agreement allows developing countries to use export subsidies on manufactured and semi-manufactured products, and on primary products as well, provided that the subsidies do not result in more than an equitable share of world exports of the product for the country.

f.a.s. Abbreviation of *Free Alongside Ship*. In international trade, refers to the point of embarkation from which the vessel or plane selected by the buyer will transport the goods. Under this system, the seller is obligated to pay the costs and assume all risks for transporting the goods from his place of business to the f.a.s. point. In trade statistics, "f.a.s. value" means that the import or export figures are calculated on this basis, regardless of the nature of individual transactions reflected in the statistics.

f.o.b.   An abbreviation used in some international sales contracts, when imports are valued at a designated point, as agreed between buyer and seller. The seller is obligated to have the goods packaged and ready for shipment from the agreed point, whether his own place of business or some intermediate point, and the buyer normally assumes the burden of all inland transportation costs and risks in the exporting country, as well as all subsequent transportation costs, including the costs of loading the merchandise on the vessel. However, if the contract stipulates "f.o.b. vessel" the seller bears all transportation costs to the vessel named by the buyer, as well as the costs of loading the goods onto that vessel. The same principle applies to the abbreviations "f.o.r." ("Free on Rail") and "f.o.t." ("Free on Truck"). (The abbreviations f.o.b., f.o.r. and f.o.t. may also be uppercase.)

Foreign Sales Corporation (FSC)   A firm incorporated in Guam, the United States Virgin Islands, the Commonwealth of the Northern Mariana Islands, American Samoa, or any foreign country that has a satisfactory exchange-of-information agreement with the United States and elects to be taxed as a United States corporation, except for the fact that it exempts from taxable income a portion of the combined net income of the FSC and its affiliated supplier on the export of United States products.

Free Trade   A theoretical concept that assumes international trade unhampered by government measures such as tariffs or non-tariff barriers. The objective of trade liberalization is to achieve "freer trade" rather than "free trade," it being generally recognized among trade policy officials that some restrictions on trade are likely to remain in effect for the foreseeable future.

Free Trade Area   A group of two or more countries that have eliminated tariff and most non-tariff barriers affecting trade among themselves, while each participating country applies its own independent schedule of tariffs to imports from countries that are not members. The best example is the European Free Trade Association (EFTA)—and the free trade area for manufactured goods that has been created through the trade agreements between the European Community and the individual EFTA countries. GATT Article XXIV defines a free trade area in GATT and specifies the applicability of other GATT provisions to free trade areas.

Free Zone   An area within a country (a seaport, airport, warehouse or any designated area) regarded as being outside its customs territory. Importers may therefore bring goods of foreign origin into such an area without paying customs duties and taxes, pending their eventual processing, transshipment or re-exportation. Free zones were numerous and prosperous during an earlier period when tariffs were high. Some still exist in capital cities, transport junctions and major seaports, but their number and prominence have declined as tariffs have fallen in recent years. Free zones may also be known as "free ports," "free warehouses," and "foreign trade zones."

Generalized System of Preference (GSP)   A concept developed within UNCTAD to encourage the expansion of manufactured and semi-manufactured export from developing countries by making goods more competitive in developed country markets through tariff preferences. The GSP reflects international agreement, negotiated at UNCTAD-II in New Delhi in 1968, that a temporary and non-reciprocal grant of preferences by developed countries to developing countries would be equitable and, in the long-term, mutually beneficial.

Government Procurement Policies and Practices   Means and mechanisms through which official government agencies purchase goods and services. Government procurement policies and practices are non-tariff barriers to trade if they discriminate in favor of domestic suppliers when competitive imported goods are cheaper or of better quality. The United States pressed for an international agreement during the Tokyo Round to ensure that government purchase of goods entering into international trade would be based on specific published regulations that prescribe open procedures for submitting bids, as had been the traditional practice in the United States. The Government Procurement Code (effective 1981) negotiated during the Tokyo Round sought to reduce the ''Buy National'' bias underlying certain practices by improving transparency and equity in national procurement practices and by ensuring effective recourse to dispute settlement procedures.

Graduation   The presumption that individual developing countries are capable of assuming greater responsibilities and obligations in the international community—within GATT or the World Bank, for example—as their economies advance, as through industrialization, export development, and rising living standards. In this sense, graduation implies that donor countries may remove the more advanced developing countries from eligibility for all or some products under the Generalized System of Preferences. Within the World Bank, graduation moves a country from dependence on concessional grants to non-concessional loans from international financial institutions and private banks.

Import Substitution   An attempt by a country to reduce imports (and hence foreign exchange expenditures) by encouraging the development of domestic industries.

Industrial Policy   Encompasses traditional government policies intended to provide a favorable economic climate for the development of industry in general or specific industrial sectors. Instruments of industrial policy may include tax incentives to promote investments or exports, direct or indirect subsidies, special financing arrangements, protection against foreign competition, worker training programs, regional development programs, assistance for research and development, and measures to help small business firms. Historically, the term industrial policy has been associated with at least some degree of centralized economic planning or indicative planning, but this connotation is not always intended by its contemporary advocates.

Infant Industry Argument   The view that ''temporary protection'' for a new industry or firm in a particular country through tariff and non-tariff barriers to imports can help it to become established and eventually competitive in world markets. Historically, new industries that are soundly based and efficiently operated have experienced declining costs as output expands and production experience is acquired. However, industries that have been established and operated with heavy dependence on direct or indirect government subsidies have sometimes found it difficult to relinquish that support. The rationale underlying the Generalized System of Preferences is comparable to that of the infant industry argument.

Intellectual Property   Ownership conferring the right to possess, use, or dispose of products created by human ingenuity, including patents, trademarks and copyrights.

Investment Performance Requirements   Special conditions imposed on direct foreign investment by recipient governments, sometimes requiring commitments to export a certain percentage of the output, to purchase given supplies locally, or to ensure the employment of a specified percentage of local labor and management.

Joint Venture   A form of business partnership involving joint management and the sharing of risks and profits as between enterprises based in different countries. If joint ownership of capital is involved the partnership is known as an *equity joint venture*.

Least Developed Countries (LDCs)   Some 36 of the world's poorest countries, considered by the United Nations to be the least developed of the less developed countries. Most of them are small in terms of area and population, and some are land-locked or small island countries. They are generally characterized by low per capita incomes, literacy levels, and medical standards; subsistence agriculture; and a lack of exploitable minerals and competitive industries. Many suffer from aridity, floods, hurricanes, and excessive animal and plant pests, and most are situated in the zone 10 to 30 degrees north latitude. These countries have little prospect of rapid economic development in the foreseeable future and are likely to remain heavily dependent upon official development assistance for many years. Most are in Africa, but a few, such as Bangladesh, Afghanistan, Laos, and Nepal, are in Asia. Haiti is the only LDC in the Western Hemisphere. *See* DEVELOPING COUNTRIES.

Liberal   In trade policy, usually means relatively free of import controls or restraints and/or a preference for reducing existing barriers to trade, often contrasted with the protectionist preference for retaining or raising selected barriers to imports.

Mixed Credits   Exceptionally liberal financing terms for an export sale, ostensibly provided for a foreign aid purpose.

Mercantilism   A prominent economic philosophy in the 16th and 17th centuries that equated the accumulation and possession of gold and other international monetary assets, such as foreign currency reserves, with national wealth. Although this point of view is generally discredited among 20th century economists and trade policy experts, some contemporary politicians still favor policies designated to create trade "surpluses," such as import substitution and tariff protection for domestic industries, as essential to national economic strength.

Most-Favored-Nation Treatment (MFN)   The policy of non-discrimination in trade policy that provides to all trading partners the same customs and tariff treatment given to the so-called Most-Favored-Nation. Since 1923 the United States has incorporated an "unconditional" Most-Favored-Nation clause in its trade agreements, binding the contracting governments to confer upon each other all the most favorable trade concessions that either may grant to any other country subsequent to the signing of the agreement. The United States now applies this provision to its trade with all of its trading partners except for those specifically excluded by law. The MFN principle also has provided the foundation of the world trading system since the end of World War II. All Contracting Parties to GATT apply MFN treatment to each other under Article I of GATT.

Multi-Fiber Arrangement Regarding International Trade in Textiles (MFA)   An international compact under GATT that allows an importing signatory country to apply quantitative restrictions on textiles imports when it considers them necessary to prevent market disruption. The MFA provides a framework for regulating international trade in textiles and apparel with the objectives of achieving "orderly marketing" of such products, and of avoiding "market disruption" in importing countries. It provides a basis on which major importers, such as the United States and the European Community, may negotiate bilateral agreements or, if necessary, impose restraints on imports from low-wage producing countries. It provides, among other things, standards for determining market disruption, minimum levels of import restraints, and equal growth of imports. The MFA went into effect on Jan. 1, 1974, was renewed in December 1977, in December 1981, and again in July 1986, for five years. It succeeded the Long-term Agreement on International Trade in Cotton Textiles ("The LTA"), which had been in effect since 1962. Whereas, the LTA applied only to cotton textiles, the MFA now applies to wool, man-made (synthetic) fiber, silk blend and other vegetable fiber textiles and apparel.

Multilateral Agreement An international compact involving three or more parties. For example, GATT has been, since its establishment in 1947, seeking to promote trade liberalization through multilateral negotiations.

Multilateral Trade Negotiations (MTN) Seven Rounds of "Multilateral Trade Negotiations" have been held under the auspices of GATT since 1947. Each round represented a discrete and lengthy series of interacting bargaining sessions among the participating contracting parties in search of mutually beneficial agreements looking toward the reduction of barriers to world trade. The agreements ultimately reached at the conclusion of each Round became new GATT commitments and thus amounted to an important step in the evolution of the world trading system.

Newly Industrializing Countries (NICs) Relatively advanced developing countries whose industrial production and exports have grown rapidly in recent years. Examples include Brazil, Hong Kong, Korea, Mexico, Singapore and Taiwan.

Non-Market Economy (NME) A national economy or a country in which the government seeks to determine economic activity largely through a mechanism of central planning, as in the Soviet Union, in contrast to a market economy that depends heavily upon market forces to allocate productive resources.

Non-Tariff Barriers (NTBs) Government measures other than tariffs that restrict imports. Such measures have become relatively more conspicuous impediments to trade as tariffs have been reduced during the period since World War II.

Orderly Marketing Agreements (OMAs) Negotiated between two or more governments, in which the trading partners agree to restrain the growth of trade in specified "sensitive" products, usually through the imposition of import quotas. OMAs are intended to ensure that future trade increases will not disrupt, threaten or impair competitive industries or their workers in importing countries.

Paris Club A term for meetings between representatives of a developing country that wishes to renegotiate its "official" debt (excluding debts owned by and to the private sector without official guarantees and representatives of the relevant creditor governments and international institutions). Meetings normally take place at the initiative of a debtor country that wishes to consolidate all or part of its debt service payments falling due in a specified period. Meetings are traditionally chaired by a senior official of the French Treasury Department. Comparable meetings occasionally take place in London and in New York for countries that wish to renegotiate repayment terms for their debts to private banks. Sometimes called "creditors clubs."

Par Value   The official fixed exchange rate between two currencies or between a currency and a specific weight of gold or a basket of currencies.

Peril Point   A hypothetical limit beyond which a reduction in tariff protection would cause injury to a domestic industry. United States legislation in 1949 that extended the Trade Agreements Act of 1934 required the Tariff Commission to establish such "peril points" for United States industries, and for the president to submit specific reasons to Congress when any United States tariff was reduced below those levels. This requirement, which was an important constraint on United States negotiating positions in early GATT tariff-cutting rounds, was eliminated by the Trade Expansion Act of 1962.

Protectionism   The deliberate use or encouragement of restrictions on imports to enable inefficient domestic producers to compete successfully with foreign producers.

Quantitative Restrictions (QRs)   Explicit limits, or quotas, on the physical amounts of particular commodities that can be imported or exported during a specific time period, usually measured by volume but sometimes by value. The quota may be applied on a "selective" basis, with varying limits set according to the country of origin, or on a quantitative global basis that only specifies the total limit and thus tends to benefit efficient suppliers. Quotas are frequently administered through a system of licensing. GATT Article XI generally prohibits the use of quantitative restrictions, except under conditions specified by other GATT articles; Article XIX permits quotas to safeguard certain industries from damage by rapidly rising imports; Articles XII and XVIII provide that quotas may be imposed for balance of payments reasons under circumstances laid out in Article XV; Article XX permits special measures to apply to public health, gold stocks, items of archaeological or historic interest, and several other categories of goods; and Article XXI recognizes the overriding importance of national security. Article XII provides that quantitative restrictions, whenever applied, should be non-discriminatory.

Reciprocity   The practice by which governments extend similar concessions to each other, as when one government lowers its tariffs or other barriers impeding its imports in exchange for equivalent concessions from a trading partner on barriers affecting its exports (a "balance of concessions"). Reciprocity has traditionally been a principal objective of negotiators in GATT "Rounds." Reciprocity is also defined as "mutuality of benefits," "quid pro quo," and "equivalence" of advantages. GATT Part IV (especially GATT Article XXXVI) and the "Enabling Clause" of the Tokyo Round "Framework Agreement" exempt developing countries from the rigorous application of reciprocity in their negotiations with developed countries.

Retaliation   Action taken by a country to restrain its imports from a country that has increased a tariff or imposed other measures that adversely affects its exports in a manner inconsistent with GATT. GATT, in certain circumstances, permits such reprisal, although it has very rarely been practiced. The value of trade affected by such retaliatory measures should, in theory, approximately equal the value affected by the initial import restriction.

Round of Trade Negotiations   A cycle of multilateral trade negotiations under the aegis of GATT, culminating in simultaneous trade agreements among participating countries to reduce tariff and non-tariff barriers to trade. Seven "Rounds" have been completed thus far: Geneva, 1947–48; Annecy, France, 1949; Torquay, England, 1950–51; Geneva, 1956; Geneva, 1960–62 (the Dillon Round); Geneva 1963–67 (the Kennedy Round); and Geneva, 1973–79 (the Tokyo Round).

Section 301 (of the Trade Act of 1974)   Provision of United States law that enables the president to withdraw concessions or restrict imports from countries that discriminate against United States exports, subsidize their own exports to the United States, or engage in other unjustifiable or unreasonable practices that burden or discriminate against United States trade.

Smoot-Hawley Tariff Act of 1930   United States protectionist legislation that raised tariff rates on most articles imported by the United States, triggering comparable tariff increases by United States trading partners. Also known as Smoot-Hawley Tariff.

Special Drawing Rights (SDRs)   Created in 1969 by the International Monetary Fund as a supplemental international monetary reserve asset. SDRs are available to governments through the fund and may be used in transactions between the fund and member governments. IMF member countries have agreed to regard SDRs as complementary to gold and reserve currencies in settling their international accounts. The unit value of an SDR reflects the foreign exchange value of a "basket" of currencies of several major trading countries (the United States dollar, the German mark, the French franc, the Japanese yen, and the British pound). The SDR has become the unit of account used by the fund and several national currencies are pegged to it. Some commercial banks accept deposits denominated in SDRs (although unofficial and not the same units transacted among governments and the fund).

State Trading Nations   Countries such as the Soviet Union, the People's Republic of China, and nations of Eastern Europe that rely heavily on government entities, instead of the private sector, to conduct trade with other countries. Some of these countries, (e.g., Czechoslovakia and Cuba) have long been Contracting Parties to GATT, whereas others (e.g., Poland, Hungary and Romania) became Contracting Parties later under special Protocols of Accession. The different terms and conditions under which these countries acceded to GATT were designed in each case to ensure steady expansion of the country's trade with other GATT countries, taking into account the relative insignificance of tariffs on imports into state trading nations.

Subsidy   Economic benefit granted by a government to producers of goods, often to strengthen their competitive position. May be direct (a cash grant) or indirect (i.e., low-interest export credits guaranteed by a government agency.)

Tariff   A duty (or tax) levied upon goods transported from one customs area to another. Tariffs raise the prices of imported goods, thus making them less competitive within the market of the importing country. After seven "Rounds" of GATT trade negotiations that focused heavily on tariff reductions, tariffs are less important measures of protection than they used to be. The term "tariff" often refers to a comprehensive list or "schedule" of merchandise with the rate of duty to be paid to the government for importing products listed.

Terms of Trade   The volume of exports that can be traded for a given volume of imports. Changes in the terms of trade are generally measured by comparing changes in the ratio of export prices to import prices. The terms of trade are considered improved when a given volume of exports can be exchanged for a larger volume of imports.

Tied Loan A loan made by a government agency that requires a foreign borrower to spend the proceeds in the lender's country.

Trade Policy Committee (TPC) A senior inter-agency committee of the United States government, chaired by the United States Trade Representative, that provides broad guidance to the President on trade policy issues. Members include the Secretaries of Commerce, State, Treasury, Agriculture, and Labor.

Transparency Visibility and clarity of laws and regulations. Some codes negotiated during the Tokyo Round sought to increase the transparency of non-tariff barriers that impede trade.

Trigger Price Mechanism (TPM) A United States system for monitoring imported steel to identify imports that are possibly being "dumped" in the United States or subsidized by the governments of exporting countries. The minimum price under this system is based on the estimated landed cost at a United States port of entry of steel produced by the world's most efficient producers. Imported steel entering the United States below that price may "trigger" formal anti-dumping investigations by the Department of Commerce and the United States International Trade Commission. The TPM was in effect between early 1978 and March 1980, reinstated in October 1980, and suspended for all products except for stainless steel wire in January 1982.

Turnkey Contract A compact under which the contractor assumes responsibility to the client for constructing productive installations and ensuring that they operate effectively before turning them over to the client. By centering responsibility for the contributions of all participants in the project in his own hands, the contractor is often able to arrange more favorable financing terms than the client. The responsibility of the contractor ends when he hands the completed installation over to the client.

Unfair Trade Practices Unusual government support to firms—such as export subsidies—or certain anti-competitive practices by firms themselves—such as dumping, boycotts or discriminatory shipping arrangements—that result in competitive advantages for the benefiting firms in international trade.

Valuation The appraisal of the worth of imported goods by customs officials for the purpose of determining the amount of duty payable in the importing country. The GATT Customs Valuation Code obligates governments that sign it to use the "transaction value" of imported goods—or the price actually paid or payable for them—as the principal basis for valuing the goods for customs purposes.

Value-Added Tax (VAT) An indirect tax on consumption that is levied at each discrete point in the chain of production and distribution, from the raw material stage to final consumption. Each processor or merchant pays a tax proportional to the amount by which he increases the value of the goods he purchases for resale after making his own contribution. The value-added tax is imposed throughout the European Community and EFTA countries, but tax rates have not been harmonized.

Voluntary Restraint Agreements (VRAs) Informal arrangements through which exporters voluntarily restrain certain exports, usually through export quotas, to avoid economic dislocation in an importing country, and to avert the possible imposition of mandatory import restrictions. Such arrangements do not normally entail "compensation" for the exporting country.

Bibliography

Prolog

Brooks, George E. Jr. *Yankee Traders, Old Coasters and African Middlemen: A History of American Legitimate Trade with West Africa in the Nineteenth Century.* Massachusetts: Boston University Press, 1970.

Carlson, Jack and Graham, Hugh. "The Economic Importance of Exports to the United States." In Center for Strategic and International Studies, ed., *The Export Performance of the United States: Political, Strategic and Economic Implications.* New York: Praeger, 1981.

Dart, Margret S. *Yankee Traders at Sea and Ashore.* New York: The William-Frederick Press, 1965.

Drucker, Peter F. *Frontiers of Management.* New York, NY: E.P. Dutton, 1986.

Economic Indicators, January 1975, Prepared for the Joint Economic Committee by the Council of Economic Advisors. Washington, DC: GPO.

Economic Indicators, May 1983, Prepared for the Joint Economic Committee by the Council of Economic Advisors. Washington, DC: GPO.

Hartland-Thunberg, Penelope. "The Political and Strategic Importance of Exports." In Center for Strategic and International Studies, ed., *The Export Performance of the United States: Political, Strategic and Economic Implications*, New York: Praeger, 1981.

Schlosstein, Steve. *Trade War: Greed, Power, and Industrial Policy on Opposite Sides of the Pacific.* Congdon & Weed, Inc. NY, 1984.

U.S. Department of Commerce. *Historical Statistics of the United States: Colonial Times to 1970.* Bicentennial Edition; part 2, chapter U, page 858. Washington, DC: GPO, 1975.

U.S. Department of Commerce. International Trade Administration. 1983. *Current International Trade Position of the United States.* Washington, DC: GPO.

U.S. Department of Commerce. International Trade Administration. 1988. *Current International Trade Position of the United States.* Washington, DC: GPO.

Chapter One

Drucker, Peter F. "The Changed World Economy." *Journal of the Flagstaff Institute*. Feb. 1987.

Whalen, Richard J. "Politics and the Export Mess." In Center for Strategic and International Studies, ed., *The Export Performance of the United States: Political and Economic Implications*. New York: Praeger, 1981.

Chapter Two

Axtell, Roger E., Editor and Compiler. *Do's and Taboos Around the World: A Guide to International Behavior*. The Parker Pen Company, 1985.

Chung, Dr. Sunny. "Here's Help in Understanding International Culture Shock." *Currents*, the Newsletter of United States International University, May 1989.

Harris, Phillip and Moran, Robert. *Managing Cultural Differences*. Intercultural Press, Inc., 1982.

Jang, Song-Hyon. "The Ten Commandments for Doing Business in Korea." *Business Korea*. January 1985.

Lowe, Janet. "It's Just a Matter of Manners." *The San Diego Tribune*, 1985.

Oberg, Dr. Kalervo. "Culture Shock." *Anthropologist*, Health, Welfare and Housing Division, U.S. A.I.D./Brazil.

Nelson, Commander Carl A. U.S. Navy, "Student Notes for Cross-cultural Survival," U.S. Navy, Pre-Vietnam duty, 1971.

Seligman, Scott D. "A Shirt-sleeve Guide to Chinese Corporate Etiquette." *The Chinese Business Review*, January-February, 1983.

"Time Can Reap Japanese Sales." Ed., *San Diego Union*, January 21, 1989.

Chapter Three

Bilkey, Warren J., and Tesar, George. "The Export Behavior of Smaller-sized Wisconsin Manufacturing Firms." *Journal of Industrial Business Studies*, Spring/Summer, pp. 93–98, 1977.

Becker, Tom and Porter, James. "How You Can Use the New Export Trading Companies." *Industrial Marketing*, January 1983.

Breen, George. *Marketing Research*. McGraw-Hill, 1982, 2d ed.

Boone and Kurtz. *Contemporary Marketing*. The Dryden Press, 1980, 3d ed.

Brooks, Mary R. and Rosson, Philip J. "A Study of Export Behavior of Small- and Medium-size Manufacturing Firms in Three Canadian Provinces." In Michael R. Czinkota, and George Tesar, ed., *Export Management: An International Context*. New York: Praeger, 1982.

Cateora, Philip R. *International Marketing*. Richard D. Irwin, Inc., 1983, 5th ed.

Cavusgil, S. Tamer. "Some Observations on the Relevance of Critical Variables for Internationalization Stages." In Michael R. Czinkota, and George Tesar, ed., *Export Management: An International Context*. New York: Praeger, 1981.

Dodge, H. Robert, Fullerton, Sam D., Rink, David R., and Merrill, Charles E. *Marketing Research*. Bell & Howell Companies, 1982.

Johnson, Wesley J. and Czinkota, Michael R. "Managerial Motivation as Determinants of Industrial Export Behavior." In Michael R. Czinkota, and George Tesar, ed., *Export Management: An International Context*. New York: Praeger, 1982.

Joynt, Pat. "An Empirical Study of Norwegian Export Behavior." In Michael R. Czinkota, and George Tesar, ed., *Export Management: An International Context*. New York: Praeger, 1982.

McKay, Edward S. *The Marketing Mystique*. New York: American Management Association, Inc., 1972.

Pavord, William C., and Bogart, Raymond G. "The Dynamics of the Decision to Export." *Akron Business and Economic Review*. 6, No. 1 (Spring): 6–11, 1975.

Ried, Stan. "The Impact of Size on Export Behavior in Small Firms." In Michael R. Czinkota, and George Tesar, ed., *Export Management: An International Context*. New York: Praeger, 1982.

Terpstra, Vern. *International Marketing*. The Dryden Press, 1983, 3d ed.

U.S. Department of Commerce. International Trade Administration. *A Basic Guide to Exporting*. Washington, DC: Superintendent of Documents, 1981.

U.S. Small Business Administration. *Export Marketing for Smaller Firms*. Washington, DC: 1979, 4th ed.

Walsh, James I. "Export-Competitive U.S. Manufacturers: Industry and Product Characteristics." In Michael R. Czinkota, and George Tesar, ed., *Export Management: An International Context*. New York: Praeger.

Chapter Four

Juran, Dr. Joseph M. *Juran on Quality Improvement*. Juran Enterprises, Inc., 866 United Nations Plaza, New York, NY 10017.

Raia, Ernest. "Better Value, Bigger Profits." *Purchasing*. June 8, 1989.

Rugnetta, Frank. "Personal interview with Dr. Carl A. Nelson," Solar Turbines, Inc., subsidiary of Caterpillar, Inc., May 10, 1989.

Suzaki, Kiyoshi. *The New Manufacturing Challenge: Techniques for Continuous Improvement*. The Free Press, a division of MacMillan, Inc., 1987.

Chapter Five

Hayes, Robert H. and Wheelwright, Steven C. *Restoring Our Competitive Edge: Competing Through Manufacturing*. John Wiley & Sons, 1984.

Peters, Thomas J. and Waterman Jr., Robert H. *In Search of Excellence: Lessons from America's Best-Run Companies*. New York: Harper & Row, 1982.

Chapter Six

Pasquinelli Jr., Arthur. *Services: How to Export, A Marketing Manual*. Northern California District Export Council, Nov. 1982.

Reed, John S. "The Service Sector: The Key to America's Economic Future." *Analysis, Reports and Briefings from the Congressional Economic Leadership Institute*. Washington, DC: June 22, 1989.

U.S. Department of Commerce. *The Services Industries Development Program*. Report by the Secretary of Commerce, April 1989.

U.S. Department of Commerce. *U.S. National Study on Trade in Services*. A Submission by the United States Government to the General Agreement on Tariffs and Trade, 1988.

Chapter Seven

Cronin, Steven. "Problems of the Export Management Company in Southern California." Thesis, San Diego State University, Fall 1982.

U.S. Department of Commerce. International Trade Administration. *Directory of U.S. Export Management Companies*. Washington, DC: April 1981.

U.S. Department of Commerce. International Trade Administration. *Partners in Export Trade: The Directory for Export Trade Contacts*. Washington, DC: 1987.

Chapter Eight

Becker, Tom. "Proposed Export Trading Company Legislation: A Panacea for Expanding Exports and Transfer of Appropriate Technology to Latin America." In Center for Strategic and International Studies, ed. *The Export Performance of the United States: Political and Economic Implications*. New York: Praeger, 1981.

Cao, A.D. "U.S. Export Trading Companies-The Time Is Now." *Business*. September-October 1981.

Federal Register VII, 15 CFR 325, *Guidelines for Issuance of Export Trade Certificates of Review*: Notice, Friday January 11, 1985, 2d ed.

Federal Register VII, 15 CFR 325. *Export Trade Certificates of Review; Final Rule*. Friday, January 11, 1985.

Green Memo. "The Export Trading Company Act of 1982. P.L. 97-290." Washington D.C. General Council's Office, National Association of Manufacturers. November 3, 1982.

Hoffheinz, Roy Jr., and Calder, Kent E. *The Eastasia Edge*. New York: Basic Books Inc., 1982.

Meissner, Frank. "U.S. Export Trading Companies: Is the Japanese Success Story Reproducible, Adoptable, or Improvable?" In Michael R. Czinkota, and George Tesar, ed., *Export Policy: A Global Assessment*. New York: Praeger, 1982.

Nelson, Carl A. "The Relationship of Export Obstacles to the Export Trading Company Act of 1982." Dissertation, United States International University, 1984.

Public Law 97-290. United States 97th Congress. *Export Trading Company Act of 1982*. October 8, 1982.

Reishauer, Edwin O. *Japan Past and Present*. Japan: Charles E. Tuttle Inc., 1964, 3d ed.

Sung, Cho Dong. *Korean General Trading Companies*. Bub Moon Sa, 1988.

U.S. Congress. House. Committee on Foreign Affairs, Subcommittee on International Economic Policy and Trade Hearings and Markup, 96th Cong., 2d Sess., May 22, June 4, 10, 18, 24, and July 1, 1980. Washington, DC: GPO.

U.S. Congress. House. Committee on Foreign Affairs, Subcommittee on International

Economic Policy and Trade. Hearings and Markup, 96th Cong., 2d Sess., May 22; June 4, 10, 18, 24 and July 1, 1980. Washington, DC: GPO.

U.S. Congress. Senate. Committee on Banking, Housing and Urban Affairs, Subcommittee on International Finance and Monetary Policy. Hearings on Export Trading Companies and Trade Associations as a part of continuing effort to improve the Competitiveness of the United States in the World. 96th Cong., 1st Sess. September 17 and 18. Washington, DC: GPO, 1979.

U.S. Congress. Senate. Committee on Banking, Housing and Urban Affairs. Hearings to Encourage Exports by Facilitating the Formation and Operation of Export Trade Companies, Export Trade Associations, and the Expansion of Export Trade Services generally. 96th Cong., 2d Sess. on S.2718. Washington, DC: GPO, 1980.

U.S. Congress. Senate. Committee on Banking, Housing and Urban Affairs, Sub-committee on International Finance and Monetary Policy. Hearings on Export Trading Companies and Trade Associations as a part of Continuing Effort to Improve the Competitiveness of the United States in the World. 96th Cong., 1st Sess. September 17 and 18. Washington, DC: GPO, 1979.

U.S. Department of Commerce. International Trade Administration, *The Export Trading Company Guidebook*. March 1984.

U.S. Department of Commerce. International Trade Administration. *Export Trading Company Act of 1982. The complete text of Public Law 97-290*. 97th Congress, October 8, 1982, December 1982.

U.S. Senate. Hearing before the Committee on Banking, Housing and Urban Affairs. 96th Cong. 2nd Sess. on S.2718. To Encourage Exports by Facilitating the Formation and Operation of Export Trade Companies, Export Trade Associations, and the Expansion of Export Trade Services generally. July 25, 1980.

Wall Street Journal, Western Edition. P.7., Col. 1, January 30, 1984.

Wall Street Journal, Western Edition. P.1., Col. 6, May 24, 1984.

Whitney, Michele. "Export Trading Companies in U.S. Struggle to Survive." *The Journal of Commerce*. July 31, 1989.

Young, Alexander K. *The Sogo Shosha: Japan's Multinational Trading Companies*. Colorado: Westview Press, 1979.

Chapter Nine

California State World Trade Commission and the California European Trade and Investment Office, *Europe: 1992, Implications for California Businesses, A Guidebook*. Office of the Government, State of California, 1989.

Hoge Sr., Cecil C. *Mail Order Moonlighting*. Berkeley CA: Ten Speed Press.

Joffee, Gerardo. *How You Too Can Make at Least $1 Million (But Probably Much More) in the Mail Order Business*. San Francisco, CA: Advance Books.

Lewis, Herschell Gordon. *Mail Order Marketing*. Englewood Cliffs, NJ: Prentice Hall.

Magee, John F. "1992: Moves Americans Must Make," *Harvard Business Review*. May-June 1989.

Marcotta, George. "Europe, Inc.," *San Diego Union*. August 20, 1989.

Nash, Edward L. *Direct Marketing*. New York, NY: McGraw-Hill.

Sweeney, Paul and Dierks, Carsten. *Europe 1992: The Removal of Trade barriers in the*

Common Market in 1992 and the Implications for American Businesses. A research paper by Texas A&M University, Department of Marketing, College of Business Administration, Fall 1988.

Superintendent of Documents. *Foreign Trade Barriers*. Washington, DC: GPO, 1987.

U.S. Department of Commerce, International Trade Administration. *Foreign Business Practices: Materials on practical aspects of exporting, international licensing and investing*. Superintendent of Documents, GPO, April 1985.

United States International Trade Commission. *Assessment of the Effects of Barter and Countertrade Transactions on U.S. Industries*. USITC Publication 1766, Washington DC, Oct. 1985.

Verzariu, Pompiliu. *International Countertrade: A Guide for Manager and Executives*. U.S. Department of Commerce, ITA, Washington, DC, November 1984.

Chapter Ten

Consjeria Comercial De Mexico, Mexico City. "Mexico's In-bond Processing Industry, the Maquiladoras." *Flagstaff Institute*. P.O. Box 986, Flagstaff, AZ 86002.

Horowitz, Rose A. "Soviets Design Incentives for New Free Zones." *The Journal of Commerce*. July 26, 1989.

United States International Trade Commission. *The Impact of Increased United States-Mexico Trade Southwest Border Development*. Report to the Senate Committee on Finance on Investigation No. 332-223, Under Section 332 of the Tariff Act of 1930, USITC Publication 1915, November 1986, Washington DC 20436.

The Use and Economic Impact of TSUS Items 806.30 and 807, Report to the Subcommittee on Trade, Committee on Ways and Means, U.S. House of Representatives, on Investigation No. 332-244 under section 332(b) of the Tariff Act of 1930, USITC Publication 2053, January 1988, United States International Trade Commission, Washington DC 20436.

Chapter Eleven

Fialka, John J. "Soviet Bottom Line Is That Few People Know What One Is." *The Wall Street Journal*. Wednesday, April 5, 1989.

Nelson, Dr. Carl A. "Personal notes taken of talk presented by Dr. Clayton Yeutter." U.S. Trade Representative, Hotel Del Coronado, Coronado, CA, 1983.

"The '90s & Beyond," ed., *The Wall Street Journal*. Monday, February 6, 1989.

U.S. Department of Commerce. International Trade Administration. *Doing Business with China*. November 1980.

U.S. International Trade Commission. "Assessment of the Effects of Barter and Countertrade Transactions on U.S. Industries." U.S.I.T.C. Publication 1766. October 1985.

Verzariu, Pompiliu. *Countertrade Practices in Eastern Europe, the Soviet Union and China: An Introductor Guide to Business*. U.S. Department of Commerce. International Trade Administration, Office of East-West Trade Development, April 1980.

Chapter Twelve

Cooper, William H. And Harrison, Glennon J. et al, "The Omnibus Trade and Competitiveness Act of 1988 (Public Law 100-418): An Analysis of the Major Trade Provisions." Congressional Research Report for Congress #88-390 E. The Library of Congress, revised September 1, 1988.

Hills, Ambassador Carla A. "Statement of Carla A. Hills," Office of the United States Trade Representative, Executive Office of the President, Washington, DC, May 25, 1989.

Morrison Ann V. and Layton Robin. "GATT: A Look Back." Office of Multilateral Affairs, International Trade Administration, *Business America*. June 23, 1986.

Morrison Ann V. and Layton, Robin. "GATT's Seven Rounds of Trade Talks Span more than Thirty Years." Office of Multilateral Affairs, International Trade Administration, *Business America*. July 7, 1986.

Morrison Ann V. and Layton, Robin. "Tokyo Round Agreements Set Rules for Nontariff Measures." Office of Multilateral Affairs, International Trade Administration, *Business America*. July 7, 1986.

Office of the United States Trade Representative, "Fact Sheet: Super 301 Trade Liberalization Priorities." Washington DC: May 25, 1989.

Office of the United States Trade Representative, "Fact Sheet: Special 301 on Intellectual Property." Washington DC: May 25, 1989.

Pregelj, Vladimir N. "Trade Remedies Available to the United States Under International Agreements and Corresponding Domestic Laws." The Library of Congress, Report No. 85-1008 E, October 18, 1985.

Pregelj, Vladimir N. "Import Relief: A Brief Historical Survey of Presidential Discretion in Providing a Remedy in Escape Clause/Import Relief Investigations." The Library of Congress, June 26, 1987.

Rappard, William. "GATT: What it is, what it does." GATT Information Service, Centre 154 rue de Lausanne, 1211 Geneva 21, Switzerland.

Sek, Lenore. "Unfair Foreign Trade Practices: Section 301 of the Trade Act of 1974." The Library of Congress, updated February 15, 1989.

U.S. International Trade Commission "Proposed Rules Governing Trade Remedy Assistance." International Trade Commission, 19 CFR Part 213, Federal Register, Vol. 53. No. 245, Wednesday, December 21, 1988.

U.S. Department of Commerce (International Trade Administration) and the U.S. International Trade Commission, *Guide for Antidumping Petitions*. Prepared jointly by the Offices of Investigation at the U.S. Department of Commerce (International Trade Administration) and the U.S. International Trade Commission, undated.

United States International Trade Commission. "Summary of Statutory Provisions Related to Import Relief." USITC Publication 1972 updated 1987, Washington DC 20436.

United States International Trade Commission. *Annual Report 1988 United States International Trade Commission*. USITC Publication 2140, 500 E. Street S.W., Washington DC 20436.

United States International Trade Commission. *Rules of Practice and Procedure*. 19 CFR Chap II, revised through November 30, 1984.

United Nations Office at Geneva. *UNCTAD at a Glance*. UNCTAD Information Unit, United Nations Office at Geneva, TAD/INF/PUB/86-1, Printed at U.N. Geneva, GE. 86-57083, November 1986.

U.S. Department of Commerce. International Trade Administration. *Subsidies and Countervailing Measures*. Volume 1 The Tokyo Round Trade Agreements, May 1980.

U.S. Department of Commerce. International Trade Administration. *Government Procurement*. Volume 2 The Tokyo Round Trade Agreements, May 1980.

U.S. Department of Commerce. International Trade Administration. *Trade in Civil Aircraft*. Volume 3 The Tokyo Round Trade Agreements, May 1980.

U.S. Department of Commerce. International Trade Administration. *Technical Barriers to Trade*. Volume 4 The Tokyo Round Trade Agreements, May 1980.

U.S. Department of Commerce. International Trade Administration. *Anti-dumping Duties*. Volume 5 The Tokyo Round Trade Agreements, May 1980.

U.S. Department of Commerce. International Trade Administration. *Agreement on Import Licensing Procedures*. Volume 6 The Tokyo Round Trade Agreements, May 1980.

U.S. Department of Commerce. International Trade Administration. *Customs Valuation*. Volume 7 The Tokyo Round Trade Agreements, May 1980.

Index

About the Author

Dr. Carl Nelson is a specialist in international trade, an author, and teacher. He is president of Global Business and Trade (GBT), an international business assistance and training company and was previously Vice President and Director of Marketing for an international consulting and trading company which specialized in Pacific Rim import/export and Mexican Maquiladora operations. He has more than thirty years of global experience in government and private business. He lived for two years in Japan, one year in South Vietnam and is intimately knowledgeable about Hawaii, Guam, South Korea, Hong Kong, Australia, Philippines, New Zealand, and the Indian Ocean area. His most recent international work has been in Central America and along the California/Mexican border where he specializes in Maquiladora operations.

As a professional writer, he has published both fiction and non-fiction and is a member of the San Diego Editors/Writers Guild. He is author of the book *Import/Export: How to get Started in International Trade*, TAB BOOKS, and his articles on international business matters have been published in *Global Trade Executive*, *Twin Plant News*, and the *Daily Transcript* (the local San Diego business newspaper). His fiction short stories have been published in various military magazines and journals. He has written three other books, two non-fiction and a war novel. In 1987, he won awards for both fiction and non-fiction.

Dr. Nelson is also an Adjunct Professor of International Trade at United States International University (USIU) where he teaches undergraduate and graduate level courses. He also gives seminars and workshops on the basics and applications of global trade.

His international experience is complemented by his academic training. He earned his Doctorate in Business Administration, Finance, (emphasis on international finance and trade) from the United States International University in San Diego, California. His Doctoral Dissertation, "The Relationship of Export Obstacles to the Export Trading Company Act of 1982," focused on United States small business export problems. He is also a graduate of the Naval War College, holds a Master of Science degree in Management (Economics/Systems Analysis) from the Naval Post Graduate School in Monterey, California, and an engineering degree from the United States Naval Academy at Annapolis, Maryland.

Dr. Nelson is a former Captain in the United States Navy. During that period of his life he was commanding officer of five naval commands: three warships, one USN/VN combat riverine unit, a USN/VN logistic support base, and served four tours of duty in the Vietnamese war. He also held demanding positions on major logistics and operational staffs as well as the staffs of the United States Military Academy at West Point and the United States Naval Academy at Annapolis, Maryland.